GENERAL HISTORIES

The United States Army Air Arm

April 1861 to April 1917

Juliette A. Hennessy

New Imprint by
OFFICE OF AIR FORCE HISTORY
UNITED STATES AIR FORCE
WASHINGTON, D.C., 1985

Library of Congress Cataloging-in-Publication Data

Hennessy, Juliette A.
  The United States Army Air Arm, April 1861 to April 1917.

  (General histories)
  Bibliography: p. 256
  Includes index.
  1. United States. Army—Aviation—History. 2. Aeronautics, Military—United States—History. I. Title. II. Series.

UG633.H395   1986   358.4′00973   85–18965
ISBN 0–912799–34–X

This volume is a reprint of a 1958 edition originally published by the USAF Historical Division.

For sale by the Superintendent of Documents, U.S. Government Printing Office
Washington, D.C., 20402

Foreword

THIS MONOGRAPH, written by Mrs. Juliette A. Hennessy of the USAF Historical Division, recounts the development of aviation in the United States Army from April 1861, when the Army first became interested in balloons as a means of observation, to April 1917, when America entered World War I. The origins and organizations of the Army's air arm are told in detail, with particular emphasis on early air force personnel, planes, and experiments. In the process the monograph traces the early development of what today is The United States Air Force.

Of necessity, the monograph tends strongly toward the chronological variety. This is owing to several factors, the thinness of aviation activities for most of the long period covered and an equal thinness in records being the principal factors.

Only a few books which deal with this early period of Army aviation have been written, and all of them together do not cover the period. This, then, is the first attempt to put the story into a single volume. Because the story of the air arm from April 1917 to the beginning of World War II also has not been fully covered it is expected that the present monograph will be the first of three, which, when completed, will become the basis for a published history of the Army Air Arm, 1861-1939.

Like other Historical Division studies, this history is subject to revision, and additional information or suggested corrections will be welcomed.

Contents

Illustrations

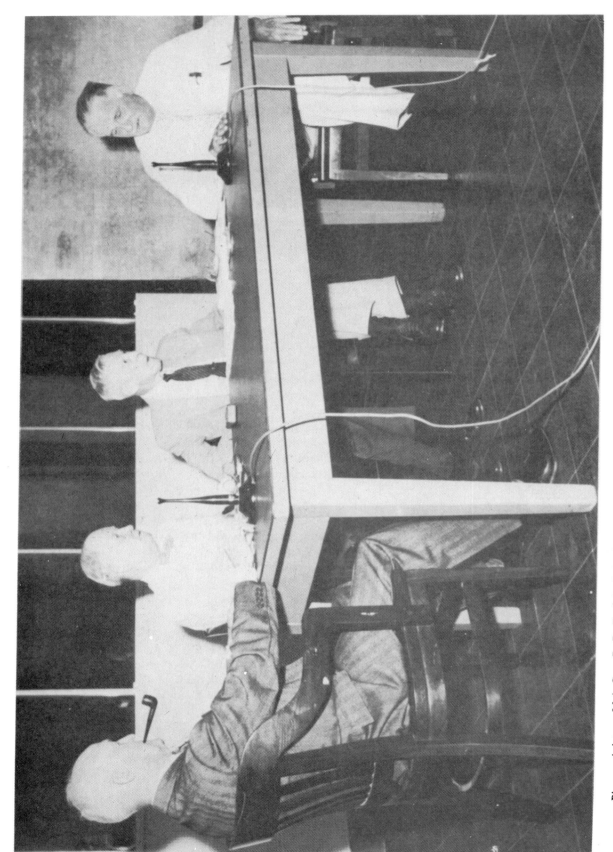

Pioneer Aviators: Maj. Gen. B. D. Foulois, Brig. Gen. T. D. Milling, Brig. Gen. F. P. Lahm, and General Carl Spaatz, Montgomery, Ala., 1954

CHAPTER I

Balloons and Airships in the United States Army, 1861-1913

BALLOONS IN THE CIVIL WAR

MILITARY AVIATION in the United States began in the early days of the Civil War when the Army for the first time employed balloons for military purposes. Balloons had been used for reconnaissance by the French Army as early as 1794 and they were primarily utilized by American balloonists for the same purpose. On 19 April 1861, four days after Lincoln's initial call for troops, two members of the Rhode Island 1st Regiment (State Militia), James Allen, a veteran New England balloonist, and Dr. William H. Helme, a dentist and balloonist, carried two of Allen's balloons from Providence, Rhode Island, to Washington. There, on 9 June, they made the United States Army's first trial captive balloon ascent. The newspapers reported that on the following day one balloon was moved with the Rhode Island regiment to Harper's Ferry where for a week it continued ascents, but no official confirmation of this report has been found.[1]

There is no further mention in the records of Dr. Helme's activities as an aeronaut, but it is known that Allen left the army after the accidental loss of both of his balloons in July 1861 at Falls Church, Virginia. He reentered the service in March 1862, and remained until June 1863. Despite the fact that his initial aeronautical attempts were considered failures, he twice served during the latter period as acting head of the balloon corps, a position which he held when the corps was disbanded in June 1863.[2]

Another balloonist, John Wise of Pennsylvania, had also been contacted by the army soon after the outbreak of hostilities. On 12 June

1861, Maj. Hartman Bache, acting chief of the Topographic Engineers, requested Wise to submit an estimate of the cost of constructing and operating a small balloon. Wise offered to build a balloon for $300 and volunteered his services free of charge. At the end of the month Major Bache (probably after consulting with another officer of the Topographic Engineers, Capt. A. W. Whipple, under whose jurisdiction the aeronauts were later placed) wired Wise for prices on a larger, 20,000 cubic-foot, silk balloon. Wise offered to have the larger balloon ready in two weeks for $850. By early July he had been taken into the government service as a military balloonist and had been ordered to construct a large balloon.

On 21 July the balloon, the army's first, was completed, delivered to Washington, and detailed to be used for observation in the Battle of Manassas, then in progress. A ground crew walked the balloon, already inflated, up Pennsylvania Avenue to Georgetown, up the Chesapeake and Ohio Canal, and across the Potomac to Fairfax Road, where Maj. Albert J. Myer, Chief Signal Officer, fastened it to a wagon and the trip was continued. As the party neared its objective, Major Myer became impatient to reach the scene of the battle; against the better judgment of Wise, he ordered the driver to whip up the horses. Almost immediately the balloon was snagged in the upper branches of the roadside trees; when Myer tried to force it free, great holes were torn in the bag. Actually, this was not the tragedy it then appeared to be, for had the balloon arrived in time to be of use, the Confederates very likely would have captured it.[3]

Wise quickly repaired the balloon and on 24

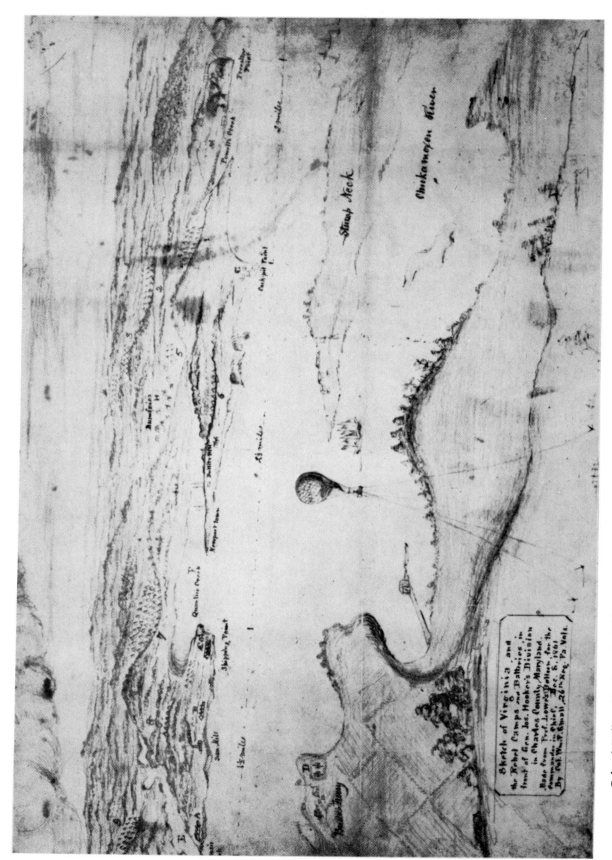

Colonel William Small of the 26th Regiment, Pennsylvania volunteers, ascended in Lowe's balloon on December 8, 1861, to make this sketch looking westward across the Potomac about 25 miles south of Washington. National Archives photo.

July made ascensions at Arlington, Virginia. Two days later, while the balloon was being towed to Ball's Crossroads, it was blown against telegraph wires, which cut the towropes, and the balloon floated away toward the Confederate lines. To prevent its capture by the enemy, Union troops shot it down near the Lee mansion at Arlington.[4]

Neither the Allen nor the Wise balloon was satisfactory, mainly because each had to be filled with coal gas from the city mains and towed inflated to the area in which it was to operate. Wise had designed a portable hydrogen generator, which would permit inflation in the field and would widen the area of operations; he now urged the army to construct such a unit. But the army blamed him for the two disasters to his balloon and abruptly terminated his connection with its aeronautics. Wise returned to his home in Lancaster, raised a cavalry troop, and rejoined the army, but after several months of service his health failed and he was compelled to retire from active duty.[5]

In May 1861 another aeronaut, John La Mountain, twice offered his services, two balloons, and a portable gas generator to the Union Army. The War Department answered neither of his letters, but on 5 June Maj. Gen. Benjamin F. Butler, in command of the Department of Virginia with headquarters at Fortress Monroe, offered La Mountain a job as an aerial observer. La Mountain became the only free-lance balloonist ever to serve in the Union Army. He made his first military captive ascent in his balloon *Atlantic* at Hampton on 25 July, but a stiff wind made it impossible to attain the altitude necessary for observation. However, six days later he was able to rise to 1,400 feet and observe the territory within a radius of 30 miles around Hampton. He reported that the Confederate forces were much weaker at this point than had been supposed.[6]

On 3 August La Mountain's balloon was moored to the transport *Fanny* and carried out into the channel of the Potomac River from where it made the Army's first ascension from a boat. Though succeeding ascents disclosed new Confederate fortifications with guns trained on Fortress Monroe and shipping in Hampton Roads, there is no evidence that La Mountain observed Magruder's advance which led to the burning of Hampton on 7 August.[7]

After a trip north to get his larger balloon, the *Saratoga*, La Mountain was transferred to the Army of the Potomac. On 4 October he inaugurated a series of free ascents from Brig. Gen. W. B. Franklin's headquarters at Cloud's Mill. These free ascensions were possible because of a prevailing east wind, which would carry the balloon over the Confederate forces located to the west of the Union Army, and a west wind at higher altitudes, which would return it. After completing his observations, La Mountain would jettison some of the ballast, letting the balloon rise until it encountered the east-bound current of air which would carry him back to his own lines; then he would release gas until the balloon settled to earth. The major difficulty which La Mountain encountered was lack of control in landing. On 18 October, after returning to the Union lines, he descended in the midst of Brig. Gen. Louis Blenker's German Brigade, and was welcomed with a volley of shots that riddled the lower part of the balloon's envelope.[8]

On 16 November the *Saratoga* was blown from its moorings and lost over the Confederate lines, leaving La Mountain with only the old *Atlantic*. He tried unsuccessfully to get another balloon from Thaddeus S. C. Lowe, a rival army balloonist with whom he had quarreled. Finally, on 19 February 1862, General George B. McClellan dismissed La Mountain from the service.

Although his work was unappreciated by the army, La Mountain had made a definite contribution to military aeronautics. He was one of the first men to make significant aerial observations for the Union Army. As a result of his observations at Cloud's Mill, the Confederate General Beauregard had ordered his division commander, General Longstreet, to utilize camouflage,* since the deception of dummy guns could no longer be assured under the eyes of the federal balloons. Although his generator was never usable, La Mountain's two balloons, the *Atlantic* and the *Saratoga,* had proved so satisfactory that they had been bought by the army in October.[9]

The balloonist who was to become the most important of the Civil War aeronauts was La Mountain's rival, Thaddeus S. C. Lowe. As a preliminary to a planned transatlantic flight (which never

*Haydon also gives Lowe credit for making camouflage necessary in the confederate lines. See F. S. Haydon, *Aeronautics in the Union and Confederate Armies* (Baltimore, 1941), pp. 215–16.

materialized), Lowe had made a trial flight on 20 April 1861 in his balloon *Enterprise,* taking off from Cincinnati and landing at Unionville, South Carolina. Although the North and South already were at war, Lowe, after some difficulties, was permitted to return to Cincinnati by way of Columbia, South Carolina, and Louisville, Kentucky. As he traveled through the South he became increasingly convinced that the war would be long and arduous, and he determined to organize a balloon corps in the Union Army and to offer his services as a military aeronaut.[10]

The editor of the Cincinnati *Commercial,* Murat Halstead, who had sponsored Lowe's earlier aerial activities, now used his influence to get Lowe to Washington, where he was received by President Lincoln on 11 June. The War Department granted Lowe $250 with which to carry out balloon demonstrations, the first of which took place on 18 June at the grounds of the Columbian Armory in Washington. On this day Lowe transmitted the first telegraphic message ever sent from a balloon. A wire was connected from the key in the balloon to the line between the Alexandria telegraph office and the War Department, from which a special line ran to the White House. The first message was sent to President Lincoln; others were sent to the War Department. On the following day the experiment was repeated. General Irwin McDowell, favorably impressed, requested that Lowe be assigned to his Army of the Potomac. After several delays Lowe and the *Enterprise* arrived at McDowell's headquarters in Arlington on 22 June. During the next three or four days several ascensions were made, most of them unsuccessful because of stiff winds, but one flight enabled Maj. Leyard Colburn to produce a very good map of the surrounding countryside.[11]

On 26 June, Lowe was asked to submit a report on his proposed operations and an estimate of the cost of constructing another balloon. Soon afterwards, however, the order for a government balloon was given to Wise, who underbid Lowe by almost $200. Still hoping for an army appointment, Lowe continued to give demonstrations on the grounds of the Smithsonian Institution. Meanwhile, General McDowell, preparing to advance into Virginia, was expecting Wise to appear with his ballooon; and when on July 17 he had not reported, Lowe was ordered by Captain Whipple

to join McDowell's Army of the Potomac. While Lowe was inflating his balloon Wise arrived in Washington and his balloon was sent forward instead of Lowe's. Subsequently, when Lowe learned that Wise's balloon had been damaged and had failed to reach McDowell's army, he started to the front with his own balloon. Before he could get there, McDowell had been defeated; on the afternoon of 21 July Lowe met the retreating Union Army and returned with it to Arlington.

On the 24th Lowe made the Union Army's first free ascent, going up from Fort Corcoran to investigate rumors of a march on Washington by the victorious Confederate Army. He helped to calm the fears at the Capital by his report that no large Confederate force was approaching. On his return to his own lines he had the dubious honor of becoming the first American airman to be fired on by friendly troops.[12]

Before the Battle of Manassas President Lincoln had sent Lowe to see General Winfield Scott, commander in chief of the Union Armies. It seems doubtful, however, that Lowe saw Scott, since he made no ascents during the battle and subsequent events indicated that the General was not kindly disposed toward military aeronautics. After the battle Lowe was summoned for another interview with the President, who thought that balloon reconnaissance might have saved the day at Manassas. He asked Lowe to have another talk with General Scott and wrote on a card: "Will Lieut. Genl. Scott please see Professor Lowe once more about his balloon? A. Lincoln 25 July 1861."[13] On the following day Lowe made four attempts to see General Scott, who for one reason or another, was not available. Angered by these rebuffs, Lowe went back to the President. Lincoln then personally escorted him to Scott's headquarters, and the General promised to take official action on the establishment of a balloon corps.[14]

The President's intercession was effective, and on 29 July, Lowe received a telegram from Captain Whipple offering him employment with the army at $30 per day for every day his balloon was used. Although the salary was tempting this arrangement did not appeal to Lowe, who wanted regular service with the army, hoping that such an arrangement would lead to the formation of an organized balloon corps. He refused the offer and made a counterproposal that the government authorize him to build a balloon, pay for the material, and pay him at the rate of $10 per day for regular service and $5 a day during construction of the balloon. Professor Joseph Henry, Secretary of the Smithsonian Institution, supported Lowe, and on 2 August 1861 Lowe became a military aeronaut with official status and was commissioned to build a balloon.[15]

Lowe promptly left Washington for Philadelphia, where he constructed the *Union,* a new 25,000 cubic-foot balloon, made of India silk, with linen rigging and cordage. He returned to the Capital with the *Union* and made his first ascension at Arlington on 29 August. He was aloft for an hour or more; during the flight a Confederate battery opened fire on the balloon but failed to damage it.[16] On 24 September, Lowe established an American "first" when he directed artillery fire from a balloon by telegraph. A system of visual flag signals was used for communicating the observer's findings to the gunners.*

Although Lowe's artillery direction was successful the main function of balloons continued to be reconnaissance, and during the fall and winter of 1861 he made numerous observations which have since been proved by official Confederate documents to have been very accurate. Even though Lowe's reports did not reveal information of any particular note, the constant surveillance of enemy lines was important, if for no other reason than that it caused considerable concern in the Confederate ranks. By moving his balloons from place to place near Washington without damage to them, Lowe also demonstrated that a well-trained ground crew could avoid such accidents as had happened earlier to the balloons of Allen and Wise.[17]

A number of general officers made ascensions with Lowe, among them his staunchest supporter, Brig. Gen. Fitz John Porter, who is credited with at least 100 ascents. Probably the most exciting of these occurred on 17 April 1862, when the General went up alone to make observations. The balloon's mooring line broke and he was carried over the Confederate lines where he had an excellent, if uneasy, view of the enemy's positions. The balloon continued to rise, en-

countered a current of air flowing in the opposite direction, and the General was carried back to his own lines, where he landed safely.

From the beginning, General Porter had been convinced of the importance of military aeronautics and had done everything in his power to further Lowe's advancement. On 15 September 1861 he had asked the aeronaut to submit a statement of material necessary to make more frequent ascensions and to conduct simultaneous observations from different points along the lines. Lowe advised that two additional balloons be constructed and urged that a portable gas generator be manufactured.[18] On 25 September the Quartermaster General informed Lowe that "upon recommendation of Major General McClellan, the Secretary of War has directed that four additional balloons be at once constructed under your direction, together with such inflating apparatus as may be necessary for them and the one now in use. It is desirable that they be completed with the least possible delay."[19] Both Wise and La Mountain had experimented unsuccessfully with a field hydrogen generator designed on the water decomposition principle. Lowe had designed a mobile generator which, using the sulphuric acid and iron process, was capable of producing enough hydrogen to fill a balloon within a few hours. A machine built to Lowe's specifications by the Washington Navy Yard at a cost of about $500 became the first successful portable generator ever used by an American army in the field*.[20] The letter from the Quartermaster General, which had given Lowe more than he had asked, was to become the initial step in the creation of the first balloon corps in American history, the end toward which Lowe had been working.

By the first of November Lowe had completed one balloon and shipped it to Washington along with the newly overhauled *Union.* About a week later the remaining three were finished. Some three weeks after this, Lowe requested permission to build two more balloons of smaller size, stating that the interests of this new branch of the Army (the balloon corps) required additional equipment immediately. McClellan approved the request and the two smaller balloons were completed shortly after the first of January 1862,

---

*The following year, on 25 and 26 March, the same system was used at Island No. 10 in the Mississippi near Cairo, Illinois, where the fire of a Navy mortar division was successfully directed by John H. Steiner, one of Lowe's assistants, cooperating with Commodore Andrew H. Foote.

*The French apparently had used a portable generator in 1794.

bringing the number of Lowe's balloons to seven. The *Union* and the *Intrepid*—the Union Army's two largest balloons—each cost approximately $1,500. Next in size were the *Constitution* and the *United States,* each of which was built for about $1,200, as was the smaller *Washington.* The two latest additions, the *Eagle* and the *Excelsior*, were the smallest of all, costing $1,000 apiece. Thus the initial outlay for balloons in the corps totaled about $8,600.[21]

Manufacturing problems now gave way to those of manipulation. It has been found that ascensions from the Potomac River and its tributaries had many advantages over ascensions from the land. With the new equipment it was possible to expand the scope of aerial operations by establishing widely separated observation stations along the river. In order to supply these stations, the USS *George Washington Parke Custis,* an eight-year old navy coal barge, was turned over to the balloon corps in November 1861 and became the first "aircraft carrier" in history.* The boat had no engines and was towed by a tug, except when it was used in shallow waters where large oars or heavy poles were used to propel it. Under the direction of Lowe, the ship became a "flattop" that could be maneuvered into positions of advantage for observation; furthermore, its large hold was capable of carrying materiel and equipment to the various balloon stations.[22]

Lowe also had to recruit aeronauts for his new balloons. Professional jealousies and antagonisms eliminated the services of his two best known contemporaries, Wise and La Mountain. Nevertheless, Lowe was able to hire nine aeronauts, some of whom rendered valuable service; others were less satisfactory. William Paullin was the first to receive an appointment—in October 1861 —but, because he started a business on the side in order to supplement his army pay, he was dismissed by Lowe on 31 January 1862 for neglect of duty. Lowe also employed John R. Dickinson in October of 1861, but there is only one other mention of him in the records. Ebenezer Seaver was added to the roll in November 1861 but was dismissed from the service when he refused to work until he was paid. John Starkweather joined the corps in November and served with the

Southern Department under General Thomas W. Sherman. He was ignored and not allowed to operate his balloon until General Benham succeeded General Sherman. One of the more colorful characters among the aeronauts was John H. Steiner, a German enrolled in December 1861. He resigned a year later because of the continual delays in receiving his pay and the enforced inactivity and ill treatment he was accorded while serving under General John Pope at Cairo, Illinois. Ebenezer Locke Mason, Jr., served from December 1861 until the spring of 1862 when he was dismissed by Lowe for refusing to perform his duties until he was paid. Jacob C. Freno, Lowe's poorest choice,* joined the service in January 1862. James Allen, whose early attempts at independent service with the 1st Rhode Island Regiment had proved ineffective, enrolled in the corps in March of 1862 in response to an invitation from Lowe. In the same year his brother Ezra Allen also entered the service of the corps, and both served until the close of its operations in 1863. Although there was a total of nine aeronauts, the greatest number employed in the field at any one time seems to have been seven. From the Fredericksburg Campaign (December 1862) until near the end of the Chancellorsville Campaign (May 1863) Lowe and the two Allens were the only aeronauts left in the balloon corps, and Lowe left the corps in May 1863.[23]

None of the aeronauts or their assistants, of whom there were several, ever received military status. Lowe was paid $10 per day, or slightly more than the pay of a full colonel. Starkweather, Steiner, and Seaver each received $5.75 per day, James Allen was paid $4.75, and the others $3.75 each. In addition to the civilian aeronauts and their assistants, enlisted men from various regiments served in numerous capacities—some of them remained permanently with the balloon

---

*As noted earlier, La Mountain had made ascensions from the ship *Fanny* prior to this, but the *Fanny* was merely a transport with a balloon moored to it, while Lowe's vessel was a specially converted balloon boat.

*Freno, who had been allowed to resign from the army in disgrace for cowardice, convinced Lowe he had resigned voluntarily to join the balloon corps. Since the man had been a former employee of Lowe's, he was hired in good faith. Freno's work was good for several months, but afterward he became a problem and was finally dismissed for being repeatedly absent without leave, expressing disloyal sentiments, opening a faro bank for gambling, and demoralizing his subordinates. Following his dismissal Freno obtained entrance to the building where the balloon *Constitution* was stored and deliberately damaged it by ripping a piece from the envelope. He also wrote a malicious letter directed against Lowe to the Provost Marshal of the District of Washington. Freno's charges were refuted by Lowe to the satisfaction of his superiors.

Inflation of the balloon Intrepid *during Battle of Fair Oaks*

First "aircraft carrier," the George Washington Parke Custis

corps and trained the constantly changing ground crews.[24]

Throughout the period of his service Lowe operated under all sorts of other difficulties, the chief of which were lack of supplies and transportation. Because of army red tape he was forced on numerous occasions to pay for supplies and services from his own pocket. Many of these bills were not honored by the government, so that in the end Lowe had spent about $500 of his own money. The Quartermaster Corps from time to time would take the wagons and teams that had been issued to the balloon corps, leaving it stranded. This happened before the Battle of Antietam, so that it was impossible for the corps to accompany the army in time to be of service. Food and tents frequently were not available. There was always trouble over pay; even the teamsters were not paid for one period of four months during which Lowe was ill. One enlisted man who had been ordered to permanent duty with the balloon corps and who was faithfully carrying out his orders was reported as a deserter, another was erroneously reported missing, and all had difficulty with their pay and rations. If Lowe had been an officer, many of these difficulties would never have arisen.[25]

Apparently the air service was never given an official designation during the Civil War, nor Lowe an official title, although he did appropriate various titles to himself. In his first communication to the army, on 29 July 1861, he signed himself "Aeronaut." In March 1862, after his balloons had been delivered to the government and all his aeronauts hired, he signed his reports "Chief Aeronaut." By the end of the year, in his official correspondence he was calling himself "Chief of Aeronautics, Army of the Potomac." But in his final report to the Secretary of War, Lowe reverted to his original signature of "Aeronaut."[26]

By the late spring of 1863 General Daniel Butterfield, who was in charge of the operations of the aeronauts, had decided that the balloons had been of no value. On the other hand, General John Sedgwick, a corps commander in the Chancellorsville campaign, wrote Lowe that his observations had furnished full and frequent reports of enemy movements, valuable information that could not have been obtained in any other way. He stated that the importance of careful balloon ̄onnaissance and accurate reports obtained

thereby could not be overestimated. The Confederates also had a great deal of respect for the Union Army balloons. General E. P. Alexander wrote: "Even if the observer [Professor Lowe] never saw anything, his balloons would have been worth all they cost, trying to keep our movements out of sight."[27] It is evident that Lowe's observations made a definite contribution to the Army of the United States in the Civil War, as did those of his rival, La Mountain. Yet despite these contributions, balloons were never popularly accepted by the military.* Only a few of the generals, such as McClellan and Porter, were convinced of the value of balloon operations. But when these officers were relieved of their commands and replaced by others who were not balloon-minded, the corps was doomed, and in June 1863 it was disbanded, having made its last ascensions during the Chancellorsville Campaign a month earlier.

During its existence the balloon corps (or department) was under the jurisdiction of three different branches of the service. The Topographic Engineers of the Army—which in 1861 had begun to study balloons—had exercised administrative jurisdiction over the military aeronauts beginning with the first Allen ascent on 19 June 1861;† the Quartermaster had furnished supplies. The Topographic Engineers also had exercised tactical control, although various commanders ordered individual operations from time to time. On 31 March 1862 the balloon corps was put under administrative control of the Quartermaster and became subject to the direction of Lt. Col. Rufus Ingalls, Chief Quartermaster of the Army of the Potomac. It remained under his jurisdiction until 25 May 1862, when Brig. Gen. Andrew A. Humphreys, Chief Topographic Engineer on General McClellan's staff, assumed tactical control.[28] After the Peninsular Campaign, Humphreys was transferred, and the balloon corps was returned to Ingalls for administration and supply. On 7 April 1863 the balloon department was transferred to the Corps of Engineers and put under the direction of Capt. Cyrus B. Comstock, Chief Engineer of the Army of the Potomac. One of

---

*For example, Generals Sherman and Pope, in the West, never permitted their balloonists, Starkweather and Steiner, to operate.

†For one day during this period, the Signal Corps exercised control over the balloon. On 21 July 1861, the Wise balloon was operated under the orders of Maj. A. J. Myer of the Signal Corps. See above, p. 2.

Comstock's first acts was to inform Lowe on 12 April that his earlier agreement with the Army was abrogated and that his pay henceforth would be only $6 a day instead of $10. Lowe protested and then resigned but offered to stay in the service until the end of the battles then in progress; he remained until 7 May although his pay had stopped one month earlier. Shortly before disbandment of the balloon corps in June 1863, command fell to Brig. Gen. Gouverneur K. Warren. One final change was attempted toward the end of June when Col. Albert J. Myer, Signal Corps, was ordered by General Joseph Hooker to take over the balloon department, but the Colonel insisted that he had neither the men nor the appropriation to take care of it, whereupon the balloon train was ordered back to Washington, and the corps was disbanded 23 months before the end of the war.[29] For the next 30 years there was no military aeronautics in the United States Army.

There are various reports, most of them unconfirmed, of the use of balloons by the Confederate Army. The first use of a Confederate balloon may have been about the 23d and 24th of July 1861, at which time several correspondents reported that the Confederates had raised an observation balloon near Fairfax, Virginia. Whether this was a Confederate balloon or one of Lowe's has never been determined, but it was very probably Lowe's, which on 24 July, while making observations between Manassas and Fairfax, was fired on by Union troops and reported as a Confederate balloon. Three Richmond papers noted that several aeronauts had offered their services to the Southern government as early as May 1861.[30] General Beauregard was said to have obtained from private sources a balloon which was reported hovering over Munson's Hill in Virginia on 4 September 1861, but which, because of defective construction, never operated successfully.[31] Early in November 1861 a Confederate balloon was reported over Leesburg.[32]

Shortly before the withdrawal of the Confederates from Yorktown early in May 1862, a balloon appeared behind their lines. According to the Confederate aeronaut, Capt. E. P. Bryan, it was made of varnished cotton and was inflated with hot air produced by a fire of pine knots and turpentine. Bryan recounted both day and night operations, his observations in daytime being reported by flag signals. His balloon's cable was secured to a tree, then coiled on the ground, and after passing around a windlass, was attached to a number of ropes coming down from the balloon. On one occasion when he was subjected to particularly heavy artillery fire and wished to expedite his descent, the cable was hitched to a team of artillery horses which were put into a gallop and soon had the balloon on the ground.[33]

Lowe reported that a Confederate balloon operated during the Peninsular Campaign. His account agrees with that of General Longstreet, who wrote:[34]

The Federals had been using balloons in examining our positions, and we watched with envious eyes their beautiful observations as they floated high up in the air, well out of range of our guns. While we were longing for the balloons that poverty denied us, a genius arose for the occasion and suggested that we send out and gather silk dresses in the Confederacy and make a balloon. It was done, and soon we had a great patchwork ship of many and varied hues which was ready for use in the Seven Days' Campaign.

We had no gas except in Richmond, and it was the custom to inflate the balloon there, tie it securely to an engine, and run it down the York River Railroad to any point at which we desired to send it up. One day it was on a steamer down the James when the tide went out and left the vessel and balloon high and dry on a sand bar. The Federals gathered it in, and with it the last silk dress in the Confederacy. This capture was the meanest trick of the war and one I have never yet forgiven.

Lowe stated that this episode ended the attempt of the Confederacy to compete with the Union Army in balloon operations.[35]

The interest in air machines for military use during the Civil War was not limited to balloons. There were attempts by both sides to design what is now known as a helicopter. The idea for a helicopter seems first to have been proposed in November 1861, to General Ormsby M. Mitchell of the Union Army's Tenth Corps at Port Royal, but the originator of that idea cannot be determined. The unknown inventor had developed a tin model that was wound up with a string; when the string was pulled the toy spun like a top, then rose vertically a hundred feet or more, according to the force exerted upon it, and would lift a bullet or two if the string was pulled with sufficient force. Nothing was done with the idea until June 1864, three years later, when the Union Army no longer had a balloon corps. Then the Tenth Corps, which had moved to Virginia and was attacking

Petersburg, found itself in need of information about the Confederate forces. The tin toy was brought out, experiments were conducted, and a 4-inch fan was spun up to an elevation of over a hundred feet. After seeing what the toy could do, Maj. Gen. B. F. Butler, who was commanding the Army of the James (which included the Tenth Corps), expressed the belief that a machine could be made that would navigate the air. He ordered Edward W. Serrell, an engineer, to report officially upon the matter.

Serrell used the little toy as a model, adding gliding planes to it. Extant drawings of the apparatus show four fans for lift—two above the engine, two below—and two fans to propel and steer—one in front and one behind. The rear fan was on a shaft which could be moved in a horizontal segment to change the direction of push, thus making the fan not only a propeller but also a rudder. Across the machine there was a horizontal shaft, at either side of which were gliding planes and automatic balancing balls which were to slide in and out to maintain the equilibrium. The length of the machine was 52 feet and from wingtip to wingtip it measured a little more. The body, shaped like a thick cigar, was to contain fuel, water, and a high-pressure boiler and engine. A weight that could be raised or lowered was to be suspended from the middle of the body; it was designed to act both as do the legs of a bird in flight and as a balance comparable to the tail on a kite. The weight was also to extend or draw in the balancing balls after the manner of the balancing pole used by a tightrope walker.[36]

General Butler was so impressed with the drawings and the explanation that he ordered the machine to be built at once under the supervision of Serrell. No appropriation and no tools were available, but a group of wealthy and patriotic oil men agreed to pay the bills. A sheetiron screw 32 feet in diameter was built; it could lift some 500 pounds, which was more than its own weight. Maj. Gen. Quincy A. Gillmore, engineer officer, certified that the device was "all right," but the engine proved to be the stumbling block. Finally, the firm of Bennett and Risley of New York undertook to build a high-pressure steam engine, but it had not been produced when Lee surrendered at Appomattox.[37]

The Confederacy also worked on a helicopter, which was to be used as a bomber rather than for observation. The blockade of Southern ports by the Union Navy prevented the South from receiving much needed supplies from abroad. Attacks on Northern ships by the ironclad C.S.S. *Merrimac* in 1862 and the submarine *Hundley* in 1864 might have broken the blockade, for both were locally successful; but the *Merrimac* failed to whip the *Monitor* and had to be scuttled when Norfolk fell, and the *Hundley* was destroyed during its initial attack and went down with its victim. At some time during this period, William C. Powers of Mobile, Alabama, conceived the idea that an aircraft capable of dropping bombs might break the blockade, and he constructed a model bomber which he intended to equip with a steam engine. The engine was to rotate a shaft and gears and drive two pairs of rotors or airscrews, one pair to raise the craft vertically, the other pair to drive it horizontally. A rudder was provided for steering and a rolling weight for balancing the craft fore and aft. After completing his design, Powers considered building a full-size machine, but the South's limited facilities for manufacturing stopped him. Fearing that the North might get its hands on his invention and knowing that its much larger industrial resources would enable it to reproduce the machine in far greater quantities than could the South, he decided to keep his design a secret, for he believed that if it were used against the South it would destroy the Confederacy. Although his design did contain several features of the modern helicopter, Powers' machine would not have been successful because of the inefficient design of its airscrews and its limited power.[38] No evidence of any other heavier-than-air craft designs or models in the Civil War period for either army has been found.

THE SPANISH-AMERICAN WAR BALLOON

In the period from 1863 to 1890 there were no military balloon operations in the United States, although by 1884 a number of other countries—England, France, Germany, Spain, Russia, Italy, and Japan—had established balloon corps as a part of their armed forces. On 1 October 1890 Congress gave to the Signal Corps the duty of collecting and transmitting information for the army, a duty which the Chief Signal Officer, Brig. Gen. Adolphus V. Greely, interpreted to in-

Model of the Confederate helicopter

clude aerial navigation; in 1891 Greely asked for appropriations to develop a balloon corps and in 1892 a balloon section was established in the Signal Corps.*

In 1891, Lt. William A. Glassford had been sent to Europe for a year to study the latest

balloon developments; while there, he had purchased a small balloon from the French. This balloon, named the *General Myer,* was exhibited at the Chicago World's Fair in 1893. During the ascensions, of which there were several hundred, a telephone was used to communicate between the balloon and the ground.* After the fair the bal-

*Although the establishment in 1907 of the Aeronautical Division, Office of the Chief Signal Officer, marks the birth of the present-day United States Air Force, the USAF is a direct descendant of the balloon section of 1892.

*This was probably the first time a telephone was used for such a purpose in the United States.

loon was sent to the Signal Corps School at Fort Riley, Kansas, and from there to Fort Logan, Colorado; at Fort Logan Glassford (now a Captain) developed a balloon section as part of a Signal Corps telegraph train; there, too, in 1897 a balloon park was established. The *General Myer* was destroyed in a windstorm during its inflation,* and Glassford had Sgt. William Ivy (better known as Ivy Baldwin, the stunt balloonist) build a new one. This balloon, made of silk by Ivy and his wife in 1896 at Fort Logan, was the only one which the Army had at the opening of the Spanish-American War.[39]

At the outbreak of the war the balloon was shipped to New York under the direction of Lt. Col. Joseph E. Maxfield of the Signal Corps. Maxfield left New York for Tampa, Florida, with the balloon on 31 May 1898; upon arriving he was informed that one balloon train was to go immediately to Santiago, Cuba. At that time he did not have even one officer or enlisted man under his command, and none of his equipment, which was scattered all over the railway yard, had been unloaded. Although three officers and 24 enlisted men were assigned to his command and the equipment was unloaded, the balloon train sailed for Santiago only partially equipped and entirely unarmed.[40]

The troops arrived at Santiago on 22 June but the balloon corps was not allowed to disembark until the 28th. Even then, they went ashore without their generator, acid, and iron filings, so that it was necessary to use tubes of hydrogen to fill the balloon, a procedure which permitted only one inflation. Because of the rugged terrain the unit did not reach headquarters until 29 June; bogholes had made necessary repeated unloadings and reloadings of the seven wagons in which the equipment was carried. When the balloon was unpacked, it was found that the extreme heat had softened the varnish so that the two sides of the envelope were stuck together and portions of it had disintegrated. After the tears were sewed and covered with adhesive plaster, it was possible to make ascensions, although under ordinary circumstances the balloon would have been

considered unsafe. An added difficulty was the inexperienced crew; the detachment, with the single exception of Sergeant Ivy, had never seen an ascension, much less handled a balloon.[41]

Despite these problems, three ascensions were made on 30 June: the first was made by Sergeant Ivy and Lieutenant Colonel Maxfield; the next by Maxfield and Lt. Col. George M. Derby; and the third by Lt. W. S. Volkmar and General Castillo, the latter a member of the Cuban Army. Their observations confirmed the presence of the Spanish fleet in the harbor at Santiago. Enthusiastic reports of the ascensions were transmitted by Derby to General William R. Shafter, who was in command of the expedition.[42]

On the following day, during the Battle of San Juan Hill, one ascension was made from a point which Derby decided was too far from the battle area to permit effective observation. Against Maxfield's advice, he ordered the balloon forward to within 650 yards of the Spanish infantry trenches and a second ascension was made. The observers discovered a new trail, the use of which relieved congestion on the main road and made it possible to deploy two advancing forces against the enemy instead of one. Also at the suggestion of the observers, artillery fire from El Pozo Hill was directed against the San Juan Hill trenches. These actions may have been the determining factor in the capture of San Juan Hill. Although the results seem to have justified the move forward, the balloon was so badly riddled by continuous enemy fire that it could not be repaired in the field.[43]

The loss of the balloon ended aerial activities in the Spanish-American War. A second company, equipped with two new balloons, was organized at Tampa, but the war ended before it could be moved to Cuba.[44]

BALLOONING IN THE UNITED STATES ARMY, 1902-1913

In his annual reports between 1892 and 1898, General Greely, citing European aeronautical achievements and advances, urged appropriations that would enable the War Department to make a start in aeronautics. But the only action taken by Congress was the inclusion in the Deficiency Act of 9 February 1900 of $18,500 for a balloon house and administration and instruction buildings at Fort Myer, Virginia.

In May 1902, a new balloon detachment, com-

---

*Ivy Baldwin, in a letter to E. L. Jones dated 20 April 1950, says that the gas used in the *General Myer* had not been washed and dried properly before using it in the balloon and the hot gas had rotted the goldbeater skin when the balloon arrived at Fort Logan. He so informed Captain Glassford who ordered him to fill the balloon with cold air; when it was half full, it burst.

posed initially of 12 enlisted men and later of 22, was organized under Lt. A. T. Clifton at Fort Myer, where all balloon equipment had been assembled since 1900. This equipment consisted of a German kite balloon, bought by Captain Glassford in 1898 for use in the Spanish-American War,* three French silk balloons, five small cotton signal balloons, five baskets, three nets, cotton filling hose, steel tubes, sandbags, a gas compressor, and a hydrogen generating tank.

Soon after it was organized the balloon detachment was ordered to take part in Army-Navy maneuvers which were planned for the Atlantic coast during the summer of 1903. Because the equipment, not in use for two years, had deteriorated in storage, it was necessary to hire a civilian balloon expert to repair it, and additional equipment had to be supplied if the balloons were to take part in the maneuvers.[45] In the fall of 1902, Maj. Samuel Reber and a detachment from the Signal Service Balloon Corps composed of Lieutenant Clifton and Sergeant Bledsoe of Fort Myer were stationed at Frankfort, New York, to supervise the construction of captive hydrogen gas balloons by "Professor" Carl Myers, who later directed the practical balloon work of the Signal Corps during the maneuvers.[46]

During the next few years little ballooning was done in the Army because neither officers nor men were available and because it was impossible to get compressed hydrogen. General Greely urged the army to build a plant of its own for compressing hydrogen,[47] but it was not until 1906 that so much as an adequate supply of hydrogen tubes was obtained,† although several balloons had been purchased in the meantime.[48] In August 1906 theoretical and practical instructions, which had been inaugurated at Fort Myer in September 1902, were required at the three service schools at Fort Leavenworth, but actual instruction was limited to theory because of lack of suitable equipment.[49]

In the meantime the advent of sport ballooning in Europe had inspired the organization of the Aero Club of America in 1905, and this group, which in years to come would play a major role in American aviation, helped to further aeronautics in the United States, especially in the

Army. Too, several young Army officers, among them Capt. Charles deForest Chandler and Lt. Frank P. Lahm,* had become interested in aeronautics while in Europe. While on leave of absence in 1905, Chandler went to London and studied the British balloon facilities at Farnsborough. Three years later the information obtained on this trip was to prove most useful when new equipment was ordered for the Signal Corps balloon station at Fort Omaha where Chandler was commanding officer. In 1906, Lahm, on leave in France, competed in the first international balloon race. He and Maj. Henry B. Hersey, of "Rough Rider" fame, piloted the balloon *United States* from Paris to Flying Dales, England, to win the Gordon Bennett trophy. In October of the same year, Captain Chandler and Major Reber officially represented the War Department in a free balloon ascent in Massachusetts, which was sponsored by the Aero Club of America.[50]

Only eight balloons had been acquired by the Signal Corps during the period from the end of the Civil War to 1907 but two more were obtained in that year. In the spring the Signal Corps ordered from Louis Godard of Paris, its balloon No. 9, a rubberized-silk hydrogen balloon of 10,500 cubic-foot capacity with a two-place cupola to be used by officers in obtaining their Federation Aeronautique Internationale† (FAI) balloon pilot certificates. Signal Corps No. 10, a 76,000 cubic-foot cotton balloon, was acquired in 1907 from A. Leo Stevens. In this balloon in June, Stevens, James C. McCoy, a pioneer member of the Aero Club, and Captain Chandler, as government observer, made the first army balloon ascent of the year from Washington, D.C. The trip, which covered a distance of 104 miles, ended in Harrisburg, Pennsylvania, after the trio had been in the air for four and one-half hours.[51] In the same balloon on 17 October, Chandler and McCoy won the Lahm Cup by bettering the record which Lieutenant Lahm had established in the Gordon Bennett international contest of 1906.[52]

On 2 July 1907, Corporal Edward Ward and Private Joseph E. Barrett, both of the Signal Corps,

---

*Sergeant Ivy stated that the German balloon was never used while he was in the service. He left the army in 1900.

†The Signal Corps had some hydrogen tubes in 1898.

*Lieutenant Lahm's interest in balloons had been furthered by his father, Frank S. Lahm, who was a member of the French Aero Club, an older organization than the American club. Lieutenant Lahm had made several balloon ascensions with his father.

†The Aero Club of America was a member of this international organization which set up standards for balloon, dirigible, and airplane pilots.

were detailed from Fort Wood on Bedloe Island, New York, for instruction in balloon manufacture at Leo Stevens' plant in New York City.[53] The two men formed the nucleus of the Aeronautical Division, which was set up in the Office of the Chief Signal Officer on 1 August 1907 with Captain Chandler in command.* (Private Barrett, evidently not fond of ballooning, deserted soon thereafter.[54]) The new division, forerunner of the present day air force, had charge of "all matters pertaining to military ballooning, air machines, and kindred subjects."

In the fall a detachment of enlisted men was ordered to the Jamestown Exposition, where they assisted J. C. "Bud" Mars with his passenger-carrying captive balloon and Israel Ludlow with the construction of a man-carrying kite. Eight other enlisted men were added to the detachment† before it returned to Washington for training in aeronautics under Chandler and ground handling of balloons under Stevens.[55]

In 1908 the Signal Corps opened a balloon plant at Fort Omaha, Nebraska. On 13 May, Captain Chandler became commanding officer of the new plant; Lieutenant Lahm was assigned as chief of the Aeronautical Division in Washington during Chandler's absence.[56] All of the balloon and hydrogen equipment, including 368 steel cylinders for compressed hydrogen, which previously had been assembled at the Signal Corps post, Fort Myer, had been shipped to Fort Omaha. Orders were placed for the installation of electrolytic cells and electrical machinery for making hydrogen,[57] and the first gas was produced there on 9 September 1908.[58]

In addition to its other activities in 1907 and 1908 the Signal Corps renewed its experiments in balloon photography, which had been started in 1893. In 1908 experiments were also conducted with radio receivers in balloons, and messages were received at altitudes varying between 300 and 3,000 feet from ground stations at the Washington Navy Yard and Annapolis.[59]

For several years before and after the Spanish-American War the Signal Corps had urged the purchase of an airship,* citing in its arguments the increasing number of dirigibles in use in the military services of Germany, France, England, Italy, and Russia. It was believed in Europe that the mission of the airship was not only reconnaissance but also speedy transport of "high-rank" officers and couriers; in some quarters far-sighted men believed that the dirigible could even be used for strategic bombing. Despite the European sentiment and the fact that the American officers who had qualified as balloon pilots were anxious to go on with their training in a balloon that had an engine and steering controls, no funds were made available to the Signal Corps to purchase a dirigible.

If the Signal Corps had no dirigible, at least there was no lack of small airships constructed by private individuals for exhibition purposes at fairs. One of these people, Thomas S. Baldwin, who made his living performing such spectacular stunts as parachute jumps from balloons, had constructed a small dirigible in 1904. Later he built a somewhat larger airship propelled by a 2-cylinder Curtiss motorcycle engine. But this engine was not entirely satisfactory, and Baldwin secured from Glenn H. Curtiss a 2-cylinder lightweight engine especially designed for use in a dirigible. Brig. Gen. James Allen,† Chief Signal Officer, attended the St. Louis air meet where Baldwin flew his dirigible in October 1907 and was so impressed that he discussed with Baldwin the practicability of building a nonrigid airship for the Signal Corps.[60]

Since no funds had been allotted for this purpose, the immediate problem was to get the money to pay for such a craft. The agency responsible for investigating new military devices was the Board of Ordnance and Fortification of the War Department, whose annual appropriation usually allowed it to purchase samples of new weapons. General Allen applied to the board for an allotment of $25,000, "or so much thereof as may be necessary" to purchase an experimental nonrigid dirigible balloon, and his request was approved on 7 November 1907.[61]

Baldwin discussed plans for the army dirigible

with officers of the Signal Corps and it was decided that rubberized silk would be the most serviceable material for the envelope. This fabric was used in Europe but was not being made in America. The Hodgman Rubber Company, however, was able to produce a satisfactory fabric of two-ply rubberized silk. Specifications giving the minimum flight requirements desired and providing that the government would furnish the material for the envelope then were prepared and published. The bids in response to this advertisement were opened on 15 January 1908, but complaints from nearly all the bidders against the proposed rubberized silk, a material new to them, caused all the proposals to be rejected. A new advertisement with revised specifications (Signal Corps No. 483)* was issued on 21 January. It provided that the manufacturer would supply the envelope fabric, but that it was not to be of varnished material, and specified that the airship must be capable of a speed of 20 miles an hour and be delivered within 150 days. The proposals received in response were opened on 15 February 1908, and on 24 February General Allen awarded the contract to Baldwin whose bid of $6,750 was the lowest.

The dirigible, delivered at Fort Meyer on 20 July, weighed 253 pounds and had a capacity of about 20,000 cubic feet of gas. The envelope was made of two layers of Japanese silk with a layer of rubber between them. The air ballonet, inside of the main envelope, had a capacity of 2,800 cubic feet; its function was to maintain the pressure in the envelope. The car in which the two pilots rode was 66 feet in length by 2½ feet in width and in height; it was composed of four longitudinal spars of Oregon spruce separated by small struts and held together by brace wires. The dirigible was equipped with a new type lightweight Curtiss engine designed especially for it. The water-cooled engine with four cylinders arranged in a vertical line, generated somewhere between 20 and 30 horsepower.[62] Mounted about one-third the length of the car from the front, it drove a tubular steel shaft, 22 feet in length, on the front end of which was a single wooden propeller designed by Lt. Thomas E. Selfridge.

At the rear of the car was a fixed stabilizing surface, back of which was located the vertical rudder for directional steering. Sitting in a canvas seat about two-thirds of the distance from the front of the car, the rear pilot operated the rudder; the forward pilot, seated immediately behind the engine, operated the altitude control with a fore-and-aft rod which, by changing its angle, controlled hinged superimposed planes resting on the car. The car was attached just below the bottom of the envelope by short suspension ropes, and a rope net of square mesh over the entire envelope supported the car.[63]

In its official speed test on 14 August 1908, the airship averaged only 19.61 miles an hour, so that, in accordance with the specifications, which required a speed of 20 miles per hour, 15 percent was deducted from the original price of $6,750. More than fulfilling his contract requirements which called for the training of only two officers, "Captain" Baldwin taught Lieutenants Lahm, B. D. Foulois, and Selfridge to pilot the craft. The airship officially became Signal Corps Dirigible No. 1 when it was formally accepted on 28 August 1908 by a board composed of Maj. George O. Squier, Maj. Charles McK. Saltzman, Capt. Charles S. Wallace and Lieutenants Lahm, Foulois, and Selfridge, all of whom were on duty in the office of the Chief Signal Officer.*[64]

The dirigible was sent to Fort Omaha for use in instruction of servicemen. On 26 May 1909, Lahm and Foulois made their first ascent and became the airship's first army pilots.[65] Their first flight lasted only nine minutes because of a break in the gasoline supply pipe, but on 31 May they made a more successful test flight. Lahm was issued FAI Dirigible Balloon Pilot Certificate No. 2 in 1908; Foulois, although eligible for certificate No. 1, did not get a certificate.† Three student officers, 2d Lieutenants John G. Winter, Raymond S. Bamburger, and Oliver Dickinson, later qualified as airship pilots but made no attempt to get FAI certificates,[66] probably be-

---

*For a brief of Specification No. 483, see App. 3.

*During the period of the assembly and trial flights of Dirigible No. 1, the ground crews were increased by the addition of a number of enlisted men. Those who remained in aviation for any length of time, were Cpl. Thomas L. Chadwick, Pfcs. Stephen J. Idzorek, Glen R. Madole, and Herbert Marcus; the others were Pfcs. William H. Donney, O. H. Dennigher, Samuel H. Elliott, George Jones, John A. Joyce, Ernest Cote, Paul Heppel, Charles F. Moore, Albert Payton and Pvt. Hersley T. Hyde.

†Foulois did not attach any significance to obtaining an FAI pilot certificate for either dirigible or airplane. It was not until later that the military became interested in obtaining such certificates. For FAI dirigible pilot requirements, see App. No. 4.

Balloon at Fort Myer, Virginia, summer of 1908

Signal Corps Dirigible No. 1 at Fort Myer, Virginia, summer of 1908

cause they were relieved from duty with the Aeronautics Division on 29 October 1909. The airship, a miniature in comparison with those in France, Germany, and Britain, continued to be used for exhibition and instruction purposes for four years.

Although several classes from the Fort Leavenworth Signal School visited the Fort Omaha Air Station in 1909 and 1910 for practical instruction in ballooning as a part of the aeronautics course,[67] it is not until May 1911 that an account of the station's activities is available. At that time two instructors and twelve student officers were sent to the station from the Army Signal School for training in ballooning.[68] Practical instruction began when the large Signal Corps balloon No. 11 was used for a free ascension by Captain Chandler, who was attending the signal school after having been succeeded as chief of the Aeronautical Division by Capt. A. S. Cowan.* His passengers were: Capt. J. F. Janda, Lts. Ira F. Fravel, Leonard J. Mygatt, and William N. Mitchel.† After 51 minutes in the air they landed near Woodbine, Iowa, 35 miles from Fort Omaha. A radio receiving set was carried and operated by Fravel, who reported that the signals were clear over the whole distance. On the same day Signal Corps balloon No. 12 was laid out and inflated by the students under the direction of Chandler. On the following day the balloon, attached to a gasoline engine winch wagon, was used as a captive by Chandler, who took up two passengers at a time in spite of a high wind. The class also made a thorough inspection of the hydrogen generating plant.[69] On 7 June 1911, Chandler was relieved from duty at Fort Leavenworth and ordered back to Washington.[70]

On 10 July 1911 the National Balloon Race to select the American team for the Gordon Bennett

international contest was won by Lieutenant Lahm and Lt. J. F. Hart, the latter of the Missouri National Guard. They flew a distance of 480 miles in 22 hours and 26 minutes. However, in October at Kansas City, Germany won the Gordon Bennett competition for the second time. After the contest Captain Chandler, Major Reber, and Maj. Edgar Russel went to Fort Omaha where all made balloon ascensions and Reber qualified as FAI spherical balloon pilot No. 43.[71]

By 1911 Dirigible No. 1 was in such bad shape that brief flights were possible only by selecting an engineer of exceptionally light weight; it finally became necessary to fly without the engineer. By 1912 the airship had so deteriorated that its prospective usefulness was not considered sufficient to warrant rebuilding it.[72] Furthermore, the Army's interest in aeronautics was now focused on the airplane. On 4 October 1913 Fort Omaha was abandoned as an active post, and all balloon school facilities were consolidated at Fort Leavenworth, Kansas. The plant at Fort Omaha was subsequently used by the Weather Bureau until 1916. Interest in balloons and dirigibles in the United States Army was not aroused again until just before the country entered World War I.[73]

Meanwhile Europe had continued to use balloons. Count von Zeppelin, the German dirigible designer, who had become interested in balloons while serving as an observer with the Union Army during the Civil War, had developed the airship that bears his name. Shortly after the outbreak of World War I the Germans began to use Zeppelins for bombing. All the belligerents found balloons to be very useful for observation purposes. After the United States realized that it might be brought into the conflict, a balloon school was established at Fort Omaha in December 1916. But during the intervening years nothing was done by the Army with lighter-than-air craft.[74]

---

*Chandler and Lahm put this in 1910, but according to other sources (cited in the footnote) it was 1911.

†Not to be confused with Billy Mitchell.

★

CHAPTER II

Early American Planes and Their Inventors

THE NINETEENTH CENTURY inventors who attempted to solve the riddle of mechanical flight may be divided into two groups: those who first built and learned to control a glider before trying to apply power, and those who initially attempted to build a machine equipped with an engine. Among the experimenters of the first group were Otto Lilienthal of Germany, Jean Marie Le Bris and L. P. Mouillard of France, Percy S. Pilcher of England, and Octave Chanute and John Montgomery of the United States. Although none of these men advanced beyond the glider stage in their experiments, their efforts promoted interest in aeronautics all over the world. The Wright brothers, who were members of this group, were influenced and aided materially by the findings of these early experimenters. In the second and larger group were such inventors as Sir Hiram Maxim and John Stringfellow of England, Alphonse Penaud and Clement Ader of France, Lawrence Hargrave of Australia, and Samuel P. Langley of the United States.[1]

THE LANGLEY PLANE

Dr. Samuel Pierpont Langley was one of the first Americans to attempt to build a flying machine equipped with a motor. Professor Langley began experiments in aerodynamics while at Allegheny Observatory in 1885, working first with small models driven by rubber bands. When he became Secretary of the Smithsonian Institution in 1887, he received from William Thaw, a Pittsburgh philanthropist, a gift of $5,000, most of which he used to construct a whirling arm device for the measurement of air pressures against moving surfaces. In 1891 he published his *Experiments in Aerondynamics* and in 1893 produced *The Internal Work of the Wind.* In 1890 he had started the construction of a steam-driven model airplane. In 1892 he had built two models driven by carbonic-acid gas and air, and the following year had constructed two more steam models. In all Langley built nine models. His efforts to develop a launching device for these planes lagged, and it was not until 1894 that he had a satisfactory launching system. On 6 May 1896, his Model No. 5 flew a half mile over the Potomac River, and on 28 November of the same year Model No. 6 flew three-quarters of a mile.

On 31 March 1898 a joint board of army and navy officers was appointed to examine Langley's models. Their report, on 29 April, recommended that Langley be given $50,000 with which to continue his experiments. Shortly thereafter he appeared before the Board of Ordnance and Fortification to explain his invention, and on 9 November 1898, the board submitted a report recommending an allotment of $25,000 to be used by Langley for further investigation. The recommendation was approved by the Secretary of War, and President McKinley asked the inventor to construct a test machine. The $25,000 was transferred to the Chief Signal Officer who was to make the actual expenditures when so requested by Langley. A second allotment of $25,000 was made by the board a month later on 9 December.[2]

Langley designed and constructed in the shop of the Smithsonian Institution a large aircraft called "Aerodrome A."* It was a tandem monoplane 62 feet long with a span of 48 feet, which, in spite of its size, weighed only 830 pounds.

---

*The word "aerodrome" was later used to refer to an airfield rather than to an airplane.

The wings were composed of four wood frame panels, each 22 feet long and 12 feet wide, ribbed and covered with linen, arranged in tandem pairs on either side of a tubular metal framework. Two pusher counter-rotating propellers were located at either side of the fuselage and behind the front wings. The blades, consisting of a triangular framework of three tubes covered with fabric, were 2 feet wide at their outer ends. A vertical rudder placed below and to the rear of the fuselage was controlled by cables connected to a small handwheel mounted on the right side of the frame. The wheel was to be operated by the pilot, who sat in an egg-shaped nacelle, 6 feet long and 2 feet wide, with sides 18 inches high. At the rear of the nacelle, which occupied the space between the lower engine section and the forward quadrilateral frame, was the large carburetor for the engine. Elevation was controlled by manipulation of the 15-foot tail, composed of four vanes arranged in the form of a cross, each 4 feet long and covered by fabric. Although the tail operated automatically to maintain longitudinal stability, it could be moved on a vertical axis by a control wheel mounted on the fuselage frame adjacent to the vertical rudder control wheel. Because the wings were set at a dihedral angle, the plane had an inherent lateral balance which was only under the control of the pilot to the extent that he could influence it by the use of the vertical rudder. The machine was to be launched by a spring-operated catapult mounted on a houseboat. Small hollow metal tanks were distributed about the fuselage frame to float the machine which could land only on water.[3]

After an unsuccessful attempt to find an American manufacturer who could make an airplane engine, Langley hired Charles M. Manly, an engineering student at Cornell University, to take over what was then the only aeronautical engineering job in the country. Manly left school before graduation in order to take the position; his diploma was granted *in absentia* after he had reported to Langley on 1 June 1898. Manly assisted in building the aerodrome and later designed a 5-cylinder fixed-radial, water-cooled engine that developed 52.4 horsepower for 125 pounds of weight, one of the most efficient gasoline engines produced up to World War II.[4]

Manly served as the operator on the two trials of the full-sized Langley machine. The first trial took place on 7 October 1903 when the plane was launched from a houseboat on the Potomac River at Widewater, Virginia, 30 miles southeast of Washington. The trial was a failure. The engine performed well, but at the moment of launching, the front guy post caught on the launching car, causing the front of the plane to be dragged down so that it plunged into the water about 50 yards in front of the boat. On 8 December another attempt was made to fly the plane, this time at the junction of the Anacostia and Potomac rivers. Again the launching was unsuccessful. The rear wings and rudder were wrecked before the machine was clear of the launching device, and it fell into the water a few feet in front of the boat.

After the second failure the Board of Ordnance and Fortification refused to make further appropriations, especially since Congress was displeased with the lack of results from the money already spent. (In addition to the money allotted by the Board of Ordnance and Fortification, $20,000 from a private source had also been expended on this project.) Langley did no further work on his plane, which was put in the Smithsonian Institution and labeled "the first heavier-than-air machine capable of flight." Obviously, the statement was open to question, for the plane as originally built never flew. In 1914 Glenn Curtiss flew it, but only after he had made a number of structural changes. The label on the Langley machine was subsequently changed, the statement that it was capable of flight being omitted, and finally the Smithsonian publicly announced that the 1914 flights of the rebuilt Langley machine did not prove it could have flown in 1903.[5]

THE WRIGHT BROTHERS' PLANE

The Wright brothers, Orville and Wilbur, followed the precepts of Chanute, Lilienthal, Pilcher, and others by experimenting with kites and gliders before building a powered plane. In 1899 they began construction of a glider in their bicycle shop at Dayton, Ohio. After determining from the Weather Bureau that steady winds were likely to prevail at Kitty Hawk, North Carolina, they took time off from their business in September 1900 and began their glider operations in North Carolina. For the next three years they divided their time between Kitty Hawk and Dayton.

The Wrights went about their work scientif-

Langley hydroplane as reconstructed and flown by Glenn Curtiss at Hammondsport, N.Y., in 1914

ically, even designing (in 1901) a wind tunnel equipped with balances for measuring the magnitude and direction of forces on airplane wings.* They made useful measurements of lift and drag and of the travel of the center of pressure, and compiled tables of statistics which would aid in designing an airplane capable of flight.[6]

In 1902 the brothers, by then highly proficient in handling a glider, had built their third one. Its construction was based on the results of their own wind tunnel measurements, the accuracy of which convinced them that they were ready to build a machine equipped with an engine. The first powered Wright plane was a biplane with a wingspan of 40 feet, 4 inches, length of 21 feet, and height of 8 feet; it weighed 605 pounds. The wings were constructed of spars and ribs covered on top and bottom with unbleached and untreated muslin cut on the bias. The outer wing extremities could be warped for lateral balance. Behind the wings were two propellers which rotated in opposite directions. They were made of two layers of spruce glued together, each layer one and three-quarters inches thick. The ribs and undercarriage were of second growth ash and the spars and struts were of spruce. In front, mounted on outriggers, was the elevator with 48 square feet of fabric surfaces, movable for vertical steering. In the rear was a rudder with a fabric area of 20 square feet. The whole was mounted on a pair of skids which formed the landing gear. The pilot, who lay prone on the lower wing, operated the front elevator by rocking a small lever with his left hand; he controlled the warping of the wings and rudder, which were interconnected, by moving his body from side to side so as to shift the control cradle on which his hips lay. His position on the lower wing slightly left of center balanced the weight of the engine which was fastened to the wing beams.[7]

It was impossible to get an engine from American manufacturers, so the Wrights, who had built an engine to power their tool shop, in six weeks constructed one of their own. They were aided in this project by Charles E. Taylor, a machinist in their employ. Their joint efforts produced a 4-cylinder engine with a 4-inch bore and stroke developing nearly 12 horsepower.[28]

The airframe* and engine were shipped to Kitty Hawk in September 1903. There were delays and difficulties with the equipment, but on 14 December everything was ready for a test flight. The plane, facing into the wind, was mounted on a dolly, which rode on the 60-foot launching track laid out on level ground. On the toss of a coin Wilbur Wright won the first chance to pilot the plane. It rose from the track but turned up at too great an angle, stalled, and fell, breaking a skid and other small parts, but leaving Wilbur unhurt. Repairs were quickly made, and on 17 December, a cold and windy day, another try was made, this time with Orville Wright at the controls. After traveling 40 feet, with Wilbur running alongside to steady the end of one wing, the plane rose from the ground and traveled 120 feet against a 22-27-mile-per-hour wind; it had remained in the air for 12 seconds. Thus Orville Wright was the first man to achieve flight in a power-driven heavier-than-air machine. The brothers took turns piloting the plane, and on the fourth and last flight of the day Wilbur had the plane in the air for 59 seconds, covering a distance of 852 feet. A rough landing broke the skids and braces of the front elevator and while the brothers were standing nearby discussing the flight, a sudden strong gust of wind upset the plane, turning it over several times and damaging it so extensively that immediate repairs could not be made. The brothers sent a telegram from Kitty Hawk to their father, Bishop Milton Wright, telling him of their success and asking him to inform the press. Flights were discontinued at Kitty Hawk and the damaged machine was shipped back to Dayton.[9]

In 1916 the Wrights' first airplane, the *Kitty Hawk,* was restored, using as many of the original parts as possible. Later it appeared in several exhibitions. In 1928 Orville Wright (Wilbur had died in 1912), still offended at the Smithsonian's labelling of the Langley plane, sent his plane to the Science Museum, South Kensington, London, England. Orville seems to have had his vanity assuaged when the Smithsonian removed the old label from the Langley Machine, for at a dinner in Washington on 17 December 1943, celebrating the 40th anniversary of the Wright's first flight, President Roosevelt, at Orville's re-

---

*This was necessary because they had discovered that existing tables were inaccurate.

*What is now called an air frame was referred to at that time as an airplane.

Man's first "... tor driven, heavier-than-air machine, Kitty Hawk, N.C., 17 December 1903

quest, announced that the *Kitty Hawk* would be brought back from England and placed in the Smithsonian. Because of the war the transfer was delayed; meanwhile Orville Wright had died on 30 January 1948. The transfer was arranged by the executors of the Wright estate, and on 22 November 1948, the plane arrived in Washington. The return was officially celebrated on 17 December 1948, the 45th anniversary of the first flight.[10]

Early in 1904 the Wrights constructed another plane and engine, and resumed their private flying experiments in Huffman's pasture near Simms Station, about eight miles from Dayton. During these flights the Wrights continued to gain knowledge about flying. They constructed a derrick catapult for getting the plane off the ground faster and made a number of changes in the machine itself, and by the end of the year had made two flights of five-minutes' duration each. In May 1905 they began assembling another airplane, all new with the exception of the engine and the propeller-driving mechanism. On 5 October the new plane made a flight of 24-⅕ miles in 38 minutes 3 seconds.

Up to this time little or no attempt had been made by the Wrights to keep their operations secret. In fact it would have been impossible to do so since an interurban car line and two highways passed the field they used for flying; certainly, their flights were witnessed by some of their close friends and by farmers living nearby. The Wrights had even invited the newspapers to send reporters to watch them fly on 23 May 1904. 2 newspapermen came but atmospheric conditions prevented flying. The newspapermen were invited back the next day and given an invitation to come anytime in the future that suited them, and two or three did return on the 24th. This time the plane rose five or six feet from the ground and traveled about 60 feet before it came down with only three cylinders working. The reporters (who, incidentally, never returned) evidently were disappointed, because the articles they wrote about the flight were unimpressive and varied considerably in content. In October 1905 the flights were discontinued for almost three years because the Wrights had not received their patent and they thought it prudent to stop before the details of the machine's construction became popular knowledge.[11]

Late in 1904 the Wrights had been approached by representatives from Great Britain and asked to state the price of their airplane. The brothers, preferring that the United States Government have priority, on 18 January 1905 wrote to Congressman R. M. Nevin of the Dayton district informing him of their accomplishments and offering their invention to the United States. Nevin contacted the Board of Ordnance and Fortifications, which had the responsibility for investigating new weapons of war. Maj. Gen. G. L. Gillespie, president of the Board, replied to Nevin with a form letter stating that the Board did not grant financial assistance to inventors. Apparently the Board members did not believe that the Wrights had achieved mechanical flight; probably, too, they remembered that the $50,000 given to Dr. Langley had not produced a plane that would fly. Friends of the Wrights convinced them that they should try once more; on 9 October 1905, in a letter to the Secretary of War they repeated their offer and restated their plane's accomplishments. They received from Maj. Gen. J. B. Bates, then president of the Board of Ordnance and Fortification, a communication practically identical to the earlier one which Congressman Nevin had received. The Wrights replied that they did not want financial assistance and asked what performance requirements the Board would require for a flying machine. But the Board recorded in its minutes of 24 October 1905 that it did not care to formulate any requirements or take any action until a machine was produced which would fly and carry an operator.* For the next 18 months no further communications were received from the United States Government. In the meantime both the British and French governments had sent representatives to investigate the Wrights' claims and to negotiate with them.

The patent on the Wright plane (No. 821,393) was issued by the United States Patent Office on 22 May 1906. In the spring of the same year the Aero Club of America printed a bulletin on the 1904-1905 flights of the Wrights which listed a number of witnesses, and the following year prominent members of the Club brought the invention to the attention of President Theodore Roosevelt. The President ordered Secretary of War Taft to investigate, and he in turn passed the President's

---

*For a file of this correspondence, see App. 5

instructions on to the Board of Ordnance and Fortification. Correspondence with the Wrights was reopened in May 1907 and continued through the summer. The Wrights offered the Government "a dirigible [*sic*] flying machine" and the instruction of an operator for $100,000. The proposal did not include any particular period of time during which the use of the invention would belong exclusively to the United States since recent negotiations with the French precluded the offer of such a right. They also reserved the right to exploit their invention in any manner they thought proper. The Board, which did not have $100,000 and could not get such a sum except from Congress, referred the correspondence to the Chief Signal Officer, Brig. Gen. James Allen, for his views. After reviewing the letters, General Allen reported that he did not think that the Wrights' flying machine was suitable for military use and recommended a helicopter-type plane.[13]

Orville and Wilbur Wright had spent the summer of 1907 in Europe, visiting France, England, and Germany for the purpose of starting negotiations to establish a European Wright company.[14] The project did not materialize until March of 1908, when they closed a contract with Lazare Weiller, a wealthy Frenchman, to form a French syndicate. When Wilbur returned from France, shortly before Thanksgiving, 1907, he had a talk with General Crozier and Major Fuller of the Ordnance Department and General Allen of the Signal Corps,[15] and on 5 December, he appeared before the Board of Ordnance and Fortification and explained to its members the capabilities of the Wright plane. He also stated that the original price of $100,000 had included "the disposal of certain secrets" but that he and Orville now were prepared to produce for $25,000 a plane capable of carrying two persons. The price would include the instruction of one operator. If a number of planes were purchased by the government, they could be furnished for $10,000 apiece. The Board was convinced of the reliability of Wilbur Wright's statements and asked General Allen to issue specifications based on statements of the Wright brothers and any other airplane designers. On 23 December 1907, General Allen issued Specification No. 486* and asked for bids. After the Board gave its approval, a copy of the specification was

sent to the Wrights on 3 January 1908, together with the notice that it might be modified so as to permit any bidder to reserve as confidential any of his machine's features which he wished to keep secret.[16]

Signal Corps Specification No. 486 required that the flying machine should have a speed of 40 miles per hour; that it be capable of carrying two people, whose combined weight would equal about 350 pounds, in addition to sufficient fuel for a non-stop flight of 125 miles; that it be controllable in flight in any direction; that it be capable of an endurance flight of one hour; and that it land at its take-off point without damage so that the flight could be resumed immediately. It was considered desirable that the machine be so designed that it could be taken apart and packed in army-wagons, with a reassembly time of about one hour. The starting device had to be simple and transportable. The plane had to be capable of landing in a field without requiring a specially prepared spot and without damage to its structure. The bidder was to quote prices for the various speeds from 36 to 40 miles per hour; any plane with a speed less than 36 miles per hour was to be rejected. There were to be three trials for speed and the average of these would determine the price paid for the machine.

In order to discourage irresponsible bidders, Specification No. 486 required that each bid be accompanied by a certified check for 10 percent of the 40 miles-per-hour price. This did not mean that in case of failure on the part of the contractor to fulfill the terms of the contract the bond would be absolutely forfeited, but rather that the bondsman would be liable only for the damage done the government by such failure. In case a machine was rejected, it would be totally rejected and the certified check received from the bidder would be held until an award was made, at which time the bidders whose proposals had been rejected would have their checks returned while the successful bidder would be required to furnish bond in an amount equal to the price bid. Two operators were to be furnished instruction by the bidder at no extra cost to the government. Finally, the plane was to be delivered at Fort Myer, Virginia, within the time specified by the bidder.[17]

Although the Wrights had conducted their early experiments and flights without much regard to secrecy, after October 1905 their concern over

---

*For a brief of Specification No. 486, see App. No. 6.

their patent rights had made them increasingly reluctant to allow the public to view their activities. Representatives of foreign countries visited them in absolute secrecy. Even so, news of a flyable airplane was bound to leak out, but when it did it was received with considerable skepticism. For example, in November 1906, at the request of the Paris *Herald,* the New York *Herald* sent a reporter to Dayton to get information about the Wrights' flights. The reporter wrote some excellent articles for the New York *Herald,* which included eyewitness accounts of the flights, but the Paris *Herald* was not entirely convinced even though it printed parts of these reports on 22 and 23 November 1906. In the issue of 28 November the Paris paper carried an editorial which stated that in Europe curiosity about the machine was "clouded with skepticism owing to the fact that information regarding the invention is so small while the results which its inventors claim to have achieved are so colossal."

It was not surprising then that when the specifications for the Signal Corps airplane were published the general public was amazed that the government should expect so much. The War Department immediately became the subject of editorial attacks by the newspapers. The New York *Globe* said,

Nothing in any way approaching such a machine has even been constructed (the Wright brothers' claims still await public confirmation), and the man who has achieved such a success would have, or at least should have, no need of competing in a contest where the successful bidder might be given his trial because his offer was a few hundred or a thousand dollars lower than that of someone else.

The *American Magazine of Aeronautics* in January 1908 criticized the army officials for prescribing flight performances that could not possibly be fulfilled and predicted that there would be no bids entered.[18]

In spite of such predictions, forty-one proposals were received by the Equipment Board of the Signal Office by the closing date of 1 February 1908, but only three of the bidders complied with the specifications: the Wrights, who offered to produce a plane for $25,000 within 200 days; Mr. A. M. Herring of New York City, who bid $20,000 and asked for 180 days; and Mr. J. F. Scott of Chicago, who bid $1,000 and asked for 185 days. The three bids were turned over to the Board of Ordnance and Fortifications. It can be

assumed that the Board would have preferred to accept the Wrights' proposal because of the evidence of their successful flights and because the specifications had been written around their plane, the only one known to be capable of flight at the time; but unfortunately their bid was the highest of the three. Herring had assisted Octave Chanute in his experiments; the Wrights had built and flown a machine; Scott's price was the lowest and his plane looked promising; therefore it appeared desirable to accept all three bids. But the total price of the three proposed planes amounted to $46,000, which was more money than the Board had available for the current year. The best that it could do was to allot $21,000 to the Signal Corps for contracts with the two lowest bidders— which left out the Wrights. After the Signal Corps officers had racked their brains for some way to include the Wright bid, someone remembered that the President had at his disposal a small appropriation made by Congress during the war with Spain; there was no limitation on the use of the sum and it could be spent for whatever purpose the President desired. The Secretary of War approved a request for $25,000 from this special fund to be used to pay for the third airplane in the event that all three bidders made delivery, and General Allen, accompanied by Captain Chandler, Chief of the Aeronautical Division, and Lieutenant Lahm, called personally upon the President to ask his approval, which was granted immediately.[19]

Shortly thereafter contracts were sent to the three bidders. Soon after receiving his contract, Scott notified the board that he was not in a position to construct a machine and asked to be relieved from all obligation. He had not learned of the government's advertisement of 23 December 1907 until 20 January 1908, which only gave him ten days in which to draft his plans and submit a bid; although he knew the cost of building an airplane would far exceed his bid of $1,000 he had only the $100 required for the ten-percent deposit and was unable to get additional funds. His request for relief was approved. Herring signed his contract but was unable to finish his plane by 13 August 1908, the date on which his 180 days expired. The War Department granted him a time extension and on 12 October 1908 he arrived at Fort Meyer with a 22-pound, 5-cylinder, air-cooled radial engine of 24 horsepower and the center section of a small biplane equipped with skids. After he explained that he had wrecked his machine on Long Island, the Signal Corps accepted "technical delivery" and he was again granted additional time. On 1 August 1909, Herring requested still another extension, but asked that the War Department cancel his contract if they could not accede to his request for further time. The extension of time was not approved and his contract was canceled, leaving only the Wrights in the running.[20]

The formal contract between the government and the Wright brothers had been signed on 10 February 1908, by Capt. Charles S. Wallace on behalf of the Signal Corps, and by Orville Wright for himself and his brother. Three months later the Wrights began flying again at Kitty Hawk, using the same airplane employed in their flights at Dayton in September and October of 1905. The plane had been modified, however. The type of control remained the same, but the position of the elevator lever and the combined rudder and warping lever, and the direction of movement, were altered in order to permit the operator to take a sitting position instead of lying prone on the lower wing. A passenger's seat was added between the pilot's seat and the engine, and the controls could be operated from either seat. One lever to the right and the other to the left of the two pilots' seats operated the elevator; one of two levers located between the two seats controlled the wing warping; the other lever operated the rudder. The plane was equipped with a new engine, which had 4 cylinders placed vertically and was 2½ times more powerful than the 1903 engine. A larger fuel tank and radiator had also been installed.

On 14 May, on the first flight of the day, Wilbur Wright and Charles Furnas, an employee of the Wrights, flew together very briefly on the first airplane passenger flight in history. Then Furnas flew with Orville for nearly three minutes. The last flight of the day, made by Wilbur Wright, ended in an accident after he inadvertently pulled the wrong lever. Since repairs to the machine would have taken a week and since the brothers could spare no more time, the flights were ended for the time being.[21]

As the Wrights were the only bidders known to have flown successfully, their flights in May 1908 were covered by the still doubtful press. D. B.

Salley, a free lance reporter, from Norfolk, Virginia, was the first to arrive, and his wires to several papers brought more correspondents to the scene. The New York *Herald* sent its star reporter Byron R. Newton, who predicted, after seeing the flights, that Congress would erect a monument to the Wrights at Kitty Hawk.* The New York *American* had William Hoster there, and the London *Daily Mail* sent P. H. McGowan. Among the last to arrive were Arthur Ruhl and J. H. Hare, photographer, both from *Collier's Weekly* magazine. The reporters, thinking the Wrights preferred privacy, hid in the pine woods near the Wright camp and watched the flying through field glasses. At first their stories were doubted by the editors of the various newspapers and it was thought best by some of them to print the information on some obscure inner page. The *Collier's* article appeared with pictures, and Ruhl told how the correspondents had informed the world that man could fly. Despite the publicity, the public was still not entirely convinced.[22]

The Wright army plane was delivered at Fort Myer, Virginia, on 20 August 1908 within the contract time limit. Since Wilbur was abroad giving demonstrations, Orville Wright was the pilot for the preliminary tests. Less than a thousand people were present for the first flight on 3 September, but they were so enthusiastic about what they saw that many thousands appeared on the following day; and on every day thereafter when the weather was good Orville flew before record crowds. After this exhibition all skepticism was ended and the newspapers as well as the general public accepted the fact that powered flight had been achieved.

During the period of these flights new world endurance records were established for the pilot alone as well as for pilot with passenger.† In the morning of 9 September 1908, Orville Wright flew for 57 minutes and 25 seconds; in the afternoon he stayed aloft for 1 hour, 2½ minutes, breaking his own record; later the same day, Lieutenant Lahm, who had met the Wrights in Paris in 1907, became the first army officer to fly as a passenger in an airplane, the flight lasting

---

*The Wright monument on the top of Kill Devil Hill at Kitty Hawk, ordered by act of Congress, was dedicated in November 1932.

†These records were not official for the simple reason that there were no official records at this early date. But the best other record at the time was a flight of 29 minutes and 54 seconds by Leon Delagrange of France.

Wright plane at Fort Myer, 3 September 1908

Wright plane showing seats and control, Fort Myer, Virginia, 1908

Orville Wright's first flight at Fort Myer, 3 September 1908

5442 A.C.

Wreck of Wright airplane in which Lt. T. E. Selfridge was killed

6 minutes, 24 seconds. On 11 September, Orville flew 1 hour, 10 minutes, 24 seconds, and on the 12th, 1 hour, 15 minutes. Major Squier, acting Chief Signal Officer, was taken as a passenger on 12 September; on this flight the two-man endurance record set on the 9th was broken by a flight of 9 minutes, 6 seconds.

The final preliminary flight on 17 September ended in tragedy. Lt. Thomas E. Selfridge,* who had already designed and flown a plane for the Aerial Experiment Association,† had asked the War Department to detail him as an observer for the army at Fort Myer during the trials of the Wright airplane, and on this afternoon he was assigned at his own request to ride as a passenger with Orville Wright. After they had been in the air for about three or four minutes and were making the fourth round of the course at a height of about 125 feet, a crack in the right propeller caused it to loosen and foul a rudder guy wire; both broke, and the plane crashed. It hit with such force that Selfridge was fatally injured and died a few hours later, thus becoming the army's first aviation casualty.** His death was a severe blow to the air service, for through his experiments with Alexander Graham Bell he had gained great technical knowledge and knew far more about airplanes than anyone else in the army. Orville Wright was seriously injured and remained in the hospital for seven weeks. Because of the accident the War Department postponed the delivery date of the machine until the following summer.[23]

In June 1909 the Wrights, who had just returned from Europe, received from the United States a long-delayed recognition of their accomplishments. On 10 June at the White House President Taft presented to them the Aero Club Medal; on the 17th and 18th, their hometown, Dayton, Ohio, staged in their honor a two-day celebration, during which they received medals given by the city and the state, and a Congressional medal,†† which was presented by General Allen. Later they were to be the first recipients of the Langley Medal, presented on 10 February 1910.[24]

On 20 June 1909, Wilbur and Orville arrived

in Washington where Orville was to resume the government trials that had been interrupted by the accident the preceding year. Their 1909 Wright A plane was very similar to the 1908 machine but included a number of improvements. Structural changes had been made to prevent brace wires from fouling the propeller, the method of staying the rear rudder had been changed by using a solid wire in place of an elastic stay, and the height of the skids had been increased in front, making them resemble runners on a sleigh. Between the two control surfaces on the front elevator two semicircular vertical fins were installed to prevent tailspins. Two control levers—one to the right, and the other to the left of the two pilots' seats—controlled the elevator, as in the 1908 machine, but the rudder in the rear was operated by one of the two parts of a split hinged lever located between the two seats; the other part operated the wing warping for lateral balance.* The combined action of these two parts performed the banking turn at the correct angle. There were no instruments but the Wrights had fastened to the horizontal crossbar between the front ends of the two skids a piece of string about eight inches long which served as a turn-and-bank indicator and showed by its angle whether the airplane was sliding inward or skidding outward during a banking turn. If the string inclined toward the pilot it indicated a loss of forward speed and danger of a stall.

The engine, which was practically the same as that in the 1908 plane, was controlled by a foot-pedal placed on the footrest crossbar out in front midway between the two seats. The pedal was connected to the magneto and served to advance or retard the spark. In order to start the engine, it was necessary for someone on the ground to hold a piece of waste saturated with gasoline over an open tube into which air was sucked as the engine was turned over by cranking both

---

*Selfridge had volunteered his services to the Wrights in January 1907 before he visited Dr. Alexander Graham Bell, but the Wright brothers refused his offer; they wanted only permanent assistants.

†This was an association headed by Alexander Graham Bell. See below, p. 37.

**Selfridge Field, Michigan, was named for Lt. Selfridge.

††This was not The Congressional Medal of Honor.

*Some sources say that the wing warping lever was separate from rudder control but so near to it that both could be operated at the same time with one hand. Pictures show the 1908 plane with a control of this type. The 1909 plane in the Smithsonian Institution has the two levers connected with a hinged top, but the Smithsonian Institution states that Lieutenant Lahm, with the permission of Orville Wright, changed this control after it had been sent to the museum from Dayton with the other type of separate controls on it. The Wright Brothers' papers in the Library of Congress state definitely that the lever of the 1909 machine was hinged, but for the instruction of the student officers this control was changed to Wilbur's stick control. A lateral movement of the stick operated the wing controls, and moving it fore and aft operated the vertical rear rubber. Both rudder and wings could be operated simultaneously by a diagonal movement of the stick.

propellers. The gasoline tank held 13 gallons, enough for a flight of three and one-half hours; the oil reservoir held .66 gallons; and the radiator had a capacity of 2½ gallons.[25]

The launching apparatus remained the same. On windy days the airplane was headed into the wind, balanced on the monorail, and set in motion by the propellers without the use of the catapult. On calm days the catapult was used. The skids rested on a small car with two grooved wheels set tandem on the rail. A rope hooked to the car ran through a pulley at the front end of the starting track, under the track and through a pulley at the other end; it then passed through a third pulley at the top of a 30-foot pyramid of braced posts, which stood about 10 feet behind the monorail. Weights, totaling 1,984 pounds, were attached to the end of the rope which hung down inside the pyramid. The plane was started by drawing it back to the beginning of the track, the weights were hoisted by a block and tackle, the propellers were started, and the weights were allowed to drop. The force of the falling weight plus the power of the propellers pulled the plane rapidly along the track. When flying speed was attained, the pilot pulled back on the elevator lever and the plane soared into the air.[26]

The period between 28 June and 27 July 1909 was spent in practice flights. The official trials* began on the 27th when Orville Wright, with Lieutenant Lahm as a passenger-observer, flew 1 hour, 12 minutes, and 40 seconds, more than fulfilling the contract requirement for endurance and establishing an unofficial world record for a two-man flight. On 30 July the final trial, which was the speed test, was flown with Orville at the controls and Lieutenant Foulois as passenger and official observer and navigator.† The average speed of 42½ miles per hour won for the Wrights a $5,000 bonus when Signal Corps Airplane No. 1 was formally accepted on 2 August 1909.[27]

---

*The board of officers observing the trials consisted of Majors Squier and Saltzman, Captains Chandler and Wallace (the latter's name was not on the official acceptance), Lieutenants Lahm, Foulois, and Humphreys, all of the Army, as well at Lt. George C. Sweet, USN, who acted as an official observer for the Navy.

†Fred C. Kelly states in his book, *The Wright Brothers,* p. 260, that this was the first cross-country trip in an airplane. The distance covered was 10 miles, from Fort Myer to Alexandria, Virginia, and return. The balloon marking the turning point for the plane was blown so near the ground that Orville could not see it in time to make the turn and went beyond the limits of the prescribed course.

Because neither Scott nor Herring had produced an airplane, the Board of Ordnance and Fortification did not have to pay the $21,000 it had allotted for these planes. When the Signal Corps had found that the Army Dirigible No. 1 would cost only $6,750, it had decided to pay for the dirigible out of its own funds and returned the $25,000 which had been allotted to it for this purpose by the Board, making this money available to pay for the Wright plane. In addition, the extension of time given the Wright brothers made a new annual appropriation available to the Board, which then had plenty of money to pay the sum of $30,000 for the Wright airplane without using any of the President's special fund.[28]

Their plane having satisfactorily passed the flight performance tests, the Wrights had only to meet the obligation of training two army officers as pilots. Wilbur Wright took over this part of the assignment while Orville went to Germany to make demonstration flights. The drill ground at Fort Myer was considered too small for safe instruction of beginners, and it was decided to use a field at College Park, Maryland, near the Maryland Agricultural College. This was one of a group of fields selected by Lieutenant Lahm on the basis of observations from a balloon and later inspections made during long horseback rides. A lease was arranged, the field was cleared, and a small hangar was built. The monorail starting track was laid near the temporary hangar. Lahm and Foulois were chosen by the Chief Signal Officer as the two officers to be trained as pilots. Before the arrangements were completed, however, Foulois was selected as the official delegate of the United States to the International Congress of Aeronautics at Nancy, France, and his place as a student pilot was given to 2d Lt. Fredric E. Humphreys of the Corps of Engineers.[29]

Instruction began on 8 October 1909. Lahm received the first lesson, but Humphreys made the first solo flight on 26 October, a few minutes before Lahm made his. Humphreys received 3 hours, 4 minutes, and 7 seconds instruction before he soloed, and Lahm had 3 hours, 7 minutes, and 38 seconds training before making his solo flight. On 25 October Wilbur Wright showed his pupils how to cut off the motor and glide safely to earth without power, a skill essential in the days of unpredictable engine performance.

Foulois, back from France, reported for in-

Orville Wright, Lt. F. P. Lahm, and Lt. B. D. Foulois at Fort Myer, 27 July 1909

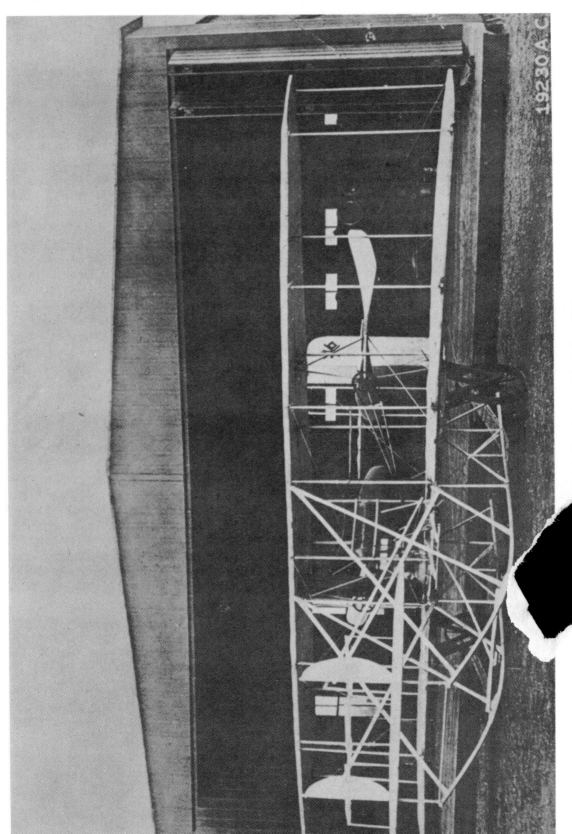

Army's first airplane at Fort Myer, 1909

19230 A. C.

struction late in October. Wilbur took him up on three instruction flights, after which Humphreys took over. During this time Foulois received three hours and two minutes instruction but did not solo. Lahm was given FAI Airplane Pilot Certificate No. 2* in October 1909, Humphreys did not get a certificate, and Foulois did not receive his until 26 June 1912, when he received Certificate No. 140. On 27 October Wilbur took Captain Chandler up for six and one-half minutes, and on 3 November Lahm carried his first passenger, Lt. George C. Sweet USN, who had been assigned as a naval observer at the Wright trials.[30] He was the first officer of the United States Navy to fly in a heavier-than-air machine. On 5 November, a low turn caused the left wingtip of the plane to hit the ground, but neither Lahm nor Humphreys, both of whom were in the plane, was hurt in the crash.[31] The skids and right wing were so damaged, however, that new parts had to be ordered from the Wright factory in Dayton.

OTHER EARLY AIRPLANES AND INVENTORS

Dr. Alexander Graham Bell, the inventor of the telephone, was a friend of Langley's and had closely followed his attempts to build an airplane. When Langley discontinued his work, Bell decided to conduct experiments of his own. He approached the over-all problem from a different angle, having concluded that it would be better and safer ‸ devise a stable platform such as a kite that ‸ support the weight of a pilot and an engine ‸ later equip it with a motor, thus allowing ‸or to learn control without the danger ‸ the fast movement of gliders and ‸ped machines. Lieutenant Selfridge ‸n the spring of 1907 to witness some ‸rimental flights; Bell was so impressed wi‸ young officer's enthusiasm that he arrang‸ with President Theodore Roosevelt to have him assigned as an official observer at Baddeck, Nova Scotia, Bell's summer place. Selfridge returned in September and became a member of the Aerial Experiment Association of which Bell was president and whose members included

F. W. "Casey" Baldwin and J. A. D. McCurdy, two young Canadian engineers in Bell's employ, and Glenn H. Curtiss, who had built an engine for one of Bell's large tetrahedral kites.* On 6 December 1907, during trials on the lake, Selfridge in one of these kites rose to a height of 168 feet and remained in the air for seven minutes. The group then turned to experiments with gliders, learning to control them before trying an engine-equipped machine. Selfridge designed the first of four flying machines (called the *Red Wing* because of its red silk wings) built by the Aerial Experiment Association, but before he could test it he was recalled to duty in Washington. The honor of making the initial flight in the plane then fell to Baldwin, who piloted the machine on 12 March 1908. After a run of 200 feet over the ice, the plane rose to a height of between six and ten feet and flew 318 feet, 11 inches. It then went into a stall, the tail structure collapsed, and the machine slid down on one wing. Five days later during another trial, the plane was completely wrecked.

On 19 May 1908, Selfridge piloted the *White Wing,* designed by Baldwin, and although he was only able to rise to a height of 30 feet and fly a distance of 237 feet, his was the first solo flight by a United States Army officer in a mechanically powered flying machine. This flight was followed by others, and subsequently Selfridge flew the *June Bug,* another Aerial Experiment Association plane.[32]

At about the same time that the Bell experiments were taking place, another inventor was trying to build an airplane. Dr. William W. Christmas and Robert N. Ions stated in depositions in regard to the Christmas aileron patent (No. 1,095,548) that prior to 1 March 1908 on Ion's farm near Fairfax Station, Virginia, they had constructed a plane which Christmas flew in the presence of Ions and other witnesses. An affidavit by David B. Fawcett, an assistant road foreman of engines for the Baltimore and Ohio Railroad, stated that he had witnessed a number of test flights made by this machine. The plane was a cantilever biplane whose outstanding features were inset trailing edge ailerons set in L-shaped recesses in the outer rear corners of the upper wing.

---

*Only five FAI airplane pilot certificates were issued in 1909;

No. 1 to Glenn Curtiss	No. 4 to Orville Wright
No. 2 to Lt. Frank P. Lahm	No. 5 to Wilbur Wright
No. 3 to Louis Paulhan	

These were the first five certificates issued. It is ironic that the Wrights, who invented the airplane and were the first two men to fly, received certicates 4 and 5.

---

*This kite, invented by Bell, was composed of a number of small units, each with four triangular faces, only two of which were covered with fabric.

The ailerons were connected by cables to the control wheel, so that by turning the wheel one aileron was pulled downward while the opposite one moved upward. Christmas and Ions stated that the plane was wrecked in a landing accident and subsequently was burned by Christmas in order to protect his invention. The Christmas patent on the aileron appears to have predated all others, since it was applied for on 30 October 1909 and it was claimed that the aileron was produced prior to 1 March 1908. The United States Government paid Christmas $100,000 for the patent rights on 18 December 1923; by that time his aileron was universally used.[33] Bell and his associates also had a patent on an aileron,* first used by them on the wingtips of the *White Wing*; however, no suit was ever filed by Bell, although J. A. D. McCurdy in 1940 wrote an article in which he declared Bell and his associates were the real inventors of the aileron.[34] Certainly their patent was an earlier one than that issued to Christmas.

---

*Patent No. 1,011,107 was filed on 8 April 1909 and was issued on 5 December 1911.

———————★———————

CHAPTER 3

The Signal Corps' First Air Installations and First Military Aviator Rating

WHEN THE ARMY acquired its first airplane it had only two pilots who had soloed, Lieutenants Lahm and Humphreys, and it promptly lost both of them. Lahm was forced to return to the Cavalry because of a current regulation that permitted a line officer only four consecutive years of detached duty; Humphreys, who had been assigned for temporary duty only, returned to his proper station at Washington Barracks in the District of Columbia to attend the Engineer School and within a few months resigned his commission in the Army.* This left on duty with the Aeronautical Division only one pilot, Lieutenant Foulois, a Signal Corps officer who had had a little more than three hours of aviation training but had not yet soloed.[1]

FORT SAM HOUSTON, 1910-1911

While new parts were being procured for the Army's first plane after the Lahm and Humphreys crash on 5 November 1909, the weather at College Park had become too cold and windy for flying. The plane had no cockpit and flying clothes had not yet become part of an aviator's equipment; the pilot and passenger sat on the leading edge of the wing, with their feet out on a crossbar, fully exposed to the wind and weather. With winter coming on it was decided to discontinue operations in Maryland and move the airplane to Fort Sam Houston, Texas, where the weather was warmer. Orders for the move were issued in December, and after exhibiting the airplane at the Electrical Trade Exposition in Chicago, Lieu-

tenant Foulois and a group of enlisted men* moved on to Fort Sam Houston in February 1910.[2] By the end of the month an inexpensive wooden hangar had been built on the drill ground at Fort Sam Houston to house the airplane, the starting tower and track had been put in place, and Foulois was ready to complete his own training. On 2 March, he made his first solo flight and between March and September made 61 practice flights to accumulate a total of nine hours in the air.† During this time Foulois received instructions from the Wrights by mail, making him the first "correspondence-course" pilot in history.

The specifications for the Army plane had required that it be able to take off from a small, uncleared, and unleveled field, but without wheels it was obviously impossible to take off after an emergency landing away from the launching mechanism. In an attempt to do away with the catapult and monorail launching devices, in August 1910 the army's first civilian airplane mechanic, Oliver G. Simmons, and Corporal Glen Madole, working under Foulois' direction, developed a "tricycle landing gear," which was constructed by attaching a pair of wheels to each skid and a front wheel to the cross bar on Signal Corps Airplane No. 1. This was the army's first use of wheels on an airplane; unfortunately, it was only partially successful. In the same month

---

*When America entered World War I, Humphreys returned to duty with the Aviation Section of the Signal Corps and served for several months.

*Among the enlisted men were Sergeants Herbert Marcus and Stephen J. Idzorek, and Corporals Vernon Burge and Glen R. Madole; others were Pvts. R. W. Brown, Felix Corke, and William C. Abolin.

†Foulois tied himself to the plane with a truck strap—the first safety belt used in Army aviation. Lt. T. D. Milling is credited with inventing in 1914 the standard safety belt with the quick-release buckle. See below, p. 88.

that the Army mechanics had designed their landing gear, the Wrights had exhibited during an air meet at Asbury Park, New Jersey, an airplane equipped with two pneumatic-tired wheels. These were attached to the skids by elastic cords which acted as shock absorbers. The Signal Corps subsequently bought a pair of the new wheels from the Wrights and installed them on the army plane.

After attending the International Aviation Meet at Belmont Park on Long Island in October and an air meet in Baltimore, Maryland, in November 1910, Foulois had a short tour of temporary duty in Washington. He returned to Fort Sam Houston in November and spent a month or so further improving the Signal Corps' Airplane No. 1 and making it conform to the new Wright B planes. Flying operations were then suspended until early in 1911.[3]

During Foulois' activities in Texas the Aeronautical Division had found itself in the position of having an airplane but no funds with which to operate it, to say nothing of funds for buying more planes. Aviation enthusiasts felt that more airplanes and equipment should be bought by the army, but Congress was unconvinced.[4] General Allen, Chief Signal Officer, had requested $200,000 for aeronautics for the fiscal year 1908 and for each of the two succeeding years, but no appropriations were made. One member of Congress was reported to have said, "Why all this fuss about airplanes for the Army—I thought we already had one."[5] The best the Signal Corps had been able to do for Foulois, with only a meager annual fund of $250,000 to take care of the maintenance of military telephone and telegraph installations, was to allot $150 to him for gasoline, oil, and repairs to the plane. Since very little could be done with such a tiny sum, Foulois had had to use his own money for buying essential equipment and supplies.[6]

Early in 1911, Robert F. Collier, owner of *Collier's* magazine, bought one of the new 1910 Wright Type B airplanes which he offered to lend to the Army. Although the original Army plane of 1909 was still in service, its condition was none too good even after Foulois had rebuilt it. The Army accepted Collier's offer, and agreed to pay him a nominal rental of $1.00 per month. The plane arrived at San Antonio on 21 February 1911. The Wrights sent along one of their pilots, Mr. Phillip O. Parmelee, to instruct Foulois

in the operation of the new plane, which had a different control system from that on the Army Wright plane. Flying started on 22 February, but five days later it stopped while the air detachment moved to Fort McIntosh at Laredo, Texas, on the Mexican border, to demonstrate the practicability of using an airplane to work with ground troops.[7]

On 3 March, with Foulois plotting the course and Parmalee piloting the Collier plane, a new unofficial American cross-country record was set by flying the 106 miles from Laredo to Eagle Pass in two hours and ten minutes. The fliers dropped messages to detachments of troops along the way, and were able to pick up on the receiving set carried in the plane all the wireless stations en route. On their return trip on 5 March* one of the two airmen accidently struck a cord connected to the cam lever, which released the compression and stopped the engine. By the time they had corrected the lever position the plane was just above the Rio Grande River, and when the engine started, the machine dove into about four feet of water and turned upside down but without injury to the two fliers. Fortunately, a cowboy in the vicinity saw the crash and rode to the nearest army camp for assistance. The rescue party had to right the plane and drag it downstream to a low bank before it could be pulled out of the water. Although the machine had not been much damaged by the landing, the rough handling tore the wing fabric and broke several ribs. The plane was carried to the nearest railway in an army wagon; from there it was shipped to San Antonio where it was repaired.

To demonstrate the usefulness of the airplane for courier duty, Foulois and Parmalee on 17 March carried a message from General William H. Carter, Division Commander at San Antonio, to Major Squier, Signal Officer at the Leon Springs Camp 26 miles away, and returned with a reply, all in 1 hour and 45 minutes.[8]

Two weeks earlier, on 3 March 1911, Congress had made its first appropriation for Army aeronautics—$125,000 for the year 1912. (On the same day the U.S. Navy received its first appropriation for aeronautics, $25,000, which enabled it to purchase its first three planes). With $25,000 of its appropriation made immediately

---

*This date does not agree with Chandler and Lahm, who give 7 March, but it is believed that the Signal Corps files are more accurate.

Lt. B. D. Foulois and Phil Parmalee in the Collier Wright, Fort Sam Houston, March 1911

available,[9] the Signal Corps ordered five planes, each of which was to cost about $5,000. Three of these planes were Wright Type B's, one of which was to be built by W. Starling Burgess, the first manufacturer in the United States licensed by the Wright Company; the other two were Curtiss planes. It was then proposed to send Signal Corps (S.C.) Airplane No. 1 to Dayton, Ohio, for reconditioning, but the Wrights advised against this because improvements in the newer models had completely outmoded the old plane. They further suggested that the Smithsonian Institution would like the plane for exhibition, and the War Department approved the suggestion on 4 May 1911. The plane was sent to Dayton where it was restored as nearly as possible to its original condition and given to the Smithsonian.*[10] Since the Government now had planes of its own, on 21 June 1911 the Collier plane was loaded and returned to Mr. Collier at Wickatunk, New Jersey.[11]

The second military airplane purchased by the Signal Corps, the Curtiss IV Model D "Military," was accepted on 27 April 1911 at Fort Sam Houston. S.C. Airplane No. 2 had a wingspan of 30 feet; its length was 29 feet, 3 inches; its height, 7 feet, 10 inches; and its weight, 700 pounds. It was equipped with a Curtiss 51.2-horsepower, 8-cylinder, water-cooled engine, and had one pusher-type propeller, which was located behind the center section of the wings. There was no fuselage; the passenger seat was on the lower wing directly behind the pilot's seat. Ailerons were hung between the wings, one at each end. These were a modification of the Bell-type ailerons and were operated by the pilot's shifting a shoulder yoke which formed a frame above his seat. A wheel mounted on a post in front of the pilot enabled him to operate the front elevator and the rear rudder. The plane had a three-wheeled tricycle landing gear.

S.C. plane No. 3, a Wright Type B, arrived at Fort Sam Houston in April and was accepted by the Army on the 27th. This plane had wheels attached to the skids. The elevator, which had been in the front on the Wright A model, had been moved back so that all of the control surfaces now were in the rear. The plane had only two control levers—one hinged lever controlled both

the wing warping and the rudder, the other moved the elevator.[12]

The Curtiss and Wright companies both sent pilots to instruct the Army fliers. The Curtiss company's representative was Eugene Ely. The Wright Company had recalled Parmalee from Ft. Sam Houston and replaced him with Frank T. Coffyn, who arrived on 18 April and began flying the new Wright B on the 20th. Coffyn found that although Foulois handled the airplane very well in the air his lack of directed training had made him "ground shy," that is, he levelled the plane off too high in the air so that it hit the ground too hard. The Wright instructor was able to correct this fault and generally to improve Foulois' flying skill.[13] During the test period, on 22 April 1911 the Curtiss plane piloted by Eugene Ely and the Wright plane flown by Frank Coffyn with Foulois as passenger-observer brought up the rear of a column of 10,000 troops being reviewed by Gen. William H. Carter and his staff. This was the first time in American history that airplanes had flown in review with an army before a commanding general.[14]

When the new planes arrived at Fort Sam Houston, the Army was prepared to train more fliers; 18 young officers volunteered for aviation duty. They were not relieved from their regular duties but were required to fly in their spare time. Under the tutelage of Coffyn and Ely, they studied the Wright and Curtiss machines and were permitted to select the plane they preferred to fly. They were then taken for a flight by an instructor in the plane of their choice. Competition between the Curtiss and Wright students and pilots stimulated flights whenever the weather permitted. Actually, however, out of the 18 volunteers, only two became pilots before World War I: 2d Lt. Leighton W. Hazelhurst, Jr., and 1st Lt. Harry Graham.*[15]

Three other lieutenants, Paul Beck, G. E. M. Kelly, and John C. Walker, Jr., had been sent to the Curtiss school at San Diego† to learn to fly in January 1911, but before they completed their

---

*The plane was assembled at College Park under the direction of Lt. F. M. Kennedy; Secretary Walcott of the Smithsonian acknowledged receipt of the plane on 20 October 1911.

*The San Antonio *Express,* 30 April 1911, gave the following additional names of the trainees: Capt. Frederick B. Hennessy, Lts. Horace M. Hickam, Ned M. Green, Edwin S. Greble, Jr., John R. Lynch, Stanley L. Jones, Olin O. Ellis, Enock B. Gary, Alva Lee, Parker Hitt, Frederick Test, W. J. Fitzmaurice, R. D. Smith, O. H. Sampson, and Ralph E. Jones. If Captain Hennessy was one of the 18 officers who volunteered at San Antonio, he should be included as one of the officers who learned to fly before World War I. However, no record other than this has been found which names Hennessy as a member of this group of 18 volunteers.

†For the story of the San Diego school see Chapter V.

Curtiss IV Model D, Military, Signal Corps No. 2, bought by the Army in 1911

Wright B, Signal Corps No. 3, bought by the Army in 1911

training, the War Department ordered them to Fort Sam Houston.* Shortly after their arrival, Major Squier, the Division Signal Officer organized a provisional aero company on 5 April.[16]

On the morning of 10 May Lieutenant Kelly took off on his primary pilot qualification flight in S.C. No. 2, the Type IV Model D Curtiss plane, which had been wrecked by Lieutenant Beck a short while before but had been completely rebuilt. After approximately five minutes in the air, Kelly came down for a landing at what appeared to be full speed; he failed to level off in time and the single front wheel struck the ground hard; he pulled up, made his turn, and came in for another landing. This time, the controls apparently failed and the machine hit the ground with such force that Kelly was pitched 100 feet from the plane. His skull was fractured and he died within a few hours.† The board investigating the accident reported that the first landing had broken the front steering wheel fork and perhaps other parts of the control system, and that Kelly had sacrificed himself in order to avoid endangering the lives of soldiers camped nearby. Foulois, who had asked that he not be put on the investigating board, felt that Beck was responsible because faulty material had been used in repairing the machine and it had not been thoroughly tested before Kelly's flight. However, the Curtiss machine mechanic, James Henning, placed the blame on Kelly's bad flying, stating that Kelly had brought his machine down at full speed and had maintained that speed at such a low altitude that the plane struck the ground when he tried to bank away from the encamped troops.[17]

After this accident the commanding general of the Maneuver Division prohibited further flying at Fort Houston.[18] The army was already committed to establish a flying school at College Park, Maryland; hence, after the Curtiss plane had been repaired, it was shipped to College Park, to which Captain Beck, most of the enlisted mechanics, and the Wright B, S.C. No. 3, had been transferred in June.[19] On 11 July Foulois was relieved of duty with the Maneuver Division at San Antonio and ordered to report to the Militia Bureau in Washington.[20] For the time being army flying in Texas was ended.

In addition to the flying training experiments during 1910 and 1911, the Army had conducted its first bombing experiments. In January 1910, Lieutenant Beck had been ordered to Los Angeles as an Army observer at the first flying meet of its kind in the United States. He had improvised a bombsight and during the meet flew with Glenn Curtiss in two unsuccessful attempts to use the device.[21] On 19 January Louis Paulhan, a French pilot, flying a Farman biplane, took Beck up and they flew around the course three times, each time dropping a weight used as a dummy bomb. In order to clear the guy wires and propeller, which could not be done from Beck's seat, the actual dropping was done by Paulhan. The "bombs" were dropped from about 250 feet while the plane was traveling at 40 miles per hour. Although the results were far from accurate because the sight was adjusted for a faster rate of speed than that of the Farman plane, this was the army's first successful use of a bombsight for dropping bombs from an airplane. Beck continued his bomb dropping experiments at the air exhibition held in January 1911 at the Tanforan race track near San Francisco.* He and his collaborator, Lt. Myron Crissy of the Coast Artillery Corps,† had devised a much improved bombsight and live bombs were dropped for the first time on 15 January 1911 by Crissy, the designer of the bomb, from a Wright airplane piloted by Phillip O. Parmalee. The experiments proved that a weight up to 36 pounds could be dropped within a 20-foot area from an altitude of 1,500 feet. At the Tanforan meet Beck also experimented with a small radio set of his own manufacture. It was after the meet that Beck volunteered for pilot training.[22]

At the same air meet a different but equally important type of experiment took place when Lt. John C. Walker, Jr. flew with Walter Brookins, the Wrights' first civilian student and pilot, and took aerial photographs of Selfridge Field** from 1,200 feet.[23] The following day, Brookins, with

---

*Walker soon was relieved from aviation duty at his own request.

†Kelly Field at San Antonio was named in honor of Lieutenant Kelly.

*At the meet Eugene Ely demonstrated the feasibility of carrier planes by landing on and taking off from the after deck of the anchored *Pennsylvania* in his Curtiss III pusher.

†In letters to E. L. Jones, Colonel Crissy says that Beck made no bombing experiments at Tanforan and that no sighting device was built or tried by either himself or Beck, but he mentions discussing with Beck a bombsight and computations.

**Selfridge Field was a civilian field in San Francisco, California, named for Lieutenant Selfridge shortly after his death. Later the Army named a field near Detroit, Michigan, for Selfridge and the name of the California field was changed.

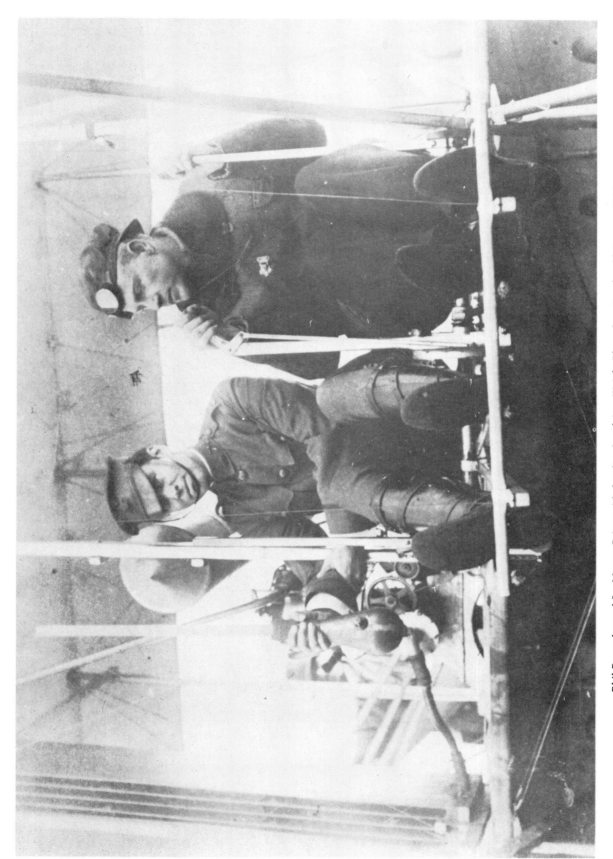

Phil Parmalee and Lt. Myron Crissy with first live bomb in a Wright Plane, Los Angeles, 15 January 1911

Lt. G. E. M. Kelly as a passenger, flew at about 2,000 feet over the San Bruno hills in California on a photo reconnaissance mission. Their object was to locate a troop of the First Cavalry and a battery of the Fifth Field Artillery marching from the Presidio to "attack the 30th Infantry at Selfridge Field," but they were unable to find them.[24] Reconnaissance was the principal function of the military airplane at that time and problems of this kind were later included in the various pilot tests.

Other and more successful experiments had already been performed by Glenn Curtiss, who by 1910 was one of the nation's outstanding aviators. He was one of the first four people to fly a distance of one kilometer (⅝ of a mile), and on 28 August 1909, he won the James Gordon Bennett Aviation Cup and $5,000 at the International Aviation Meet in France. Besides being an aviator, Curtiss was a builder of motorcycle and aviation engines and designer of his own planes.*[25] On 30 June 1910, at Lake Keuka near Hammondsport, New York, he conducted bombing demonstrations under the auspices of the New York *World*. In the presence of Army and Navy officers lead missiles were dropped on a battleship mock-up target.[26] Later at an air meet held in August at the Sheepshead Bay race track near New York City, Major Reber of the Signal Corps persuaded Curtiss to take up Lt. Jacob E. Fickel for the Army's first air experiment in firing a rifle from a plane. On 20 August Curtiss flew with Fickel at an altitude of about 100 feet over a 3 x 5-foot target in the center of the race track. Fickel fired on each of four passes directly over the target and scored two hits. His report of the experiment so interested the War Department that he was ordered to the Remington Arms Company factory at Bridgeport, Connecticut, to help design a rifle sight that would compensate for the rate of travel of the airplane. In September Fickel and Curtiss repeated the experiment at Boston, but this time an Army automatic pistol was used instead of a rifle.[27]

COLLEGE PARK, 1911

The Army still had too few pilots on aviation duty, and, with the new machines on order, more

officers who were interested in learning to fly had to be procured. The War Department had on file a number of applications, and from these, several officers were selected for flight training. The first of them was 1st Lt. Roy C. Kirtland, who was ordered to Washington on 28 March 1911 and put in charge of building four hangars at College Park. He later became secretary of the flying school, a position which he held for the next two years in addition to serving as a flying instructor.[28] In May, 2d Lt. Henry H. Arnold and 2d Lt. Thomas DeW. Milling were ordered to the Wright Company's flying school at Dayton for instruction. After finishing their course and doing some solo flying, these two officers were sent to Washington and from there to College Park, where they arrived on 15 June 1911.[29] On the same day Captain Beck was ordered to duty at College Park from Fort Sam Houston.[30] Captain Chandler became commanding officer of the College Park school on 20 June, but he also continued to serve as Officer in Charge of the Aeronautical Division in Washington.*[31] The last student to arrive was 2d Lt. Frank M. Kennedy, who reported on 3 August 1911.[32] In addition to the flying officers, 1st Lt. John P. Kelly, the first medical officer to be assigned to a flying unit, reported to the school on 7 June. He remained on duty for two years, going with the school to Augusta, Georgia, and to Texas City.[33]

Besides the military personnel at Fort Sam Houston there had been one civilian mechanic, Oliver Simmons, who had resigned to take a position with Robert Collier. Thus the College Park school was left without an expert mechanic to take care of the airplane engines. Accordingly, in June the Signal Corps hired Henry S. Molineau, the only civilian mechanic on duty with the school during its first two years of operation.[34] Fifteen enlisted men arrived in June to assist him. This number had increased to 39 by November.[35]

On 19 June 1911, the third Wright plane, S.C. No. 4, was delivered at College Park and this plane together with S.C. No. 3, which had already arrived from Texas, made two Wright planes available for flight training. There was one difficulty about training pilots on these machines. The control system consisted of two elevator levers, one

---

*Glenn Curtiss had built the engine for Army Dirigible No. 1, as well as the engines for the Aerial Experiment Association planes. In 1909, in cooperation with his new partner, A. M. Herring, who had bid on the Army's first airplane, he designed a new biplane for the Aeronautic Society of New York.

*Chandler was able to handle duties at both stations, which were several miles apart, only because the flying at College Park was done early in the morning and late in the afternoon.

Charles F. Willard, Curtiss pilot, and Lt. J. E. Fickel with rifle in Curtiss plane, Sheepshead Bay, N. Y., August 1910

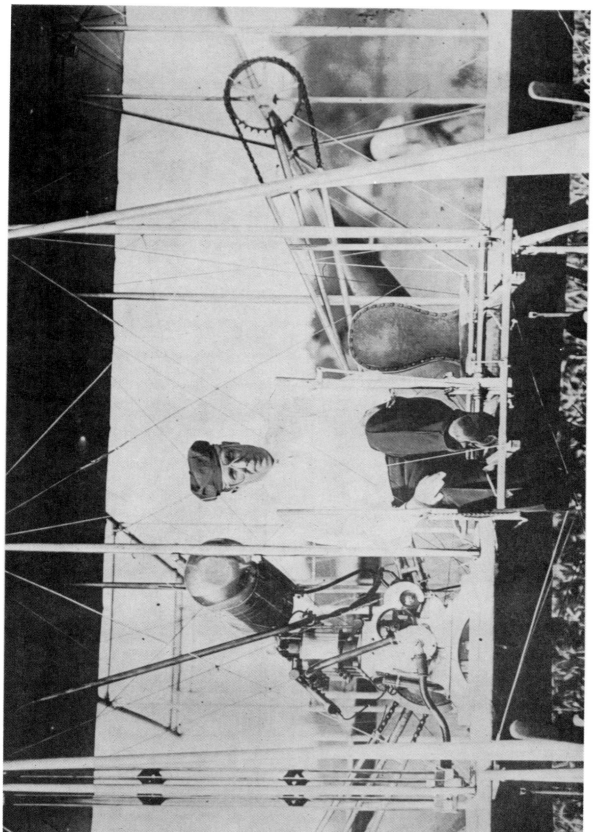

Capt. Charles deF. Chandler in Wright plane, College Park, Md., June 1911

for each pilot, but only one warp-rudder lever, which was between the two seats for the use of either operator. This arrangement produced "right seat" or "left seat" pilots, according to the seat in which they were trained. Since Lieutenants Arnold and Milling had been taught as left seat pilots at the Wright factory, their pupils, Captain Chandler and Lieutenant Kirtland, were instructed as right seat pilots, using their left hands for warping and steering and their right hands for changing altitude. The problem of the controls was corrected in 1912 by the installation of a complete set of duplicate controls—a left-hand elevator control and a right-hand warping and rudder lever for each pilot.[36]

The new Burgess-Wright airplane arrived at the school early in July but cracked up as a result of an engine stall during its first test flight on 8 July*. Neither Mr. Burgess, the pilot, nor Lieutenant Milling, who was flying with him as Army observer, was hurt. On 7 August, another Burgess-Wright plane, S.C. No. 5, was delivered and successfully completed its acceptance trials on 10 October 1911.† On 25 July the rebuilt Curtiss plane, S.C. No. 2, in which Lieutenant Kelly had been killed, arrived at College Park and was equipped with a new 8-cylinder engine. On 15 November this engine was transferred to the second Curtiss plane, S.C. No. 6, which had arrived at the school on 27 July; the latter plane's 4-cylinder engine then was installed in the rebuilt S.C. No. 2, making it a slower and safer training plane for beginner pilots.[37]

Up to this time the Army had no prescribed tests for qualification as an airplane pilot. Now it adopted the FAI regulations and required all army fliers to pass these tests in order to be rated as pilots.†† All qualification certificates for airplane, airship, and balloon pilots were issued by the Aero Club of America, the only U.S. representative for the FAI.[38] Arnold and Milling passed the test on 6 July 1911 and received FAI pilot certificates Nos. 29 and 30 respectively. Beck qualified for his pilot certificate No. 39 on 3 August; Kirtland passed the tests for his certificate No. 45 on 17 August. Chandler was ordered to the Wright

School for further instruction on 22 August and soon after returning to College Park from Dayton he received FAI aviation pilot certificate No. 59, dated 20 September 1911. In order to facilitate the tests at College Park, Chandler was appointed by the Aero Club of America as its representative for observing and reporting the qualifications of other pilots. Lieutenant Kennedy soloed on 23 October 1911, but did not take the FAI test until 12 February 1912, when he qualified for certificate No. 97.[39]

Learning to fly an airplane at the College Park school in 1911 was not as complicated a process as modern flight training. In the Curtiss section of the school student pilots taught themselves to fly by the "grass-cutting" or "short hop" method, because the Curtiss machines were not powerful enough to carry more than one person. To prevent the student from taking off during his initial training, the foot throttle was tied back so that there was only enough power to permit the plane to run along the ground at a speed of about 15 miles per hour. The pilot ran the plane down the field in as straight a line as possible; at the far end of the runway, he stopped the plane, got out, picked up the front end of the machine, turned it around, and ran it back to the starting point. This was continued until the student could guide the plane in a straight line. He was then given enough power to get off the ground to a height of about 10 feet; whereupon, he took his foot off of the throttle and landed. When he had perfected his takeoffs and landings, he was permitted to use a little more power and was taught one-eighth and full quarter turns. The student was then ready to solo.[40] Lieutenant Kelly learned by this method, as had Captain Beck earlier at San Diego.

In the Wright section of the school the instructor first took the student up as an observer to get him accustomed to the sensation of flying. After several flights he was permitted to put his hands on the warping and elevator levers, noticing on his duplicate set how they were manipulated by the instructor and how the machine reacted when the levers were moved. He was then allowed to work the warping lever and make turns, the instructor correcting any errors. When the student had become proficient in handling the warping lever, he was allowed to work the elevator lever with the instruction being continued in the

---

*This plane was wrecked before it was accepted, so, as it was never government property, no Signal Corps number was assigned. The loss was the factory's.

†Chandler and Lahm state that this plane was accepted on 10 August 1911, but Signal Corps and Air Force files say 10 October.

††See Appendix No. 7 for FAI airplane pilot requirements.

Airplanes and hangers, College Park, Md., 1911

Capt. Paul Beck, Lt. H. H. Arnold, Capt. C. deF. Chandler, Lt. T. D. Milling, and Lt. Roy Kirtland, College Park, July 1911.

same manner as before. Next he was permitted to make landings and take-offs. Training continued until the instructor considered the student competent to handle the machine alone whereupon he was allowed to solo. From this point he began to increase his altitude from time to time and acquired confidence in the air. At first only wide turns were made; these were gradually shortened as the student acquired proficiency and ability to handle the machine at a steeper bank. Before the student took off, the instructor gave him directions as to the duration of his flight, the altitude, and some particular maneuver he was to execute.[41]

The Curtiss throttle operated in the same manner as the foot throttle on cars of today. By pressing down with the foot the engine was speeded up; it was slowed by relaxing pressure. In order to make flying easier for the pilot, in 1911 Lieutenant Kennedy supplemented the foot control on the Curtiss plane with a hand throttle, similar to that on the Model T Ford, which could be used to set the engine speed at any desired rate. The Wright foot throttle worked just the opposite to that of the Curtiss. The engine was throttled down by pushing with the foot, and it had so little compression that when the pilot glided in for a landing with the engine throttled, it continued to pump gas, which spilled over the side of the engine and ran down on the wing into a metal pan placed underneath to catch it. When the Wright plane landed, the pilot gave it more gas in order to taxi in; since in about 50 per cent of the landings the dripping gas caught on fire, ground crews or "volunteers" had to stand by with fire fighting equipment.[42]

As there were no accommmodations for the officers at the College Park school, they were billeted in Washington. (One officer assigned as officer-of-the-day remained at the school for a 24-hour period). Because of this arrangement the officers had to leave home very early every morning in order to be at the school by 0630.[43] They flew until around 0900, when the wind usually began to rise, then resumed flying about 1500 or 1600 in the afternoon when the air was again calm. Frequently the late sunsets and long twilights of summer allowed flying as late as 2030. Although this made a long working day, the pilots were too enthusiastic to mind the hours.[44]

The first "long" cross-country flight from College Park was flown in the Burgess-Wright plane on 21

August 1911 by Lieutenant Arnold with Captain Chandler as co-pilot. The school had received an invitation to send airplanes to the District of Columbia National Guard encampment at Frederick, Maryland. Arnold and Chandler left at 0634 and arrived at Camp Ordway at 0723, covering the 42 miles without incident. Lieutenants Milling and Kirtland in a second plane were not so fortunate; they were forced by engine failure to land at Kensington, Maryland. Arnold and Chandler started back to College Park at 1830 but a headwind from the east so reduced their speed that darkness and haze made it impossible for them to identify landmarks, and they had to make an emergency landing to get directions. Tall grass so slowed their take-off that when Arnold tried to turn to avoid some telephone wires, the plane, because of lack of power, went out of control and crashed. Neither flier was injured but the plane's skids were broken and the officers had to return to Washington by rail. The next morning a truck from the aviation school hauled the machine in for repairs.[45]

Several interesting experiments were conducted at the flying school in the autumn of 1911. One of these was in the field of aerial photography, which was inaugurated at College Park on 19 September 1911 when an aerial photograph of the school was made from an altitude of 600 feet. Other photographs, taken at 1,500 to 2,000 feet, showed the topographical features of the area very distinctly.*[46] Several years later the Chief Signal Officer, in order to show the success of aerial photography, sent copies of the pictures taken from Signal Corps airplanes at College Park and Augusta to the editor of the *Army Navy Register*.[47] In October another experiment at the school involved smoke signaling tests; these were made from an airplane by use of the James Means system, in which the pressure of the exhaust of the engine was utilized to make puffs of lampblack corresponding to the dots and dashes of the Morse code. Messages were visible for a distance of one to one and a half miles, but the airmen believed that with a larger apparatus the visibility would be increased. This was the first stage of the present day skywriting.[48]

On 10 October the school conducted the first

---

*No standard airplane camera had been adopted at this time; Lieutenant Kennedy states that the camera used was a standard commercial Graflex.

military trials of a bombsight and dropping device which had been invented by Riley E. Scott, a former coast artillery officer. The tests took place at College Park in an Army Wright B plane flown by Milling; Scott, lying prone on the lower wing, operated the bombing device, which was placed directly in front of the wing. The apparatus utilized a small telescope, which could be moved forward and backward, to help determine the ground speed of the airplane and other factors necessary in fixed-angle bombing, the technique employed by the sight. Scott carried tables so as not to have to make in-flight computations and, because the tables were prepared for 400 feet, that was the altitude from which the two 18-pound bombs were dropped. The bombs had to be released simultaneously in order not to disturb the balance of the sighting mechanism. On his first try, Scott missed the target by 62 feet; the second time, the bombs fell about 32 feet to the right of the target. On one flight Sergeant Idzorek of the Signal Corps replaced Scott, partly because of his lighter weight and partly to test the efficiency of an inexperienced bombardier. Idzorek missed the target by only 11 feet. On Scott's final try both bombs landed within 10 feet of the 4- x 5-foot target. Scott wished to make further experiments from an altitude of 3,000 feet, which he realized was much safer for the airplane, but he was forced to discontinue the experiments in order to leave for Paris where he was to enter a bomb-dropping competition.* Scott's bombsight was a forerunner of those used in World War II.[49]

During the era of these early aviation experiments it was the custom to grant army officers leave to enable them to fly manufacturers' planes at aviation meets. Captain Beck was granted such a leave to attend an aviation meet in Chicago from 12 to 20 August 1911, where he studied foreign airplanes, flew a 50-horsepower Curtiss plane, and won some prize money. A week later Lieutenant Milling flew a Burgess-Wright plane in the 160-mile tri-state race at the Boston meet, 26 August to 6 September 1911. Flying the last leg of the race after dark and landing by the light of gasoline flares, Milling finished second. Also in September Arnold and Milling flew Burgess-Wright machines for the Burgess Company and Curtis at the Aero Club of America's meet at

Nassau Boulevard on Long Island;* there Milling won a prize for making the most accurate landings with a dead engine. On 26 September in the same meet he established a world record of 1 hour, 54 minutes, and 42.6 seconds for endurance flying with two passengers. This meet marked the opening of the first airplane mail service not on a set route, in the United States; Beck inaugurated it by flying Postmaster General Frank H. Hitchcock in a Curtiss plane to Mineola, New York, where Hitchcock dropped the first bag of air mail.[50]

By November the weather was no longer suitable for student flying at College Park, and the War Department selected Augusta, Georgia, for the winter site of the Signal Corps Aviation School. With the school's departure from College Park, the use of the field there was requested by various civilian organizations, among them the United States Aeronautical Reserve (an unofficial organization) and the Christmas Airplane Company. On 25 April 1912, the Secretary of War granted the Reserve organization a license to erect an aeronautical station and conduct airplane flights at College Park, subject to regulation by the Chief Signal Officer. In May, the War Department granted the Christmas Company permission to construct a hangar and to conduct flights there.[51]

WINTER SCHOOL AT AUGUSTA, GEORGIA, 1911-1912

On 28 November 1911, 5 officers, 20 men, and 4 airplanes (1 Wright, 1 Burgess-Wright, and 2 Curtiss pushers),† and motor vehicles, wagons horses, and mules were moved by special train from College Park to Augusta, Georgia. The officers were Captain Chandler, commanding, Lieutenants Arnold, Kirtland, and Milling—all Wright pilots—and Medical Officer J. P. Kelley. The two Curtiss pilots, Captain Beck and Lieutenant Kennedy, did not leave Washington until January 1912; Beck's father had died, and Kennedy was receiving treatment at Walter Reed hospital. In Augusta the officers were quartered at a hotel and the enlisted men were billeted in a nine-room house on the Barnes farm, which had been leased by the Quartermaster for $15 a month as a site for the

---

*In the Paris competition Scott won a $5,000 Michelin prize.

*After the meet Arnold doubled for the leading man as a stunt flier in the movies "The Military Scout" and "The Elopement," both written by Israel Ludlow.
†There were five planes at College Park, but only four were sent to Augusta. The other Wright airplane, probably S.C. No. 4, remained at College Park.

Signal Corps Aviation School, Augusta, Georgia, 1911–12

Wreck of Curtiss Signal Corps No. 2 flown by Lt. F. M. Kennedy at Augusta, 19 February 1912

school. The planes were sheltered in canvas tent hangars. Outbuildings served as repair shops or were used for storage, and the horses and motor vehicles were kept in the barns.[52]

Flying began on 7 December 1911, when each officer made a flight in the Burgess-Wright, which was the first machine assembled. The officers then learned to fly planes other than the types they had flown originally. Milling, a Wright pilot, practiced in the Curtiss machine under the direction of Beck and Beck took instruction in the Wright plane from Arnold.[53] Arnold also gave lessons to Lt. William C. Sherman, a member of the Engineer Corps and a friend of Milling's who had taken some flying instruction from him at College Park in 1911. Sherman took Christmas leave and continued his flying instruction at Augusta.*[54]

Another student pilot was Lt. Col. Charles B. Winder of the Ohio National Guard, who had obtained the approval of the War Department for his instruction as a pilot. When Winder arrived on 12 March 1912 Lieutenant Kirtland was assigned as his teacher. Winder returned to College Park with the school in April, completed his instruction, and received FAI aviation certificate No. 130.[55]

Because of inclement weather and other difficulties during the winter at Augusta, the air training group made flights on only 58 of the 124 days they were stationed there. Classroom instruction (ground school) began on 11 December 1911, and all officers assembled each weekday morning thereafter for instruction in telegraphy, gasoline engines, the structure of seaplanes, and the design of field equipment for aviation service. This cut down on the flying time, and in January and again in February heavy snow falls stopped flying for several days. Then excessive rains and the melting snow sent the Savannah River out of its banks and inundated the flying field. However, the flood did no damage to the planes, which had been set on platforms built high enough to remain above the water level. In February cross-country flights from Augusta were impossible because of the loss of power in the Wright engine; in fact, Wilbur Wright, who had visited the school on 20 January, had estimated that the engine had lost five horsepower. Consequently not as much

flying was done at Augusta as had been expected.[56]

Although Lieutenant Foulois was on duty in the Militia Bureau of the War Department, he still kept up an active interest in aeronautics, frequently visiting the Signal Corps machine shop where he helped design a radio generator that could be operated by attaching it to an airplane engine. One of the new radio sending sets was sent to Augusta and installed in a Wright plane in January. The radio was tested there and at College Park the following summer, but the set proved unsatisfactory and later the Signal Corps had the Holtzer-Cabot Company design a new generator.[57]

On 25 January 1912, Arnold, who had previously established Army altitude records, broke his own record by climbing to a height of 4,764 feet. Military authorities at this time felt that an altitude of one mile gave the airplane adequate safety from infantry small arms fire, but that higher altitudes would prevent military observers from obtaining information of military value.[58]

Several accidents occurred at the school during the winter. The most serious of these happened on 19 February when Lieutenant Kennedy in a single-seater Curtiss plane failed to level off soon enough in landing and his front wheel struck the ground with such force that it buckled and the machine turned upside down. Kennedy was thrown from the plane, and struck with such force that his head made a five-inch indentation in the ground. Although he wore a football helmet, which was part of an aviator's equipment at that time, the impact and a blow on his back from the vertical rudder fractured several vertebrae. He resumed flying in June, but because of his injuries was relieved from aviation duty in October 1912.*[59] Beck had two crashes, neither of which injured him. On 4 February he took off in the Curtiss plane in a 20-mile wind; when he had ascended to only 20 feet, a current of air forced the machine into a small tree and sheared off the right wings. The mechanics were able to repair it with new parts from the factory, and on 2 March, Beck took it up again for a trial flight. At an altitude of 300 feet the plane's engine stopped, and Beck attempted to glide down. As he came in toward the field the chassis struck the

---

*Sherman, who was not detailed to aviation duty until 27 September 1912, received FAI pilot certificate No. 151 dated 7 August 1912.

*Kennedy returned to the Aviation Section in 1917, served with the Balloon Division during the war, and continued on aeronautical duty thereafter.

top of a tree, and the plane again had to be repaired.[60]

In March two new officers reported to Augusta for flying training. Lt. Leighton W. Hazelhurst, Jr. arrived on 1 March and began flying the Wright machine with Milling as his instructor. On 28 March, Lt. Harry Graham* reported at the winter school and was given his first airplane ride by Chandler. This was the last day of flying at Augusta. On 1 April 1912 the winter flying camp was closed, and the squadron departed with all its equipment on a special train for College Park, where it arrived on 2 April.[61]

MILITARY AVIATOR RATING

By the end of 1911 the Army had come to realize that it needed aircraft with longer range and greater weight-carrying capacity if its air arm was to do field service. No specifications had been issued since those under which the original Army Wright had been purchased, so that it was now necessary to draw up new specifications that would meet the Army's latest requirements. It was found, however, that the two characteristics which were most desired, weight-carrying and high speed, could not be combined in a single plane. After consulting with all the officers on duty at College Park and discussing the conditions with Orville Wright, on 11 September 1911 Captain Chandler submitted to the Chief Signal Officer a set of specifications which, after being rewritten, were accepted, and on 8 February 1912 new Signal Corps airplane specifications were issued for two types of planes—a light "Speed Scout" airplane and a weight-carrying "Scout" plane.

The "Speed Scout" was to be a fast single-seat plane to be used for strategic reconnaissance.† It must have a radius of operation of about 100 miles, and a speed of at least 65 miles per hour. It had to carry enough fuel for three hours and be able to climb to 1,800 feet in three minutes while carrying enough fuel for one hour. The second type, the "Scout," was to be used for tactical reconnaissance.** The plane was to carry two aviators, who would relieve one another as pilot and observer, a radio, and sufficient fuel for four hours. Its speed was to be at least 45 miles

an hour. Its rate of climb was to be 2,000 feet in 10 minutes with a load of 450 pounds, except that with a load of 600 pounds the speed requirement could be reduced to 38 miles per hour and the rate of climb lowered to 1,600 feet in 10 minutes. Both planes had to be constructed so as to be easily transported as well as rapidly and easily assembled. Their engines must undergo a 2-hour flight test and be capable of being throttled. Both planes had to be able to land and take off from ploughed fields and to glide to safe landings from 1,000 feet with a dead engine. The starting and landing device for each was to be a part of the machine.[62]

A Curtiss Scout, which would meet the army's new requirements had been ordered on 1 December 1911 and was delivered at Augusta on 19 March 1912. This plane, S.C. No. 8, was the first of the new "Scouts." It was tested at Augusta by Curtiss pilot Charles F. Walsh, and met all of the 1912 specifications except the climb test. It finally passed this test at College Park in May 1912 with Lincoln Beachey, the Curtiss Company's test pilot, at the controls. Before the delivery of S.C. No. 8 the Signal Corps, in January 1912 had ordered five more airplanes. Three of these were "Scouts," two from the Wright Company, and one, the first tractor, from the Burgess Company and Curtis. The fourth and fifth planes, "Speed Scouts," were ordered from the Wright Company.[63]

After the new plane specifications had been issued, it became evident that there was also need for a new measurement of pilot skill, one which would be more adequate than the simple FAI test. Consequently, a new rating of "Military Aviator" was announced in War Department Bulletin No. 2 on 23 February 1912. In the report of the Secretary of War to the House of Representatives on 20 April 1912, the requirements for the Military Aviator rating were published. Applicants for that rating had to be commissioned officers of the Regular Army or Organized Militia; those who qualified were to be reported to The Adjutant General and were to receive certificates from the Secretary of War and be carried on the *Army Register* as "Military Aviators." The Adjutant General disapproved of the notation in the *Army Register* but directed that it be noted on their records that they were entitled to be rated as Military Aviators and that certificates be furnished

---

*Graham later received FAI pilot certificate No. 152 dated 7 August 1912.

†At that time this meant that the pilot was expected to locate and report large bodies of troops outside the immediate vicinity of the friendly forces.

**That is, for reporting enemy forces that were approaching or were in immediate contact.

them. The test for this rating required that the candidate attain an altitude of at least 2,500 feet, fly in a 15-mile-per-hour wind, carry a passenger to a height of at least 500 feet and immediately make a dead-stick landing within 150 feet of a previously designated point, and make a military reconnaissance cross-country flight of at least 20 miles at an average altitude of 1,500 feet.*[64]

Instructions issued by the Chief Signal Officer on 26 October 1912 relative to flying training stated that when a student passed the Military Aviator's test, he was to be considered a graduate of the school. The instructions also made it plain that when a student reported for flying instruction he would either be sent to one of the airplane manufacturers' schools for preliminary instruction or would be assigned to an instructor at the Signal Corps Aviation School for such training.[65]

On 20 September 1912 the Chief Signal Officer suggested to the Aero Club of America that Army pilots who were rated Military Aviators should receive the Aero Club rating as Expert Aviator without further trial, since the test for Military Aviator demanded skill equal to that for the club's rating.† On the recommendation of the contest committee of the club, the board of governors approved the suggestion.[66]

The first Military Aviators' certificates were presented to Captain Chandler and Lieutenants Arnold and Milling, who qualified for the rating on 5 July 1912.[67] These certificates consisted simply of a few typewritten lines, signed by an officer in the Adjutant General's office, which stated that a notation had been made on the officer's record to the effect that he had qualified for Military Aviator. The Chief Signal Officer considered this to be scant recognition and not in accordance with usual military practice. He pointed out that special recognition was given abroad to those who had attained such distinction and suggested a more appropriate certificate, one which would be signed by the Secretary of War, the Chief Signal Officer, and the Commanding Officer of the aviator's unit. He also enclosed a sketch of a badge, similar to the Army marksmanship badges.[68] Finally, on 27 May 1913, in General Order No. 39, the War Department authorized both a certificate and a badge for Military Aviators, the badge to be "worn on all occasions, except on active duty in

the field in time of war or during maneuvers."[69] The order also stated that when an officer qualified as a Military Aviator, the fact would be announced in General Orders of the War Department, but this was rescinded by General Order No. 68 on 17 September 1914.

A number of designs for the badge were submitted by various people, including Lieutenants Kirtland and Hugh M. Kelly, and by the Ordnance Department. There was a great deal of discussion and disagreement about the designs, but eventually one was selected. It depicted an eagle with the Signal Corps flags in its talons, suspended from a bar with "Military Aviator" embossed on it in large letters. In 1913 the Ordnance Department manufactured the dies. The two original gold proof-badges were presented to Chandler and Milling on 16 October 1913. As fast as they were completed, badges were sent to 12 more officers, until all of the 14 officers in the first group recommended for the award on 29 September 1913 had received their badges. From time to time thereafter the Chief Signal Officer sent to Ordnance the names of other officers[70] until badges had been issued to all of the 24 original Military Aviators who qualified under General Order No. 39.*[71]

Officers took the FAI test for pilot qualifications as a matter of course before getting their rating as Military Aviators, but apparently until 26 December 1913 there was no army regulation requiring that they do so. The December regulation was issued as a result of some unexplained difficulty experienced by Lieutenants Lewis H. Brereton and Samuel H. McLeary while they were taking the FAI test, with Lieutenant Harold Geiger acting as the Aero Club's representative. Because of the difficulty, Brereton, through Geiger, asked for the return of his license fee and photographs (which the Aero Club required) in the event that the contest committee decided that the test was not in the proper form. Geiger also stated that he did not desire to take the time to act as an official observer. The matter was brought to the attention of Colonel Scriven, Acting Chief Signal Officer, who advised the commanding officer at San Diego that all army officers engaged in flying would be required to take the test and receive the Aero Club's Expert Aviator rating after becoming Military Aviators. Although officers were not required to receive the Expert Aviator's rating, they had to be qualified to do so.[72]

---

*See Appendix No. 8 for the requirements for Military Aviator.

†See Appendix No. 9 for Expert Aviators Requirements.

*See Appendix No. 10 for the list of "Military Aviators."

CHAPTER IV

College Park and Other Air Schools, 1912-1913

COLLEGE PARK

SHORTLY AFTER FLYING was resumed at College Park in April 1912, three new officers reported for flying duty. Lt. Harold Geiger was ordered to College Park on 27 March 1912 but did not report until relieved from his duty in Columbus, Ohio.[1] On 11 April Capt. Frederick B. Hennessy,* who had made a balloon ascension with Captain Chandler in 1907, was assigned. Captain Beck instructed both officers in flying the Curtiss machine until 1 May, at which time he was relieved from aviation duty to rejoin his regiment.†[2] On 15 May 2d Lt. Lewis C. Rockwell, reported. Rockwell had previously visited the flying school and later, while a patient at Walter Reed Hospital, he had on one occasion flown with Lieutenant Arnold. He had applied for aviation duty soon after returning to his regiment.[3]

During the summer and fall of 1912 several other officers reported for flying training. On 10 July, 1st Lt. Samuel H. McLeary, Coast Artillery Corps (CAC), received his orders[4] and reported shortly afterward. On 27 September, Lieutenants Lewis H. Brereton, Lewis E. Goodier, Jr., and Loren H. Call from the Coast Artillery Corps, Lieutenants Joseph D. Park and Eric L. Ellington from the Cavalry,[5] and Lieutenant William Sherman of the Corps of Engineers were assigned to the school. Sherman, who had learned to fly at College Park and Augusta in 1911, relieved Lieutenant Kennedy, who was ordered to rejoin his regiment.[6]

According to the new training policy each officer attached as a student pilot had to take a shop course and a flying course at an airplane manufacturing plant. Kennedy and Geiger had been ordered to the Curtiss plant at Hammondsport, New York, on 9 May 1912; the former, already a Curtiss pilot, was to take the shop course in plane and engine construction, while Geiger was to get further instruction in flying. In August Lt. Harry Graham was sent to the Wright company for instruction, and in September McLeary was ordered to the Curtiss factory.[7] In October, Goodier, Park, and Brereton received instruction at the Curtiss factory at Hammondsport; while there they acted as a board of acceptance for the Army's first flying boat,* S.C. No. 15, on 27 November 1912. Before going to Hammondsport, Brereton had received about one and a half hour's training from Lincoln Beachey in an Army hydroairplane; at Hammondsport he got about 100 hours of instruction on land planes from Lansing Callan, three hours' dual instruction in flying boats over Lake Keuka from "Doc" Wildman,† and additional instruction from John D. Cooper and Beckwith Havens.[9] Call and Ellington went to Marblehead, Massachusetts, in October and November, respectively, for instruction in flying at the Burgess Company and Curtis factory.[10] The chief instructor, Frank T. Coffyn, was assigned to teach them the Wright system of control. Since the coast of Massachusetts in the winter was not suitable for student flying, Coffyn and the two students were sent to Palm Beach, Florida, in January 1913, to complete the instruction. They took with

---

*Captain Hennessy received FAI certificate No. 153 dated 7 August 1912.
†Beck served as an Infantry officer through World War I, but transferred to the Air Service as a Lt. Col. in 1920. He was shot and killed on 4 April 1922 while Commander of Post Field, Ft. Sill, Okla.

*The flying boat was actually a boat hull with wings, as distinguished from the hydroairplane, which was a land plane equipped with pontoons. At this early date there was little distinction between Army and Navy planes.
†Subsequently, "Doc" Wildman was a flying boat instructor at the Aviation School at North Island, San Diego, California.

them a Type B Burgess-Wright plane equipped with pontoons and the new S.C. No. 17, a Burgess coast defense hydroairplane with an 8-cylinder, 60-horsepower Sturtevant engine. The latter plane, a standard Wright on twin floats, had an enclosed fuselage in which the engine, equipped with a handcrank starter, was mounted.[11]

Between May and September 1912 the Army took part in various activities of the Aero Club of America. The Washington association had arranged for an exhibit on the grounds of the Chevy Chase Club on 6 May, as a part of the celebration to honor the memory of Dr. Samuel P. Langley. The War Department approved participation by aviators from the Signal Corps Aviation School, and Captain Chandler, the school's commanding officer, with two other pilots took off in three planes from College Park and landed on the golf course of the Chevy Chase Club to complete the first army group cross-country flight. A little later in the month (9-18 May) the Aero Club held in New York the most extensive aeronautic exposition ever attempted in the United States up to that time. On 13 May, announced as "Army Day," a special luncheon honored Chandler, Arnold, Milling, Kennedy, and Geiger, representing the War Department at the exposition.[12] In September the Army sent four officers to the fourth international Gordon Bennett airplane meet, held at Chicago from 9 to 21 September 1912. The officers attending were Major Reber of the Signal Corps, chairman of the Aero Club of America contest committee, and three pilots—Chandler, Arnold, and Milling—who were assigned various duties which allowed them to contact other aviators and inspect their airplanes. Chandler was the official starter for the Gordon Bennett race and the two lieutenants were responsible for sealing, mounting, and safeguarding the official barographs on the contestants' planes.[13]

On 28 May Chandler received copies of War Department Form No. 395 AGO, dated 2 February, which stated that "all candidates for aviation only shall be subject to a vigorous physical examination to determine their fitness for duty." This was the first document in American aviation medicine, for prior to the issuance of this form no physical examination had been required for student pilots. Chandler as commanding officer of the aviation school, promptly saw to it that all officers on duty at the school were properly examined.[14]

The first night flying at College Park took place quite accidentally on 1 June 1912, the same day that Lieutenant Arnold established a new Army altitude record of 6,450 feet, breaking his own previous record. That afternoon the annual Army-Navy baseball game was to be played at Annapolis. The Navy pilots stationed there had invited the Army pilots to fly over for the game. Captain Chandler flew over alone, landing on the parade ground after only 18 minutes in the air. After the game, engine trouble delayed his departure, and by the time Lt. T. G. Ellyson, in charge of the Navy pilots, had the plane repaired, the sun had set. Chandler, nevertheless, decided to try to make it to College Park before dark. On his way he ran into turbulent air, which buffeted his plane about, almost causing it to crash, and by the time he got out of trouble, it was dark. He was able, however, to follow the signal lights of the Baltimore and Ohio Railway to College Park. When he arrived over the field, the mechanics heard his engine and saw flashes from the exhaust; they promptly threw oil and gasoline on the field and ignited it, lighting the way for Chandler, who landed his plane safely. Later acetylene signaling lamps were set up along the runway, and Milling and others conducted several experiments in night flying.[15]

A week after Chandler's night flight the Army made its first attempt at firing a machine gun from an airplane. Col. Isaac N. Lewis had designed a machine gun for infantry and cavalry use; since it had a low recoil, it was thought possible that it might be effective in an airplane, and Colonel Lewis brought one of his guns to College Park for a flight test. The air-cooled weapon weighed 25 pounds, 6 ounces and fired the Army standard rifle ammunition, which was loaded in a 50-round drum. It could be adjusted for rates of fire between 300 and 700 shots a minute. For the tests at College Park, the rate of fire was set at about 500 shots a minute, which would empty the drum in six seconds. Chandler volunteered to operate the gun from a Wright B plane piloted by Milling, and on 7 June the two fliers took off with the muzzle of the gun resting on the plane's crossbar footrest. Milling flew over the 6 x 7-foot cheesecloth target three times at an altitude of 250 feet while Chandler fired at it. Although the gun had no sights, Chandler scored five hits and several near-misses. On 8 June a better target made of cotton cloth 2 yards wide and 18 yards long was provided, and the altitude was increased to 550 feet. This time, out of 44 shots fired, 14 hits were scored. Though these experiments made good newspaper copy, a General Staff officer made it clear to reporters that airplanes were suitable only for reconnaissance and that thoughts of air battles were purely the product of the young fliers' fertile imaginations. The aviators at the school, however, continued to believe that air warfare was a possibility, and they requested 10 Lewis guns for further experimentation. Because the army had not accepted the Lewis gun, it turned down the request, but later sent several Benet-Mercier machine guns, which the school group, then in Augusta, found unsuitable for use in an airplane. The subsequent development of the Lewis gun for aviation was effected in Europe during World War I.[16]

The first of the Wright Company's Scout airplanes Type C, S.C. No. 10, was delivered at College Park in May. Similar in shape to the Type B of 1911, it was slightly larger and was powered with a 6-cylinder, 50-horsepower Wright engine. On 17 May, Orville Wright arrived to confer with Mr. A. L. Welsh, the Wright pilot conducting the acceptance tests, and the next day Welsh made the first of a series of 16 flights in the new plane. On the afternoon of 11 June 1912, Welsh decided to finish the tests. He took off with Lt. L. W. Hazelhurst as a passenger, rose to an altitude of about 200 feet, and descended at a very steep angle. This was a maneuver he had previously executed successfuly, but this time he apparently waited too long to pull out of his dive, for the plane crashed into the ground. Welsh and Hazel hurst were killed.* Another Model C, also numbered S.C. No. 10, was subsequently delivered by the Wright company to take the place of the wrecked plane. S.C. No. 11, another Wright C, was delivered at College Park and accepted on 3 October 1912.[17]

By the spring of 1912 the three major airplane manufacturing companies, Wright, Burgess, and Curtiss, were producing hydroairplanes. These were land planes equipped with pontoons, particularly adapted to coastal defense and interisland flying because they could operate from both land and water. The Wright Types B and C were built so that the wheels and pontoons were interchangeable. The Burgess Company and Curtis, in addition to using pontoons, followed the European plan by equipping its planes with a cockpit nacelle in which the passenger was seated directly behind the pilot and both were protected from the wind and weather. Burgess also used the European tractor propeller out in front instead of the old pusher type in the rear. An Army plane of this new type, S.C. No. 9, had been ordered from Burgess Company and Curtis. It was to be a biplane with Wright warping wings and controls, equipped with a French, 70-horsepower Renault engine.[18]

In August 1912 during army maneuvers near Bridgeport, Connecticut, the War Department had an opportunity to test the efficiency of airplanes operating in conjunction with ground troops. Captain Hennessy and Lieutenants Kirtland, Arnold, Foulois, Graham, Geiger, and Milling were to represent the aviation service. Arnold and Kirtland were at the Burgess factory when they received their orders. On Chandler's recommendation, they left for the maneuvers on 12 August in the Army's first tractor, the Burgess hydroairplane, S.C. No. 9, which had just passed its acceptance tests. High winds forced them to land on Massachusetts Bay. When they attempted to take off with the tide, one wing hit the water during a low turn into the wind causing them to crash. The plane was shipped back to the Burgess Company and Curtis for repairs, and the two lieutenants did not get to the maneuvers.* The only other planes in condition to be used for the maneuvers were the Burgess-Wright and the dual-control Curtiss, neither of which was suitable for carrying an observer.†[19] The aviation school sent these two planes—the Curtiss, Signal Corps No. 6, piloted by Milling, and the radio-equipped Burgess-Wright, Signal Corps No. 5, piloted by Foulois, who, although he was not on aviation duty, had been ordered to participate in the maneuvers. The New York National Guard sent a Curtiss singleseater, which was piloted by Pfc Beckwith Havens of the Guard and was attached to the aviation detachment.[20]

The officers made numerous reconnaissance

---

*One of the World War I training fields in New York was subsequently named Hazlehurst Field.

*This statement is based on Signal Corps files, although Chandler and Lahm say the two lieutenants went to Connecticut by train.

†The Burgess machine was old and needed overhauling, and the Curtiss plane could not always carry an observer because of the inadequate flying field. However, Geiger did fly with Milling as an observer on one or more occasions.

Officers at College Park, May 1912

Captain Chandler and Lt. Roy Kirtland in Wright B with Lewis machine gun, College Park, 7 June 1912

Wright C at College Park, 1912

Wreck of Wright C, Signal Corps No. 10, in which Welsh and Hazlehurst were killed at College Park

The Army's first tractor, Burgess hydro Signal Corps No. 9, at Salem, Mass., July 1912

The Army's first Curtiss tractor, Signal Corps No. 21, accepted in February 1913

Lts. H. H. Arnold and T. D. Milling at College Park, 1912

Curtiss hydroplane on ramp at Army War College, 1912

flights, and during good weather frequently reported the position of ground troops, but when the weather was bad it was impossible to see anything from the prescribed 2,000-foot minimum altitude. On 12 August Foulois flew more than an hour in the Burgess-Wright on reconnaissance over the Stratford-Derby-New Haven area, reporting the location, composition, and strength of the forces in the area. The next day, Foulois and Milling were both up for more than an hour on different occasions scouting the country between Zoar Bridge and Sandy Hook. In the course of his flights Foulois tried reporting by radio but he found that the radio, which he had tested at College Park the week before maneuvers, could not be operated satisfactorily by the pilot because of his flying duties. Although information was transmitted for a distance of 8 to 12 miles, no attempt was made to send complete messages because further adjustments were found to be necessary. Three days later, on the 17th, Foulois, after landing to report that both Blue flanks were seriously threatened, was left stranded when the Blue forces retreated and was captured by the Reds.[21]

During the maneuvers the aviation detachment had operated first with the Red force and then with the Blue force, and it was found that in each case the airplanes gave the force to which they were attached a decided advantage over the opposition. The pilot officers were commended for their work by the officer in charge of the maneuvers. After the maneuvers the pilots recommended that trained observers were necessary for reconnaissance work and that fuselage machines were desirable to protect the observers from the wind.[22]

While the maneuvers were in progress, the new Burgess hydroairplane, S.C. No. 9, in which Arnold and Kirtland had crashed, was being repaired. It was later sent to College Park, but since there was no body of water there, it and the single pontoon Curtiss Type D were kept at the Army War College in Washington, D.C. Captain Hennessy, in addition to his duties at College Park, was placed in charge of the seaplane equipment and the enlisted personnel. The Corps of Engineers built a 67-foot float which was anchored to the seawall on the Anacostia River near the War College, and the commandant of the Navy Yard, Rear Admiral Beatty, put his launch at the disposal of

the aviators so that they could get to and from the planes housed on the float.[23]

Meanwhile, at College Park, Lt. L. C. Rockwell, under the instruction of Milling, had qualified on 25 September 1912 for FAI pilot certificate No. 165. On the 28th he took off in S.C. No. 4 with Corporal Frank S. Scott, Wright airplane mechanic, as a passenger. After flying for a few minutes at 500 feet, he descended to 100 feet, and then appeared to throttle down the engine to descent to within about 25 feet of the ground, before resuming full power for the upward climb. Apparently he misjudged his distance and when the engine was suddenly given full power the plane dived to the ground. Scott was killed instantly, and Rockwell died three hours later at Walter Reed Hospital.* This was the fourth fatal airplane accident in the Army. Scott, who had been with the aviation school for some time, was the first enlisted man to be killed in an airplane crash.[24] In order to reduce the possibility of any more such tragedies, Col. George P. Scriven, Acting Chief Signal Officer, directed that thereafter officer aviators would not be permitted to carry passengers until they had qualified as Military Aviators and that for this test they would carry 150 pounds of additional weight instead of a passenger.[25]

Shortly after the Rockwell-Scott tragedy the first competition was held for the Mackay Trophy, which had been presented by Clarence H. Mackay, a member of the Aero Club of America, to the War Department in January 1912 for annual competition by army pilots. The conditions of the initial competition, drawn up by the Signal Corps, included a cross-country flight of 20 miles at an altitude of not less than 1,500 feet; military reconnaissance of a triangular area of 10 miles on each side for the purpose of locating troops within the area; an accurate landing; and a report on the location and composition of the troops. The requirements were to become increasingly difficult each year. In the absence of a contest, the trophy could be awarded to the officer or officers who, in the opinion of the War Department, made the most meritorious flight of the year. The first competition was held on 9 October at College Park; the judges were Lt. Col. Frederick Foltz, Major Saltzman, and Captain Chandler. The two

_____

*Rockwell Field, in California and Scott Field, in Illinois were named for these two men. Rockwell is no longer in existence, having been taken over by the Navy as part of its San Diego Air Station.

entrants, Lieutenants Arnold and Milling, took off at 9:30 A.M., but Milling returned and asked to be withdrawn from the contest on account of illness. Arnold located the troops, complied with the other requirements, and was declared the first winner of the Mackay Trophy.[26]

Later in the month, Arnold, Hennessy,* Milling, and eight enlisted men under Sgt. Herbert Marcus[27] were sent from College Park to Fort Riley, Kansas, where they were joined by 1st Lt. Joseph O. Mauborgne, Sgt. George M. Dusenberg, and a radio section from Fort Leavenworth. These men were ordered to conduct experiments in aerial observation and direction of artillery fire. The two new Wright C's, S.C. Nos. 10 and 11 (with one spare 6-cylinder engine), were shipped to Fort Riley where they were staked down in the open on the parade ground.

On 27 October, Arnold and an artillery officer, Lt. Follett Bradley, a Navy past midshipman† and wireless operator on the U.S.S. *Michigan,* conducted a radio test flight prior to the artillery adjustment flights. The operation was not completely successful. The radio's 300-foot antenna was paid out behind the plane and 15 words were sent, but because the weight at the end of the antenna was not heavy enough to hold it down and prevent its being snarled in the propeller on turns, the wire had to be cut. No signals were received by the ground operator, who was only a mile away. On 2 November the two lieutenants went up again in S.C. No. 10 for a 33-minute flight at 1,000 feet with a heavier weight attached to the antenna. This time Lieutenant Mauborgne who was operating the receiving set at Fort Riley heard the signals clearly from a maximum distance of six miles, but it was noted that when the speed of the engine of the plane was reduced, the signals had a tendency to fade.[28]

From 5 to 13 November, artillery fire was directed from an airplane for the first time in the United States.[29] The planes were used to locate targets, give the range and direction to the battery, spot the hits with reference to the targets, and give the necessary corrections. Three methods were used to transmit the information from the airplane to the firing battery: the first and most successful was radio telegraphy; the second

was a card dropping system which required the plane to remain directly over the firing battery so that the cards could be picked up immediately; the third was the Means smoke signal method, the least successful of all, except for short distance, because the blast from propellers quickly dissipated the lampblack. Since no successful method of receiving messages in an airplane had been devised at this time, a panel system of two strips of canvas arranged in various ways on the ground was used for communicating from the ground to the plane; for example, strips laid in the form of a "T" indicated that the message had been received on the ground, whereas a "V" meant to repeat the message. The test proved the value of using trained observers in the airplanes, especially in connection with artillery fire at hidden targets.[30]

On 5 November when Lieutenant Arnold was conducting a test with an artillery officer as an observer he had a harrowing experience in plane No. 10 which he described as follows:[31]

The machine was spiralling down to land near the camp from a height of about 400 feet. The spiral was not steep and was of a large diameter. . . . The engine was fully throttled when suddenly the machine turned a complete circle, 360° in spite of the fact that the rudder was turned hard over the other direction. Then for some unaccountable reason the machine plunged head foremost in a vertical line down towards the earth. . . . The machine was out of control from the time it took its first turn of 360° until the bottom of the drop when I pulled it up and landed. There is no explanation of this occurrence for after landing I found every control wire intact and no wires cut or entangled in any manner. I am unable to account for it.

He ended his report by stating that he did not see how he could get in a plane for a month or two and requested 20 days' leave of absence.

After his near-crash Arnold did no more flying for some time. In December 1912 he got a desk job as assistant to Major Russel in charge of aviation in the Office of the Chief Signal Officer and later he was relieved from aviation duty at his own request because of his approaching marriage. He did not return to aviation until May 1916, when he was made supply officer of the Aviation School at North Island, San Diego, California.[32]

At the conclusion of the experiments in air-ground cooperation the pilots returned to College Park. Signal Corps plane No. 11 was sent to Augusta. Signal Corps airplane No. 10 was shipped to Fort Leavenworth in the care of Sergeant Mar-

---

*Captain Hennessy was selected for this duty because he was a Field Artillery officer and could coordinate the work between the aviation and artillery units.
†Past midshipman was an early naval rank.

cus and Private McCloud who were ordered there with it.* No one at Leavenworth knew what to do with the plane and apparently it was not used; it was still there in 1913.*[33]

In the fall of 1912 the Army made the performance test for military aircraft more difficult. The useful load of the Scout type plane was increased 150 pounds over that prescribed the previous year. Maneuverability and rate of climb were stressed in the Speed Scout. One test required the plane to make figure 8's over a rectangular field 500 yards long and 250 yards wide, without losing more than 100 feet of altitude.[34]. In the meantime the Wright company's planes were having considerable trouble in passing even the earlier tests, with structural defects apparently the main cause of the difficulty. Mr. William Kabitzke, a Wright pilot, had succeeded in getting only two out of six airplanes successfully through the tests in two months' time. The Wright C, S.C. No. 16, was accepted at Augusta on 22 November 1912, but in January 1913, the D's (new Wright Speed Scouts) were still undergoing tests there. In addition to these difficulties, during one of Kabitzke's tests on 18 October, Lincoln Beachey in the Curtiss S.C. No. 2 (which had been rebuilt and fitted with a 75-horsepower engine) flew so close to buildings and to Kabitzke that Beachey was prohibited from flying government airplanes.[35]

The Chief Signal Officer announced on 26 October 1912 that instruction at the aviation schools would be put under control of an advisory board consisting of the commandant and all Military Aviators on duty at the school, but a year later on 18 October 1913 the composition of the advisory board was reduced to the commandant and only three Military Aviators. Each instructor was to have direct charge of the student assigned to him until he had passed the test for Military Aviator. The student was to be given his choice of the type airplane he wished to fly and then sent to one of the civilian manufacturers' schools for preliminary instruction (which was given without charge), or assigned to an instructor of the Signal Corps school. In either case when the student reached the advanced course in flying he was assigned an instructor who had complete control of the method of instruction and the time spent in flying.

At the end of October 1912 the Signal Corps had purchased the following planes:[37]

> Wright A, S.C. No. 1 in 1909
> Curtiss D, S.C. No. 2 in 1911
> Wright B, S.C. No. 3 in 1911
> Wright B, S.C. No. 4 in 1911
> Burgess F, S.C. No. 5 in 1911
> Curtiss E, S.C. No. 6 in 1911
> Wright B. S.C. No. 7 in 1911
> Curtiss E, S.C. No. 8 in 1912
> Burgess H, S.C. No. 9 in 1912
> Wright C, S.C. No. 10 in 1912
> Wright C, S.C. No. 11 in 1912

Of these 11 planes, 8 were at College Park at this time; S.C. No. 1 was in the Smithsonian, S.C. No. 4 had been destroyed, and S.C. No. 7 was in the Philippines.

By November 1912, the College Park school had 8 sheds. The personnel on aviation duty consisted of one civilian mechanic, 39 enlisted men, and 14 flying officers. The officers were: Capts. Charles deF. Chandler and Frederick B. Hennessy; 1st Lts. Roy C. Kirtland, Harold Geiger, Harry Graham, Loren H. Call, Lewis E. Goodier, Joseph D. Park, and Samuel H. McLeary; 2d Lts. Thomas DeW. Milling, Henry H. Arnold, Eric L. Ellington, Lewis H. Brereton, and William C. Sherman.

By this time the weather at College Park was no longer suitable for flying, and since Glenn Curtiss had invited the Signal Corps to send officers to his school at San Diego, California, for winter flying it was decided to divide the Signal Corps aviation school. The Curtiss pilots and mechanics were sent to San Diego and the Wright pilots and mechanics to Augusta. The move to San Diego marked the inception of what was to become the army's first permanent aviation school.*[38]. The school at College Park closed on 18 November 1912, and although legislation was introduced on 6 May 1913 to buy the ground there, the Chief Signal Officer recommended the annulment of the lease when it expired on 30 June 1913 and the station was abandoned on that date.[39]

THE AUGUSTA AIR SCHOOL, 1912-1913

On 18 November 1912 a special train of nine cars transported Captain Chandler and Lieutenants Graham and Sherman—all Wright pilots—five

---

*In the Wright Brothers' papers in the Library of Congress there is a letter from Lieutenant Foulois in which he says that S.C. No. 10 was sent to Fort Leavenworth for his use; he asked the Wrights for information on how to fly it since he had never flown a Wright C. Foulois was stationed at Leavenworth with the 7th Infantry at that time.

*See below, Chapter V.

planes, and equipment from College Park to the Barnes farm outside Augusta for the second winter. These pilots were followed later by Lieutenants Kirtland and Milling. Lieutenant Arnold was left in charge of the Aeronautical Division in Washington. The planes shipped to Augusta were the Wright B, S.C. No. 3, the Burgess-Wright, F. S.C. No. 5, the Burgess tractor H, S.C. No. 9, the Wright C, S.C. No. 11, and the Wright C trainer, S.C. No. 16.[40]

The weather in Augusta at the beginning of 1913 was not favorable for flying; furthermore, the school had considerable trouble with its plane engines. Plane No. 11, which had been used at Fort Riley, had been overhauled by the Wright Company, but the pilots had no confidence in its 6-cylinder engine. The Wrights advised that they had no hesitation in guaranteeing the engine to be better than the 4-cylinder one, which was also giving trouble. Finally, a Wright Company mechanic, Mr. Conover, was sent to Augusta to put the engines in shape.

When Conover arrived he was accompanied by Oscar Brindley, a Wright Company pilot, who had been sent to test the new Wright D–1 and D-2 Speed Scouts, which Kabitzke had previously and unsuccessfully tried to get through the tests at College Park.* On 23 January 1913, Brindley began practice with the D-2 machine. Bad weather and unfamiliarity with the plane delayed the trials, but on 30 January the speed test was passed with an average of 66.9 miles per hour, which was much faster than that of any previous army plane. On 4 February the plane passed the climb test; the following day it passed the glide test. On the 6th, however, while landing on ploughed ground the sudden braking effect of the soft dirt caused the machine to roll over and come to rest upside down. Although the pilot received only minor injuries, the plane was badly damaged. In spite of the fact that the D-2 plane had passed all the tests except landing on plowed ground, it was not accepted. Instead, it was rebuilt and sent to College Park, where, on 3 May 1913, after seven months of tests it was accepted as S.C. No. 19. It was then sent to Texas City, with instructions that it was to be flown only by the most experienced aviators.

*These planes were the property of the Wright Company and in order to pass their acceptance tests they had to be flown where the Signal Corps aviation officers could observe their performance.

Later it was shipped to San Diego where it was never flown. The D-1, S.C. No. 20 also was sent to College Park where it was finally accepted on 6 June 1913. Later it was shipped to San Antonio, and from there to San Diego, where it was dropped from the records of 2 June 1914, apparently never having been used.[41]

Up to the end of February 1913 no flights which included a landing away from the school had been made from Augusta. Captain Chandler, who wished to encourage cross-country training, made the first such flight on 25 February when he flew to Waynesboro, Georgia, 28 miles south of Augusta, and landed in an open field near the home of a friend who had invited him to spend the night. That evening, Chandler received a call from the school advising him that all personnel and equipment were to be sent to Texas City, Texas, as quickly as possible because of the tense relations with Mexico, resulting from a revolution and seizure of power on 22 February by Gen. Victoriano Huerta, whose government was not recognized by the United States. Early the next morning Chandler put blocks in front of the wheels while he turned the propeller to start the engine, took off without assistance, and with the aid of a tail wind was back at Augusta in 36 minutes. After two hectic days of preparations, the detachment left Augusta on 28 February in a special train of 11 cars carrying 5 officers, 21 enlisted men, the airplanes, and all necessary equipment for field service. Two cars of garrison equipment were shipped back to College Park.[42]

THE TEXAS CITY AIR SCHOOL, 1913

The two officers who were being trained by Frank Coffyn at the Palm Beach school, Lieutenants Ellington and Call, together with S.C. No. 17, also were ordered to Texas City to take part in the 2d Division maneuvers.[43] Captain Hennessy, on duty in the Aviation Section in Washington, left on 26 February to arrive in advance of the Augusta and Palm Beach contingents to select a suitable camp site at Texas City, preferably on the water front so that the seaplanes could be used.

The train from Augusta arrived at Texas City on 2 March and camp was established, the planes were assembled, and flying began a few days later.[44] Here the group operated as the First

Wright D

Aero Squadron* instead of as a school, although the provisional squadron organization was not announced in general orders until 4 December 1913. This designation appears to have been based on a memo from the Chief Signal Officer to the Chief of Staff dated 3 March 1913, which suggested that "as the present concentration of aeronautic material at Galveston presents the first opportunity to officially recognize an organization," the name "First Aero Squadron" should be the official designation provisionally adopted for this organization.[45] On 5 March 1913, the First Aero Squadron was organized and the officer personnel were assigned as follows:

Squadron Commander—Capt. Charles deF. Chandler
Adjutant and Supply Officer—
      Capt. Frederick B. Hennessy
Surgeon—1st Lt. Charles J. Boehs

Company A:
   1st Lt. Harry Graham
   1st Lt. Loren H. Call
   2d Lt. Eric L. Ellington

Company B:
   1st Lt. Roy C. Kirtland
   2d Lt. William C. Sherman
   2d Lt. Thomas DeW. Milling

Company A was assigned S.C. airplanes Nos. 5, 9, 17, and 18,† together with 24 enlisted men. Company B got S.C. airplanes Nos. 3, 11, 12, 13, and 16, and 27 enlisted men. Each airplane was charged to an officer and could not be used without his permission. Milling was Senior Instructor and his orders were obeyed without regard to rank.[46]

On 6 March 1913, Major Samuel Reber, Signal Corps officer and balloonist, was ordered to Galveston on temporary duty in connection with Signal Corps organization and installations.[47] He was followed by six other officers who were assigned to the First Aero Squadron. Three of the officers received their orders in March: 2d Lt. Fred Seydel was assigned on the 15th, but was relieved from aviation duty early the following year;**[48] 2d. Lt. Ralph E. Jones received his orders on the 18th but was relieved by the board

on 3 May because of ineptitude;[49] and Lt. Hugh M. Kelly was detailed for aviation duty on 26 March. In May the other three officers arrived. 1st Lt. Moss L. Love, who had learned to fly in the Philippines,† and 1st Lt. Townsend F. Dodd were ordered to Texas City on the 8th and 9th, respectively.[50] Lt. J. C. Morrow was assigned on 15 May; he was relieved on 7 January 1914, but was put back on aviation duty the following day. On 1 April 1913, Captain Chandler, who had been ordered to the Philippines, was succeeded as commander of the First Aero Squadron by Capt. A. S. Cowan, Chief Signal Officer of the 2d Division.[51]

Although the flying field at Texas City was adequate when it was selected, it was soon found necessary to place two infantry brigades on the ground alloted for flying, which considerably reduced the space available for landings and take-offs. The field area proper was large enough, 250 x 350 yards, but three of its sides were obstructed by wires, tents, and houses, and the fourth bounded by Galveston Bay; consequently it was not considered safe for beginners practicing landings in training machines, or for more advanced students landing higher powered machines for the first time.[52] Constant high winds during March also interfered with flying. Nevertheless several of cross-country flights were made from the field. On 12 March three planes, S.C. No. 9 with Milling and Sherman, No. 5 with Graham, and No. 16 with Kirtland as pilot and Sergeant Idzorek as passenger flew to Houston and back, a round trip of 80 miles. Kirtland experienced the only difficulty encountered on the trip; he was forced down by a rainstorm five miles out of Houston.[53]

On 28 March Milling and Sherman in the Burgess tractor, S.C. No. 9 established a new American two-man duration and distance record flying 200 miles in 4 hours and 22 minutes. With Milling as pilot they arrived over San Antonio from Texas City after flying for 3 hours and 20 minutes but continued to circle the city for more than an hour in order to break the old record. On the return trip, made in 3 hours and 57 minutes on 31 March, Sherman made the first Army aerial map. Made in sections, it covered the entire route. Each section showed the country passed

---

*This squadron became the first air combat unit in the United States Army when it took part in the operations of the Punitive Expedition on the Mexican border.
†Burgess J, S.C. No. 18, was a duplicate of the Wright C but it had a Sturtevant engine. There is no record of its receipt or acceptance. It was ready for delivery at Marblehead on 21 January 1913.
**Seydel returned to aviation duty in May 1917 and was again relieved in 1918.

'See below, pp. 79 ff.

Wright hydroairplane, Texas City, 1913

over in 10 minutes of flying time. All bearings were taken from a compass mounted near the observer, who used a cavalry sketch case. The map was a detailed one, showing railroads, bridges, wagon roads, towns, streams, woods, hills, prairies, and other topographical features.[54]

On 17 April, the Burgess-Wright S.C. No. 5 was damaged in a takeoff by Lieutenant Call when the 4-cylinder Sturtevant engine failed to deliver its full power and the plane ran over a bank at the water's edge, flew about 75 yards, stalled, and struck the water nose first at an angle of about 15°. Call was thrown clear into four feet of water, which broke his fall. When the damaged machine was rebuilt, it emerged as a Wright type C, with a 4-cylinder Wright engine. Thereafter it was used as a training machine. This changeover left Texas City with only one type B plane, S.C. No. 3, which greatly facilitated the handling of spare parts, for most of the other planes were type C's.[55]

On 1 May two airplanes played an important part in solving a maneuver problem. Signal Corps No. 9, flown by Milling with Sherman as observer, reconnoitered the town of Webster, flew back to Algoa to locate the position of the "enemy," and ended the flight at the field headquarters of the 2d Division. Sherman made a map and took photographs of the towns and the encampment over which they flew. The other plane was a Wright, piloted by Kirtland with Ellington as observer. These officers flew from the camp to Algoa and vicinity. Ellington also made a map of the country traversed, which was incorporated in the situation report covering both the enemy and the various units of the defensive force. Milling then made a short flight to locate the 6th Cavalry, and the air part of the problem was declared solved. The commanding general of the 2d Division, William H. Carter, commended the excellent showing of the Signal Corps officers and asked that all of them be congratulated.[56]

Although the Signal Corps aviation unit did not take part in it, the first war bombing in the Western hemisphere took place on 10 May 1913, when Didier Masson and bombardier Thomas J. Dean, both American nationals flying in a Glenn Martin Curtiss-type pusher, for Mexican revolutionist Pancho Villa bombed a Mexican federal gunboat in Guaymas Bay.*[57]

During this period when war with Mexico seemed imminent several air-minded citizens wrote to the War Department offering units of aviation reserves composed of pilots and mechanics for duty on the border. Among these were Mortimer Delano of New York, who called himself Acting Commander, First Provisional Aviation Corps, and Albert B. Lambert, a pilot and former president of the Aero Club of St. Louis, who had formed a United States Aviation Reserve Corps. The volunteers of the reserve units could not be accepted by the Army because Congress had not enacted legislation nor had it called for volunteers.[58]

These civilian organizations were separate and distinct from the National Guard units, several of which had formed their own aviation detachments. Among the first of these were the balloon detachments of the New York National Guard which were established in 1908 and those of the Missouri Militia and the California National Guard, both established in 1909.[59] Some of the National Guard units had planes of their own, but others tried to persuade the Army to furnish them with aircraft and to teach their officers to fly. Such requests for planes had to be refused because the army had barely enough planes for its own pilots and no money with which to buy more, so that until 1913 the only National Guard officer who had been taught to fly by the Signal Corps was Lt. Col. C. B. Winder of the Ohio Guard.

On 22 April 1914 the Chief Signal Officer requested legislation for the organization of an aviation branch of the Volunteer Signal Corps and three days later on 25 April the Volunteer Act was approved. This act allowed an aviation branch to be formed, but the volunteer forces were to be organized only in the event of war. Actually, the reserve organizations were not needed at that time, since the threatened war with Mexico

*The Masson bomb was a 3 x 18-inch iron pipe with a cap on each end. Set in the nose cap was a rod, one end of which was close to a detonator screwed to the base of the cap; the other end projected an inch or so beyond the nose cap and had a nut screwed on it. A clip, secured about the rod between the nose cap and the nut as a safety device, was removed before the bomb was launched. The bomb was kept on course by directional vanes which extended from the base of the bomb. When the rod struck the ground or an object, it was driven back against the detonator, setting it off. Eight bombs loaded with sticks of dynamite packed in steel rivets were carried in a rack under the plane. They were aimed with a crude bombsight and released by pulling a cord.

did not materialize, and when the United States entered World War I they practically went out of existence as the army absorbed many of their members into the Signal Corps.[60]

When it became evident that the United States would not be involved in any military operations on the Mexican border, most of the aviation personnel and equipment at Texas City was transferred on 15 June 1913 to San Diego, California. Experience had shown that training conditions were simply too hazardous at Texas City for student pilots. Lieutenant Kirtland was left there in command of the First Aero Squadron, composed of himself and Lieutenants Graham and Call, 26 enlisted men, and two airplanes, S.C. No. 11, and S.C. No. 20.*[61] On 26 June Kirtland and Call took part in another maneuver problem. They flew S.C. No. 11 to reconnoiter the "enemy" force which was reported to have camped at Dickinson, Texas, on the preceding day. They found the troops preparing to march toward La Marque although their wagon trains had not yet left camp. The fliers marked a map to show the "enemy's" positions and circled the area to determine which road the mounted scouts took. They flew at less than 1,000 feet because of clouds, but maintained safety from hostile fire by remaining a horizontal distance of about half a mile from the enemy. Three minutes after landing on their home field the aviators had submitted a complete report.[62]

Not long afterward two of the three pilots remaining at Texas City were dropped from the rolls of the First Aero Squadron. On 30 June Lieutenant Graham had a serious motorcycle accident, from which he recovered so slowly that he was finally relieved from aviation duty.† On 8 July Lieutenant Call, in order to complete the requirements for his Military Aviator rating, took off alone in S.C. No. 11. The machine had attained an altitude of two or three hundred feet and was in a banked turn—from which the pilot was apparently unable to level out—when, according to witnesses, there was a loud sound, the wings or parts of them separated, and the plane struck the ground upside down. The airplane was totally demolished, and Call was killed.**[63] After Call's

death Kirtland requested one or more additional officers for Texas City but the Chief Signal Officer refused because there were only three officers available and they were at San Diego conducting the training program. Finally Kirtland was sent to San Diego on 28 November 1913, and operations at Texas City ceased.[64]

OVERSEAS AIR SCHOOLS: PHILIPPINES AND HAWAII

In August 1911 Gen. James Allen, the Chief Signal Officer, had recommended the establishment of an air station in the Philippines. In September, Lt. Col. William A. Glassford, Chief Signal Officer of the Philippines Department, anticipating maneuvers early in 1912, urged that two or more airplanes and one trained aviator be sent to the Philippines to participate in the maneuvers. General Allen wanted to comply with this request, but the scarcity of officers and men in the War Department precluded detailing the additional officers necessary for instruction in aviation. On 14 November 1911, however, Glassford was notified that an order had been placed for a Wright B airplane with enough spare parts for six months of operation. This plane, S.C. No. 7, was shipped on 11 December, and two early members of the Signal Corps air detachment, Corporal Vernon Burge and Private Kenneth L. Kintzel, went along as mechanics. At Manila five more mechanics were obtained (Sergeant Cox and Privates Dodd, McDowell, Johnson, and Corcoran). The Quartermaster built a two-plane hangar on the edge of the polo field at Fort William McKinley to house the plane. Lieutenant Lahm, who had rejoined his regiment, the 7th Cavalry, in the Philippines in November 1911, was detailed to temporary duty for aviation with the Signal Corps and opened the Philippine Air School on 12 March 1912. On the 21st, plane No. 7, equipped with floats, was assembled and flown for the first time.[65]

The first two students at the Philippine school were 1st Lt. Moss L. Love and Corporal Burge. Love, who was on 4-year detail with the Signal Corps, obtained permission to take flying instruction provided that it did not interfere with his regular duties. Burge, who had requested flying training, was selected by Lahm because of the lack of officers in the Signal Corps available for instruc-

---

*S.C. No. 20 was not used; a Wright "C" S.C. No. 12 was reported to have been delivered at Texas City also, but it is not known when.

†He returned to aviation during World War I and remained until he retired in 1929.

**One of the World War I training fields in Texas was named for Lt. Call.

tion.* He became the first enlisted man to be taught to fly by the army, passing the FAI test on 14 June 1912 and receiving aviation certificate No. 154. Love passed his test on 28 June and received FAI certificate No. 155. Lahm acted as the Aero Club observer.[66]

During the training period there were two minor accidents, the more serious of which happened on 8 May when Lahm stalled his plane and landed in the mud of the Taguig River. Eight days were required to repair the plane. On the 29th an emergency landing caused damage that involved five more days' delay for repairs. Finally, another engine was substituted for the original one and results were more satisfactory.

With the beginning of the rainy season in July, flying was suspended and the plane was stored until early in 1913. The enlisted men of the detachment were reassigned and Lahm was returned to his regiment on 1 August 1912.[67] For the next seven months the school was closed, although as late as 12 October physical examination forms were sent to the Philippines with the request that each officer on aviation duty take the examination. Each aviator also had to have his eyes examined every three months.[68]

On 10 March 1913 the Philippine air school reopened at Fort McKinley with Lahm on temporary duty as instructor to three new students, 2d Lts. Carleton G. Chapman, 7th Cavalry, Herbert A. Dargue, CAC, and C. Perry Rich, Philippine Scouts, all of whom had applied for air training. Six Signal Corps enlisted men were detailed as mechanics. The plane used for instruction was the same Wright B that had been used the previous year. Chapman and Dargue made their first solo flights on 15 April 1913, and in July received FAI pilot certificates No. 241 and 242, respectively. Rich qualified for his pilot rating on 5 May 1913, obtaining certificate No. 243.[69]

The Chief Signal Officer on 20 September 1912 had ordered for the Philippine air station one 50-horsepower Wright C Scout with pontoons.[70] This airplane, designated Signal Corps No. 13, was delivered at Fort McKinley in May 1913.[71] When it was unloaded, several wing ribs were found to be broken and leaks were discovered in the oil, fuel, and water tanks. It was repaired and

assembled on 16 May and first flown as a landplane on 21 May. The three student officers were given instruction in flying the faster Type C, so that when the requirements for the new Military Aviator's pilot rating were received, Chapman and Dargue were able to pass the test and to receive their Military Aviators' ratings. Both men qualified also for Expert Pilot certificates* before leaving Fort McKinley. In June Captain Chandler, who had arrived in the Philippines from Texas City, was put on flying status. There were then six Wright pilots at the Philippine air school—Chandler, Lahm, Chapman, Dargue, Rich, and Sergeant Burge.[72]

Several reconnaissance flights were made during the maneuvers in 1913. On 29 May Lahm made a military reconnaissance flight of 21 miles to Alabang and return. The objective was to search for favorable landing places along the Taguig River and the shores of Laguna de Bay and to report whether or not troops were in the vicinity of Alabang.[73] On 17 June Dargue reconnoitered troops of the 7th and 8th Cavalry regiments returning from maneuvers, and submitted an accurate sketch which showed the location of the various elements as they passed Alabang, about 10 miles from the post.[74]

The summer rainy season put an end to flying from the low ground at Fort McKinley, but on 12 July 1913 a temporary base was established at the Manila Polo Club at Pasay and a temporary hangar was built on the beach of Manila Bay. Pontoons were substituted for the wheels on the two planes. The S.C. No. 7, Wright B, did not have enough power to lift two persons in addition to the pontoons, so it was used only for solo practice. Dargue was flying this plane on 28 August 1913, when an engine failure forced him to land on the water near the Army and Navy Club in Manila. Fortunately he was wearing a bathing suit so that he was able to swim to a small beach, towing the plane behind him. He telephoned for aid and a crew in a rowboat arrived from the air station to tow the machine back to its hangar. During the return trip, a squall came up and the wind dashed the plane against the rocks along the shore, damaging it beyond repair.[75]

The new Wright C, S.C. No. 13, was given its

---

*Colonel Glassford, Signal Officer in Manila, approved Burge's training. By the time a letter arrived from the Chief Signal Officer disapproving of enlisted men's learning to fly, Burge was already a pilot.

*Chapman received No. 14, and Dargue received No. 16.

first test on pontoons on 11 September by Lahm, but it would not rise from the water. The following day after a long run of three-quarters of a mile the plane finally cleared the water, but there was such a strong pull on the elevator that an immediate landing was necessary. As Lahm tried to bring the machine down, it dived into the water and turned over on its back. The pilot's kapok jacket kept him afloat until the crash boat arrived. It was found that the accident was caused by the center of gravity on the plane's being so far to the rear as to make it tail-heavy, putting too much of the lift on the tail surfaces. Lieutenant Rich had reported the same heavy pull on the elevator control when flying it as a land plane. The plane was so badly damaged that repairs were considered impractical and it was declared a total loss.[76]

After this accident the school was without a plane until 2 October when a second Wright C Scout, No. 12,* which had been flown at Texas City earlier in the year, arrived in the Philippines. It was in poor condition, and parts from the wrecked S.C. No. 13 were used to repair it. Its first flight took place on 8 October. On 14 November Rich, after flying this plane for nine minutes over Navy ships in Manila Bay, headed toward the hangar and started his descent. The angle increased until the flight ended in a perpendicular dive into the water. The engine broke loose, struck Rich at the base of the skull and killed him instantly.† The plane, last of the school's three, was completely wrecked and the work of the school was suspended until additional planes arrived from the United States.[77]

Meanwhile, in the first week of September, the Burgess coast defense seaplane, S.C. No. 17, had arrived in the Philippines, but it had been so damaged in transit that new upper and lower wings had to be ordered. Unlike the planes previously received in the Philippines, which had seats side by side on the leading edge of the lower wings, this plane had a cockpit with tandem seats for two passengers, but because the added weight of pontoons prevented carrying two in the plane,

the pilot had to fly alone. This seaplane was assigned to Corregidor Island for service with the Coast Defenses in radio communication and to observe the fire of the large caliber mortars and guns.

On 18 October Dargue, Burge, and Privates Dodd and Roberts reported to Fort Mills, Corregidor, for duty with the seaplane. A hangar was built at San Jose beach and a series of flights was begun on 6 November. These flights were made for various purposes: to observe the results of mortar fire, for practice in locating targets, and to observe results of siege gun fire from Corregidor on targets on the Mariveles shore. Dargue, in cooperation with Capt. Harrison Hall of the Coast Artillery, arranged a crude system of small parachute and Very pistol signals in order to indicate errors in firing. The seaplane was found to be very valuable in locating hostile positions invisible to ground observers.[78]

In December 1913 Dargue was the only officer on aviation duty in the Philippines, since Chandler had been made Assistant Department Signal Officer and the other officers had been returned to duty with their regiments.*

Several improvements were made at Fort Mills in the winter of 1913-14 in order to facilitate use of the plane for reconnaissance. By January 1914, S.C. No. 17, had been reconditioned with new pontoons so that it could carry two people. Burge was then able to relieve Dargue at the controls or act as observer for reconnaissance flights. A cement floor had been laid in the hangar and a 225-foot marine railway had been built into the water for launching the seaplane.

On 30 January the first aerial photographs of Corregidor were made from 2,000 feet. From 15 to 20 February maneuver reconnaissance flights were flown. They revealed that, although the fleet could easily be located, mobile land forces were not visible unless they were encamped in open fields. Both the pilot and observer reported that bombs could easily have been dropped.[79]

The seaplane was damaged in a landing on 20 February and was not repaired until the following month. From 28 April to 15 May 1914, flights were made for adjusting artillery fire and

---

*This disagrees with Chandler and Lahm who state that two Wright C's were delivered in May 1913. Signal Corp files give the October date and there is no earlier mention of this plane elsewhere.

†Rich had discussed with Lt. Dargue the facility with which he could pull the Wright plane out af a dive and Dargue stated that Rich was trying to prove that the Wright plane would pull out of a dive better than a Curtiss plane. Rich Field, a World War I training field at Waco, Texas, was named for Lt. Rich.

*On 15 March 1914 Chandler became Philippine Dept. Signal Officer, relieving Col. Glassford, who was ordered back to the U.S. Lieutenant Chapman had been returned to duty with the 7th Cavalry but was sent back to the States in December 1913 and was assigned to duty at the Aviation School at North Island, California, in 1914.

Lt. F. P. Lahm with the Wright hydro, Signal Corps No. 7, at Fort McKinley, Philippine Islands, 1912

Burgess coast defense hydro, Signal Corps No. 17, with Lt. Dargue at controls, Corregidor, P.I., 1914

a few photographs were taken, but the results of the latter were not very satisfactory. The rainy season began earlier than usual and only two flights were made in June.

Beginning on 18 September the first flights after the rainy season were made by Dargue and Burge. During these flights a small radio set which had been made at the Signal Corps shop in Manila by Dargue and Lieutenant Mauborgne* was tested. It was found that the antenna arrangement was not satisfactory and further experiments were necessary. These continued until the latter part of October when the seaplane was grounded for repairs. Eight flights were made in November.[80]

From 1 to 16 December Dargue and Mauborgne demonstrated for the first time in Army history two-way radio telegraphy between an airplane and the ground. Heretofore receivers had not been used in Army airplanes because of the noise of the engine, the interference of the ignition, and the lack of a detector which was rugged enough not to burn out because of its proximity to the transmitter nor get out of adjustment from the vibration of the plane. A molybdenum detector proved satisfactory and Mauborgne sealed it in the receiver. The transmitter was of the simplest design, consisting of an old spark coil, a small storage battery, a glass-plate condenser, a small inductance coil, and an open gap. The 200-foot wire antenna, weighted with large iron washers, was paid out from a reel. Seven flights were made during the testing of the two-way radio, with Dargue as pilot and Mauborgne as radio operator.[81] On 11 December, during the third test, messages sent from the plane were heard distinctly at the Corregidor ground station ten miles away. On the return trip signals were received in the plane from a distance of four miles at an altitude of 600 feet with the engine unmuffled. This was the first time that an Army airplane had received radio signals. The most successful test of all was made on 16 December. A switch had been installed to throw the ground wire and the antenna to either the sending or the receiving side and a radio message exchange was carried on with Corregidor over a distance of from five to seven and one-half miles at an altitude of 1,200 feet. During the exchange the following

message was received in the plane:[82] "Far greater results are obtained from the set than were expected but it is proposed to continue the experiments by varying the length of the antenna."

Unfortunately, these tests came to an end on 12 January 1915, when Dargue wrecked S.C. plane No. 17 in San Jose Bay.* Corporal Dodd was flying with him as a passenger when the wind caught the plane and headed it straight for the cliffs. In attempting a steep turn to avoid a crash, Dargue lost control, then managed to regain it sufficiently to get the plane down, but it hit the water tail first and was completely wrecked. Since there were no other Army planes in the Philippines, Dargue's services as a pilot were no longer needed and he was ordered to the North Island School at San Diego on 15 January.[83]

Although the Philippine air school was short lived, it was useful in that it produced new pilots for the tiny aviation unit and gave good experice to air and ground crews under difficult conditions, which promoted resourcefulness and initiative. It also allowed the Army troops stationed in the islands to become acquainted with airplanes and what they could do, a knowledge which would prove useful in World War I.

In the meantime another overseas aviation station was getting started. On 29 June 1913, Lt. Harold Geiger, about 12 enlisted men, and a civilian engine expert, George B. Purington, left San Diego to establish an air school in Hawaii. Their equipment consisted of two airplanes used as seaplanes—S.C. No. 8, a Curtiss E, two-seater, dual-control machine, and S.C. No. 21, a Curtiss G, fuselage tractor—with spare parts, tentage, some machinery, and two motorcycles. The unit arrived at Honolulu on 13 July and was first ordered to Schofield Barracks, but as this area was not suitable for an airdrome site, Fort Kamehameha was selected. After considerable difficulty a tent camp was set up, the enlisted men messing with a coast artillery company and Geiger living at the Fort.[84]

The base at Fort Kamehameha was far from satisfactory. Except at high tide the harbor was so shallow that it was dangerous to land or take off anywhere except in the narrow channel. Winds were troublesome and the tent hangars were old and easily torn in storms. On 8 August 1913,

---

*J. O. Mauborgne, later Chief Signal Officer, 1932-1936, had formerly been engaged in radio work with the Signal Corps and was in charge of the Fort Mills radio station.

*Chandler and Lahm say 15 January, but Signal Corps files show 12 January.

the first flight was made with S.C. plane No. 8 over Pearl Harbor, but very little flying was done in the early weeks. The Curtiss tractor, an experimental plane that had been in several accidents during its test flights at San Diego in June, was tried out on 28 August. Geiger found so many things wrong with it that he suggested that he be sent to the Curtiss factory to tell them how they could improve the plane, but the Signal Corps did not approve of the suggestion.[85]

About the middle of September the aviation camp was moved to a nearby spot to permit other construction on the first site. Only short flights were possible because of the treacherous winds, and for this reason the department commander would not sanction any regular flying instruction. Neither did he want the planes to take part in maneuvers. Consequently, about the only thing the planes were used for was amusement—various officers were taken for rides from time to time. On 25 November 1913, both machines were packed for storage in Honolulu, while two

new temporary airplane sheds and a machine shop were built to take the place of the worn out tents. Shortly after November the civilian engine expert left. In the face of so many unsatisfactory conditions Geiger naturally felt that it was a waste of time for the school to remain in Hawaii.

No records have been found for the Hawaiian detachment during the period between November 1913 and June 1914, but by the latter date S.C. No. 21 had been repaired and put in commission with new spares from the States. Soon afterwards, however, flying was discontinued, and the three airplane engines were packed for shipment to the States. The two planes, minus engines, were sold on 12 November 1914—No. 21 for $250 and No. 8 for $200. Geiger and his detachment, with the exception of Sergeant Yates, left Hawaii for the States on the August transport in 1914; Yates followed on the next Army boat.[86]

★

CHAPTER V

Signal Corps Aviation School at San Diego, 1913 to July 1914

GLENN H. CURTISS, in accordance with an agreement made with the Coronado Beach Company, owner of North Island, had established, on 17 January 1911, an aviation school and experiment station on North Island, San Diego, California. The contract gave him the right to use such portions of North Island as he might designate for a period of three years or until such time as the owner demanded possession. Anticipating the establishment of his school, Curtiss had invited the Army to send officers there for instruction. On 29 November 1910 and in January 1911 Lieutenants Beck, Walker, and G.E.M. Kelly were sent to receive flying instruction and to participate in experiments. However, they were ordered to Fort Sam Houston before they had finished the course.[1]

Although Curtiss repeated his invitation on several occasions, no other army officers were sent to San Diego until mid-November 1912, when Lieutenant Geiger arrived to set up a Signal Corps school and to take charge of a Signal Corps detachment of eight enlisted men who had arrived at Fort Rosecrans for duty at North Island. Geiger was accompanied by Lieutenants Goodier, McLeary, Brereton, and Park, all of whom had recently been at the Curtiss plant in Hammondsport for instruction. After the personnel for the school arrived, three Curtiss airplanes, Signal Corps Nos. 2, 6, and 8, were sent from College Park to San Diego.[2] On 8 December 1912 the Signal Corps School was established.[3]

Up to the fall of 1913 the army paid $25 a month to Curtiss for use of the school site and space in the Curtiss hangars. Curtiss' repair facilities were also made available to the Army. The Signal Corps quarters consisted of an old barn and a shed, left over from some earlier activity, and a canvas hangar and lean-to without floors or doors put up by the army to house the three planes. The officers lived in San Diego and the enlisted men were quartered at Fort Rosecrans. All personnel traveled back and forth to North Island in an old and not very dependable motor boat or by a ferry which operated at the other end of the island, a mile from the camp. After some trouble at Fort Rosecrans, the enlisted men were moved to the island where conical tents were set up and arrangements were made with a lunchroom in San Diego to feed them.[4]

In addition to the three airplanes sent from College Park, the Army's first flying boat, S.C. No. 15 was shipped to San Diego in December 1912. The Curtiss flying boat was a two-seated, dual-control plane which had the advantage of placing the instructor beside the student, as was the custom in the Wright planes. (Curtiss had devised a dual control in 1911, but the Army planes purchased that year still had only a single seat.) The Signal Corps equipped plane No. 15 with the Sperry automatic pilot, and on 17 February 1913 Geiger began flying the machine to test the new device, the first of its kind to be tested by the Signal Corps.[5]

Accidents were frequent at San Diego. Goodier had two in the early part of 1913, one of them more amusing than serious. On 29 January, he was making a practice flight in S.C. No. 2 in preparation for his official Military Aviator tests. The hand throttle was set wide open (so that he would not have to hold his foot on the foot pedal) when suddenly the engine stopped. He was over a clearing and was able to make a landing. After repairing the machine, he started the engine by turning the pusher propeller. Ordinarily when that was done the engine was throttled down very low, but Goodier had neglected to change the hand throttle back to a retarded position. Consequently, when the engine caught, the plane began to move forward. Goodier tried to reach the controls but only managed to get hold of a wing, which caused the airplane to turn in a circle dragging him along the ground. The strain on his arms forced him to let go and he rolled quickly to one side to escape the propeller. As he lay on the ground unhurt, he saw the plane take off, rise about 30 feet in the air, turn its nose down and crash. His fellow officers, instead of being glad he was not killed, were furious because he had wrecked one of their few planes. Fortunately the machine was repaired within a few days and Goodier was able to pass the tests for Military Aviator.

On 18 February, Goodier crashed in the flying boat while trying to turn too close to the water and was seriously injured. Glenn H. Curtiss and John D. Cooper were in the air at the time, saw the accident, and flew to his aid; they pulled him from the plane, laid him across the bow of Curtiss' flying boat, and taxied back across the water to the hangar on North Island. There he was transferred to the old motor boat, which got only as far as the bay entrance when the motor stopped and the boat began to drift out to sea. Finally the engine started again and Goodier was taken to Fort Rosecrans where it was found that he had a fractured skull. This was the first time a seaplane had been used to rescue a flier. Although Goodier was badly hurt, he recovered and later returned to duty. The flying boat which he had been piloting was completely wrecked and had to be rebuilt. After the accident Curtiss designed and installed the "Goodier strut," a post extending from the engine to the bow of the boat which prevented the hull from jackknifing into the engine in crashes. The rebuilt machine had more power than the original one and rose from the water in a shorter time.[6]

In March 1913 three new student officers, 2d Lts. Rex Chandler, Joseph E. Carberry, and Walter R. Taliaferro arrived at San Diego.[7] On 8 April Brereton took Chandler up on a training flight in the Curtiss flying boat. The wind was strong and

at times treacherous gusts from the ravines on Point Loma seemed to converge at the bay near the spot where they were flying. Flying with the wind, Brereton attempted a right turn but when the turn was only partially completed, a sudden gust of wind struck the machine augmenting its bank so that it fell out of control from a height of about 100 feet, ending its dive in 30 feet of water. The hull of the machine was broken in half, and Brereton was thrown clear, but the motor struck Chandler on the head, knocking him unconscious. He drowned before he could be pulled from the wreckage.* This was the first flying fatality at the Signal Corps' North Island school. The Chief Signal Officer decided against rebuilding S.C. airplane No. 15, and it was listed as out of commission in his report for 1913.[8]

Brereton resumed flying the first week in May, and on the 21st of the month when he was riding as a passenger in the Curtiss school flying boat an accident almost identical to his first occurred.† This time both he and the pilot, John D. Cooper, were thrown clear; both suffered only minor cuts and bruises. The plane was almost totally demolished. Because of his approaching marriage and the fact that his father objected to his flying, Brereton, who was rated as Military Aviator and Expert Pilot, was relieved from aviation duty at his own request in June 1913.††[9]

The tests with the Sperry automatic pilot had been interrupted by Goodier's accident in S.C. No. 15, and after the death of Chandler the Signal Corps decided from the report that was made that the stabilizer should be developed further. Because of the limited number of airplanes at San Diego, the tests were discontinued there, but the automatic pilot was taken to Hammondsport for further development, and in January 1914 in France Sperry won a prize of $10,000 for his device. As finally evolved it consisted of a double set of gyroscopes, which by controlling the ailerons and rudder kept the plane on an even keel and on course.[10]

---

*Chandler Field, at Essington, Pennsylvania, a World War I field, was named in honor of Lt. Chandler.

†Chandler and Lahm state on p. 263 of *How Our Army Grew Wings* that Cooper took Brereton up on the same day as the Chandler accident, which they say took place in April. Signal Corps records give 8 April for the first accident and 21 May for the second. It is believed that the records are correct.

††Brereton returned to aviation duty in 1917 and served through World War II. He retired in 1948 with the rank of Lieutenant General.

The loss of the Signal Corps flying boat left the North Island school with only the three Curtiss practice airplanes. The engines and parts of these machines had been interchanged so often that an assured identification of any plane was almost impossible, although each retained its original Signal Corps number. In May No. 8 was converted into a seaplane by Geiger so that it could be used for training Carberry and Taliaferro and other pilots.[11]

Because of the shortage of airplanes at San Diego some student officers flew Glenn Curtiss' planes under the supervision of a Curtiss pilot. In return for this service the more advanced army pilots instructed Curtiss civilian students, which gave the army fliers additional practice. In February, tests were begun with higher test gasoline and different oils. A marked improvement in performance was obtained by using a half-and-half mixture of 80 and 60 octane gasoline.*[12]

During 1913 two of the officers at San Diego used their spare time to improve the equipment at the school. In the spring Goodier built a launching device for the flying boat. It consisted of a wooden railway, which extended out into the water, and a combination car and turntable made of steel. The flying boat rested upon the car, which sank when it entered the water, leaving the plane afloat. When the plane returned to its base the car was pulled up under its hull by a cable, and the whole apparatus was then hauled up and swung around leaving the plane ready to start again.[13] After Lieutenant Milling arrived at the school, he became interested in the various methods used to hold aviators in their seats. He finally conceived the idea of the safety belt with a large, easily released, buckle which allowed the aviator to free himself immediately in case of fire or a crash. This type of belt and buckle are standard equipment in the airplanes of today,[14] the easy release feature being important not only in fires and crashes, but also in bail-outs and ditchings.

Nearly all the officers at San Diego did cross-country flying in the spring of 1913. Just before being relieved from aviation duty on 17 April, Lieutenant McLeary in a 63-mile flight, set a new Army altitude record, taking his Curtiss up to 8,400 feet. Lieutenant Park flew 100 miles in two hours and five minutes at 6,000 feet,[15] and during the first week in May, drew a map while flying solo in S.C. No. 2 on a cross-country flight from San Diego.[16] On 9 May Lieutenant Park started cross-country flight from San Diego to Los Angeles, a trip that had never before been undertaken by an Army pilot. Flying in S.C. No. 2 he lost his way in a mist and was forced to land in a barley field at the little town of Olive, 14 miles north of Santa Ana. After getting directions from a nearby schoolhouse he tried to take off, but the barley prevented him from getting off the ground in time to avoid a tree. The impact tore away the entire left side of the machine which crashed about 100 feet away. Park was killed instantly.* A board of officers decided that the accident was caused by the officer's poor judgment in trying to take off from the field. The plane was rebuilt and flown until the pusher type of plane was discontinued in 1914.[17]

After this fatal accident, the second at North Island, long cross-country flights were discouraged. In fact it was necessary to get official permission before making a flight of this kind. Short cross-country flights to obtain Military Aviator certificates were permitted, but every precaution was taken to avoid accidents, and physical examinations were given more frequently.[18]

On 23 May 1913 the Signal Corps Aeronautical Board,† composed of Captains Cowan and Hennessy and Lieutenants Kirtland, Graham, and Milling, recommended that 9 pilots, 30 enlisted men, 6 airplanes, and 1 motor truck from the 1st Aero Squadron at Texas City be sent to San Diego without delay in order to "expedite the preliminary and intermediate training of the officers now detailed on aviation duty who have not yet qualified."[19] Consequently, Signal Corps airplanes 3, 5, 16, 17, and 18 with Captains Cowan and Hennessy and Lieutenants Milling, Ellington, Kelly, Dodd, Love, Morrow, and Seydel were ordered to San Diego on 6 June.[20] In the meantime two other officers, 1st Lt. Virginius E. Clark and 2d Lt. Henry B. Post, had been detailed for aviation duty at San Diego.[21]

With the arrival of this increment the Signal Corps Aviation School had both Curtiss and Wright pilots and machines. Upon reporting for duty, student officers were assigned to the type of plane

---

*High-test gasoline was not referred to as high octane gasoline at that time.

*Park Field, at Millington, Tennessee, a World War I field, was named in honor of Lt. Park.

†This board was apparently the same as the earlier air "Advisory Board" set up by the CSO in Circular No. 11, 26 October 1912.

Flying boat hangars at North Island, 1913

Wright B, Signal Corps No. 3, San Diego, 1913

they desired and reported to the chief instructor for training. Depending on the machine selected, the student was trained under either the Curtiss or the Wright system.*[22] At both sections of the school the student officers were taught from the beginning how to inspect their machines in order to determine whether they were in perfect flying condition, a policy which had been in effect at the earlier Signal Corps aviation schools. At first the instructor made the inspection, showing the student officer how it was done and pointing out the things which might go wrong. Later, the students were required to make the first inspection which was verified by the instructor who called to their attention anything which might have been overlooked. No machine was taken into the air under any circumstances until it had been thoroughly inspected by one or more competent persons and until anything found wrong, no matter how trivial, had been repaired. Student officers were also taught the construction and maintenance of their machines by actually assisting in making all repairs; they were given the same training in the care and operation of the engines. When an engine was taken down, a certain number of student officers were detailed to assist the mechanic. As they became more competent, they were allowed to do parts of the work themselves. Much of the maintenance, such as the adjustment of the carburetor and the proper oiling and cleaning of the motor, was turned over to the students and they gradually acquired proficiency by assisting or by doing the work themselves.[23]

About 29 June 1913 Captain Cowan relieved Lieutenant Geiger as commanding officer of the North Island school, Geiger (as noted above) having been ordered to Hawaii to set up a school there.[24] One of Cowan's first actions on assumption of command was to establish a new camp, separate from the field occupied by the Curtiss school. He also urged that the enlisted men be housed in some empty barracks at San Diego instead of the tents which they had occupied on North Island since the move from Fort Rosecrans. Conditions on the island were very primitive. Because the price demanded for the installation of a power plant was prohibitive, there was no electric power. (A gasoline engine and generator were used to take care of the Signal Corps machine

shop.) The wind which blew sand into everything, contributed toward making the island a rather unsatisfactory place in which to live, although it was almost perfect for flying.[25]

In the fall of 1913*, the Army tried to enter into a lease with the Coronado Beach Company, owner of North Island, but it was unsuccessful. However, the company gave the Army permission to use the land without rental and to construct some temporary buildings, with the provision that the government would remove them and vacate the premises when given notice to do so. The Signal Corps discontinued the payment of $25 a month rent to Glenn Curtiss for the use of his hangars and airplanes, for with the new buildings and new planes on order it would no longer be necessary to use those of the Curtiss school. Since there was no assurance that the site at North Island would be used permanently, the Army did not feel that it was advisable to spend much money for improvement of the camp. Only temporary wooden buildings were constructed and as little as possible was spent on the runways. This status continued until 1917 when Colonel William A. Glassford assumed command. He had long been an advocate of aeronautics and envisioned North Island as becoming the center of a large training establishment, so he started a campaign to buy the island. The owners set a price of $1,500,000 on the property, but even the entrance of the United States into World War I failed to convince Congress that aviation was sufficiently important to warrant the spending of that much money. However, on 11 July 1919, Congress authorized the purchase of North Island, then called Rockwell Field, for $6,098,333—four times what it would have cost two years earlier.[26]

When Geiger left for Honolulu he took with him two Curtiss planes,† one of them being the only passenger-carrying Curtiss plane at North Island, thus making it impossible to give any instruction in the air to the Curtiss student officers. Under the Curtiss system the instructor could stay on the ground and direct his pupils as long as they were making "straight-aways," but when they were ready to make turns involving the proper use of the rudder, ailerons, and power, it was considered much safer and better for the instruc-

---

*For a full description of both systems, see above, Chap. III, pp. 50-53.

*Chandler and Lahm state this was in June but Signal Corps files indicate it was in the fall.
†S.C. Nos. 8 and 21.

tor to take the student up in a dual-control machine and show him exactly how it should be done. Lieutenants Carberry and Taliaferro learned to fly without this instruction (as had earlier Curtiss pilots), but they were exceptionally good fliers and Milling took them up in a Wright machine and gave them instruction in banking which improved their flying tremendously. But if the other Curtiss students were to complete their training it was very necessary for the school to have a dual-control Curtiss, preferably a hydro. The Chief Signal Officer had refused to buy one (although there was $30,000 left of the funds appropriated for 1914), but after Captain Cowan persuaded him to reconsider, he ordered a Model E plane without an engine.* It was planned to use the engine from the machine in which Lieutenant Park had been killed, but meanwhile Lieutenant Goodier had built a machine from spare parts and had already used the engine. After testing his machine Goodier stated that it was the best Curtiss plane he had ever flown and Taliaferro and Carberry agreed with him. Nevertheless, on 12 August 1913 the Chief Signal Officer ordered that no further flying was to be done in this machine. Goodier had not been informed that the engine was to be used in a new machine, and he asked that the prohibition against using his machine be removed; Curtiss also wrote to the Chief Signal Officer explaining that his mechanic had inspected the machine and had found it to be perfectly safe. Finally, on 21 October, the Chief Signal Officer authorized the use of the Goodier plane and it was assigned Signal Corps number 23. On 29 December Carberry and Seydel won the Mackay Trophy with this plane, in which a new engine and dual controls had been installed.[27]

In August 1913 Lieutenants Foulois, Arnold, and Milling advocated the adoption of a universal or standard control for airplanes. No universal control was adopted, but there were two different types, both invented by Europeans, which later were generally used. The Deperdussin control, which is used today almost exclusively for all but single engine planes, had a wheel attached to a column (similar to that of the Curtiss planes). The elevator was operated by pushing the wheel and column forward or backward, thus moving the nose down or up. The ailerons, whose movement raised or lowered the wings, were controlled

by turning the wheel. The rudder bar was operated by the feet: to make a left turn, the pilot pressed with his left foot and for a right turn with his right foot. The other type of control, that of Robert Esnault-Pelterie (also called the Bleriot control), used the universal movement of a stick to control both elevator and aileron action. A forward or backward motion moved the nose down or up and a sideward motion dropped or raised the wings. The stick could be used simultaneously for aileron and elevator action. The rudder bar was the same as that used in the Deperdussin control. Wilbur Wright had devised a similar stick control for the Wright plane taken to Europe in August 1908, but Orville did not like this kind of control and it was not used on the American Wright planes.* Single engine and jet fighters today use the stick control because it results in a faster reaction, making the plane more maneuverable.[28]

Lieutenant Carberry recommended in August 1913 that some kind of airfield symbol be put on maps to designate landing places for airplanes and that a description of what constituted such a landing place be furnished officers on mapping detail so they could mark the best landing places. Such a system, checked by officers on aviation duty, would be of great value to pilots in planning and executing cross-country flights. Lt. Thomas S. Bowen of the 6th Infantry, who was on mapping duty in the vicinity of San Diego, volunteered to undertake the work, and it was decided that a test of the practicability of the plan would be made at the San Diego school. Two signs were to be used, a "Y" for a good landing field and a "V" for a possible field. A "good" landing place was described as one offering a runway of at least 300 yards in all directions, so that a safe landing might be made no matter in which direction the wind was blowing. In addition, the land had to be level and free from all kinds of obstruction, including shrubbery over two feet high; the soil had to be firm enough to support a plane on take-off; and there must be no high obstacles surrounding the field. A "possible" landing field was designated as one having a runway of at least 250 yards in any one direction and at least 50 yards wide. It also had to be

---

*There is nothing further in the records about this plane.

*Wilbur did put the stick control on the Army's first airplane to train the student flyers. Orville Wright stated (in the Wright Brothers' papers in the Library of Congress) that he believed Wilbur's control to be the first of the stick controls.

CONTROL SYSTEMS

Wright

A pair of levers controlled the flight of Wright biplanes. Left-hand lever moved the elevator; a push forward on the lever brought the nose down, a pull back brought it up. Motion of the right-hand lever both warped the wings and moved the rudder for normal turns, forward for left bank, back for right bank. Additional rudder control was provided by side-to-side motion of right lever's top portion which "broke" right or left for the equivalent rudder motion. This early Wright system of control was more mechanical than instinctive.

Curtiss

A column with wheel and set of shoulder-yokes made up the Curtiss control system. Fore-and-aft motion of the column lowered and raised the nose. To bank, the pilot leaned his body in the desired direction, pushing the shoulder-yoke, which controlled the ailerons, left or right. The rudder was linked to a steering-wheel on top of the column, and it followed the wheel motions, left or right. Advantage of the Curtiss control system over the Wright system of levers was that the motions of control more nearly approached the instinctive.

"Dep"

Déperdussin, European airplane designer, linked the ailerons to a Curtiss-type wheel and added rudder control worked by the pilot's feet. The column's forward and back motion still moved nose down and up, while a roll of the wheel dropped and raised the wings. On the rudder bar, the pilot pushed his foot forward in the desired direction of turn. This more instinctive "Dep" system, in general use by 1915, was accepted by the U. S. Army shortly after that. Today, all but a few single-engine airplane types are flown by "Dep" control.

Stick

Robert Esnault-Pelterie used the universal movement of a stick to control aileron and elevator action. Forward and back motion moved nose down and up. Sideward motion dropped and raised the wings. Stick could be used simultaneously for aileron and elevator action. Rudder bar was used the same as in "Dep" control. The "stick" system was used by the Allied and Central powers from the beginning of World War I and it was adopted by the Army in 1917 for all but heavy-type aircraft. Little if any transition is required between stick and "Dep" control.

Lever-happy, this early airman is headed for a stall.

Except for calloused shoulders, this man is doing O.K.

Content at last, this flyer feels confident with "Dep."

As in "Dep," pilot takes to instinctive stick action.

First decade of power flight saw an evolution of control systems from primitive weight-shifting techniques to the present-day methods. There was never any disagreement about the three motions that needed control, the movements about longitudinal, lateral, and vertical axes, but each designer approached the problem with different mechanical solutions. Early pilots engaged in heated controversies over the relative merits of the Wright and Curtiss methods; and since all pilots were originally either Wright- or Curtiss-trained, they had to master both systems in order to fly all available equipment. Above panels trace the development of controls

free from obstructions, but grass or low shrubbery not over three feet high would not be considered an obstacle. The soil might be sandy, but there could not be any high obstacles surrounding the field.*[29]

In July three new student officers were added to the rolls at North Island: 1st Lt. Hollis LeRoy Muller and 2d Lts. Leon R. Cole and Robert H. Willis, Jr. Captain Hennessy† was relieved from aviation duty to rejoin his regiment on 14 July. Second Lieutenant Stanley W. Wood had been assigned for aviation duty in June but was relieved the following December.[30]

On 12 August 1913, including the three air schools in San Diego, the Philippines, and Hawaii, there were 16 pilots,** 8 student pilots, and 17 airplanes in the air service. Five airplanes had been destroyed in accidents since 1909, and the original Army Wright was in the Smithsonian Institution. In addition there were 7 airplanes on order. Fifteen officers had been rated Military Aviators since 1912, 4 of whom—Captain Beck and Lieutenants Foulois, McLeary, and Brereton—had been returned to their own arms of the service, and 2—Lieutenants Park and Call—had been killed.[31] On 15 August, the Chief Signal Officer, disturbed by the small number of pilots and students, appealed to officers throughout the country to volunteer for aviation duty, calling attention to the appropriation act of March 1913, which permitted the detail of 30 army officers for aviation and provided an increase of 35 percent in their pay and allowances while on such duty. Volunteers were limited to men under 30 years of age who were physically and temperamentally fit. By the end of the year several new officers were detailed to aviation duty.[32]

On 4 September 1913, Lieutenant Love became the tenth Army officer to lose his life in an airplane accident, when he was killed at North Island in the Wright C, S.C. No. 18 while attempting to qualify for his Military Aviator rating.†† After climbing to 2,000 feet, he had started a slow glide downward on a wide turn; when he was within 300 feet of the ground, he apparently put

on power, but instead of pulling out of its dive the plane drove straight into the ground. It was thought that a slight gust of wind might have been responsible for the final dive, but the cause was actually unknown.[33] This accident left San Diego with but one Wright trainer, S.C. No. 16, whose engine had been built largely from spare parts that had already seen considerable service. Six officers, exclusive of Lieutenants Ellington and Sherman, were receiving instruction on the Wright machine, and Captain Cowan urgently requested the purchase of a Wright C with a 4-cylinder Sturtevant engine, and extra engines, one of which was to be used in S.C. No. 16.[34]

Lt. Col. Samuel Reber, who had become Eastern Department Signal Officer on 1 July 1913 and was put in charge of aviation on 10 September, visited San Diego to investigate the Love accident and other matters pertaining to the aviation school. From there he was sent to San Antonio to look into the possibility of establishing an air center there.[35] General Scriven, Chief Signal Officer, had suggested to Maj. Gen. Leonard Wood in April 1913, that such a center would be a means of concentrating the training then being done at the scattered civilian schools of the Wright, Curtiss, and Burgess companies, as well as as the Signal Corps schools at College Park, Augusta, and Texas City, all of which had only temporary facilities. It was considered desirable that the air center be located on a military reservation such as Fort Sam Houston, where the fliers not only would have the advantage of service with other troops, but also would be assured of year-round flying. It was proposed that, if the center were established at San Antonio, the aero squadron would be moved there from San Diego; the aviation school at San Diego also would be moved when accommodations could be secured; thus all planes and aviation officers would be concentrated at one place. Until this move was accomplished a primary school would be maintained at San Diego or elsewhere, but a depot and the main center would be established at San Antonio with a squadron of eight airplanes to serve with the ground troops. It was also proposed that this center should be under the control of a man of sufficient rank and experience to build and manage it, a man who should be an administrator, but not necessarily an aviator. The second in command should be a flier, and the center should be a permanent place, school, or

---

*There is no record of what was done about this idea, but it is believed that Bowen undertook the experiment.

†Captain Hennessy, who held FAI pilot certificate No. 153, did not qualify for Military Aviator, and he did not return to aviation duty before he retired on 16 June 1921.

**Some of these pilots were capable of flying alone but had not yet been rated.

††Love Field, at Dallas, Texas, a World War I field, was named for Lt. Love.

depot where all necessary instruction and training could be carried on.[36] Later, this plan was revised; three air stations were suggested for the United States, an additional one in the Philippines, and a section or company in Hawaii and one in the Canal Zone.

The Secretary of War approved the original air center project and designated San Antonio as the site for the first permanent aeronautical station. It was proposed that most of the materiel and personnel from Texas City be moved to San Antonio, but because no provisions had been made for them there they were sent to San Diego instead. Although money was appropriated by the act of 27 April 1914 for the construction of buildings at Fort Sam Houston, nothing further was done at this time about the actual establishment of the air center at San Antonio.*[37]

During the fall of 1913 the aviation service lost several of its outstanding men but gained a number of replacements. Lieutenants Arnold and Sherman were relieved from aviation duty to rejoin their regiments.[38] Lieutenant Milling was sent to Paris on aeronautical duty on 9 September 1913.[39] Lieutenant Frederick S. Snyder was ordered to San Diego in August, but was relieved from duty in December because he was temperamentally unsuited for aviation.[40] In September Lieutenants Lahm, Chapman, and Dargue were sent to San Diego from the Philippines, and 2d Lt. J. P. Edgerly was detailed to aviation at North Island.[41] In November 1st Lt. William C. Nicholson and 2d Lt. Byron Q. Jones were ordered to North Island for aviation duty, but Nicholson was relieved to rejoin his regiment in March 1914.[42] Later in the same month Lieutenants Taliaferro and Carberry returned from Hammondsport, New York, where they had just completed a course in engine and airplane construction at the Curtiss plant.[43] Lieutenant Foulois was returned to aviation duty, and 2d Lt. Douglas B. Netherwood was assigned to the Signal Corps Aviation School.[44] By the end of the year Captain Chandler and Lieutenant Lahm had been relieved from aviation duty at their own requests.[45]

Meanwhile, specifications for airplanes had been revised on 1 January 1913 by the Chief Signal Officer. The most revolutionary of the new requirements was that the bottom of the fuselage of

the scout plane was to be covered with chrome steel about 0.075 inches thick, designed to protect the personnel and the engine from ground fire. There was to be space provided in the plane for instruments and a radio, which were to be furnished by the Signal Corps. Another new requirement subjected the engine to a 6-hour test at the Bureau of Standards in Washington. If the engine was equipped with a cutout, silencer, and starter it would add to the machine's rating. The plane had to be capable of a 2,000-foot climb in 10 minutes with a payload of 450 pounds, a minimum speed of no more than 38 miles per hour, and a maximum speed of at least 55 miles per hour. The new specifications also covered seaplanes, for which the general physical requirements were the same as those for the land plane, except that certain bulkheads were required to withstand rough water and beaching. The rate of climb was to be 1,500 feet in 10 minutes with a payload of 400 pounds. The required assembly time was one hour and a half as compared with one hour for the land plane.[46] The 1913 FAI test for land plane pilots was practically the same as that for 1912, but it permitted operating on water for one of the three tests. A seaplane pilot classification was also set up by the Aero Club of America with its own conditions.*[47]

With the specifications for new Army airplanes made more rigorous, and with the planes being steadily improved, the pilots had to become increasingly proficient. The Signal Corps, consequently, had to establish new and more difficult tests for the rating of Military Aviator. An order of 27 October 1913, which was to be effective on 1 January 1914, called for a cross-country reconaissance flight of 100 miles and a dead-stick landing from an altitude of 1,500 feet.† No tests were to be made with passengers. An entirely new phase of the examination was a theoretical or academic section that required the candidate to be able to use maps and instruments and to have a knowledge of airplane construction, repairs, navigation, meteorology, topography, and theory of operation of aircraft. Military Aviators who had received their ratings prior to 1 January 1914 and who were on aviation duty in the Signal Corps were required between 1 January and 1 July

---

*For later developments, see pp 149 ff.

*The seaplane pilot classification was not yet recognized by the FAI.
†See Appendix No. 11 for these requirements.

1914 to make flights equal to, or better than, those prescribed in the test and to show that they were familiar with the repair of engines and machines; otherwise, they, too, would be required to pass the new test.[48]

Since some of the theoretical subjects covered in the new tests had not previously been taught at the aviation school, it became necessary to change the entire training program. A series of lectures on aeronautical subjects was included in the winter course at North Island which began on 8 December 1913. Dr. A. F. Zahm of the Smithsonian Institution, who was already at San Diego getting information for a report on the safety of airplanes, gave lectures on aerodynamics and design; Professor W. F. Durand of Leland Stanford University gave a course on propellers; Dr. W. J. Humphreys of the Weather Bureau lectured on meteorological physics and the laws of atmosphere as applied to aeronautics; and other authorities conducted courses on the theory, design, and operation of aviation engines; courses in topography, aerial reconnaissance, photography, and radiotelegraphy were also offered. The academic work began at the close of the flying day and continued until 10 o'clock at night. It was thought that pilots would be able to pass all parts of the Military Aviator examination after a 9- to 12-month course.[49] The Army air school at San Diego, established for theoretical and practical instruction in aviation, became a part of the educational system of the United States Army on 13 December 1913, when it was designated as the Signal Corps Aviation School.[50]

In addition to their ground school and flying duties officers at San Diego in 1914 were ordered to spend six hours a week in professional study or reading and at least eight hours a week in physical exercise, either walking or horseback riding—tennis, golf, swimming, motorcycling, and bicycling might be partially substituted. Cavalry officers kept their own horses on the post. The Army gave them yearly allotments for not more than two private mounts—$150 for the first and $50 for the second. The Army shipped these mounts from station to station and provided stables for them. For those who did not have horses of their own, army horses were available for riding.[51]

Four badly needed airplanes arrived at North Island in the latter part of 1913 and early in 1914. Three of the planes were Burgess tractors

equipped with Renault engines. Two of them, which were to have been delivered to the First Aero Squadron in Texas City in July and August 1913, arrived at San Diego in November and the third in January 1914. The air testing of the planes was waived by the Army on the understanding that the manufacturer would test the planes before delivery. The new Burgess H weight-carrying scouts were the same size as the original Burgess tractor, S.C. No. 9 of 1912, but there were some refinements. The top and bottom wing sections had the same dimensions and were interchangeable. A center upper panel, the same width as the fuselage, did away with the need for a central juncture of the upper wing. The airplane was supported on two pairs of vertical wheel struts instead of the old diagonal braces, which reduced the number of spare parts needed. The fuel supply was carried in two gravity fed tanks carried on either side of the fuselage. Speed had been increased from 57 to 60 miles per hour.* The planes were given Signal Corps numbers 24, 25, and 26.[52]

The fourth plane, a Curtiss tractor Model H, S.C. No. 22, which resembled S.C. No. 21, was delivered at San Diego on 1 December 1913. It was equipped with a "full floating" fuselage, that is, three sets of heavy rubber bands, working on rocker arms on each side, acted as shock absorbers and supported the fuselage on a heavy 4-wheeled chassis. The wings were made in one piece on each side of the chassis; this construction gave greater strength than the panel construction. A new system of wires and braces which did not require holes in the longerons was used. At each side of the fuselage there was a 12-inch open space in the wings for better downward vision. The Curtiss OX 90-horsepower engine was located in front of the seats, which were side by side over the lower wing about midway between the front and rear wing spars, with the carburetor projecting through the dashboard into the cockpit† to make it easier to adjust. The dual control consisted of the standard Curtiss shoulder yoke and the wheel mounted on a column. Under the seat was a 40-gallon fuel tank supplemented

---

*The tandem seats were upholstered in leather, a windshield was furnished, and there was ample room for instruments, although none were provided.

†The air circulated around the cylinders and was deflected to each side and away from the passengers by the curved metal shield which formed the dashboard and closed the cockpit off from the engine.

San Diego school, 1913

S. C. No. 24, Burgess tractor delivered at San Diego in 1913

by a 2-gallon auxiliary tank which was mounted on the dashboard and fed by a mechanical pump driven by the engine. A plate glass window in the auxiliary tank enabled the pilot to watch the functioning of the pump, and check the fuel level. The radiator, mounted on top of the nose of the fuselage, formed the forward support for an automobile-type engine hood, the rear of which was curved to deflect the air over the heads of the operators.[53]

About the time the first two Burgess tractors were delivered, another fatal accident took place at North Island. While on a training flight on 24 November 1913, Lieutenant Ellington and his student, Lt. Hugh M. Kelly, were killed in Wright C, S.C. No. 14.* Ellington, who was chief instructor at the school, and Kelly made a short flight around the southern part of the island, then headed toward the Wright section of the school with the engine missing badly. While still about a mile from the Wright hangars and at an altitude of some 200 feet, the plane went into a normal gliding angle with the engine throttled down but still misfiring. When the plane was about 75 feet from the ground, the angle of glide suddenly steepened into a headlong plunge to the earth. The machine was completely wrecked and both men were killed instantly. It was stated in the report that the accident was caused by an inherent tendency in this type of machine to plunge downward upon any sudden increase of power during a glide, and it was believed that such an increase took place at the moment of the plunge or just before.[54]

In December several important flights were made at San Diego. Lt. Henry B. Post in S.C. No. 23, which had been built by Goodier from spare parts, established a new Army solo altitude record of 10,600 feet on 18 December, breaking the old record by nearly 2,000 feet.[55] On 26 December Lieutenant Carberry and his passenger, Lieutenant Taliaferro, in S.C. No. 22 set a new Army altitude record of 7,800 feet for pilot and passenger.[56] Three days later Carberry (pilot) and Lieutenant Seydel (observer) in Signal Corps No. 23 won the Mackay Trophy at Encinitas, California. The only other entry in the contest was S.C. No. 22 flown by Taliaferro with Lieutenant Muller as observer, but this plane was elimi-

nated by an accident during its test flight on the day of the contest.[57]

Although the 1st Aero Squadron had functioned as part of the army field forces at Texas City in the summer of 1913, it was not until six months later that the War Department recognized the possibility of using aviation in this capacity by prescribing for the first time, on 4 December, a provisional organization for an aero squadron of the Signal Corps. It was to consist of 20 officers, 90 men, 8 airplanes, and enough tractors and motorcycles to make the squadron a self-sufficient, mobile, mechanized combat unit.[58] On 7 January 1914, the Chief Signal Officer approved the organization of the 1st Aero Squadron at San Diego under the command of Captain Cowan, with Lieutenant Kirtland as adjutant and supply officer. The squadron was divided into two companies. Lieutenant Foulois commanded the first company, which was composed of Lieutenants Dodd, Nicholson, Morrow, Seydel, and Netherwood. The second company, commanded by Lieutenant Taliaferro, consisted of Lieutenants Goodier, Muller, Willis, Carberry, Post, and Edgerly. There were two vacancies in the first company and one in the second company. The first company was to have 4 airplanes, all Burgess tractors—Nos. 9, 24, 25, and 26, and the second company was given 4 Curtiss planes—Nos. 2, 6, 22, and 23.[59]

On 12 December 1913 Oscar A. Brindley, formerly a Wright company pilot, had reported as a civilian instructor at the Signal Corps Aviation School (SCAS) at San Diego. Given complete charge of the instruction of officers flying Wright machines, he tested all the Wright pilots and passed Lieutenants Morrow, Seydel, and Dodd; Lieutenants Wood, Snyder, Cole, Jones and Nicholson were to continue under instruction.[60]

At the end of the year, the following 20 officers were on aviation duty at the SCAS in San Diego:[61]

> 2d Lt. J. E. Carberry, Inf.
> 2d Lt. C. G. Chapman, Cav.
> 2d Lt. V. E. Clark, CAC
> 2d Lt. H. A. Dargue, CAC
> 1st Lt. T. F. Dodd, CAC
> 2d Lt. J. P. Edgerley, Inf.
> 1st Lt. B. D. Foulois, Inf.
> 1st Lt. Harold Geiger, CAC
> 1st Lt. L. E. Goodier, Jr., CAC
> 2d Lt. B. Q. Jones, Cav.
> 1st Lt. R. C. Kirtland, Inf.

---

†Ellington Field, Houston, Texas, was named for Lt. Ellington.

2d Lt. T. D. Morrow, Inf.
1st Lt. H. LeR. Muller, CAC
2d Lt. D. B. Netherwood, CAC
1st Lt. W. C. F. Nicholson, Cav.
2d Lt. H. B. Post, Inf.
2d Lt. Fred Seydel, CAC
2d Lt. W. R. Taliaferro, Inf.
2d Lt. R. H. Willis, Jr., Inf.

In June 1912 the Chief Signal Officer had stated in a letter to the Philippine Division that it was contrary to War Department policy to teach enlisted men to fly. Nevertheless, from 1912 through 1915 four enlisted men in the Signal Corps became pilots by one method or another. As noted earlier, Sgt. Vernon L. Burge, who was taught to fly in the Philippines by Lahm because of the shortage of officers who could be detailed as students, received his FAI pilot certificate No. 154 on 14 August 1912.[62] Corporal William A. Lamkey graduated from the Moisant Aviation School, a private organization, and received FAI certificate No. 183 on 6 November 1912. He enlisted in the Signal Corps and was ordered to the Signal Corps Aviation School at San Diego on 17 May 1913, where he flew under the instruction of Oscar Brindley. Lamkey later purchased his discharge and became a civilian aviator. After flying for Pancho Villa in Mexico, he became a naval pilot in the AEF during World War I.[63] On 6 December 1912, Sgt. William C. Ocker was ordered to San Diego,[64] where he received instruction from T. C. Macaulay of the Curtiss School in return for off-duty work done for Macaulay.[65] Ocker received FAI pilot certificate No. 293 on 29 April 1913 and later became an instructor. He was discharged in January 1917 to accept a commission as Captain, Air Service, Signal Officers Reserve Corps, and was ordered to active duty in February 1917. He was rated as a Junior Military Aviator on 2 November 1917.[66] Corporal James S. Krull was flying in the spring of 1914 at North Island and received FAI certificate No. 360 on 24 October 1915. The Rockwell Field Monthly Progress Report of 31 December stated that he was ready to take the Junior Military Aviator test. Krull was discharged on 16 May 1917 to become a civilian instructor. He reentered the service and on 30 November 1920 was again discharged, this time with the rank of 1st Lieutenant in the Air Service.[67]

In addition to the four men who qualified as pilots, other enlisted men were also given some

flying training. On 26 January 1914, the Chief Signal Officer approved the training of Master Signal Electrician John McRae and Sgt. Thomas Boland, as enlisted pilots. Those men, both members of the 1st Aero Squadron, were to be trained under the authority of OCSO Circular No. 11 of 26 October 1912.*[68] On 12 January 1914, Sgt. Stephen J. Idzorek filed an application for flying training, but there is no record of its being approved. Idzorek was never rated as a pilot nor did he get an FAI certificate.† An application for flying training made on 16 February 1914 by Pvt. Samuel Katzman, who had transferred from the Field Artillery at the United States Military Academy to the Signal Corps at San Diego, was approved by the Chief Signal Officer.[70] In March 1914, Lieutenant Geiger requested the return of Privates Arnold Rueff, Wilfred G. Threader, and Samuel P. Jones from Honolulu to San Diego for instruction in flying; each had expressed a desire to learn to fly, and Geiger felt that it would increase their value to the aeronautical service if they were allowed to do so. Captain Cowan verified the fact that these men had received some flying training and added the names of three others, Herbert Marcus, Austin A. Adamson, and Leo G. Flint, who had also had some flying instruction.** Actually the airplane shortage was so acute that it was almost impossible for an enlisted man to get a plane; but as compensation for not flying the qualified enlisted pilots were made aviation mechanicians with 50 percent increase in pay. The training of enlisted men as pilots was temporarily discontinued in 1914.[71]

Two general orders, issued at San Diego in 1914, included regulations for phases of aviation that had seldom if ever been referred to before— security and safety. General Order No. 1 issued on 7 January contained a security regulation which stated that "officers, enlisted men, and civilians on duty at this school will under no circumstances give out for publication any information concerning the work of the school. Such information as is considered proper for publication will be given

---

*Circular No. 11 did not differentiate between officer and enlisted flying students. However, the general use of the word "officer" in this circular indicated that, when it was written, enlisted pilot training was not anticipated.

†Idzorek claimed that he was given flying instruction by Wilbur Wright at College Park in 1909. He also stated that he soloed in land and seaplanes after being instructed by Oscar Brindley and "Doc" Wildman, respectively, at North Island.

**Available records do not show whether or not these men became pilots.

out by the Commanding Officer."[72] On 15 January General Order No. 2 included a safety measure requiring that all officers, enlisted men, and civilians connected with the school would wear helmets on all flights and that the leather coats would be worn for all flying over land and the nonsinkable coats for all seaplane work.[73]

During January the Army, including the Coast Artillery, and the Navy worked together in conducting experiments in submarine mine detection at San Diego. On 6 January Lieutenant Carberry, with Lieutenant Dodd as observer, reconnoitered the minefield in the vicinity of Fort Rosecrans from an altitude of 1,800 to 2,400 feet in the Curtiss S.C. No. 23. Upon their return, Dodd plotted on a harbor map the outline of the channel and the location of three mines, the distribution boxes, and the cable terminal. On 13 January Dodd, who was a Coast Artillery officer, reported that the type of submarine mines used by the Coast Artillery could easily be seen from an airplane at a height of 2,400 feet on a clear day in clear, indisturbed water. A week later Major Davis, the commander of the coast defenses of San Diego, flew with one of the Signal Corps aviators on a dark and overcast day and reported that he could see kelp on the bottom of the bay and easily spot newly planted mines, but was unable to locate the older mines which were covered with marine growth. Naval aviators also flew with Coast Artillery officers as observers during the experiments. Future investigations along this line were planned for a time when a mineplanter and a Burgess tractor seaplane would be available.[74]

A number of cross-country flights were made from San Diego in January and February. On 9 January Lieutenant Post in the Burgess Signal Corps No. 5 made a 76-mile, nonstop flight from San Diego to Winchester, California. He had intended to fly on to Beaumont, but his gasoline gave out at Winchester after an encounter with rough air in the mountains. The machine bucked up and down and sideways so that the effort of staying in the seat was greater than that of controlling the machine; the maximum wing warp was entirely without effect on many occasions; and Post was forced to allow the machine to plunge downward for a considerable distance in order to pick up flying speed. The return trip was made the next day without incident, but the flight proved that a low-powered machine like Signal Corps No.

5* was not satisfactory for cross-country work.[75]

On 12 January Lieutenant Carberry in the Curtiss D pusher, S.C. No. 2, flew 120 miles nonstop from San Diego to Venice, California in 1 hour and 58 minutes. Carberry had a map case strapped to his leg and a watch on the steering wheel of the plane which enabled him to plot his course without any difficulty. He picked out a ploughed field near Venice and headed in for a landing, but the soft ground caused the plane to swerve into a pole, damaging the upper leading edge of the wing panel next to the engine section. Carberry, with the aid of Glenn L. Martin, a plane manufacturer of Los Angeles, repaired the panel and took off the next afternoon for San Diego. On the return trip a different route was followed, and the flight of 134 miles took 2 hours and 36 minutes. Since his fuel supply was exhausted as he approached San Diego, Carberry had to make a deadstick landing.[76]

On 20 January Lieutenant Taliaferro flew 220 miles in the Curtiss scout, S.C. No. 23, from San Diego to Elsinore, via Los Angeles and Pasadena, in 3 hours and 39 minutes. He refueled and started back to San Diego but had to land about six miles southeast of Temecula when his engine went dead; after making repairs he flew back to Elsinore to spend the night. Taking off the next morning, he continued his flight to a point eight miles west of Corona where the engine again stopped because of the poor quality of gasoline obtained at Elsinore. Since it was impossible to take off from the plowed field on which he had landed, he had to disassemble the machine and ship it to San Diego by rail.[77]

On 14 February Lieutenant Dodd and Sgt. Herbert Marcus established an official nonstop American duration and distance record in the Burgess H tractor, S.C. No. 26, when they flew 244.18 miles in 4 hours and 43 minutes. Dodd was credited with setting the American duration and the American cross-country duration and distance records for aviator and one passenger, but this performance also exceeded all previous American duration records for pilot alone.[78]

In the spring of 1914 the pilots at San Diego continued their experiments. After adding an extra wing panel at either extremity of the upper wing and installing a carburetor mechanism to per-

---

*S.C. No. 5 was declared out of commission on 24 February 1914 as were S.C. airplanes Nos. 2, 3, 6, 16, 19, and 23.

mit adjustment in flight, on 16 February Carberry and Taliaferro set a new official Army altitude record of 8,800 feet at San Diego in S.C. No. 23.[79] On 23 February Glenn Martin demonstrated his patented automatic attached pack-type parachute at the Signal Corps Aviation School. Accompanied by Lieutenant Muller and Charles Broadwick, Martin ascended to 1,150 feet, at which point Broadwick jumped. The device worked perfectly. Tests on the parachute were completed in September 1914, and the purchase of a number of parachutes was recommended, each of which was to be demonstrated by Broadwick, who was also to give instruction in their care and handling. There is no record that any were bought, although some money was authorized for that purpose. Apparently the officers who recommended the purchase were years ahead of their time, for it was not until after World War I that parachutes were made a part of the regular equipment on Army planes.[80]

On 9 February 1914, Lieutenant Post was killed at San Diego when his Wright C seaplane, S.C. No. 10, crashed in San Diego Bay during an attempt at a solo altitude record in which he reached an unofficial height of 12,140 feet, exceeding by 500 feet Lincoln Beachey's existing official American record of 11,642 feet.* The investigating board of officers reported that Post descended from approximately 12,000 feet to 1,000 feet without any difficulty, and from 1,000 to 600 feet at an increasingly steeper angle; at that altitude the plane assumed a vertical nose down position and crashed into the bay. The board felt that the accident was not the fault of the operator, but it was unable to determine the cause of the accident.[81] The plane† was one of six Wright C's which had been purchased by the government; five of the C's had killed a total of six men. The sixth had been destroyed on 12 September 1913, when Lieutenant Lahm had plunged into Manila Bay. The elevator in the Wright C was too weak and as the speed of flight increased the tendency of the elevator to fail also increased.[82]

---

*Post Field, a World War I training field, was named for Lt. Post.

†This was the machine in which Lieutenant Arnold nose dived at Fort Riley in 1912. It had remained at Fort Leavenworth, Kansas, since that time and was not flown as there was no pilot there. However, on 30 July 1913, the CSO had written the Director of the Signal School at Leavenworth to prepare No. 10 for shipment to San Diego.

Prior to 1914 the majority of biplanes built in the United States had been of the pusher type with the propeller immediately behind the wings, constructed either by Wright or Curtiss. There was so much disagreement among the officer pilots as to which manufacturer built the better plane and used the better methods of training that two separate and distinct camps had grown up in the aviation school, and competition between the Curtiss and Wright advocates had become so keen as to be dangerous. Each faction tried to demonstrate in the air the advantages of his particular method of instruction and the superiority of the airplane he was flying. When new students arrived, each camp tried to persuade them of the superiority of its particular method of instruction and of its machine, in the same manner that fraternities in colleges try to influence rushees. For a time the competition had stimulated interest and effort but by the fall of 1913 the rivalry had become so intense that it was detrimental to the efficiency of the school and it was necessary to put an end to it. Consequently in February 1914, the Wright and Curtiss sections of the school were consolidated.

The rivalry had been accentuated by the close association of the Curtiss section with the Curtiss Aeroplane Company at North Island, where many of the student officers had received their training in planes belonging to the Curtiss company. T. C. Macauley, later a major in the Air Service Officers Reserve Corps, was at that time in charge of training for the Curtiss company, and it was due to his cooperation and generosity that a considerable amount of the training of regular officers was possible, for the Signal Corps did not have enough planes. After the Wright and Curtiss sections were combined, in order that the government would be under no obligation to the Curtiss company, all airplanes housed in Curtiss hangars were taken to the government end of North Island and all instruction under the Curtiss company was stopped. Soon thereafter, Curtiss ended active operations at North Island and moved his equipment.[83]

Through February 1914, 48 officers had been detailed to aviation: 18 of them were on duty, another 18 had been relieved from aviation duty, and 12 had been killed. (Corporal Frank Scott, an enlisted man, had also met his death in an airplane accident).*[84] The 12 officer fatalities were in order, as follows:

1st Lt. Thomas E. Selfridge
2d Lt. G. E. M. Kelly
2d Lt. L. W. Hazelhurst
2d Lt. L. G. Rockwell
1st Lt. Rex Chandler
1st Lt. Joseph D. Park
1st Lt. Loren H. Call
1st Lt. Moss L. Love
2d Lt. Perry C. Rich
2d Lt. Hugh M. Kelly
1st Lt. Eric Ellington
2d Lt. Henry B. Post

From June 1913 until February 1914 "an amount of flying quite unprecedented in the history of aviation in the United States" was carried on at the Signal Corps Aviation School at San Diego.[85] During this time three accidents had occurred in Wright C planes, all of which had "stalled." Orville Wright insisted that the accidents were not the fault of the plane but rather the fault of the pilots who had not been properly trained to fly them. The pilots in these latest accidents were considered among the army's best, and Captain Cowan thought that this fact warranted the belief that there was something wrong with the Wright machine. Because of these accidents the pilots lost confidence in the pushers and no longer wanted to fly in them. Only two Wright C machines were on hand at North Island in February 1914—No. 5 and No. 16, both of which had been in service for some time. At first their loss as training machines did not interfere with the progress in instruction. The Wright C's had previously been used as an intermediate step between the slower B type and faster Burgess tractors, but now it was found practicable for the students to skip that step. On 16 February 1914, however, the Chief Signal Officer directed discontinuance of the use of both the Wright B and C machines until further notice, and a board was appointed to report on the suitability and safety of these machines. The board, composed of Lieutenants Foulois, Dodd, Taliaferro, Chapman, and Carberry, in effect condemned all pusher airplanes by recommending that the planes to be flown be limited to the Curtiss tractor Signal Corps No. 22, and the four Burgess tractors, Signal Corps airplanes Nos. 24, 25, 26, and 9, the latter then at the factory for remodeling.[86] Since only a few officers were qualified to fly the trac-

tors, (which had the propellor in front of the pilot) this decision caused considerable delay in training, but instruction was pushed rapidly and much progress had been made by April 1914 when orders were received to send a detachment with three airplanes to Galveston, Texas, for duty in Mexico.[87]

As a result of the series of accidents at San Diego, the SCAS and the 1st Aero Squadron in February 1914 were inspected (for the first time) by the Inspector General's Department. Col. J. L. Chamberlain, the Inspector General, gave both installations a very unfavorable report. He stated that the organization for the 1st Aero Squadron was essentially a paper one and had not been made effective because of a lack of officers and men, and that there was no well-defined line of demarkation between the squadron and the school. Although he did not blame anyone in particular for the bad conditions, he was very critical of the airplane manufacturers, especially the Wright Company. He recommended Glenn Martin* as a progressive builder of airplanes and suggested that the government establish a factory of its own with Martin in charge, since no other American manufacturer had shown any progress. General Scriven did not concur in the findings of Colonel Chamberlain. He pointed out that, "in spite of short-comings and accidents the results obtained are believed to be fully commensurate with the means provided for the establishment of this new art in the Army."[88]

On 12 June 1914 the Secretary of War directed the Chief Signal Officer's attention to the Inspector General's recommendations for the school: 1) that a suitable permanent site be selected for the aviation school; 2) that the services of a competent aeronautical engineer and an expert construction man be secured; 3) that officers detailed for aviation duty be sent to an airplane factory for a course before taking up work in the Signal Corps school; and 4) that no officer should be given a pilot's license until he had mastered the principles of construction. The Secretary of War desired that these recommendations be accepted insofar as was possible and suggested that every

---

*See Appendix No. 12 for a full list of Signal Corps aviation fatalities through 6 April 1917.

*Glenn Martin, an exhibition flyer and designer-builder of planes, who had learned to fly in 1908, established the Glenn L. Martin Company at Santa Ana in 1911. His company later merged with that of the Wrights to form the Wright-Martin Aircraft Corporation in 1917. He withdrew from the partnership in 1918 and again set up his own company, later building Martin bombers for the United States Government.

effort be made to obtain the most up-to-date material within the limits of the appropriations available.[89]

Early in 1914 the Wright and Curtiss companies made an effort to improve their machines. The Wright Company substituted a steering wheel for the old fore-and-aft moving lever for wing warping on its new tractor and equipped it with a 120-horsepower Austro-Daimler engine, which was controlled by levers located on a sector of the steering wheel. The Curtiss Company produced an 8-cylinder, 160-horsepower engine, one of the highest-powered engines produced by an American manufacturer to that date.[90]

In the summer of 1909 the Wright Company had filed suits for patent infringements against the Aeronautical Society, Curtiss, and the Herring-Curtiss Company. This litigation had continuel for several years, until, on 13 January 1914, the United States Circuit Court of Appeals handed down the final decision in favor of the Wrights. This meant that the Wright Company could charge royalties on planes made by any company which used its patents; companies unwilling to pay the royalties would have to stop manufacturing planes which infringed on these patents. Some settlement also had to be made with the Wright Company for planes already manufactured and sold. For example, early in 1911, the Burgess Company and Curtis had obtained a license from the Wright Company to use its patents; since then they had paid $1,000 per airplane produced for this privilege. Although the Burgess Company and Curtis had been operating at a loss, in 1913 the Wright Company decided to increase the royalty on finished machines to 20 percent on all sales, including airplane parts, motors, and other products patented or subject to patents by the Wright Company. Although Burgess had departed from the Wright type of airplane and had begun to make planes of his own design (of which the Burgess tractor was the best known), he was still bound by certain Wright patents, but he did not wish to pay the Wrights 20 percent of all sales. After due consideration, the Burgess Company and Curtis decided to withdraw from aviation manufacturing rather than to operate under the new Wright conditions.[91]

On 22 January 1914 the Wright Company notified the Secretary of War that the Burgess Company and Curtis planes, Models I-35, and J-36, delivered between 1 January and 10 April 1913, and Models H-40, H-41, and H-42, delivered to the Army between 2 October 1913 and 5 January 1914, were infringements on the Wright patents and that they claimed a lien on these machines for royalties due them. The Secretary of War replied that between April 1912 and May 1913,* the Signal Corps had purchased seven planes from the Burgess Company and Curtis but that each contract contained a provision which excluded the United States from any suits for patent infringements and made the manufacturer alone responsible. Consequently, the property of the United States was not subject to seizure and sale at the suit of parties who alleged that their patent rights had been infringed, and no injunction could be obtained to restrain the use of the property by the United States.[92]

The Burgess Company and Curtis was dissolved in the latter part of January 1914, and a new organization called the Burgess Company was formed and located at the plant formerly occupied by the Burgess Company and Curtis. The new company obtained a license to build airplanes under the Dunne patents. It was held that the Dunne machine did not infringe on the Wright patents, although the Wrights alleged that it did. Burgess intended to adapt the plane to marine flying. The new company informed the Chief Signal Officer on 27 January that it was prepared to furnish parts and accessories for all machines formerly manufactured by the Burgess Company and Curtis.[93]

The Burgess-Dunne airplane was constructed on a principle which afforded inherent stability in flight: the wing ends checked each other during flight, counteracted changes in the relative lift of bow and stern, and checked all tendencies to dive when the airplane was descending with the motor cut off. On meeting side gusts of wind, the nearer wing, being broadside on and at an unfavorable angle for lifting, acted as a weather vane, turning the machine into the wind, while the far wing, offering little head resistance, was speeded up and kept from falling so that the airplane remained on an even keel. The steering and elevating of the Burgess-Dunne was controlled by a single set of levers, and ailerons were used only

---

*The fact that the planes were ordered under contract some time before they were delivered, accounts for the difference in dates.

as rudders and not for lateral control. The machine was supported on water by a single pontoon, but the ends of the wings were equipped with floats so that the machine had three points of contact with the water and could not submerge its wings as other seaplanes often did. The controls were self-locking and could be so set that the machine would fly in a straight line, in a circle, or up and down with the machine stabilizing itself.[94]

On 2 May an Aero Club committee observed this machine in flight and reported that the plane solved the problem of inherent stability. The observers saw the pilot, Clifford L. Webster, make a long glide with the machine, shut the engine off, and put his hands over his head while flying with the controls locked. He also demonstrated circular flight and a take-off with his hands off the controls. Later a plane of this type was purchased by the government and delivered in December 1914.[95]

In the meantime, two more Burgess tractors, S.C. Nos. 27 and 28, had been purchased. The tractor was unquestionably safer than the pusher, and from an engineering standpoint had numerous advantages. Its principal disadvantage was that it did not afford an unobstructed view for reconnaissance. Steps also were taken to secure from the Glenn Martin and Curtiss companies machines of an improved type, but none was delivered prior to 30 June 1914.[96]

From 11 to 13 March 1914 a board of officers composed of Lieutenants Foulois, Dodd, Taliaferro, Chapman, and Carberry convened at the Signal Corps Aviation School to determine specifications for a training tractor to be used solely as a practice machine for beginners. The board decided that a lightweight, strongly built machine, possessing as its chief characteristic maneuverability at all speeds and particularly at slow speed, was desired. Special equipment was also specified: a tachometer, an air speed indicator, gas and oil gauges, an aneroid barometer, and a clock. The manufacturer was to submit his bids, consisting of plans, specifications, and samples, to a board of military aviators actively engaged in flying. It was also stipulated that a government inspector would be at the plant during the construction of the plane or planes.*[97]

A continuation of the tests of the Riley Scott bombsight was the next major project undertaken at San Diego. After Scott had won first prize for his bombsight in the international competition in France in 1912, the Signal Corps had arranged to employ him temporarily to conduct experiments to determine the general usefulness of his device. The Ordnance Department agreed to manufacture the bombs needed for the tests, and the project was inaugurated in June 1913, but because of Scott's obligations elsewhere and because the bombsight was still in France, the experiments were delayed. Scott finally reported at North Island on 7 April 1914, and on the 17th, with the aid of Lieutenant Dodd who piloted him in the Burgess-Wright tractor No. 24, he began testing his bomb sighting and dropping device. Progress on the experiment was slow, for the airplane had to be adapted for bombing. A great deal of experience was obtained with 15-pound dummy bombs, the majority of which landed within a 100-foot target area when dropped from 900 to 2,000 feet. It took considerable practice for a pilot to steer a plane accurately over the target at 2,000 feet or higher, but Dodd demonstrated that it could be done when visibility was good. These experiments had to be discontinued the last of April when S.C. No. 24 was ordered to Galveston. Tests were tried in Signal Corps No. 9, but it could not carry the weight, and further experiments were suspended until the new Martin airplane No. 31 was received. The tests were not resumed until 17 August 1914.*[98]

In March 1914 tense relations between the United States and Mexico led to a demonstration at Vera Cruz. The Navy's aviation section was even smaller than the Army's, and to strengthen the nation's air arm at the scene of possible combat operations, the War Department directed the commanding officer of the flying school at North Island to send five qualified aviators, 30 enlisted men, and three Burgess tractor airplanes (S.C. Nos. 24, 25, and 26) to Fort Crockett at Galveston, Texas. Lieutenant Foulois, who only recently had relieved Captain Cowan as commander of the 1st Aero Squadron, was put in charge of the Galveston detachment, composed of Lieutenants Milling, Taliaferro, Carberry, Dodd, and Adna G. Wilde, the latter a medical officer. The unit de-

---

*No formal numbered specifications were issued for training planes through 1917, but specifications were written in the individual orders.

*See below, Chap. VI, pp. 125-26 for later bombing experiments.

parted for Texas on 26 April 1914, leaving Lieutenant Patterson in command of the 1st Aero Squadron. Lieutenant Morrow joined the unit at Fort Crockett on 6 May 1914.[99] This detachment was designated the 1st Company, 1st Aero Squadron, on 2 May 1914, and the men left at San Diego were designated as the 2d Company. Cowan again became squadron commander when Patterson was put in charge of the 2d Company on 20 June 1914.[100] On 13 July 1914 Patterson was relieved because of illness and Lieutenant Chapman succeeded him. Meanwhile, at San Diego it was decided to teach the remaining Wright pilots to fly Curtiss machines, since there were five pilots and only two planes left at the school— S.C. Nos. 22 and 23*—both Curtiss products. This program would produce more pilots in case they were needed in Mexico, and would provide five Curtiss pilots to supplement the 1st Company at Galveston. As no further trouble developed in Mexico, these men and planes were not needed. After the Mexican crisis passed, the 1st Company was returned from Fort Crockett on 13 July 1914, without ever having unpacked its airplanes.[101]

---

*S.C. No. 23, although declared out of commission on 24 February 1914, was evidently still in use.

★

CHAPTER VI

Aviation Legislation, and the Aviation Section Through 1914

LEGISLATIVE ACTION

UNTIL 1912 Congress had enacted no legislation to protect or reward the few men assigned to aviation duty, nor had anything been done to increase their numbers. The War Department had long insisted that it simply did not have enough men to detail additional officers for aviation training. Bills had been introduced in Congress in 1908, 1909, and 1910 (H.R. 12890, S. 230, and H.R. 16931) in an attempt to secure an increase in Signal Corps personnel, but none of these proposals had reached the floor of either house.[1] On 26 March 1912 after repeated requests for an increase in aviation personnel and numerous warnings that the United States was far behind other world powers in expenditures for aeronautics, the House of Representatives directed the Secretary of War to furnish it with a review of air progress abroad, a report on the extent and cost of U. S. Army aeronautics (including the instruction being given), and plans and recommendations for an increase in air activity and for necessity legislation to implement the program.[2]

On 20 April 1912 Secretary of War Stimson reported that there were only 10 officers on aviation duty and that this number could not be increased without legislation authorizing additional officers for the Signal Corps. He recommended the passage of a bill which the War Department had submitted to the House Military Affairs Committee on 14 March 1912 which called for an increase in the air strength of the Signal Corps to three squadrons by adding 55 officers as a first increment, provided for an increase of 20 per cent in the pay of all Regular Army military aviators and all enlisted men rated as airplane mechanicians (not to exceed one to each plane), and included a provision for six months' pay to widows or other beneficiaries of aviators or enlisted men killed in line of duty.[3] There is no record that this bill was introduced.

Meanwhile, in January 1912 Representative Thomas W. Hardwick of Georgia had introduced "a bill to increase the efficiency of the aviation service."[4] This bill, H.R. 17256, authorized the detail of 30 officers to the aviation service and doubled the pay and allowances of Regular Army officers who were actual fliers of heavier-than-air craft. An amendment was made on the floor of the House, however, which made the bill inoperative for the next five years, and another amendment included 30 additional officers to be detailed for aviation in the Navy and Marine Corps.[5] H.R. 17256 as amended was passed by the House on 5 August 1912. When the bill went to the Senate, the Military Affairs Committee asked the War Department for an opinion on it. The War Department was very critical of the bill: it disapproved the first amendment for obvious reasons and the second because the Department considered the 60 officers detailed for aviation duty in the Army, the Navy, and Marines to be inadequate. The Secretary of War recommended that the increase in pay be limited to 50 percent and that the provisions which removed limitations as to the length of detail be struck out, as he did not consider this to be in "the best interests of the service,"[6] explaining that it was not desirable to keep officers on aviation duty any longer than it took to train them to fly. The bill failed to pass the Senate.

The second appropriation for Army aeronautics, which amounted to $100,000, was made on 24 August 1912 for fiscal year 1913. General Allen reported that out of the first appropriation of $125,000 made on 3 March 1911, 15 airplanes had been purchased. Out of the new appropriation, contracts were awarded for 4 planes, and it was expected that by the end of fiscal year 1913 the Signal Corps would have not more than 24 and probably only 22 airplanes; the maintenance of each would cost approximately $2,500 a year.[7]

Despite the fact that Congress had passed little air legislation, the discussion of bills introduced so promoted interest in aviation that President Taft in December 1912 appointed a commission to report to Congress on the possibility of establishing a National Aerodynamic Laboratory. After three meetings the commission recommended such a laboratory and further recommended that it be advised by an aeronautical committee similar to the British Advisory Committee on Aeronautics, and be put under the direction of the Smithsonian Institution in Washington, which had funds that could be used to purchase equipment as soon as the project was legally launched. After a bill designed to legalize the commission had failed to pass, the Senate in January 1913 passed a bill authorizing the creation of a temporary commission to investigate and make recommendations as to the necessity of establishing the laboratory; and on 9 May 1913, President Wilson approved the designation of 12 advisory members, one each to be appointed by the Secretaries of War, Navy, Agriculture, and Commerce, and the remainder to be named by the Secretary of the Smithsonian. The advisory committee at its first meeting on 23 May decided to send Dr. Albert F. Zahm of the Smithsonian and Assistant Naval Constructor Jerome C. Hunsaker of the U.S. Navy to visit the world's principal aerodynamic laboratories, located at London, Paris, and Gottingen. After their return from abroad the two men submitted a report, which was published on 17 July 1914. But a decision by the Comptroller of the Treasury, declaring it illegal for persons already in the government service to act as an advisory committee to the laboratory, killed the committee. The idea back of it did not die, however, for on 3 March 1915 President Wilson was authorized by Congress to appoint the National Advisory Committee for Aeronautics.[*8]

No further air legislation was proposed in Congress until 11 February 1913, when Representative James Hay of West Virginia introduced H.R. 28728, the first bill to propose the removal of aviation from the Signal Corps. This bill provided for an Aviation Corps as a part of the line of the army. The corps would consist of 1 major, 2 captains, and 30 first lieutenants. The bill further authorized the detail of officers from other branches to the Aviation Corps, specified that the corps' commanding officer should be a military aviator, provided flying pay for both officers and enlisted men, and created the grades of Military Aviator and Aviation Mechanician. It also contained provisions for pay to beneficiaries of aviators killed in line of duty.[9]

The War Department did not favor the bill, but the Chief Signal Officer asked for expressions of opinion from various veteran fliers. Lieutenant Foulois, one of the army's oldest pilots, thought that military aviation was not developed sufficiently to be placed in the army line as a separate unit. He also objected to the measure because no provision had been made for captains and first lieutenants already on aviation duty. Moreover, he believed a nonflying officer who was experienced in executive and administrative work should be placed at the head of the service.[10] The Chief of the Army War College Division of the General Staff also protested against the creation of a separate corps. He called attention to the fact that the Signal Corps had the personnel, experience, and facilities for handling the aviation service, all of which would have to be duplicated in a new corps. In addition, he thought that the duties of the Aviation Corps were more those of the staff corps than the line of the army.[11] These objections to a separate corps were upheld by the officers of the aviation service. They even went so far as to say that the transfer of aviation to the line of the army "instead of increasing the efficiency of aviation, will set it back for a number of years."[12] In the face of such opposition from the officers most closely associated with aviation, H.R. 28728 was abandoned by the Military Affairs Committee and was never reported to the floor of the Senate.

---

*See below, Ch. VII, pp. 130-31.

Meanwhile in the fall of 1912 Congressional hearings began on the War Department appropriation bill for fiscal year 1914. The Chief Signal Officer again called attention to the need for additional personnel and said that by the end of fiscal year 1914 there would be on hand a minimum of 22 airplanes but only 14 officers to fly them; inasmuch as all government airplanes were designed to carry 2 officers, the Signal Corps would be short 30 officers. On 2 March 1913 the third air appropriation bill, covering fiscal year 1914 was passed. In addition to giving the Signal Corps $125,000 for aviation, it provided the first flying pay for army personnel by increasing by 35 percent the pay of Regular Army officers who were detailed as airplane pilots. The bill also limited to 30 the number of officers detailed to aviation, and provided that such details should not be restricted to officers below the grade of lieutenant colonel as had been the custom in the past.[13]

On 24 February 1913, shortly before the appropriation bill was passed, the Chief Signal Officer called together the air officers on duty in Washington to give them a chance to recommend legislation which they considered necessary to further the aeronautical work of the Signal Corps. This group drew up a bill calling for an increase in Signal Corps personnel and providing that detail of officers to the aeronautical service and their promotion be decided by a board of officers appointed by the Secretary of War on the recommendation of the Chief Signal Officer. The bill also called for a 50 per cent pay and allowance increase for officers detailed to air duty and a 25 percent increase for enlisted men, and provided for payments to the beneficiaries of deceased flying personnel. The proposed bill was signed by Maj. Edgar Russel, Capt. F. B. Hennessy, 1st Lt. Harry Graham, 2d Lts. H. H. Arnold, T. D. Milling, and W. C. Sherman.[14]

When a new bill, H.R. 5304, was introduced by Representative Hay on 16 May 1913, it was neither the bill favored by the War Department nor the one drafted by the aviation officers, but was more like Hay's old H.R. 28728 of February 1913, which the War Department had opposed. Hearings on the bill centered around the question of whether aviation should take the form of a new corps or be continued under the Signal Corps. Both Assistant Secretary of War Breckinridge

and Chief Signal Officer Scriven were against removing aviation from the Signal Corps, as were all but one of the Signal Corps officers who testified. The exception was Captain Beck, who had drafted the bill, and who urged a separate air organization. Beck wanted aviation removed from the Signal Corps partly because he felt that, if it remained there, it would probably never achieve any size or importance and partly because he believed that the longer the Signal Corps had control of aviation the more difficult it would be to break that hold. Among the officers who protested against removing the control of aviation from the Signal Corps was Capt. William Mitchell, not yet a flyer, who radically changed his views in later years. As a result of the hearings, the committee voted to strike out everything after the enacting clause and to prepare an entirely new bill.[15]

A new H.R. 5304 called for the creation in the Signal Corps of an Aviation Section composed of 60 officers and 260 enlisted men in addition to those already allotted by law to the Signal Corps. The flying officers were to be lieutenants selected from the army line for a four-year detail in the aviation section. The bill provided for the training of aviation students who, on recommendation of the Chief Signal Officer, were to be selected from unmarried lieutenants of the line, not over 30 years of age. It created two aeronautical grades for officers: one, that of Junior Military Aviator, which would have the rank, pay, and allowances of one grade higher than that held in the line, provided the line rank was not higher than that of first lieutenant; the other, that of Military Aviator, limited in number to 15, which required duty for three years as a Junior Military Aviator and carried the same provision as to rank and pay as the grade of Junior Military Aviator. Provision was made for 25 per cent increases in flying pay for students, 50 per cent for Junior Military Aviators, and 75 per cent for Military Aviators. The bill also established the rating of Aviation Mechanician, which carried a 50 per cent increase in pay for enlisted men, of whom there were to be no more than 40. Twelve enlisted men were to be instructed in flying and these men would also receive an increase in pay of 50 per cent. No person not already on aviation duty could be detailed as an aviation officer, rated Junior Military Aviator, Military Aviator, or Aviation Mechanician until he was issued a certificate of qualification by an aviation examining board composed of three aviators and two medical officers. Within 60 days of passage of the act, the Secretary of War was authorized, on the recommendation of the Chief Signal Officer, to rate as Junior Military Aviator any officer who was below the rank of captain, was then on aviation duty, and had demonstrated that he was especially qualified for military aviation service, The bill also provided that except in time of war, no one could be assigned or detailed to aviation duty against his will, and that one year's pay be given the widow or other beneficiary of any officer or enlisted man who died as a result of an airplane accident.[16] The bill encountered no serious opposition in either the House or the Senate and the brief debate in both houses indicated a desire to make the aviation service more efficient. H.R. 5304 was passed by both houses and on 18 July 1914 it became a law.*[17]

THE AVIATION SECTION

The Aviation Section was established for the purpose of operating or supervising the operation of all military aircraft, including balloons and airplanes, all appliances pertaining thereto, and any signaling apparatus installed thereon, and for training officers and enlisted men in military aviation. The establishment of the Aviation Section gave to the air service its first definite status, for prior to the passage of this act there was no actual provision of law covering the duties of the Signal Corps with respect to aeronautics except that contained in the 2 March 1913 Act, which allowed the detail of not more than 30 officers of the line of the Army on air duty and provided 35 per cent extra pay for flying.[18] Fortunately for the new section—and for its chief, Lt. Col. Reber (who also was chief of the Aeronautical Division)†—a new appropriation of $250,000, twice as much as had been appropriated for any year theretofore, had been made for aeronautics on 27 April.[19] Thus funds were available for the Aviation Section of the Signal Corps when it was created by the Act of 18 July 1914.

In addition to officers or enlisted men assigned from the Signal Corps at large for executive, administrative, scientific, or other duty in the Aviation Section, the new law of 18 July authorized 60 aviation officers and students and 260 enlisted men, to include 12 master signal electricians, 12 sergeants first class, 24 sergeants, 78 corporals, 8 cooks, 82 privates first class, and 44 privates.[20] The total of 320 personnel was to be added to that already provided for the Signal Corps proper. An aviation student was to serve not more than one year to determine his fitness for detail as an aviation officer; at the end of that time he was either to be detailed in the Aviation Section or returned to his branch of the service.

Since the law stated that the rating of Military Aviator would not be awarded until the officer had served at least three years as a Junior Military Aviator, the 24 officers who had already qualified as Military Aviators in 1912 and 1913 reverted to Junior Military Aviators. Newly graduated students were placed on a par with these older and more experienced flyers, and the flying pay of both groups was increased from 35 to 50 per cent. In 1917 those of the 24 original Military Aviators who were living and still flying, again became Military Aviators (the first since the Act of 1914); they received a 75 per cent increase in pay, but this lasted only until the National Defense Act of 1920 restored the old 50 per cent rate.[21]

The names of Military Aviators, Junior Military Aviators, and aviation students on flying status, with the dates when such flying duty began and terminated, were published in special orders. The dates specified in these special orders determined the period for which the increase of pay accrued. A copy of the order placing an officer on flying status had to be filed with the first pay voucher and cited on subsequent vouchers—a requirement which remained in effect until 1 July 1949. When the officer was relieved from flying duty, a copy of the order had to be filed with the voucher covering that particular period. Each officer had to state on his voucher the grade held under his line commission, since the increase accrued only on the pay for such grade. The various increases of 25, 50, and 75 per cent were restricted by law to base pay as increased by longevity pay, and did not apply to other elements of pay or allowances. The Chief Signal Officer

---

*See Appendix No. 13 for the full provisions of this act.

†Reber became chief of the Aviation Section on 18 July. He seems to have handled both duties until 17 March 1916, when Capt. George S. Gibbs became acting chief of the Aeronautical Division.

The Aviation Section encompassed the Army's entire air organization. The Aeronautical Division continued to exist, however, as the Washington Office of the Aviation Section.

announced the names of enlisted men required to participate in flying and those rated as Aviation Mechanicians, with the date on which the increased pay was to begin.[22]

The Act of 18 July 1914 did not repeal that of 2 March 1913. The Quartermaster General reported that the question had arisen as to whether the 1913 law was still effective and applied to those officers whose status was such as to preclude them from being brought within the terms of the 1914 Act. As an example, he mentioned a captain* of the Signal Corps who was drawing 35 per cent increase under the 1913 Act but who by virtue of his rank was precluded from sharing in the benefits of the new law, and requested an opinion from the Judge Advocate General. On 30 July 1914 the JAG held that the 1913 Act was in force, since there was no specific provision in the new act repealing the old. No officer with a line commission above the grade of first lieutenant could be a member of the Aviation Section, but it might frequently happen that the services of an officer of higher grade would be necessary for such duty. The evident purpose of the earlier law was to compensate any such officer for risk. It might also frequently happen that officers in the junior grades, not members of the Aviation Section, were competent and available for the performance of aviation duty when no members of the section were present. Therefore, the JAG held, an interpretation of the 1914 Act which excluded all persons other than members of the Aviation Section from the performance of aviation duties was not reasonable. Not only could the two acts stand together but the inference was strong that Congress intended they should.[23]

The original personnel of the Aviation Section of the Signal Corps, created by the Act of 18 July 1914, consisted of 19 officers and 101 enlisted men. The following nine officers were rated Junior Military Aviators (JMA's) and put on flying status effective 23 July 1914: †[24] Captains B. D. Foulois, L. E. Goodier, H. LeR. Muller, T. F. Dodd, and 1st Lieutenants W. R. Taliaferro, T. DeW. Milling, Carleton G. Chapman, Joseph C. Morrow, and Joseph E. Carberry. Capt. Roy C. Kirtland also was rated JMA but was not put on flying status. He was returned to his own branch

of the service because of some difficulty with Captain Cowan over the school accounts, but he was rerated JMA on 6 August 1917.[25] On 17 August 1914 Capt. Harold Geiger was rated JMA and put on flying status;[26] 1st Lieutenants Thomas S. Bowen, Douglas B. Netherwood, and Byron Q. Jones were rated JMA's on 20 August 1914 and put on flying status;[27] 1st Lt. H. A. Dargue was rated JMA on 22 July 1914 and put on flying status 21 August 1914;[28] Capt. William L. Patterson was rated JMA on 17 September 1914 and put on flying status on the same day,[29] making a total of 15 Junior Military Aviators on flying status as of that date.

There was no actual flying test required for the rating of Junior Military Aviator until 10 April 1915.[30] Unmarried lieutenants who were under 30 years of age and desired detail in the Aviation Section could apply through military channels to The Adjutant General of the Army, inclosing a certificate of good physical condition with no abnormality in vision or hearing. Before their qualifications could be considered, applicants had to undergo a thorough physical examination by a board consisting of two medical officers.[31]

All enlisted men who desired detail to the Aviation Section of the Signal Corps made application through regular channels to the Chief Signal Officer of the Army.[32] Although the Act of 18 July 1914 authorized 12 enlisted men to be given pilot training with 50 per cent increase in pay, at the end of October 1914 only 9 had been put on flying status:*[33] Master Signal Electrician John McRae; Sergeants First Class Herbert Marcus, Vernon L. Burge, S. J. Idzorek; Sergeants Thomas Boland, William Ocker; Cpls. William A. Lamkey, Samuel Katzman, and Charles Payne. Apparently two of these men soon dropped out, for records indicate that shortly after October there were only seven men being trained as enlisted pilots. A number of these men had already had flying training and on 10 March 1915 Sergeants, Ocker, Marcus, and Burge made solo flights. On 7 July Cpl. Albert D. Smith, who had enlisted on 10 March, was put on flying status and reported to Oscar Brindley for dual training. He had previously logged 40 hours in exhibition flying as a

---

*Captain Cowan
†See Appendix No. 14 for a list of army officers and enlisted pilots on aeronautical duty to April 1917.

*See Appendix No. 15 for a list of the enlisted men who under the Act of 18 July 1914 had been ordered on flying status up to the outbreak of World War I. (Inclusion in this list did not necessarily mean the man was a pilot—he might be an Aviation Mechanician.)

civilian in 1913 and the winter of 1913-14, so that three days after reporting he was able to make his first solo flight in a military airplane.[34]

On 1 December 1914 it was announced that examinations for the rating of Aviation Mechanician, of which there were to be not more than 40, would be held at such times as were necessary for service requirements. This rating carried with it a 50 per cent increase in pay. Enlisted men desiring to take the examination applied to The Adjutant General. A board composed of Captains Cowan, Foulois, and Dodd with a medical officer, 1st Lt. H. L. Schurmeir, was appointed on 2 December to examine the candidates. On 29 January the board met and examined 38 men, whose names were arranged in order of their technical ability, aviation experience, length of service in the Army and in aviation, and general efficiency in aviation. Twenty men passed the examination and on 12 February 1915 they were rated Aviation Mechanicians.*[35]

On 8 September 1914 the San Diego school had requested that no recruits be transferred there from the recruit depot. The school felt that it was desirable to eliminate recruit training and believed that it could get all the men it wanted by transfer of enlisted men from the line of the Army. Accordingly, on 21 November the Chief Signal Officer advised various Signal Corps organizations of his intention to transfer about 50 men from the Signal Corps at large as soon after 1 December as practicable and requested the names of intelligent men of good conduct who had shown aptitude along mechanical lines and who desired service in the Aviation Section. Transfers of noncommissioned officers would be made only after reduction to the rating of private first class, but the chances for promotion of ambitious men, particularly old NCO's, were very good. On 5 December 1914 the Chief Signal Officer requested the transfer of 44 men: 24 from Fort Leavenworth, Kansas, and the remainder from Fort Wood, New York; Fort Sam Houston, Fort Bliss, and Texas City, Texas; Fort Mason, California; Fort Logan, Colorado; and Fort Shafter, Hawaiian Islands. Captain Cowan was also anxious to transfer some of the men at the school who were unsuited for aviation work; he therefore asked that 9 men

*See Appendix No. 16 for a list of Aviation Mechanicians to 6 April 1917. It should be understood that the ratings may not have been held throughout the period, because of revocation of orders.

on duty at the Signal Corps Aviation School at San Diego be transferred to Telegraph Company H, Texas City.[36]

AIRPLANES PURCHASED BY THE SIGNAL CORPS IN 1914

Between October 1908 and 30 June 1914, $430,-000 had been spent for aeronautics, including $50,000 of the $250,000 appropriation for 1915, which had been made immediately available. From these funds, 30 airplanes had been purchased by the Signal Corps. In 1914, nine of the planes were considered modern enough to be serviceable in every way.[37] Eleven airplanes were delivered and accepted in 1914, not including the Burgess tractor, S.C. No. 26, already mentioned, which was received in January. The first of the new planes were two Burgess H tractors, without engines, equipped with modified wheel and rudder controls, which were delivered at Fort Wood, New York, on 15 and 25 May. These planes, S.C. Nos. 27 and 28, which cost $6,000 each, were duplicates of S.C. No. 26. They were shipped from Fort Wood to San Diego, where they arrived at the end of July. A year later on 21 June 1915 the Commanding Officer at San Diego recommended that they and No. 26 be dropped as obsolete. All three planes were underpowered; and, although they had been remodeled by Grover C. Loening, the Wright Company's famous engineer and general manager, by this date they were of no value as service machines and were not satisfactory even as trainers. Number 26 was out of commission on 20 August 1915, but later it was sent to the 1st Aero Squadron, condemned, and sold in 1916. Number 27 was dropped at San Diego on 25 August 1915 and shipped to the 1st Aero Squadron on 21 December 1915; it was then turned over to an inspector and sold.[38] Number 28 was dropped at San Diego on 25 August 1915.[39]

On 2 July 1914 the first of a series of Glenn L. Martin "T" tractors, S.C. No. 31, was accepted through local purchase after demonstrations of its performance. The landing gear with shock absorbers was a special Martin product. The instruments consisted of a gasoline gauge, an auxiliary gas gauge, an oil gauge, an electric tachometer, and a thermometer. The plane was slightly modified for testing the Scott bombsight and release mechanism; it was equipped with dual controls especially convenient for bombing and a sliding cover over the view spaces provided for bomb sighting. This plane was ordered on 20 June 1914 for delivery at the Signal Corps Aviation School, San Diego, on 23 June 1914; the cost, without an engine, was $4,800. The government ·supplied a Curtiss 100-horsepower engine. The plane was damaged two years later by Lieutenant Butts on 26 June 1916 and was condemned on 18 October 1916.[40]

On 26 August 1914, S.C. No. 32, the first of two additional Martin T2 tractors, was accepted at San Diego. It cost $4,400. It was badly damaged by Lieutenant Netherwood in an accident on 1 September 1914 but was rebuilt. After 151 hours of rough usage as a trainer, including severe damage in one wreck and minor damage in two others, the plane was condemned on 29 June 1915 by the Chief Signal Officer on Cowan's recommendation.[41] Signal Corps No. 33, a duplicate of Martin T2 No. 31, was received on 7 September 1914 and accepted on 11 September. After having been flown 156 hours as a trainer and having been damaged twice, it was condemned on 29 June 1915.[42]

The first Curtiss J. tractor, Signal Corps No. 29, was received at San Diego on 24 June 1914. In December 1914 it was lost in the Pacific Ocean, but the engine (a 90-horsepower OX Curtiss) was salvaged.[43] On 15 September 1914, the second Curtiss J. tractor, S.C. No. 30, was accepted at San Diego. It was a duplicate of No. 29 but did not have an instrument board, which presumably was to be furnished by the Signal Corps. Delivery was scheduled on 27 June 1915 and the price was to be $6,725; but on 1 July 1915, spares which cost an additional $2,790 were ordered. Lieutenant Goodier, who reached 1,000 feet in one minute in the new plane, stated that it was a fine climber. Captain Muller used it to set a new American altitude record of 16,790 feet. The plane was also used by Lt. B. Q. Jones in studying and demonstrating acrobatics; in it he executed the first deliberate stall and stalled loop. It was damaged in December 1914 by Lieutenant Carberry and again early in 1915 by Lieutenant Bowen. On 11 October 1915 while attempting a loop, Lieutenant Taliaferro* was killed in a crash that wrecked the plane. On

12 November 1915, the Office of the Chief Signal Officer approved dropping it from the list.[44]

A second Curtiss F flying boat, S.C. No. 34, was delivered on 3 September and accepted on 21 September 1914 at San Diego. On 1 September 1915, by which time it had logged 343 hours in the air, Cowan reported the plane unsafe to fly. Although the Chief Signal Officer approved condemnation of the plane on 10 September, it was rebuilt and was in use from 19 November 1915 until 25 May 1916, when it was again reported out of commission. It was finally condemned on 18 October 1916.[45]

The first Curtiss N tractor, S.C. No. 35, with a Curtiss OXX engine was delivered by 2 December 1914 and accepted at San Diego on 11 December. After almost two years of use it was condemned on 18 October 1916.[46]

The Burgess-Dunne armored seaplane, S.C. No. 36, was accepted by the Army on 30 December 1914. It had been ordered without an engine on 13 March 1913, for delivery to College Park on 1 July at a price of $6,025. The delivery date was postponed to 1 August 1913 in order to permit installation of ⅛ inch nickel-steel armor plate; actually the plane did not make its initial flight until 10 October. On that date at Marblehead, Massachusetts, it flew at an average speed of 75 miles per hour and climbed over 300 feet per minute. The Army had ordered a Renault 100-horsepower engine for this plane, but for some unknown reason it was equipped with a 120-horsepower Salmson. On 9 October 1914, a pontoon was purchased for it. At some time during the experiments with the plane, a Benet-Mercier machine gun built to government specifications by the Colt Company was mounted on the plane. The Burgess-Dunne weighed 1,700 pounds and had a carrying capacity of 2,300 pounds.[47] Unique in form and design, it was described as "self-balancing, self-steering and non-capsizable, tailless and folding, inclosed nacelle with armored cockpit."[48] The wings of the biplane formed a "V," with a biplace nacelle at the center of the "V". Ailerons in the tips of both upper and lower wings were the only controls—acting as elevator and rudder, and providing lateral balance. The plane,* however, was not found

---

*A World War I training field in Texas was named for Lt. Taliaferro.

*No market was found for this type of plane and the Burgess Company was subsequently absorbed by the Curtiss Aeroplane and Motor Company.

Burgess tractor, Signal Corps No. 28, 1914

The Army's first Curtiss J tractor, Signal Corps No. 29

The Army's first Martin T tractor, Signal Corps No. 31

practicable because it was slow in responding to controls, and on 18 October 1916, it was condemned.[49]

The Burgess-Dunne plane was one of three foreign-powered, armored airplanes ordered in March 1913. The other two were a Curtiss and a Wright. The Curtiss, which was never delivered,*[50] was to have had a 160-horsepower Gnome engine, and the Wright (which was not delivered until 1915) had a 90-horsepower Daimler engine. The latter plane was the last Wright Company plane purchased by the government; it was designated the Model F "Tin Cow," S.C. No. 39. Although the plane had been designed by Grover C. Loening, Oscar Brindley said that it handled badly, and Lieutenant Dargue stated that it was uncontrollable on the ground and was out of date. After only seven flights (between 27 May and 4 June 1915) all by Dargue, the plane was dropped from the record on 13 June 1915.[51]

On 8 June 1914, General Scriven, the Chief Signal Officer, requested authorization from The Adjutant General[52]

to hold a competition for the development of a suitable military aeroplane for service use, purchasing the machine making the highest number of points in the competition for $12,000, the second for $10,000, and the third for $8,000; the competition to be held at San Diego, California, beginning 15 October 1914, under such regulations as the Chief Signal Officer of the Army may prescribe to assure the obtaining of suitable machines and safeguarding the interests of the Government.

After the Judge Advocate General had given a favorable opinion, the Secretary of War approved the proposal on 15 June, and on 1 July the Chief Signal Officer announced the competition. It was expected that the results would enable the Corps to decide on a standard machine—and standardization was one of the most important problems confronting the Signal Corps at that time. It was hoped too, that the competition would encourage airplane manufacturers and, at the same time, permit some of the newer types of planes which were being produced to be tested.[53]

The specifications prescribed a two-seater tractor biplane with dual controls, maximum speed of at least 70 miles per hour and a minimum speed of not more than 40 miles per hour, and fuel and oil for four hours at 70 miles per hour. Desirable features were a positive driven fuel pump, an attachment for a tachometer, a quickly demountable power plant, the elimination of friction in duplicate control leads, and a streamlined design. The machine was to be capable of being assembled from transport cases in two hours by four mechanics, while disassembly and packing in cases was to take not more than an hour and a half.[54]

Manufacturers were to have their entries filed by 1 September, and by 1 October they were to furnish certain information including stress diagrams and blueprints as well as certificates of engine performance. The planes were to be delivered at San Diego by 20 October. In order to compete, the machine had to qualify with a nonstop flight of four hours and a 4,000-foot climb in 10 minutes while fully loaded. It would then be graded by a system of points on such things as construction, maneuverability, and inherent stability. On 28 September 1914, a board consisting of Captains Foulois and Dodd, Lieutenants Taliaferro, Milling, and Carberry, and the civilian engineer, Grover Loening, was appointed to conduct the tests.

Twelve airplane companies had signified their intention to enter the competition, but on 20 October only two manufacturers, the Curtiss and Martin companies, were ready. A third machine, owned by Maximilian Schmitt, was withdrawn before the tests. The other contestants were barred. Because there were so few entries the Chief of the Aviation Section called off the competition, but at their request the manufacturers present were given permission to demonstrate their machines. The tests were made under the conditions of the competition between 23 October and 8 November,[55] but with the understanding that the government was under no obligation to purchase the machines. The Curtiss Aeroplane Company's plane was the only entry which fulfilled every requirement of the specification. The competition was a great disappointment.

THE SAN DIEGO SCHOOL

All of the equipment of the 1st Company, 1st Aero Squadron, had remained packed, and neither the officers nor the enlisted men had

---

*Curtiss ordered a Gnome engine from a salesman named Devillers and paid for it. He was unable to get the engine from the Gnome Company and borrowed a smaller horsepower Gnome from Norman Prince. When this engine was tested at Annapolis it developed only 102 horsepower. Norman Prince replevined the engine and the Navy sent it back to him. The Curtiss company was unable to get the 160-horsepower Gnome engine from DeVillers, who was convicted of grand larceny, but neither did it get its money back. The government refused to accept a Salmson or Curtiss engine and canceled the contract in January 1914.

The Burgess Dunne, Signal Corps No. 36, accepted by the Army in December 1914

The Wright Model F "Tin Cow," Signal Corps No. 39

engaged in any aviation activity since their arrival in Galveston on 30 April; hence, Lt. Col. Samuel Reber had requested its return on 3 July. Two weeks later on 17 July 1914, the company arrived at San Diego. Since practically all of the experienced military aviators were members of the 1st Company, the work at San Diego had been greatly hampered by their absence. There were several new planes to be tried out and it was necessary that the officers become familiar with them.[56]

After the return of the 1st Company, the 1st Aero Squadron was organized into a Headquarters Detachment and two companies to conform with War Department General Order No. 75 of 4 December 1913. On 5 August 1914, there were 12 officers, 54 enlisted men, and 6 airplanes in the squadron. By October it had grown to 16 officers, 77 enlisted men, and 8 airplanes and was ready for field service. As this was the first air service operating unit of any kind ever organized in the United States in compliance with War Department regulations, the question as to whether a flying officer of limited administrative experience in the army should be placed in command became one of major importance, and for some time it was not satisfactorily answered. In this instance, Captain Foulois, who was just such an officer, was made squadron commander. Captain Cowan felt that it would be necessary to make a number of changes in the organization before it would be entirely satisfactory, but that it was better to wait until the organization had been tried out in the field under service conditions. According to Foulois the organization remained unchanged until 17 April 1915, when instructions were received from the Chief Signal Officer directing that the entire commissioned and enlisted personnel of the squadron be carried on one roll under the heading 1st Aero Squadron.[57]

General Order No. 10, SCAS, San Diego, 5 August 1914, assigned the personnel of the Aviation Section, Signal Corps at the field as follows:[58]

SIGNAL CORPS AVIATION SCHOOL

Capt. A. S. Cowan—Commanding Officer
1st Lt. William L. Patterson—Secretary
Capt. Roy C. Kirtland—QM Supply Officer, Disbursing Officer, and Ordnance Officer
1st Lt. T. D. Milling—Officer in charge of training
Mr. O. A. Brindley—Instructor in Flying
Mr. G. C. Loening—Aeronautical Engineer
Mr. W. C. Bauer—in charge of machine shop and motors
Mr. H. S. Molineau—on duty in machine shop

Mr. Jacob Bailey—on duty in machine shop
Mr. E. J. Briggs—on duty in machine shop
Mr. R. R. Marsh—Clerk, School Headquarters
One MSE, 2 sergeants first class, 1 sergeant, 2 corporals, 23 privates first class, and 8 privates
One airplane, S.C. No. 22

1ST AERO SQUADRON

Capt. B. D. Foulois—Commanding Officer
Capt. H. LeR. Muller—Squadron Adjutant, PX Officer, and officer in charge of general mess
Sgt. Arthur L. Bruhl—Sergeant Major

1ST COMPANY, 1ST AERO SQUADRON

Capt. Harold Geiger—Commanding Officer
1st Lt. W. R. Taliaferro—OIC Training from 3 September 1914
1st Lt. J. C. Morrow
1st Lt. J. E. Carberry
2d Lt. D. B. Netherwood—OIC Machine Shops from 7 October 1914
One MSE, 3 sergeants first class, 1 sergeant, 3 corporals, 1 cook, 13 privates first class, and 5 privates
Signal Corps airplanes Nos. 24, 25, and 26

2D COMPANY, 1ST AERO SQUADRON

Capt. L. E. Goodier, Jr.—Commanding Officer
Capt. T. F. Dodd
1st Lt. C. G. Chapman
2d Lt. T. S. Bowen
2d Lt. B. Q. Jones
One MSE, 2 sergeants first class, 2 sergeants, 4 corporals, 1 cook, 11 privates first class, and 5 privates
Signal Corps airplanes Nos. 20, 28, and 31

From July to December 1914 very little systematic training or instruction in technical work was accomplished because a large portion of the enlisted personnel of the Squadron was constantly needed in construction work and development of the Signal Corps Aviation School (SCAS). The period was utilized, however, in the technical instruction of officers, the securing of camp, garrison, and personal equipment for the entire squadron, and in such military instruction as could be given without interfering with the construction work regularly carried on at the school.[59]

On 5 July 1914, the 4th Regiment of United States Marines, under command of Col. J. Pendleton, arrived in San Diego from duty along the coast of Mexico. On 24 August it was given permission by the Coronado Beach Company to construct and maintain certain temporary structures on North Island with the usual condition that the premises would be vacated and structures removed upon notice. The Marine camp was called Camp Howard in honor of Rear Admiral Thomas Benton Howard, commander of the Pacific fleet. The

1st Aero Squadron, San Diego, October 1914

advent of the Marines was providential, for until they left on 22 December 1914, they assisted materially in construction work. They repaired and practically rebuilt the little landing wharf, cleared ground for parade and drill purposes, built a boardwalk from the wharf to the camp, and in other ways—such as policing the occupied portion of the island—aided the small Signal Corps garrison.[60]

Although there were a number of expert military aviators in the service, these men were not necessarily competent as instructors; and during 1914 the policy of employing civilian instructors to give preliminary instruction in flying was adopted. Oscar Brindley had been employed in this capacity a year earlier; and on 5 October 1914, Francis "Doc" Wildman was employed by the Signal Corps. Both men gave regular flying instruction at the school, and the results proved the wisdom of employing expert civilian instructors. The school also taught the care and repair of airplanes, and the operation, care, and repair of aeronautical engines, while eminent authorities gave lectures on meteorology, aeronautical engineering, propellers, and internal combustion engines.[61]

Several civilian engine experts were also employed at San Diego at this time. On 15 July 1914, Grover C. Loening was appointed aeronautical engineer in the Signal Service at large at $3,600 a year. He joined Oscar Brindley at San Diego; and Captain Cowan gave the two men a free hand at reorganizing the system of training, engineering, maintenance, and procurement. Brindley had reported that the planes at North Island were in very bad shape, and both Milling and Reber recognized the need for an engineering staff. An Experimental and Repair Department was established with Loening in charge and Milling as his assistant. This department was responsible for all experimental work and development of new airplane construction features. It also took care of major repair jobs, with minor repairs being handled by the crew assigned for duty with each machine. Very satisfactory results were obtained from this arrangement, its chief contribution being the training of enlisted men for duty as Aviation Mechanicians.

The most important single piece of construction work undertaken during the year was the rebuilding of Burgess tractors Nos. 24, 26, 27, and 28. These machines were underpowered with the 70 horsepower Renault engines and could not climb with a load. After S.C. No. 28 was rebuilt, Lt. B. Q. Jones used it to establish a world's duration record for a pilot and two passengers on 12 March 1915. Loening and Milling were also instrumental in persuading Glenn Martin to build and deliver to the San Diego school, without a contract, a Model T tractor airplane. Martin's gamble paid off; for the plane, S.C. No. 31, was the first of a number of Martin tractors purchased by the government.[62]

It seems that in 1914 very little actual repair work was done in the shop under the supervision of Loening, who was concentrating on major construction changes in the Burgess tractors. Consequently, Cpl. A. D. Smith, Mr. Semeniouk, a civilian employee, and Private Kuhn, with the permission of Lieutenant Taliaferro, who was in charge of the training department, opened up a repair shop in a hangar wing; there they rebuilt and overhauled wing sections and fuselages which heretofore had had to be returned to the factory for repairs. The need for this local repair shop was evidenced by the fact that it very quickly took over the entire hangar. Cpl. A. D. Smith and Pvt. Gordon Smith took over the job of covering wings with fabric and rebuilding fuselages, and Private Kuhn remained in charge of the woodwork. Mr. Semeniouk, who proved to be expert in metal work, repaired and made new metal fittings. Sergeants Barnhardt, Ocker, Parkinson, Krull, Steinle, Sweet, Marcus, and Burge participated in final assembly work. George Hallett, who had been loaned by Curtiss for a month's trial in December 1914, was made an instructor for Aviation Mechanicians at $2,000 a year, and also instructed pilot officers in engine overhaul,[63] while Corporal Smith was given the function of instructing the same officers in airplane assembly and maintenance. In the spring of 1916, while Smith was on leave of absence, the Martin company employed him as a test pilot and school instructor. In the summer of that year he was approached by Mitsui and Company (a Japanese firm which had bought the Sloane Aeroplane Company and renamed it Standard Aircraft Company) with a rather fabulous offer to go with them as test pilot. But Smith turned down the offer, purchased his discharge from the army, and became a civilian instructor at San Diego, in a capacity similar to that of Brindley and Wildman.

He continued in this position from 17 August 1916 to 25 June 1917, when he was appointed to the rank of Captain in the Air Service Officers Reserve Corps.*[64]

On 17 September 1914, Captain Cowan made the Army's first official call by air on the Navy at sea. The USS *California* was being rechristened the USS *San Diego* in the harbor at San Diego, and the President of the Chamber of Commerce had requested an airplane to fly over the ship during the ceremony and also had invited Cowan to be on board for the ceremony. Cowan arranged with the commanding officer of the ship to make his call in a flying boat and thus comply with both requests. With Francis Wildman† as his pilot he flew out to the ship, circled it twice, then landed on the water, taxied to the gangway, and went aboard. After paying his respects to the commanding officer and visiting awhile, he returned to the flying boat. Wildman took off from the water, circled the ship once more, and then flew back to the hangar.[65]

On 24 September 1914 Cowan requested a Curtiss hydroplane for use as a seaplane tender. For a year the installation at North Island had rented speed boats and had found them far from satisfactory;** they were out of commission such a large part of the time that overwater flying had to be suspended for weeks at a time or done without the use of a tender. The Chief Signal Officer approved the request and a new five-passenger, Curtiss hydroplane was put in service at San Diego in December. Its average speed on a trial run was 35 miles an hour. Part of its equipment was a temporary stretcher, so arranged that a man could be placed on it and a doctor could attend him while the boat was in motion.[66]

On 8 October 1914 Captain Muller, flying alone in the Curtiss J tractor No. 30, set a new official American altitude record of 16,798 feet†† in a flight lasting two hours and twenty-seven minutes. Prior to this flight, Muller had made several

fifteen-minute climbs to determine the most efficient climbing angle and to measure oil and gas consumption. On the second flight his plane was equipped with tachometer, gravity needle oil gauge, clock, aneroid barometer reading to 6,000 feet, and a large registering barograph from which the pilot observed the climb to 5,000 meters (16,404 feet). Between 12,500 and 13,000 feet the engine suddenly lost 50 revolutions per minute, but the deficiency was corrected by the adjustment of the carburetor needle valve; the new setting was held for the remainder of the climb. At 14,000 to 15,000 feet Muller encountered violent air which several times forced him to fly level and even point the plane down occasionally; similar trouble was encountered at 16,000 feet. At that altitude Muller had a suggestion of nausea, which wore off and was followed by a feeling of exhilaration at the peak of the climb.[67]

On 5 November 1914, Captain Goodier was severly injured while riding as a passenger with Glenn L. Martin, who was demonstrating a new model tractor to the army in an official competitive slow speed test. At the end of the mile straightaway test Martin turned too slowly and stalled his engine; when he gunned it with the rudder well over, the plane went into what was said to be the first tailspin. The plane descended from 200 feet and hit the ground on one wing, which folded up like an accordian. Goodier, who was in the front seat, was thrown forward with such force that his nose was almost severed on the aluminum cowling and his old skull fracture reopened. The engine telescoped back and broke both of his legs, the engine shaft drove a hole through his right knee, and the fuel tank broke and flooded him with gasoline. Martin received only a scalp wound; he slid forward through the thin wall between the two seats and Goodier served as a bumper to soften the jolt. Goodier recovered.[68] He was relieved from active duty in 1915 and retired in 1916, but returned to active duty a short time later.[69]

On 8 December 1914, the Chief Signal Officer had recommended to the Secretary of War that there be included in the appropriation bill for the fiscal year ending 30 June 1916, a proviso that a sum not to exceed $500 should be used to defray the cost of special technical instruction of officers of the Aviation Section. It had been found desirable to send officers to take the air engineer-

---

*Smith remained in the service and became a Brigadier General in World War II.

†Neither the report of this flight which appeared in the *Army Navy Journal* and which was written so as to make it appear that Captain Cowan flew the plane nor other reports mentioned Wildman. Later, the episode became an important item in the Goodier courtmartial proceedings. See below, Chap. VII, pp. _____.

**One Signal Corps file states that in 1913 the SCAS had secured two army launches—one a large slow boat used to transport personnel and freight and the other a fast one used as a crash boat.

††There is a disagreement among the sources: Signal Corps files state 17,441 feet, and *Aeronautics* gives 17,185 feet. The above figure is from ACA records, which are always considered final.

ing course at MIT—the first of its kind given in the United States—and it was felt that their tuition should be paid from the air appropriation. (Captain V. E. Clark was taking the course at his own expense at that time.) On 4 January 1915, the Chief Signal Officer wrote to the commanding officer, Signal Corps Aviation School, to select two officers to pursue a reading course which would qualify them for the MIT course. Lts. B. Q. Jones and H. W. Harms were selected; and after the requested $500 was appropriated, they were ordered to MIT on 27 September 1915 for the 1915-1916 term.[70]

The enlisted men on duty at the Signal Corps Aviation School in December 1914 were still quartered in the old San Diego barracks, which had been condemned some years before. Only one set of quarters in the yard was occupied as all others had been found unsuitable for NCO quarters. The enlisted strength was greater than the accommodations; and some men, not entitled to quarters, slept in town and lost much time in traveling back and forth across the bay from San Diego to North Island. On 2 December, the Quartermaster General authorized $1,238 to cover rental of additional quarters for three MSE's and six sergeants on duty at the SCAS for the balance of fiscal year 1915. This sum was totally inadequate considering the number of enlisted men improperly quartered, but Colonel Reber finally gave verbal authorization for $2,000 to build a temporary shack to house a detachment of 50 men, pending formal action by the Chief Signal Officer.[71]

The personnel strength of the Aviation Section on 7 December 1914 was 30 officers—2 non-flying Signal Corps officers, 18 Junior Military Aviators, and 10 aviation students—119 enlisted men, 7 of whom were under instruction, and 8 civilian employees. Between 18 July and 7 December 1914, there had been 51 applications for duty in the Aviation Section; of these, 12 had been detailed, 1 case was pending, 17 had not replied to letters sent them, and 21 had been rejected. The airplane strength was 11; 3 of the planes were assigned to the school proper and 8 were in service with the 1st Aero Squadron. In addition, 1 school machine was under construction and 1 experimental machine* was en route to San Diego.

A few days later an order was issued for 8 new machines to equip the 1st Aero Squadron—which would make a total of 21 airplanes when delivered.[72]

The Mackay Trophy contest was scheduled for 21 December 1914 and six machines from San Diego were entered in the competition. The plan was to have the machines fly to Los Angeles on the 21st and start the contest from that point on the following day, but the weather and other unpredictable events changed the plans. On his way to Los Angeles Captain Muller, piloting the Curtiss J, S.C. No. 29, was forced by very rough winds to land in the Pacific off Arguello, California. Lieutenant Gerstner, who was acting as Muller's observer, attempted to swim ashore for aid but became entangled in kelp and was drowned.* Muller stayed with the plane, which remained afloat, and was rescued several hours later. The plane was a complete loss but the engine was salvaged by a naval crew from the USS *Truxton*.[73] Lieutenant Milling and Captain Patterson in S.C. No. 24, the Burgess H which Loening had remodeled, had to land in a ploughed field near Agra, just west of the San Onofre Mountains, because of engine trouble. The plane turned over in landing and was so badly damaged that it was out of the running and had to be condemned. Milling and Patterson, both unhurt, saw the Muller machine come down and Patterson went for aid, which had already been sent by a railroad employee who also had seen the accident.[74] Lieutenants Carberry and Christie in S.C. No. 30, Curtiss J, were forced to land at Pacific Beach with a broken fuel lead. Repairs were made and the machine finally reached the vicinity of Oceanside; there rough air and engine trouble forced a second landing, and the plane failed to reach Los Angeles. No. 31, Martin tractor, with Lieutenant Taliaferro and Captain Foulois aboard, also landed near Oceanside with an engine failure, but another Martin airplane, S.C. No. 32, was sent from North Island to replace their plane. The two officers continued on their way; but when they neared the San Onofre Mountains a piece of glass from Tailaferro's goggles blew into his eye, forcing his to land. When he did so, S.C. No. 32 tipped over on the rough ground and was eliminated from the contest.

*Probably the Burgess-Dunne.

*There was a World War I training field named for Lt. Gerstner.

Only two planes managed to get to Los Angeles: the Burgess H, S.C. No. 25, with Lieutenants Morrow and Holliday aboard, and Burgess H No. 28, piloted by Captain Dodd with Lieutenant FitzGerald as observer.

The contest was not held until 23 December on account of rain and high winds. On that day Morrow and Holliday were compelled to land near Oceanside with a broken fuel line; their plane (S.C. No. 25)* was so badly damaged in landing that it was out of the contest. Captain Dodd and Lieutenant FitzGerald in the only plane left, S.C. No. 28, completed the required flight, made a successful reconnaissance of troops located in a triangular area bounded by the mouth of the San Diego River, La Mesa, and Lower Otay Reservoir, and thus won the trophy.[75]

On 22 December, detachments were sent from San Diego to recover the three crashed and grounded machines. The other three planes were total losses. The many accidents caused serious concern at the aviation school but the experience was a valuable one because it showed that even with good pilots and planes, adverse circumstances could put a number of machines out of commission in a very short time. This fact emphasized the necessity of having a relatively large number of machines available in case of war, when flying would have to be done in all kinds of weather and over all sorts of terrain. The Signal Corps Aviation School recognized the necessity of providing spare machines to meet such contingencies. Up to that time the plan had been to provide two pilots for each machine but it was now evident that it would probably be better to provide at least two machines for each pilot.[76]

In the summer of 1914 after war broke out in Europe, the combatants gave unprecedented attention to military aeronautics, a new and heretofore neglected science. At the outbreak of the war the Allies possessed a total of 208 airplanes: the British had approximately 48 airplanes,† the French had 136, and the Belgians 24. Germany had 180 airplanes.[77] When it was discovered that reconnaissance done by airplanes greatly aided the armies in battle, the race to build up

air forces began. More planes were built in European countries, and orders for trainers were given to American manufacturers.

In an effort to preserve American neutrality, President Wilson issued a proclamation on 4 August 1914, forbidding various acts within the territory and jurisdiction of the United States. The visits of belligerent vessels were regulated, and United States residents were prohibited from participating in the war or transporting contraband for a belligerent. However, the proclamation permitted production for belligerents by stating that "All persons may lawfully and without restriction . . . manufacture and sell *within* the United States arms and munitions of war, and other articles ordinarily known as 'contraband of war,' yet they cannot carry such articles upon the high seas for the use or service of a belligerent." This clause made it possible for a number of American airplane and engine companies to supply directly all of the warring countries, with the exception of Germany,[78] and it brought about some expansion in American airplane factories. Whether this was an advantage to the United States is debatable; for it was not as easy for the Aviation Service to get planes from manufacturers who already had foreign orders. However, the airplane industry was benefitted, for the foreign orders stepped up production and American manufacturers increased their experience in plane manufacturing.

The first bombing from airplanes in World War I took place in August 1914, when bombs and hand grenades were dropped from planes by both sides without benefit of a bombsight. During the same month German planes bombed Paris, and three Zeppelins bombed Allied territory; but each of the Zeppelins was either destroyed or lost. German Zeppelins did not begin bombing London until March and April of 1915, although they appeared over England as early as 19 January.[79]

The beginning of air bombardment by the European combatants coincided with new tests of the Riley Scott bombsight and dropping mechanism at the North Island school. Scott's two devices were designed to be carried in the rear seat of a two-place tandem plane, along with the bombardier and the bomb rack. The sight, attached to the right side of the fuselage, consisted of a small telescope mounted on a gradu-

---

*This plane suffered another accident on 13 January 1915 and was dropped from the records.

†Air Ministry publication 125, *A Short History of the Royal Air Force*, pp. 24 and 25, states that the Royal Flying Corps had 63 airplanes, but Cuneo in *The Air Weapon 1914-1916*, p. 16, gives 48.

ated vertical limb and horizontal axis, similar to that of a transit; while a small weight hanging below held the main portion of the instrument in a horizontal position. Using this instrument, the bombardier could determine the ground speed, which, together with the altitude (indicated on the aneroid barometer), enabled him to calculate the telescope angle-setting for a given target. Instead of making these calculations in the air, Scott had prepared tables, which provided the angle-setting for any target, given the altitude and ground speed. The telescope was set at the desired angle and when the bombardier saw the target through the lens, he released the bomb. Attached to the left hand side of the fuselage was a bomb rack for 15-lb. bombs, which were light enough to be put into the rack by hand. Two racks for 50-lbs. bombs were carried under the fuselage. The 50-lb. bombs were suspended in the racks in a horizontal position by means of brass jaws resembling ice tongs. The upper ends of the tongs were held together by a spring plunger and to this was attached a release wire leading to the bombardier's cockpit. Another release wire, attached to the safety pins of the bombs, could be pulled by the bombardier before releasing the bombs. The bombs, manufactured by the Frankford Arsenal, were of the simplest type, being made of commercial steel pipe with cast iron head, base, and tail piece. The latter part, designed by Scott, was made of iron rods, threaded at one end to enter the rear cap fitting, and carried 3 vanes of galvanized iron 120° apart at the other end. This tail piece was roughly made and soldered to a sleeve secured to the rod by a threaded collar, but it functioned perfectly.

On 5 August 1914, bomb-dropping tests preliminary to the scheduled tests were made by Captain Goodier, Corporal Hale, and Private Hall in S.C. No. 31, and on the 6th, Goodier took up Scott, who dropped dummy bombs from 1,000 feet. Thereafter, until the scheduled tests began on 17 August, Goodier and the Martin tractor were busy, for both were to participate in the final tests. The pilot was responsible for direction, and considerable practice was necessary to enable him to steer accurately over a small target.[80] From the time the official tests began until the 24th of August, 30 dummy and live explosive bombs, numerous grenades, and one 3-inch standard artillery shell were dropped on a 100-foot bullseye target. The dummies were dropped from 1,000 and 2,000 feet, and the live projectiles from 2,000 feet. Observers viewed the results from a bombproof shelter 150 to 200 yards distant from the target.

Captain Muller officially observed the tests for the Aviation Section, and Col. J. W. Joyes represented the Ordnance Department, which had made the bombs. Joyes reported that the accuracy was regarded as astonishingly good. A number of missiles fell within 15 or 20 feet of the center of the target and a very large proportion within 75 or 100 feet. Accuracy, however, was a secondary consideration, the results of detonation and fragmentation being the main factors to be determined. The 15-lb. bombs made a uniform crater about four feet in diameter and one foot deep. Fragments flew out as far as 300 yards, although many did not rise out of the crater. The character of fragmentation of the 50-lb. bombs was similar, with craters up to 10 feet in diameter and 4 feet deep. One 50-lb. bomb dropped from 2,000 feet failed to detonate when accidentally dropped into water, but this was the only failure of its kind.

The results indicated that the tests were a success and that bombing instruction should be given at the school. Captain Muller urged the purchase of a complete set of bombing devices, and the assignment of one or more officers to specialize in bombing; he also felt that an airplane should be designed especially for bombing. Captain Cowan recommended buying five sights and racks for $500 apiece and stated that the experiments proved beyond a doubt that it was entirely practicable to drop bombs with sufficient accuracy to obtain satisfactory results. General Scriven did not agree with these more farsighted air officers and continued to hold that the airplane's chief use was for reconnaissance.[81] As a result, no bomb-sighting devices were purchased, and the Signal Corps had not so much as a description of the Scott sight when the United States went to war three years later.

In September, shortly after the bomb tests, General Scriven and Lt. Col. J. E. Hoffer of the Ordnance Department inspected a non-recoil 6-pounder Davis airplane gun at the New London Ship and Engine Company in Groton, Connecticut. The gun was a smooth bore, vanadium steel forged weapon, 10 feet long, and weighing 155.35

pounds. It was a double-barrelled gun, with a common powder chamber in the center, and was fired by electricity. When the gun was fired, the projectile was propelled toward the target while the load in the second barrel was thrown to the rear. The latter consisted of a mass of finely divided matter—metallic filings or small lead shot, which scattered at once and did not endanger either personnel or materiel.

The weight of the Davis gun was considered too great for airplanes although it had never been fired from one. It was thought that airplanes equipped with a lightweight non-recoil weapon of this same type would be singularly effective against attack from other airplanes and that this particular gun might be used on dirigibles. Further tests were recommended. On 25 November 1914, Brig. Gen. William Crozier of Ordnance suggested to the CSO that the Signal Corps consider mounting machine guns on airplanes for offensive use, and offered cooperation in any manner desired, including the manufacture of suitable mounts. Two guns were already in use in the army: an automatic 30-caliber 1909 machine rifle, which was a light air-cooled gun weighing only 29 pounds, and the more recently adopted Vickers, which was waterjacketed and weighed 36 pounds. One of each of these was shipped to the San Diego school, and it was proposed that an officer from the Benecia Arsenal should visit San Diego to design a satisfactory mount.[82]

In October of 1914, tests were made of life preservers, and it was found that the Robinson-Roders Company's "Universal" came as close to fulfilling the requirements as any of those submitted. However, it lacked one very essential feature—it would not keep the mouth and nose of an unconscious man out of the water unless he happened by chance to land in the water on his back. Further experiments were made with a later type of preserver, but the same objection existed; and it was not until 22 October 1915, that 10 Universal life preservers were ordered, 8 for the 1st Aero Company, 2d Squadron, and the other two for the school.[83]

Up to this time the exact cause of airplane accidents had been almost wholly a matter of conjecture, but it was believed that most accidents were due to the airplane's taking such unusual positions in the air that the pilot could do nothing to bring the machine back to an even keel. Inventors throughout the country had given considerable thought toward perfecting a stabilizer that would keep an airplane on an even keel and thus eliminate the cause of many accidents. One such device, the Macy automatic stabilizer, was sent to the San Diego Aviation School and tests were scheduled to begin in November 1914*. Two similar devices had been invented, the Sperry automatic pilot, which had earlier been tested by the Signal Corps, and the Converse automatic pilot, which, because of a shortage of planes and pilots, had not been tested.[84]

The year 1914 had been a difficult one for the aviation school. Many problems had arisen to obstruct its progress. The most serious of these were the small number of planes available for instruction, the selection of the most desirable kind of airplanes, and dissension in the school among the advocates of the various types of machines. Because of this last situation, on 20 August, General Order No. 12† of the SCAS, San Diego prohibited officers, enlisted men, and civilian employees of the school from discussing in the presence of anyone not connected with the school the relative merits of airplanes and engines of different manufacturers. It was the particular duty of each officer to see that none of the officers, enlisted men, or civilians under his command, did or said anything which might in any way be interpreted as indicating a prejudice against any airplane or engine of the school equipment. The other problems also were successfully solved; and the new year brought a systematic course of instruction, more airplanes for instruction than ever before, and sufficient additional civilian personnel to provide continuous instruction for the military students, both officers and enlisted men.[85]

---

*See below, p. 138.
†This order was rescinded by G.O. No. 17 SCAS, 12 April 1915.

CHAPTER VII

Aviation in 1915 and 1916

THE AVIATION SECTION IN 1915

ARMY APPROPRIATIONS for fiscal year 1916 were being estimated just as war broke out in Europe. An army request for $1,006,300 for the Aviation Section of the Signal Corps was submitted to Secretary of War Garrison. In addition to lighter-than-air equipment, the sum would provide for two complete squadrons of 16 planes with 6 other planes for insular service. The Secretary of War reduced the airplane estimates by $100,000 and removed the lighter-than-air figures entirely, sending an estimate of $400,000 to Congress. The hearings which began before the House Committee on Military Affairs on 8 December 1914 were the first ones held after the outbreak of war, and General Scriven who did not believe in airships, took this opportunity to urge that more money be appropriated for airplanes. He pointed out that the last prewar budgets of the great European forces for aeronautics put all of them ahead of the United States. Germany had appropriated $45,000,000; Russia, $22,500,000; France, $12,800,000; Austria, $3,000,000; Great Britain, $1,080,000; Italy, $800,000; and the United States, $250,000. Congress apparently was not impressed; for on 4 March 1915 it appropriated for aeronautics only $300,000,[1] of which not more than $500 was to be used for the cost of special technical instruction of officers in the Aviation Section.

The appropriation bill also authorized and directed the Secretary of War to appoint a commission of not more than three Army officers to report upon the advisability of the Government's acquiring land near the Bay of San Diego, and elsewhere on the Pacific, Atlantic, and Gulf coasts for an aviation school and training grounds for

the Signal Corps; the commission was also to ascertain and report what would be the probable cost of acquiring such land. The sum of $1,000 was appropriated to defray their expenses. But the orders which Lt. Col. Samuel Reber and Capt. Richard C. Marshall, QMC, received on or about 1 July sent them only to San Diego, San Francisco, Seattle, and Portland, all on the Pacific Coast, to investigate sites. On 29 December they recommended Coronado Heights near San Diego,[2] but no land was purchased.

When the Chief Signal Officer had appeared before the House Committee on Military Affairs he described an adequate air force as consisting of 50 airplanes, divided among 4 squadrons with 8 planes apiece and approximately 50 per cent reserve for replacement. Besides the airplanes, 18 automobiles and tractors for the transport of spare parts, fuel, and men were required for each squadron. A complete and theoretically perfect personnel requirement for 1 squadron would consist of 8 pilots, 8 observers, 4 administrative officers, and 90 enlisted men. For 4 squadrons this added up to 80 officers and 360 men. The cost of materiel was estimated roughly at $250,000 per squadron.[3] At this time the whole Aviation Section consisted of only 29 officers and 155 enlisted men, with fewer than 20 planes.

Almost a year later General Scriven in his annual report (dated 10 September 1915) proposed that an airplane squadron should be composed of three companies, with a total of 12 planes. Two companies should have 8 reconnaissance planes, 4 to a company, and the third should be made up of 2 pursuit planes and 2 combat machines. He advocated that provision be made for 18 squadrons: one each at Corregidor, Hawaii, and the Canal Zone, one for each of the three coast artillery districts and the seven tactical divisions, and five for the field artillery. The total strength for this organization would be 368 officers and 2,360 enlisted men, and the cost of equipment would be $4,284,000. This was to be a peace-time organization; a much greater number of officers would be required in time of war. Realizing the need for trained pilots and observers, General Scriven suggested the creation of an Aviation Reserve Corps of officers from which the army could draw if the United States entered the war. However, these ideas were not put into effect before April 1917.[4]

During this period, that is, the first year of the war in Europe, none of the American military observers attached to the various European armies had enough experience in aviation to make their reports of value; actually, almost no reports were made covering operations, organization, or equipment of the flying corps abroad. The Aviation Section had to depend almost entirely on current periodicals and other literature for information, and these sources contained practically no facts of any technical value. Therefore, there was a need for officers of the Aviation Section to be detailed with the Allied and German armies in Europe.[5] Colonel Reber made several requests for an air war observer, but apparently nothing was done about the matter. An observer would have had much to report during the summer and fall of 1915, including the first verified incident of an airplane's destroying an airship, which occurred on 7 June, when flight Sub-Lieutenant R. A. J. Warneford, a Canadian in the Royal Navy flying a Morane airplane, shot down a German airship, the LZ 37 near Bruges.[6]

In the European war, aircraft were being employed for strategical and tactical reconnaissance and the prevention of reconnaissance by the enemy's aircraft; direction and control of fire in conjunction with the field artillery; destruction of enemy personnel and materiel by explosive and incendiary missiles and other means; and the rapid transportation of high-ranking officers.[7] As a result three separate types of airplanes had evolved—reconnaissance, pursuit, and combat. The function of the reconnaissance machine, probably the most important plane, was to gain information regarding the enemy; it also directed fire for field artillery batteries. The plane, which carried a pilot and an observer and sometimes a radio, was usually a tractor with a 125- to 200-horsepower engine, carrying fuel for a flight of 6 or 7 hours, with a maximum speed of 90 miles an hour and rate of climb of 5,000 feet in 10 minutes. The combat machine was larger and usually of the pusher type, with as much as 500 horsepower, and was equipped with two or three light automatic machine guns and perhaps a heavier rapid-fire gun with the necessary personnel to operate them. The duty of this plane was to convoy and protect reconnaissance machines, as well as drive away enemy planes. Although it could carry heavy loads, it had neither speed, maneuverability, nor climbing-power. Both this plane and the reconnaissance model could carry bombs. Pursuit machines were usually very small, fast tractors, which were highly maneuverable and strong climbers. They carried only one man, who had to be a skillful pilot. When enemy planes were reported, it was his duty to attempt to climb above them and dive down, firing an automatic machine gun in an effort to prevent reconnaissance and to rid the air of enemy planes.

The Aviation Section had what it considered to be a satisfactory type of reconnaissance plane, and it was experimenting with machines of the other two types, but there were none on hand when the United States entered the war in 1917. Perhaps, as General William Mitchell said, it was because those in charge were unable to determine what kind of planes to buy.

The fact is that although the war in Europe was emphasizing the importance of aeronautics, aviation development was still lagging in the United States. Government support for aeronautics was lacking and public interest had not yet been aroused. There were few aircraft engines available in the United States, and because of the war foreign-made engines could not be purchased. Both the Army and the Navy staff officers realized that something must be done to increase the supply of machines and particularly to train more flyers. In 1915 Orville Wright, who had joined the newly-formed U.S. Naval Consulting Board for the development of inventions, advised the purchase of 13 new water planes for the Navy and 700 planes for the Army; in addition, he advocated training three flyers for each machine.

It is interesting to note in the light of later developments that at this time the Navy Board of Aeronautics felt that steps should be taken toward cooperation between the Navy and Army air services as had been done in Great Britain. Commodore T. D. Parker stated these sentiments this way:

> These [steps] cannot be taken by either body acting alone; but it will clearly be a defect if, in a naval war, the army aviators are not available as a naval reserve, and vice versa. The lack of a joint flying school, or its equivalent, seems to be the weakness of our dual organization. . . . We must look forward to the time when the air fleet may leave the army or the navy for a sphere of its own.[8]

The Aviation Section was hampered in obtaining and keeping personnel by those provisions of the Act of 18 July 1914, which specified that only unmarried lieutenants of the line under 30 years of age would be eligible for service with the Section. Only 34.4 per cent of the lieutenants of the line of the army were eligible for detail. Approximately one-fifth of the applicants for flying duty failed to pass the physical examination, leaving only 27 per cent of the total number of lieutenants of the line who could qualify. The requirement that an officer be unmarried was considered to be pretty much useless because the service was purely voluntary and no married officer would apply for duty unless he had carefully considered the extra hazard, which was only partially compensated for by increased pay. The age limit of 30 years was not only unnecessary, it was a detriment to the aviation service; the effect of the law was to fill the Aviation Section with young and inexperienced officers, the majority of whom were second lieutenants. Under this system it was difficult to find an officer with the age and experience needed to command an aviation organization. Of the 29 line officers on duty with the Aviation Section on 16 August 1915, only five were first lieutenants. In order that important command or administrative positions might be filled, it was desirable to remove both the age and rank limitations.

Still another troublesome part of the Act of 18 July was a proviso which required that an officer on aviation duty return to the line as soon as he was promoted to the grade of captain. For example, there was the case of B. D. Foulois, a captain in the Aviation Section and a lieutenant in the Infantry, who was in command of the 1st Aero Squadron. He was one of the few officers of age and experience in the Aviation Section.

He was 36 years old, had served in the Army for 17 years, had been on aviation duty longer than any other officer in the Army, and was one of the best practical fliers. He possessed the necessary age, experience, professional qualifications, and skill for the position which he held. But with this law in effect, he would be lost to aviation as he would soon be promoted to captain in the Infantry. It seemed foolish to sever his connection with aeronautics merely because he was promoted, particularly when an aero squadron was a field officer's command.[9]

THE NATIONAL ADVISORY COMMITTEE FOR AERONAUTICS (NACA)

The need for an advisory committee for aeronautics was well known, but Congress did not see fit to provide for one until 3 March 1915. The Naval Appropriation Act, approved that day, established a National Advisory Committee for Aeronautics, to be composed of not more than 12 members appointed by the President—two from the Aviation Section of the War Department; two from the office in charge of aeronautics in the Navy; a representative each from the Smithsonian Institution, the U.S. Weather Bureau, and the Bureau of Standards, together with not more than five additional persons who were acquainted with the needs of aeronautical science, either civil or military, or skilled in aeronautical engineering or its allied sciences. The Committee initially was composed of: General Scriven and Lieutenant Colonel Reber, representing the Army; Capt. Mark L. Bristol and Naval Constructor Holden C. Richardson for the Navy; Dr. Charles D. Walcott, Secretary of the Smithsonian; Charles L. Marvin, Chief of the Weather Bureau; and Dr. S. W. Stratton, Chief of the Bureau of Standards; Byron R. Newton, Assistant Secretary of the Treasury; and Professors W. F. Durand, Stanford University, Michael I. Pupin, Columbia University, John F. Hayford, Northwestern University, and Joseph S. Ames, Johns Hopkins University, all of whom were acquainted with the needs of aeronautical engineering or its allied sciences. Dr. A. F. Zahm of the Smithsonian Institution was the Recorder of the Committee. These members were to serve without compensation.

It was the duty of the committee to supervise and direct the scientific study of the problems of flight, with a view to their practical solution, and to determine the problems which should be experimentally attacked, as well as to discuss their solution and application to practical questions. In the event that a laboratory should be placed under the direction of the committee, it was to direct and conduct research and experiments in aeronautics in the laboratory. Rules and regulations for the conduct of the work of the committee were to be formulated by the group and approved by the President. The sum of $5,000 a year for five years, or so much thereof as might be necessary, was to be appropriated out of any money in the U.S. Treasury not otherwise appropriated; the sum was to be immediately available for experimental work and investigations undertaken by the committee, clerical expenses and supplies, as well as necessary traveling expenses of members of the committee when attending meetings. An annual report was to be submitted to Congress through the President, with an itemized statement of expenditures.[10].

The general functions of the Committee were: 1) To furnish information or assistance in regard to scientific or technical matters relating to aeronautics to any department or agency of the government. This function might also be performed for any individual, firm, association, or corporation within the United States provided they defrayed the actual cost involved. 2) To institute research investigation and study of problems, which in the judgment of its members were necessary and timely for the advance of aeronautics. 3) To keep advised in the progress made in aeronautical research and experimental work in all parts of the world. 4) To bring to the attention of subcommittees in the organization as well as the army, navy, other branches of government, university laboratories, and aircraft manufacturers information gathered by the Committee. 5) To be at all times at the service of the President, Congress, and the executive departments of the government for consideration of any problems regarding international air navigation regulation and development of civil aerial transport as well as technical development policies of the military, naval, and postal air services.[11]

The two military services cooperated very well in aeronautical matters during the ensuing years; such teamwork made for unanimity in the formulation of programs, not only for scientific research in aerodynamics but also for experimental engineering development carried on by both services. When the Aviation Section in 1916 selected Langley Field, Virginia as an engineering development station and the proving ground for aircraft, the NACA was invited to locate its research laboratories there. Although the war necessitated a change in the Army's plans for Langley Field, the Committee's plans for the construction there of the foremost laboratory in the country for scientific research in aeronautics were carried out. The Langley Memorial Aeronautical Laboratory was named in honor of Dr. Samuel Pierpont Langley.[12]

THE AERO CLUB OF AMERICA AND THE NATIONAL GUARD IN 1915-1916

Since there were so few planes and pilots in the Army and Navy aviation units and since Congress had not seen fit to appropriate sufficient funds to rectify this condition, the Aero Club of America inaugurated a subscription campaign to raise funds with which to develop aviators, acquire a squadron of airplanes for the National Guard and the Naval Militia of each state, and obtain 100 planes to carry mail to inaccessible places. These flying mail carriers were to form a reserve of trained aviators for military service in case of need.[13] On 15 April 1915 the Aero Club announced a national airplane competition to assist the War and Navy departments in developing aviation corps for the National Guard and Naval Militia and to demonstrate to the Post Office Department the practicability of the airplane for general use. The competition had to be postponed, however, because of the war scare which followed the sinking of the *Lusitania* and because of the possibility of American intervention in Mexico. If the competition had taken place it is doubtful that it would have been a success because airplane manufacturers were sending practically their entire output to Europe, more and more men were going overseas to enter service in the aviation corps of foreign countries, and the civilian aviators who were left in the United States were making exhibition flights which were much more profitable than competing for prizes.

As a consequence of its program, the Aero Club was flooded with requests from various state National Guard organizations for information on how best to organize a corps to teach the rudiments of aeronautics. The Secretary of War referred the Aero Club to Organization Tables, USA 1914 and also sent copies of the Act of 18 July 1914 and General Order No. 75 of 4 December 1913, which gave the organization of a squadron. If the states should organize aero companies or squadrons which would meet the requirements necessary for them to be classed as Organized Militia under the Militia law of 1903 (and subsequent amendments), the War Department would be in a position to render positive aid in the same way that it did to other units of the Organized Militia. Until these units were created by the states, the War Department was unable to do more than furnish whatever information was at hand on the subject. Since the Signal Corps had not detached the 1st Aero Squadron from the Signal Corps Aviation School and therefore had gained little experience in the field, it did not wish to lay down any hard and fast rules for squadron organization at this time. However, in November 1915 a proposed circular for the information of National Guard units was drafted.[14]

Already various air reserve organizations had been formed for the purpose of training men in aeronautics. One of these was headed by Mr. Mortimer Delano, who now dubbed himself Acting Colonel-in-Chief of the First Aviation Corps, Provisional Federal Volunteers. Mr. Delano, who had offered the services of his unit in 1913, again wrote the Secretary of War in February 1915 offering this organization of "close to 12,000 members" as an unofficial federal reserve and asked that the Secretary appoint a brigadier general to act as its chief. Delano's request was not granted because no reserve organization had been authorized for the Aviation Section.[15]

During the year a number of state National Guard units were presented with airplanes by air-minded philanthropists, while others obtained planes by public subscription of funds. These units wished to send their members to the Signal Corps Aviation School to learn to fly, but Lieutenant Colonel Reber, commanding officer of the Aviation Section, stated that the facilities at the school were completely occupied in training the officers attached to the Aviation Section. However, he thought that the training of militia officers might be undertaken by the fall of 1915.[16]

On 7 September 1915 the Chief Signal Officer was notified by the Division of Militia Affairs that Section 16 of the Militia Law provided for the admission of National Guard pilot students at aviation schools. In the appropriation bill of 4 March 1915, Congress had allowed $20,000 for subsistence, mileage, and commutation of quarters to officers of the National Guard attending service and garrison schools. There were no such specific provisions for the expenses of enlisted men of the

Organized Militia, but it had been decided that the law would also cover enlisted men attending service schools under proper authority; however, pay for this service had to be taken care of by the state. When the Chief Signal Officer learned of these provisions, he agreed to make arrangements for two officers and two mechanics of the New York Militia to take the courses for JMA and Aviation Mechanician respectively, after 15 December 1915. It was not until a year later that the New York National Guard took advantage of this offer. On 16 December 1916, instead of sending two officers and two enlisted men, the Adjutant General of the New York Guard sent four enlisted men—1st Sgt. Paul R. Stockton, Sgt. E. A. Kruss, Pvt. Roland S. Knowlson, and Pvt. Thomas F. Ward—to San Diego. These men were the first National Guardsmen to attend the Signal Corps Aviation School at San Diego. The state paid for their travel and all authorized expenses while they were on duty at the school. They received commutation rations of $1.50 a day while traveling and $1.00 a day while at the school. They were also given 50 per cent additional pay while under instruction at the school and on duty requiring them to participate regularly and frequently in flights. After completion of the flying tests on 9 July 1917, Stockton was commissioned First Lieutenant, Signal Officers Reserve Corps (SORC) on 28 August 1917; Kruss obtained his discharge, became a civilian senior instructor at San Diego, and was eventually commissioned First Lieutenant, Signal Corps (Temp.) Regular Army on 25 March 1918; Knowlson was discharged and became a civilian instructor at Mineola and later at Call Field; Ward was commissioned in the SORC on 17 September 1917 and went overseas, where he toured the AEF with Lowell Thomas.[17]

The most important part of the aeronautical program was the training of fliers. Although some civilian flyers were extremely capable, the general opinion of the military was that without special training the average civilian pilot would not be good enough in time of war, because he had not flown at high altitudes nor had he done enough cross-country flying, and many had not qualified for Aero Club pilot certificates. The Chief of the Division of Military Affairs suggested that $76,-000, which would buy four airplanes and maintain them for one year, be added to the Signal

Corps estimates for 1917 to provide airplane equipment and maintenance for the instruction of the Militia. General Scriven agreed with the suggestion. He was also in favor of an auxiliary course at the aviation school for the training of Militia and Reserve officers.[18]

In 1915 a movement was inaugurated in Maine for a series of aerial stations along the eastern coast of the United States; the idea was endorsed by all leading authorities on national defense, including President Wilson and Secretaries Garrison (War) and Daniels (Navy). The plan was to divide the entire coast into sections, each of which would be patrolled in time of emergency by a powerful hydroairplane, equipped with radio and manned by a pilot and observer. With such a system in effective operation, a surprise attack on any point of the eastern coast would be practically impossible. The aerial coast patrol would be the eyes of the nation. It would be necessary to use private means for the establishment of this system. The Aero Club of America worked out plans for the coastal stations, and in 1917 the Chief Signal Officer appointed Lieutenant Colonel Squier and Capt. Virginius Clark of the Aviation Section to collaborate with the War College Division of the General Staff on the project, but nothing ever came of it.[19]

THE FIRST AERO COMPANY OF THE NATIONAL GUARD IN 1915-1916

In the summer of 1915 Raynal C. Bolling, a member of the New York National Guard, Philip A. Carroll, and Norman Cabot began to take flying lessons at Mineola, Long Island. Dr. John S. Phillips, brother-in-law of Bolling, Richmond Fearing, James E. Miller, and others joined them. They contracted with the Gallaudet brothers for the use of a Gallaudet-Gnome 50-horsepower airplane and a pilot, P. C. "Tex" Millman. When the "Business Men's Camp"* opened at Plattsburg, New York, in July, Bolling used the plane in conjunction with a mobile machine gun unit which he had formed.[20]

Upon returning to New York on 1 September 1915 (after the close of the camp) Bolling and Miller, with the support of General John F. O'Ryan, head of the New York National Guard, began work preliminary to organizing an aero company under the New York National Guard. In addition to Millman, Filip A. Bjorklund, O. M. "Rusty" Bounds, and Lieutenant A. B. Thaw (of the guard unit) were secured as pilot instructors for the group. Recruiting started and two Gallaudet-Gnome tractors were rented, one with an engine of 100 horsepower and the other of 50. Work was started with $12,500 from the Aero Club's fund, subsequently increased by the club and supplemented by other contributions. The Aero Club also financed the training of some National Guard student pilots at the Curtiss school at Newport News, Virginia, and the Thomas school at Ithaca, New York*

On 1 November 1915 the first aero company of the National Guard was organized under command of Captain Bolling and was called the Aviation Detachment, First Battalion, S.C., N.G., N.Y. Shortly thereafter it was designated the First Aero Company with a strength of 4 officers and 40 enlisted men. Good progress was made in training at Mineola through the winter months, but by April 1916 bad weather and frequent engine trouble were seriously interfering with the company's flying training. Five more airplanes were obtained —one being purchased from the original club contribution—and the Gallaudet planes were released. The new planes consisted of a Curtiss JN4 and a Thomas, each having a Curtiss OX2 90-horsepower engine; a Sloane with a 125-horsepower Hall-Scott engine; a Sturtevant with a 140-horsepower Sturtevant engine; and an old Wright machine donated by the Wright Company, on whose land at Mineola the company was operating. The aggregate value of these five machines was approximately $40,000. In addition to actual flying instruction, personnel of the company were given a 2 hour-a-week course by Dr. C. E. Lucke and Professor Willhofft at Columbia School of Engineering. The course was designed to give them thorough preparation for the scientific study of aviation and airplane motors.

The First Aero Company was provisionally recognized on 22 June 1916 and mustered into federal service on 13 July 1916 in anticipation of duty on the Mexican border. At this time the company, still under the command of its founder, Captain Bolling, went into more intensive training

---

*A military training camp for businessmen organized under the direction of Maj. Gen. Leonard Wood and under his command during the summers of 1915 and 1916.

*The Thomas Airplane Company and school operated first at Bath and later moved to Ithaca, New York, where it was in operation from 1915 to 1917.

under regular army officers, Lieutenants Joseph E. Carberry and W. G. Kilner, who were assigned to the company by the Signal Corps. For five weeks after the organization went into camp, all expenses for equipment maintenance and operation were met by the Aero Club and by private contributions. By 1 August the amount which had been spent was $5,500, not including $2,250 which represented the final payment on one airplane. At this time the Army belatedly took over the expenses of the company. Eventually 25 members qualified as pilots. On 2 November 1916, the First Aero Company with one officer and 36 enlisted men was mustered out of federal service, without ever having reached the border.[21]

THE STATUS OF THE AMERICAN AVIATION INDUSTRY IN 1915

In June 1915, Grover C. Loening, aeronautical engineer with the Signal Corps, inspected and reported on the Wright, Curtiss, Burgess, and Thomas airplane plants. Although most of these companies had foreign orders to fill, the Curtiss plant far exceeded the others in output.* The Wright Company was capable of producing only one machine a week and Orville Wright stated that he had not tried to get any war orders because he did not have an engine powerful enough for European demands. There was considerable activity at the Burgess works at Marblehead, but their work for European countries was being conducted in secrecy and little information was obtainable. The Thomas Company also had foreign orders. Among the several new engines examined by Loening were the experimental 16-cylinder, 150-horsepower Burgess-White; the 85-horsepower Aeromarine; the 90- and 110-horsepower rotating Gyro; the 12-cylinder, 150-horsepower Rausenberger; the 90 Gyro Mayo tractor; the 110 Gyro Huntington tractor; the 100 Gnome-Gallaudet tractor; and the 110 Gyro Heinrich tractor. After turning in his report, Loening resigned from the Signal Corps on 15 July 1915 to join the new Sturtevant Aeroplane Company at Jamaica Plain, Massachusetts.[22]

In August, after Loening's departure, George B.

Fuller, aeronautical-mechanical engineer employed by the Signal Corps at San Diego, was sent to San Francisco to investigate the Hall-Scott engines to determine their suitability for aeronautical use. He reported that the engine developed 125 horsepower at 1,250 revolutions per minute, but he recommended that other engines be investigated before adopting this one as standard.[23]

The American aviation industry was rapidly expanding (although not so rapidly as events would soon demand). The Thomas Aeromotor Company, a new company located at Ithaca, planned to produce a 150- to 180-horsepower, V-type engine to be used in twin tractors or pushers. The Sloane Aircraft Company had built a new plane in which the British were interested. Their tests showed that the plane had a high degree of inherent stability, a mean speed of 84.7 miles per hour, and was a good weight carrier. The Christofferson Aircraft Manufacturing Company of San Francisco was in the process of perfecting a military tractor and was building its own engine.[24] Practically all the other companies were expanding their facilities and promoting experimentation. The influence of the war in Europe was being felt more and more by the aviation industry.

PYROTECHNICS TESTED

As the war in Europe progressed, American interest in pyrotechnics increased, and several tests of flares and bombs were made in 1915. On 26 April at Fort Bliss, Texas, the Army began a series of tests on a parachute flare invented by Cassius A. Barnes. This "torpedo torch," constructed for 10 minutes' illumination, weighed 30 pounds; a pound had to be added for each additional minute of illumination. It ignited upon contact with the ground. The flare carried a destructive charge, capable of regulation and designed to destroy the framework of the torch itself after the illuminating charge was exhausted. In the tests the torch was dropped from a 22-foot pole erected for this purpose. The board of Signal Corps officers which viewed the test considered the flare of great value for illuminating the position or works of an enemy at night, and for improving the accuracy and effectiveness of rifle, artillery, or machine-gun fire. It recommended that further tests be made at San Diego where an airplane could be used for dropping the flare.[25]

---

*An unsigned and unidentified tabulation of production capacities of American airplane plants dated 1 July 1915 stated that the Buffalo Curtiss plant's daily production average was 2½ airplanes; the Wright Company at Dayton was producing 1 plane a week; Burgess at Marblehead, 15 to 20 a month; Thomas at Bath, 10 a month; and Martin at Los Angeles, 10 a month.

On 15 June Capt. C. A. Seoane, S.C., observed a demonstration of an 18-ounce parachute smoke bomb at the Staten Island plant of the Consolidated Fireworks Company. Three samples were attached to 8-pound sky rockets; the rockets ascended to 1,000 feet, at which heighth the bombs exploded. The parachutes opened and a considerable volume of amber smoke came forth, probably visible for a distance of five miles. The release of the smoke was regulated to last 40 to 50 seconds. As the parachute fell, the effect was that of a vertical streak. Shortly thereafter the company shipped to the San Diego school 11 samples of aviator's colored smoke bombs, some searchlight bombs for night use, and an aerial machine detector.* On 5 August the school tested two daylight black and yellow bombs but with unsatisfactory results. The other sample bombs were all night bombs and could not be tested until the squadron was able to undertake night flying.[26]

AIRPLANES ACCEPTED AND TESTED IN 1915

During the calendar year 1915, 18 planes were delivered to the Aviation Section and accepted; only one plane, a Curtiss trainer, was rejected. On 13 January the first of two Martin TT tractors, S.C. No. 37, was accepted. Two days later on 15 January, Lt. B. Q. Jones established a new official American duration record of 8 hours and 53 minutes in this plane. S.C. No. 37 was the first Army plane in which loops were performed intentionally. Jones had previously made stalled loops in S.C. No. 30, but since acrobatics were prohibited at the school in March 1916, he confined his looping experiments in the new plane to an area out of sight of the field.[27] The plane was later shipped to Brownsville to replace the Martin S.C. No. 31 which had been damaged there. There is no record of the final disposition of S.C. No. 37. The other Martin tractor, Signal Corps No. 38, was accepted on 27 January 1915. After several accidents it was completely demolished on 27 September 1916.[28]

On 31 March the Burgess tractor trainer, S.C. No. 40, was accepted. The order for this plane had been approved on 28 January after Captain Cowan had reported the rejection of the Curtiss trainer on 5 January because of inferior workmanship. The Burgess was a two place tandem

biplane with a Curtiss 6-cylinder O engine. Although it had been designed by Loening and Milling, it was never satisfactory. The 60-horsepower engine had ample power, the climb and range were good, and it was stable directionally, but engine trouble began as soon as the plane was unpacked.[29] Further, Milling reported that the machine had poor lateral control, the rudder was too sensitive, and it was tail-heavy with power on and nosed into a dive with power off. In spite of these deficiencies Milling still suggested that it be used as a trainer. However, every officer who flew it stated that it was unsafe, and it was finally condemned and sold on 18 September 1916.[30]

The first of eight Curtiss JN2's, Signal Corps No. 41, ordered for field service for the 1st Aero Squadron, was accepted on 5 May 1915 and the remaining seven planes, S.C. Nos. 42 through 48, were delivered on 21 June.[31] The JN2s were distinguished by low rakish lines, an effect produced by staggered wings. The fuselage was long and unusually deep and narrow. The machines were equipped with instrument boards and the observer's seat was a wicker chair.[32] At the time of their construction these planes, modifications of the British Sopwith, represented the latest in aeronautical developments. They were originally scheduled to be delivered at San Diego by 8 April; after deduction for delay, the bill for the eight machines amounted to $63,284.[33] Lieutenant Carberry flew one of these planes at the Curtiss plant on 4 June and doubted that it would meet the required rate of climb; nevertheless, he recommended immediate shipment and acceptance. The Chief Signal Officer remarked that up to 6 October the machines had never been formally accepted nor had the account been paid. In the meantime, the 8 planes, 8 sets of spares, and 12 engines had been moved to Fort Sill with the 1st Aero Squadron on 26 July 1915. After accidents, investigations, and all sorts of difficulties, they were remodeled by Curtiss into JN3's. S.C. No. 46 was wrecked at Brownsville in 1915, planes Nos. 41 through 44 and No. 48 were destroyed in Mexico in 1916, No. 45 was condemned in Mexico in 1916, and No. 47 was wrecked at Fort Sill in 1916.[34]

Two Martin planes, Signal Corps Nos. 50 and 51 were also delivered on 21 June but were not accepted until 1 July, and there is no record

---

*An illuminating parachute bomb which was propelled 600 feet from a mortar shell and opened 100 feet above the ground.

of the disposition of either.[35] On 3 September two Curtiss JN3's, S.C. Nos. 52 and 53, arrived at Fort Sill, Oklahoma. No. 52 was abandoned in Mexico on 14 April 1916 and No. 53 was delivered at Columbus, New Mexico, to be condemned as unserviceable on 24 April 1916.[36]

Two more Martin TT tractors, SC. Nos. 54 and 55 were ordered on 16 August to be delivered without engines to San Diego on 30 September. The planes were built for the 70 Renault engine, five of which were on hand at the aviation school. The specifications for the planes required a 3,000-foot climb in 10 minutes allowing 325 pounds for personnel and 200 pounds for fuel; or 3,000 feet in 8 minutes allowing 350 pounds total for personnel and fuel. The minimum speed required was not over 47 miles per hour with a 525-pound load and the maximum not under 70 miles per hour. Although there is no record of the delivery or acceptance dates of either of these machines, it is known that No. 54 was condemned on 15 October 1917, while No. 55 was awaiting condemnation on 21 February 1918.[37]

The last plane delivered in 1915 was a Curtiss F boat, S.C. No. 49. The order for this plane had been canceled on 5 October but the cancellation apparently was rescinded, for on 18 November the Curtiss Company was ordered to ship the flying boat to San Diego. It was worn out and awaiting condemnation on 30 December 1916.*[38]

On 21 December 1915 the Aviation Section had 23 airplanes, 17 spare engines, 2 passenger-carrying automobiles, 12 auto trucks and 1 auto ambulance; it also had 44 officers and 224 enlisted men.[39]

THE SAN DIEGO SCHOOL

Because the military had had insufficient experience prior to 1915, they had not formulated operating regulations for the San Diego school; all programs for instruction and training of officers and enlisted men, as well as rules and regulations for repair of airplanes and engines, had

been worked out as the various problems arose. But on 2 January 1915 regulations governing the administration of the school were published in General Order No. 1. The order covered administration and dealt with boards, councils, courts-martial, leaves of absence, physical exercise, and other miscellaneous matters.[40]

By 20 January there were 11 aviation students enrolled at San Diego; there were also 18 qualified Junior Military Aviators assigned there.[41] Housing for these personnel was inadequate, as were the physical properties of the school, but some improvement was made in February by the completion of two additional hangars, the installation of a 10-kilowatt gasoline-electric generator,* and the arrival of lathes for the machine shop.[42]

After the additional facilities had been completed, technical instruction, which had been placed under the direction of Capt. T. F. Dodd in November of 1914, but had been limited to instruction on engine overhaul and adjustment, was expanded. Now, with power for the machine shop and new hangar space to be utilized, the instruction could be outlined and an organized class system could be scheduled.

The first students in the technical course were MSE Idzorek, Sergeants first class Literland and Boland, and Sergeants Bruhl, Costenborder, and Robertson. The school was tentatively designated as the Technical Instruction School in order to distinguish it from the flying school. The Aviation Section's intent was to build up a school in which a systematic course of instruction in the care, repair, and operation of aeronautical engines and the care and repair of airplanes could be given to all officers and to selected enlisted men. Before making definite recommendations in regard to establishing the status of the school, the course of technical instruction was to be built up gradually so as to discover the best methods of instruction, what apparatus was needed, the length of time required to complete the course, and exactly what the course should consist of. After the gasoline-electric set for power and light had arrived, the machine shop started operations on 23 February. Machine shop and metal work were done by

*Various sources show that a total of 59 airplanes had been delivered to the Aviation Section by the end of 1915. In order to arrive at this total, 4 Martin S seaplanes—Nos. 56 through 59—, which arrived in the Philippines in 1916 will have to be considered as delivered in 1915. At least 2 of them had been received but they were not accepted in time to be sent to the Philippines with the 1st Company, 2d Aero Squadron. These 4 planes were not counted in the total of 18 planes delivered in 1915.

*This generator was inadequate for the demands of the machine shop by the spring of 1917 and a 75-horsepower semi-diesel Fairbanks Morse generator was installed. Within a few months after the outbreak of the war this machine, too, had become inadequate.

civilian mechanics Newton and Semeniouk, assisted by enlisted men. George Hallett lectured on engines, and during February the following officers were assigned to attend these lectures: Second Lieutenants Vautsmeier, Rader, MacDill, Gantz, Gorrell, Holliday, Christie, and Sutton. In April Lieutenants Palmer and Harms were added to the list, and 28 enlisted men were detailed to the school or were in attendance during the month. The course continued at least through April; work in the engine and machine shop sections included trouble-shooting the Curtiss OX, repairing a leaky Renault oil pump, installing a band saw, making a new connecting rod and crankshaft bearings, performing lathe operations, and making parts for the machine shop truck.[43]

During the fiscal year 1 July 1914 to 1 July 1915, 10 special type truck bodies were designed and built in the shops at San Diego. One of the trucks was a completely equipped portable machine shop with electric power for driving tools. Others were fitted with special bodies for carrying airplane spare parts, tools, crews, equipment, reserve gasoline, and oil. During the same period 69 engines were overhauled, several being almost completely rebuilt. A stand for testing and balancing airplane propellers was designed and built as was a machine for testing radiators under air pressure. A portable field tent hangar was designed and a number were built by a local firm.[44]

A number of remodeling projects were undertaken at the school. In the fall of 1914 Loening had remodeled the Burgess tractor, S.C. No. 24, which like the other Burgess tractors was underpowered for the load it was expected to carry, but Captain Cowan reported that, although the changes made in the machine had materially increased its efficiency, it was still below the standard required for service machines and could be used only as a trainer for advanced students.[45] Loening then remodeled the three other Burgess tractors, Nos. 26, 27, and 28,* intending that they be used as advanced trainers: ailerons were substituted for the wing warping and the Curtiss control replaced the Wright system, while a new landing gear was substituted for the double wheel and skid combination. The wing area was cut

down and the tail redesigned. The high speed was raised from 58 to 72 miles per hour, the slow speed reduced from 42 to 38 miles per hour, the climb was increased from 1,800 to 3,200 feet in 10 minutes, the empty weight was cut by 200 pounds, and the disposable load increased by 400 pounds.[46] The rebuilding of these machines was not entirely satisfactory, although both officers and men obtained a great deal of valuable experience in performing the work. The machines developed qualities which made them undesirable for trainers—only the most skillful pilots could handle them, and even the experts did so reluctantly. This experience also served to establish the fact that attempts to convert unsatisfactory service machines into trainers were almost invariably failures.[47]

From 22 to 26 January 1915 Col. D. C. Shanks, Inspector General, had made the annual inspection of the 1st Aero Squadron and the SCAS at San Diego. He reported that the personnel consisted of 28 officers and 170 men. His first criticism was that the organization lacked a permanent site, and he advised that new barracks be provided on North Island—the old ones were practically uninhabitable during the rainy season—and that a crash boat, a crash car, and an auto ambulance be purchased.* He recommended that the Aviation Section send observers to Europe to obtain firsthand knowledge of military aeronautics. Colonel Shanks stated that the Act of 18 July 1914 had one inherent defect, in that it made no provision for a detailed officer to continue on duty after he had reached the grade of captain. He cited Captain Foulois' case and said that the provision of the act which required that an officer leave the air service when he became a captain took away all incentive for him to become either the best aviator or the best mechanic in the country. He complimented the school, noting that efficiency in aviation had increased, the old pusher machines had been almost entirely eliminated, and new records had been established, the most recent being a new official 2-man American altitude record of 11,690 feet made in a flight lasting 1 hour and 13 minutes by 1st Lt. J. E. Carberry and 2d Lt. Arthur R. Christie in S.C. No. 35, at San Diego on 5 January. Colonel Shanks noted

---

*The other Burgess tractor of this type, No. 25, after having been wrecked on 23 December 1914, and again on 13 January 1915, was dropped on 20 January.

*The school did receive an auto ambulance, but no funds were available for either additional barracks or for a crash boat.

that the rivalry between the Curtiss and Wright camps had been wiped out, for the Wright machines had become defunct and Curtiss machines were considered the best for service conditions.[48]

In February tests were made with the Macy automatic pilot, a gravity-controlled unit affected by the tilting of the plane, which operated the ailerons and elevator to bring the craft to normal position. The device had been sent to San Diego for testing in November 1914 and a board composed of Lieutenants Milling and Chapman and Mr. Loening had been appointed to conduct the tests, but there is no record of any test being made at that time. On 26 March 1915 Captain Dodd and Lieutenants Milling and Jones were appointed to investigate and report on the stabilizer. The testing plane, S.C. No. 31 Martin, was usually flown by Raymond V. Morris, expert Curtiss test pilot, but at other times it was also piloted by Oscar Brindley, the school's civilian flying instructor, Captain Dodd, and Lieutenants Taliaferro, Milling, and Jones. After careful tests the officers reported that the device kept the airplane balanced, afforded automatically correct banks for turns when the pilot used the rudder only, and that the mechanism was of such simple, rugged construction as ordinarily to preclude its getting out of order. Brindley stated that the stabilizer would be of great assistance to the operator in cross-country flying since it added to the elements of safety, ease of control, and reduction of fatigue on long flights.[49] Although the principle of the stabilizer was sound, the pilots were not willing to turn the actual control of the airplane over to a mechanical device.[50] Further tests were made at the Signal Corps Aviation Station at Mineola in 1916.[51]

All new instruments and accessories for airplanes were tested and demonstrated by the personnel of the aviation school at San Diego, for this was the only aviation station where sufficient personnel and materiel were available for this purpose.[52] On 19 March Lieutenant Harms and Loening tried out the Turner aviaphone,* a device equipped with a transmitter and receiver for voice communication between the front and rear cockpits. With the plane on the ground and the engine running, the sound of the voices carried easily but

it was impossible to distinguish words or to understand the drift of the conversation. No better results were obtained in flight tests on 15 March. Other aviaphones were also tested but were unsuccessful. On 28 July Lieutenant Dargue, who had returned from the Philippines in February, reported on a chest telephone transmitter made by the Western Electric Company. The transmitter was tried on a tandem-seater land plane and in the side-by-side seat of the flying boat, but the vibration of the engine prevented intelligible conversation. As soon as the engine was shut off to start a glide, the instrument functioned satisfactorily. On one occasion during these tests, an old bicycle tire was cut in half and used as a speaking tube, with excellent results.[53]

Among other items tested at San Diego was a sample of airplane linen submitted by J. A. Ludlow. Various methods of doping were tried but the fabric did not seem to be exceptional. However, the school had no means of testing tensile strength and elongation. Another fabric called "Steril" was also tested and found unsatisfactory. Burd high compression piston rings were tested in a Curtiss OX engine, and in May a tachometer made by the Electric Tachometer Company was sent to the school to be tested, but there is no record of the results. On 4 August 1915, Dargue reported on the Hopkins Electric Tachometer installed in S.C. No. 51, Martin tractor. He concluded it was a reliable and satisfactory instrument for airplane use.[54]

While the 1915 tests were going on, the aviation school was also getting some publicity, for the Lyman H. Howe Attractions was making pictures of Army Aviation at San Diego for its series, "Our Army in 1915." Captain Cowan was instructed by the OCSO to make available such facilities as he could to this organization because the Secretary of War, L. M. Garrison, was particularly sympathetic to the project.[55]

Meanwhile, General Scriven, the Chief Signal Officer, made an inspection trip, starting at San Diego on 6 March 1915 and going from there to Fort Sam Houston and Texas City. He flew over San Diego Bay and harbor with civilian pilot Francis A. Wildman in a flying boat, interviewed officers of the school, and made a survey of the lands suitable for an aviation site. On 8 March he again visited the aviation school at North Island while instruction and flying were in full progress and

---

*This aviaphone had been developed to its then current efficiency in cooperation with a number of army aviation experts at Augusta, Georgia, in 1912.

made an inspection of buildings, machines, and the force on duty. While flying with Lieutenant Taliaferro in the Martin tractor No. 38, the General observed a parachute descent from 1,200 feet, which prompted him later to recommend the purchase of parachutes for the Aviation Section; however, nothing ever came of the recommendation. The Chief Signal Officer approved of the School's safety measures, which consisted of having an observer stationed in a tower with an automobile at the base for immediate use in case of an airplane accident during the hours of flight; and he stated that he was most gratified with Cowan's fine work in building up the school with the limited means provided the aviation service.[56]

In March civilian technical employees of the Aviation Section were reclassified by the Civil Service Commission. Grover C. Loening filled the position of Aeronautical Engineer, Oscar A. Brindley and Francis A. Wildman were classified as instructors in flying, and six men were named aviation mechanicians: Jack Bailey, Elmer J. Briggs, George E. A. Hallett, H. S. Molineau, Irving I. Newton, and I. G. Semeniouk. Hallett, Newton, and Semeniouk, who had been temporary employees, automatically became permanent when these grades were established.[57]

On 12 March 1915, 1st Lt. B. Q. Jones and Corporals Carl T. Hale and Robert H. Houser in the remodeled Burgess-Renault No. 28 fitted with extra fuel tanks set a new official world duration record for three men: seven hours and five minutes. For this feat and his solo American duration record of 8 hours and 53 minutes established on 15 January, Jones was awarded the fourth Mackay Trophy. The award was made almost a year after Jones' second record-setting flight, for in December 1915 the Chief Signal Officer decided that it was impossible to hold contests for the Mackay Trophy at a single station and recommended that a board be appointed to examine the record and performance of the air officers in order to choose the winner. It was this board which voted the trophy to Jones for the best record performance of the year 1915.[58]

A freak accident took place on 8 April 1915, when Captain Dodd was piloting the rebuilt Burgess-Renault No. 28. He was en route to San Francisco, accompanied by Sgt. Alvah E. Baxter, and flying slowly at about 2,300 feet to economize on fuel, when he noticed a light colored ring in the blur of the whirling propeller. The ring widened and the plane began to vibrate so violently that Dodd was afraid the tanks would be torn loose. He cut off the engine and immediately the propeller shaft snapped off in front of the crankcase, but he was able to make a normal landing in an oat field near Encinitas, 35 miles from North Island. After landing, the propeller was located and it was found that the entering edge of one blade had a piece knocked out and another long piece of wood had been broken from the trailing edge. It was believed that the rabbeting of the wood tip to fit closely the brass tip had weakened the blade where the long sliver had peeled off and that the freshly exposed wood produced the light-colored ring.

A similar accident happened on 26 June to 2d Lt. Edgar S. Gorrell in Martin S.C. No. 37 on a nonstop flight from San Diego to Long Beach. The propeller flew off, cutting away the tires of the front wheels and slightly denting both rims. Gorrell had cut the ignition switch the instant vibration started and attempted a stalled landing in an open ploughed space about 50 yards long in the center of an alfalfa field. The rims dug into the earth and the plane turned over on its back, smashing the landing gear and filling the radiator with sand. The immediate cause of the accident was not known. These two episodes marked the beginning of a long series of difficulties with propellers.[59]

In order to comply with Section 3 of the Act of 18 July 1914, certificates were prepared in March 1915 for Junior Military Aviators and Aviation Mechanicians.[60] It was not until 10 April that an examination was furnished for the rating of Junior Military Aviator. The instructions* issued by the Chief Signal Officer provided that the candidate was to demonstrate his flying knowledge by "operating a machine" in a triangular cross-country flight without landing, the minimum length of any side of the triangle to be 20 miles. He was to make a straight-away cross-country flight of at least 90 miles without landing and during this flight was to remain for half an hour at an altitude between 2,500 and 3,000 feet, to be registered by a recording barograph. Finally, he was to make such starting and landing flights as

---

*In the letter the CSO also recommended that a board be appointed to examine Lieutenants FitzGerald, Kilner, and Sutton, who passed their tests on 15 May 1915.

the board might require.[61] By July, the examination had been expanded, as General Scriven noted in a letter to the Division of Militia Affairs:[62]

Flying. Five figure 8's around pylons, keeping all parts of machine inside a circle whose radius is 300 feet.

Climb out of a square field 900 feet on a side and attain 500-feet altitude, keeping all parts of the machine inside of square during climb.

Climb 3,000 feet, kill motor, spiral down, changing direction of spiral, that is, from left to right, and land within 150 feet of previously designated mark.

Land with dead motor in a field 800 feet by 100 feet, assuming said field to be surrounded by a 10-foot obstacle.

From 500 feet altitude land within 100 feet of previously designated point with dead motor.

Cross-country triangular flight without landing, of approximately 60 miles, passing over the following points: starting from North Island, over Del Mar, La Mesa, Coronado Heights.

Straightaway cross-country flight of about 90 miles without landing from the vicinity of Santa Ana, California, to North Island, California.

Other parts of the examination covered the making of fittings; assembly, balance and alignment of planes; theory and practice of gasoline engines; meteorology; and navigation. From time to time, as aviation developed, these requirements were changed.

Since the requirements for JMA rating were more difficult than those prescribed for civilian candidates for the Aero Club of America's Expert Certificate, Lieutenant Colonel Reber, OIC of the Aviation Section and member of the club's contest committee, recommended in June that qualification as JMA be accepted as qualifying an applicant for the Club's expert certificate. There was no need for formal action on the part of the board of governors of the Club since it had decided in 1912 that army pilots rated as Military Aviator would receive the rating of Expert Aviator without further trial.[63]

During the month of June the House Appropriations Committee visited the school at North Island and each member was taken up by Francis "Doc" Wildman in the Curtiss F flying boat S.C. No. 34.[64] This visit gave the members of the committee an opportunity to see how the aviation appropriations were being spent. The school also had foreign visitors; the Spanish ambassador had been granted permission to send two Spanish officers—Capt. Emilio Herrera of the Engineer Corps and Lt. Don Juan Viniegra of the Aviation Corps— to look over the aviation establishment of the

Signal Corps.[65] In the meantime the Coronado Beach Company had given Capt. George Van Horn Moseley, CO First Regiment, Cavalry, San Diego, permission to occupy temporarily a part of North Island for target practice, providing this occupancy did not conflict with that of the Signal Corps or the Marines.[66]

While these events were taking place, tests were conducted to discover the visibility of different colored Very Pistol signals. The Very lights already had been tested in firing at the School of Fire for Field Artillery at Fort Sill, Oklahoma, in April and May, when control of fire by an aerial observer was simulated. The tests were repeated at San Diego because it had been found that communication was very slow and visibility of the Very lights was uncertain.[67] In the first San Diego tests Lieutenant Dargue reported that smoke from the cartridges was visible up to two miles under favorable light conditions and that white showed up better than either red or green. The Very Pistol, he stated, was one of the best means for visual signaling within the two-mile limit. On 7 July, another test, in which a code was used, was made in conjunction with the field artillery. Up to two miles and at 5,000 feet, 15 out of 17 white signals were seen and 13 recorded accurately by observers. The two not seen were considered out of range and were not counted in the results. The trial showed that the code should be comprised of upward shots only, fired when the plane was at right angles to the line of observation. Yellow smoke, tried on 14 July also under a code system, was found to show up even better than white. It was reliable up to three miles and 5,000 feet. Fire up or down was equally visible.[68]

In June Dargue, in addition to his other duties, was given responsibility for all aviation activity relating to the coastal defenses of San Diego. He was ordered to visit the defenses and ascertain the desires of the commanding officer in order that all possible cooperation might be given. A new seaplane hangar was built to house the Burgess-Dunne, S.C. No. 36, which was to be used for experimental work with the Coast Artillery. It was particularly difficult to carry on this type of work because only one flying boat was available.*[69]

---

*For that matter, any kind of experimental work was difficult during the fiscal year ending 30 June 1915 because of lack of machines and pilots.

The work required three land machines, at least two water machines, and the full time services of a minimum of two of the very best pilots. Pilots doing instruction work could not be counted on for experimental work for they had all they could take care of with their regular duties, and fliers who did do experimental work had to be carefully selected with reference to their ability to analyze the results they obtained as well as their ability to criticize and assist in making changes.[70]

During the more than two years the school had been in existence, a constant effort had been made to secure a satisfactory training plane. In an effort to meet this need Milling and Loening designed a plane with flying qualities approximating those of the B-type Wright machine. The first plane built to this design by Curtiss was rejected; the second, S.C. No. 40, built by the Burgess Company, was accepted, but was not safisfactory. This was the first attempt to design a complete machine at the school, and if nothing else was accomplished, at least it provided good training. An attempt also was made at the school to build an airplane which would have all of the performance qualities desired by the flyers. An old airplane was completely torn down and from it a new type was built. However, the plane as produced was a disappointment from the start. Although it had the flying qualities desired, the system of controls was inadequate and unsatisfactory. Several attempts were made to correct these defects but without success and the plane was finally destroyed.[71]

Marked progress was made toward perfecting the system of instruction in flying during the fiscal year 1915. Preliminary training was given by "Doc" Wildman in the Curtiss flying boat which, being heavier than the land machine, was less susceptible to puffs of wind and could be flown with greater safety at low as well as at high altitudes. Consequently the student, receiving his preliminary instruction under the very best conditions, was given confidence in the safety of the plane. After a few rides to accustom him to being aloft, the student was allowed to handle the machine in the air, first making straightaway flights and then right and left turns. Because the flying boat could land on the water, which had an unlimited amount of landing surface, it was possible to give a relatively large amount of instruction in landing and taking off; in a land

machine it was generally practicable to make only one landing in ten or fifteen minutes of flying, while in a water machine a half dozen landings could be made in the same length of time. The value of this practice was immediately recognized when the student was transferred to a land machine. Since the instruction was individual, the length of time required to graduate from the flying boat depended entirely upon the ability of the student; as a rule this period of instruction was finished in four or five hours. After being transferred to the land machine, the student continued his training in all phases of flying under the instruction of Oscar Brindley. As soon as the civilian instructor considered his student competent to fly alone, he handed him over to the Officer in Charge of Training, who determined whether or not the trainee would develop into a satisfactory pilot. If he got along well, he was allowed to fly alone until he was ready to try for his FAI pilot's license, a test which he was required to pass before continuing with his training. He was then ready for instruction in cross-country flying preparatory to his test for Junior Military Aviator rating. This test was sufficiently comprehensive to determine beyond question the pilot's ability to handle a machine in actual service. If the three instructors agreed that a student was not qualified to do military flying, there was very little doubt as to the correctness of their decision.[72]

The instruction of both officers and enlisted men in the care, repair, and maintenance of airplanes and aeronautical engines had gradually developed and improved until the students in 1915 knew more about these subjects after six month's training than they had formerly known after years of training. Under the old system, officers who were not trained for this work and who had to spend much of their time flying had been in charge of the machine shop. Attempts had been made to use the shop for instruction of officers and enlisted men; although the officers and men received good training from this procedure, the work of the machine shop as such, was hampered. Under the new system, instruction was separated from the machine shop. George Hallett, one of the most expert men in the country at locating engine trouble and making repairs in the field, taught the aeronautical engines course. His aim was to teach enlisted men to handle such tools as com-

Curtiss flying boat, San Diego, 1915

prised the equipment of the portable field machine shop so that they could take care of many minor repairs which had to be done in the field. No attempt to produce finished machinists was made because it would have required too much time; besides, if an engine was so badly damaged that it could not be repaired in the field, it would have to be sent back to a permanent base where there was a large machine shop. In the short time that the new system had been in effect the improvement in the shop was marked. On 6 July 1915, Capt. V. E. Clark, the first air officer to graduate in aeronautical engineering from MIT, reported at North Island and was assigned to engineering.[73]

On 12 July 1915 a board of officers of the SCAS, San Diego, adopted Aviation Mechanician examination requirements, dividing them into two parts: airframe maintenance and repair, and engine construction, maintenance, and repair. Examinations were practical, and theoretical questions were limited to those necessary to show that the candidate's practical work had a sound basis. The candidate had to make a grade of 75 in both phases. The first part of the examination required the student to be able to make fittings, ribs, spars, struts, skids, and wires; assemble, disassemble, and align an airplane, and prepare it for shipping; stretch cloth on wing frames and dope it; remove, repair, and replace tires. The second part required that the candidate be capable of cleaning an engine; grinding valves; adjusting clearances, time valves, and spark; cleaning magnetos and locating as well as repairing firing system trouble outside of the magneto; adjusting the carburetor; and locating and remedying other ordinary troubles. In addition, he had to pass a physical examination.[74]

On 1 July 1915 there were on duty at the Signal Corps Aviation School at San Diego, 30 officers, 12 civilians, and 185 enlisted men. Thirteen airplanes were reported on hand; six planes had been dropped since December 1914.[75] In this connection it is interesting to note that the approximate gas consumption at the San Diego school for the first six months of 1915 was indicated by a contract signed by the Signal Corps with the Union Oil Company of California on 30 December 1914 for 6,000 gallons of gasoline of a specific gravity of not less than 60° Baumé, the amount to be decreased or increased as might be required. Delivery was to be made on call to the SCAS, San Diego, in barrels and in such quantity and at such time as it might be needed. The price was 10.4 cents a gallon. The second bidder was Standard Oil of California, quoting a price of 11.4 cents a gallon.[76]

In June 1915, Captain Cowan had recommended that an officer who was competent to take charge of experiments in radio telegraphy as applied to airships and airplanes and who could give instruction be detailed to the San Diego school. For that duty 1st Lt. C. C. Culver reported to the school in September and took over all radio experimental work. He had previously done radio work in the Signal Corps and was probably the best qualified officer in the army for this assignment. The fact that he had also been a student of meteorology further enhanced his value to the school. The school recommended that he be given flying pay since he had to make flights and so was subject to the same risk as other flying officers, but he was not put on flying status until 9 December 1916, when he became an aviation student.*

The development of an airplane radio telegraph transmitter set, SCR-51,† intended for communication over several hundred miles, began in 1915 and the first successful test was made in the spring of 1916. As a preliminary to the tests, on 9 October 1915 a spring driven dictaphone was taken in the air and a record of speech was made in the noise of the engine and the blast of air. Lieutenant Dargue operated the dictaphone and Lieutenant Kilner was the pilot of the Curtiss tractor in which the experiment was conducted. The record made during this preliminary test revealed the difficulties which were involved in radio reception at this time.[77]

In September Secretary of War Garrison agreed with Secretary of State Lansing that a request of the Portuguese Minister for the instruction of officers of the Portuguese Army at the San Diego school be approved. It was understood that their government would assume financial responsibility for breakage and damage, and on 11 December 1915 four Portuguese Army officers were attached to the Signal Corps Aviation School at San Diego for instruction in aviation. Three of the

---

*Culver subsequently qualified as a pilot and received his JMA rating in July 1917. He later became a Colonel in the Air Corps.

†By 6 April 1917 the design of this set was practically completed and a limited number of the sets were in production.

officers finished the course in March 1916; the fourth "washed out."[78]

About 25 September 1915 the Deperdussin control was installed in one airplane at the North Island school and the personnel were familiarized with its use. This control, which resembled that of Curtiss, consisted of a wheel on a pillar which was rotated for lateral control and moved back and forth for elevation, while a rudder bar for the feet served to coordinate in turns. The "Dep" control was in general use in Europe by this time, and it was accepted by the United States shortly thereafter.[79]

On 17 September Lieutenant Taliaferro, one of the army's best flyers, set a new unofficial one-man American endurance record of 9 hours and 48 minutes. Three weeks later on 11 October Taliaferro was flying Curtiss J, S.C. No. 30, when at about 2,000 feet he attempted a loop; he reached an upside down position but was unable to complete the loop and slid off to strike the water of San Diego Bay with terrific force. His body was found 24 hours later pinned beneath the machine in fifty feet of water. He was the 16th man* to be killed in the U.S. Army aviation service. The cause of the accident was not known, but the necessity for instruction in acrobatics was becoming apparent, and with the entry of the United States into World War I acrobactics became a part of the curriculum in the aviation training schools.[80]

On 18 October 1915, in San Francisco the court-martial of Lt. Col. Lewis E. Goodier, Judge Advocate of the Western Department and father of Army aviator Capt. Lewis E. Goodier, Jr., was opened. Because most of the key figures in the trial were members of the Army's aviation service and because the trial revealed certain unhealthy conditions in the service, the proceedings are of more than ordinary interests to students of military aviation. Briefly, the background of the court-martial was this: in the spring of 1915 Lieutenant Colonel Goodier had assisted Capt. Dodd and Lt. Taliaferro to prefer charges against Capt. Cowan, head of the San Diego Aviation School, and had himself filed further charges against Cowan as well as against Capt. W. L. Patterson to the effect that both men were receiving flying pay when neither was able to fly a plane. After an

investigation the Judge Advocate General decided that the charges could not be sustained, and Colonel Goodier then was court-martialed for his part in filing them.[81] He was found guilty of conduct prejudicial to good order and military discipline, and on 17 April 1916 was reprimanded by President Wilson.[82]

Evidence presented at the trial showed that at the time the charges were preferred against Cowan and Patterson both men were drawing flying pay, but that neither was a qualified pilot, a fact known to Colonel Reber, officer in charge of the Aviation Section. Cowan's record showed 11 "straightaways" or short runs just above the ground for a total of 24 minutes "flying" time, while Patterson, who was rated as a Junior Military Aviator, had received only 54 minutes of training and was not capable of flying solo. Evidence further revealed that Cowan and Reber had wanted to get rid of Captain Goodier, and had succeeded in having him relieved from the aviation service while he was in Letterman Hospital recovering from injuries received in a plane accident.[83]

But evidence also showed that between the date when the charges were preferred and the opening of the Goodier court-martial, Brig. Gen. E. H. Crowder, the Judge Advocate General, pursuant to an investigation of the charges, had ruled that Cowan's failure to become proficient in flying was due to the pressure of his other duties and to lack of equipment, and that so long as he held himself in readiness to fly he was entitled to flying pay. The JAG also had ruled that, while Patterson's rating might have been erroneous in fact, it was not invalid in law, and he was allowed to retain his JMA rating.*[84] The rulings may have been legally sound, but they were unfortunate; for they left uncorrected some obviously bad conditions in the aviation service.

In the light of the JAG's rulings the evidence presented at Goodier's trial of the inadequacy and abuses of the Signal Corps' regulations covering flying and the JMA rating became largely a matter of academic interest. Although nothing seems to have been done to correct the abuses at the time, Reber† and Cowan were subsequently

---

*One other man had been killed in an Army aviation accident but he was a civilian—Al Welch, Wright pilot.

*Subsequently, both men learned to fly, although Cowan never received a pilot's certificate.
†It may have been because of this difficulty that Capt. George S. Gibbs was made acting chief of the Aeronautical Division, the Washington Office of the Aviation Section, on 17 March 1916.

removed from aviation duty. One bit of evidence cast the long shadow of a coming event when it revealed that a basic cause of the trouble was friction between the Signal Corps and the aviation service and that the young flying officers wanted an air organization separate from the Signal Corps.[85]

Meanwhile in 1915, Glenn Curtiss had offered the Curtiss Marine Trophy, valued at $5,000, and five annual prizes of $1,000 each or the equivalent thereof for annual competition by members of the Aero Club of America and affiliated clubs holding pilot certificates. The winner of the trophy the first year would be the person who on 31 October 1915 held the record for distance covered in a seaplane during 10 hours of any one day. The pilot was to be given the cash prize and his club would hold the trophy. If the trophy was won for three consecutive years by one of its members, the club became the owner. Oscar Brindley, civilian pilot instructor at San Diego, won the trophy in 1915 with a flight of 554 miles and Lieutenant Dargue received one of the $1,000 prizes by flying 192 miles in an unsuccessful attempt to win the trophy.[86]

In a letter dated 1 December 1915 the Coronado Beach Company advised the Commanding Officer of the Signal Corps Aviation School that the Company desired to regain possession of North Island before the United States Government became too firmly implanted, and indicated that it would like the island vacated as soon after 31 March 1916 as possible. In spite of this request, nothing definite was done by either the Government or the Coronado Beach Company for the next two years, at which time the Government finally obtained title to the island. In the meantime, the commanding officer of the school worked under the great handicap of never knowing at what moment he might be called upon to move the entire school off the island.[87]

THE 1ST AERO SQUADRON

The 1st Aero Squadron had been functioning as such for several months when Lieutenants Milling and Jones were ordered on 13 April 1915 from San Diego to Brownsville, Texas, for duty with the border patrol. They took with them one airplane, S.C. No. 31 Martin T with a Curtiss O 75-horsepower engine, the necessary accessories, and eight men. The detachment left on 14 April by rail and arrived in Brownsville on the 17th, the express cars with the plane and equipment being attached to the same train. Camp was established at the west end of the cavalry drill ground. The first reconnaissance flight was made by Jones on 20 April. In the afternoon of the same day the two lieutenants flew at 2,600 feet for 20 minutes to determine the position of Villa's trenches around Matamoras and to scout the surrounding country. Milling carried a map of Brownsville and vicinity on which he noted the variations of actual trenches from those indicated on the map.[88]

On the same day Lieutenant Jones was taxiing in from a short flight with Corporal Ruef when he ran into a ditch, damaging the plane's fuselage beyond repair. A request for a new fuselage or another plane was refused by Colonel Reber, but on 30 April The Adjutant General ordered the damaged machine freighted to San Diego and a replacement sent. On 1 May Captain Cowan expressed Signal Corps No. 37, another Martin T, to Brownsville and several flights were made in this machine.[89]

On 18 May Reber asked The Adjutant General to return the detachment of the 1st Aero Squadron to San Diego since the need for its presence at Brownsville had passed when the Field Artillery had been relieved. The detachment rejoined the squadron at North Island on 27 May after an absence of a month and thirteen days.[90]

Actually the one plane had been of very little value at Brownsville. General Funston, who was in charge of the border forces, had planned to use it for observing artillery fire and to locate the positions of Villa's guns, but no wireless was carried on the plane and the nature of the country was such that it precluded the use of the card system for signaling. However, this experience showed the necessity for planning some system whereby airplanes could work with the artillery. It had been hoped that enough fieldwork would be done at least to determine the spare parts necessary to keep a plane in commission, but this had been impossible because the plane was used so little. Villa had begun withdrawing his troops on the night of the 15th of April, completing the movement the following day, and since the detachment did not arrive until the 17th day of April, practically nothing was accomplished.[91]

Villa himself was a staunch advocate of air-power. He employed a number of American civilian flyers to work with his forces in Mexico, among whom were Farnum Fish, Eugene Heth, Howard M. Rinehart, Floyd Smith and Mickey McGuire.* Villa had at least one Christofferson Curtiss pusher and a Martin T in addition to a new Wright plane in his airport at Monterey; the air park was equipped with a railroad car airplane shop. Lester Barlow, the inventor of the Barlow bomb, who was with Villa as an engineer, was responsible for building up the air park and shop. Another Wright plane was sent to Villa from Dayton in April. Since it was impossible to deliver the plane to Villa at Matamoras, it was shipped to El Paso where it was picked up by his men. Later Rinehart made a hop in the new fuselage HS model Wright from Matamoras to Brownsville, and from there, apparently tired of the fighting, left for home after asking General Funston to do what he could about returning the Villa plane.†

Fish, who had followed Rinehart into Mexico, was the only foreign pilot who was wounded while in Villa's service. He was sent out to make observations of the Mexican government troops, but while flying over his own forces (which he had been instructed not to do), he was hit by heavy rifle fire. He banked his plane and turned back toward his own lines, came in on a long flat glide, and fainted as soon as he landed. Only one bullet had struck him but it had made two wounds; it went in the back side of the thigh and came out the fleshy part near the trunk, and then struck him on the shoulder. He was bleeding badly and the machine was spattered with blood. Fish was not dangerously wounded but he had very nearly lost control of the plane because of loss of blood. He quickly recovered but obviously he had had his fill of war, for he returned to his home in Los Angeles shortly thereafter.

The Carranza forces also had American planes and civilian pilots, but little information is available

about them.[92] It is known that Charles S. Niles, an employee of Moisant, sold several planes to Carranza and became chief of his air force. Lawrence W. Brown and the Salinas brothers also flew with the Carranzistas.

Meanwhile, as a result of instructions received in April, at San Diego, the two companies into which the 1st Aero Squadron had been organized were discontinued and the squadron was reorganized into 12 sections consisting of headquarters, supply, training, shop, and 8 airplane sections. The two-company organization had not been satisfactory for it placed too much responsibility for training and instruction in the hands of company commanders. Because of the irregularities in the rank of the various officers in the squadron, it was impossible to put the best men in command of the companies, and Captain Foulois, the squadron commander, practically had to take charge of company instruction. Under the new system, two officers were assigned to each plane, one as pilot and the other as assistant pilot. The pilot was responsible for the care, repair, and maintenance of his airplane, and the training and discipline of his crew. When an airplane was laid up for repairs, its officers were not allowed to fly any other machine except in an emergency. Each was required to repair his own machine and keep it in good shape. This regulation tended to promote efficiency in the section, as the officer knew he could fly only if he took good care of his own machine.[93]

On 26 July 1915 the 1st Aero Squadron, as reorganized by Foulois, consisting of 15 officers, 85 enlisted men, 8 JN2's, and camp equipment, left San Diego for Fort Sill, Oklahoma, to take part in fire control operations with the Field Artillery. Civilian Jacob Bailey, aviation mechanic, accompanied the group, which was composed of the following officer pilots: Capt. B. D. Foulois, CO; 1st Lts. T. D. Milling, J. C. Morrow, C. G. Chapman, J. E. Carberry, T. E. Bowen*, B. Q. Jones, R. H. Willis, R. B. Sutton, S. W. FitzGerald, Leslie MacDill, A. R. Christie, H. W. Harms, Ira A. Rader, and Harry Gantz.

The squadron arrived at Fort Sill on 29 July and remained there until 19 November. There were no quarters and most of the time until 13

---

*Smith and Rinehart later became test pilots of army aircraft in World War I. Fish applied for a civilian instructor's job at Mineola in February 1917 but failed to meet the requirements. William A. Lamkey, formerly an enlisted pilot in the aviation service, also flew for Villa. McGuire was killed in an exhibition flight at Agua Caliente while in Villa's employ. It is not known what became of Heth.

†John Hettich stated in Jones collection of papers that Villa had a Wright H.S. or "tin cow" plane and two Wright B's, one of which was destroyed on the ground in a windstorm in January. Hettich says the Wright left at Brownsville was returned to Villa.

*Lieutenant Bowen was on leave at this time but he reported to San Diego on 13 August and was immediately ordered to Fort Sill.

August was spent in making camp and building a messhall, storehouse, and garage, laying water pipe, and installing telephone lines from the post to the camp. On 14 August one section was ordered to Brownsville, Texas, together with batteries from Fort Sill. The following day a second section was sent. This left 10 officers and 68 enlisted men at Fort Sill after 20 August when Lieutenant Gantz went on 3 months' leave. Lieutenant Sutton was ill in the hospital and the remaining officers were Captain Foulois and Lieutenants Milling, Chapman, Willis, FitzGerald, MacDill, Rader, and Carberry.[94]

The first flights were made at Fort Sill on 10 August. From 15 August to 1 September frequent attempts were made to cooperate in air reconnaissance with the artillery troops, but constant engine trouble and alterations to planes prevented satisfactory work. Of the 12 engines which had been received at San Diego for the 8 JN2's (S.C. Nos. 41-48), 6 had been immediately condemned without being installed. Of the remaining 6 engines only 5 were ready for installation when the unit left for Fort Sill; the 6th had to be overhauled. During August Foulois urged the Curtiss Company to expedite the delivery of engines and plane parts, but on 1 September airplanes No. 42, 45, and 48 were out of commission awaiting propellers and bolts, No. 41 was temporarily grounded for minor repairs, No. 43's engine was being repaired and Nos. 44 and 46 were at Brownsville with the detachment there. No. 47 on 12 August had been destroyed in an accident, which cost the life of Capt. G. H. Knox, QMC, and so injured the pilot, Lieutenant R. B. Sutton, that he was relieved from temporary duty at Fort Sill on 26 October and returned to San Diego. A board found that the accident was caused by the manner in which the machine was handled and by weather conditions.

After the accident an informal meeting of the 12 officers of the 1st Aero Squadron was held and 10 of the officers agreed that the JN2 was unsafe and should not be flown, especially with a passenger, because of its low power, cheap and faulty construction, lack of stability, and unduly sensitive rudders. The other two officers present did not concur: Foulois said simply that the machines were not as good as they should be and that he was working to get other planes, while Milling held the planes were "safe within

their limitations." None of the officers made his statement for publication, however. Since the planes were in such poor condition, Foulois recommended on 1 September that no further aerial reconnaissance or artillery fire observation be undertaken until all the machines were again in commission and flights could be made despite interruptions for minor repairs. Therefore practice with the batteries was suspended until the squadron could cooperate.[95]

From 7 September to 9 November tests were made of Arthur Brock's automatic camera. The results showed that with certain improvements the camera would be of great assistance in securing accurate firing data for the field artillery and would be helpful in obtaining accurate maps of the terrain which, under service conditions, could not be obtained from the ground if it was covered by hostile fire.

On 14 October operations with the artillery were renewed. Major H. G. Bishop of the 5th Field Artillery reported that the aviation squadron was able to cooperate in only a few flights during firing and that the field artillery gained little or nothing from their presence. He admitted that this was not the fault of the aviators, who were anxious to work with the field artillery, but was caused largely by faulty materiel and the detachment of part of the squadron's machines. While the work of the squadron was limited, it clearly showed the futility of observation of artillery fire except by trained observers. Foulois, therefore, recommended a special course in air reconnaissance for artillery observers. These observers, he said, should be officers. The training should also be given to staff officers at the army, corps, division, and brigade levels. Foulois also recommended that the campsite and buildings constructed by the squadron should be left intact at Fort Sill for future use. If it had done nothing else, the exercise at Fort Sill gave the squadron an opportunity to test and improve its new mobile equipment and service machines.[96]

Meanwhile, on 14 and 15 August the detachment of 4 officers and 15 enlisted men with 2 JN2's, S.C. Nos. 44 and 46, had left Fort Sill for Brownsville. The officers were 1st Lt. J. C. Morrow, commanding officer, and Lieutenants Jones, Christie, and Harms. One White truck, spares, 2 engines, and quartermaster and ordnance supplies were also taken.[97] Upon their arrival on

18 August, Morrow wired the Chief Signal Officer that the Brownsville field which had been used by Lieutenants Jones and Milling in April was too small for the JN2's because of their poor climbing ability. He reported that 6 miles away there was another rough field, which, although it had no telegraph, telephone, or water, could be used for the JN2's; and he asked that S.C. airplanes Nos. 30 and 50 be sent down to be used on the field at Brownsville. Instructions arrived on the same day; "Go into camp at or near post. Prepare field which you report rough so that machines can start and land. You are equipped with service machines and none others will be furnished. If you cannot meet the incidents of active service you will be superseded."[98]

A great deal of difficulty was experienced with the planes at Brownsville. On 26 August, Lieutenant Jones, with Morrow as observer, flew No. 44 from Brownsville to Santa Maria, Texas, about 30 miles, in search of bandits reported operating in that area. Jones found it extremely difficult to keep the plane under control. On 1 September Jones, with Lieutenant Christie as observer, flew his JN2 in Very Pistol practice preliminary to artillery adjustment flights. The air was rough and gusty so that it took 42 minutes to reach 4,600 feet where Christie shot his signals. On 2 September Lieutenant Harms in No. 46 flew along the Rio Grande between Point Isabel and Brownsville in an attempt to locate bandits reported trying to cross to the Mexican side. After reaching 2,200 feet he returned, reporting that he could not proceed on his flight because of the way the plane handled in the rough air.[99] On 5 September Morrow and Pfc Adam Khuen-Kryk in No. 46 took off in gusty air and climbed at a moderate angle in a straight course for a mile and a half. At this point the plane had reached 200 feet altitude; Morrow leveled off and began a gradual left turn, the plane wobbled, the left wing went down, and the machine went into a nose dive. By the time Morrow began to pull it out of the dive, it was headed in the opposite direction. Although he partially recovered control, the plane struck the ground at an angle of 45°. It was completely smashed, and Morrow was injured. Since he was an excellent pilot, the accident was attributed to the faulty qualities of the machine.[100] On the 9th, No. 46 was replaced by No. 41, then back in commission.

As a result of his injuries, Morrow was relieved of duty as commanding officer, and Captain Dodd was ordered from San Diego to replace him. In the interim, Lieutenant Jones assumed command; while acting in this capacity, he made a report on the safety of the JN2 machine at the direction of the commanding officer of U.S. troops at Brownsville. In his report Jones stated that the JN2's were entirely unsuitable for military purposes and that they unnecessarily endangered the lives of the men who had to fly them. Lieutenants Christie and Harms concurred with Jones' views. Although the field artillery officers at Fort Sill had not withdrawn their offers to ride as observers in the planes after the Sutton accident, when the Jones' report was made the artillery officers at Brownsville refused to go up except in case of absolute necessity. On 13 September General Funston, Commanding General of the Southern Department, prohibited further flying of the JN2's unless it was necessary for artillery adjustment.[101]

No one seems to have been satisfied with the JN2 planes. Captain V. E. Clark had reported in July 1915, after inspecting the planes when they were delivered at San Diego, that he would condemn them all. Wind tunnel tests of the plane were made in August 1915, and Asst. Naval Constructor Hunsaker reported that the JN2 was statically stable over its whole flying range but dynamically unstable longitudinally for angles of 12, 14, and 15.5 degrees. The model tests also proved that, among other bad characteristics, the machines were laterally unstable at these high angles, both statically and dynamically. Hunsaker objected to the wing design and recommended a big, broad tail. Upon receipt of the Hunsaker report, the Chief Signal Officer had Curtiss come to Washington to discuss the situation. Curtiss agreed to send new upper wings, stabilizing fins, rudders, and OXX engines to Brownsville and Fort Sill to remodel completely the JN2 machines and remove the reported defects. Curtiss also sent a man who made all the necessary installations and even changed the whole wing structure rather than just that of the upper wing.

Apparently Colonel Reber, Acting CSO, had not been informed of the derogatory reports, for he stated in September that his office had no knowledge of any criticism of the JN2's, structurally or dynamically. He said the Morrow telegram from Brownsville on 18 August did not indicate faulty construction but only unsuitability for a particular field on account of the JN2's poor climbing ability. Captain Carberry, who was at the factory when the planes were constructed, had criticized the climb with the current weight and power but had recommended acceptance; however, the machines had neither been formally accepted nor paid for in October 1915.

From 2 October to the end of the month various tests were made of the JN2, both the original plane and the modified version, which was just like the new JN3, the first two of which, S.C. Nos. 52 and 53 had arrived at Fort Sill on 3 September. All of the trials were made to test the statements of Captain Clark and for the purpose of discovering what was wrong with the JN2. The tests showed that the plane had too much weight and not enough engine power. Since, at the time of construction, the machines had been expected to encounter very hard service, they had been given a rugged design. Their extra strength, however, made them weigh nearly 200 pounds more than the original J type. Foulois, realizing the limitations of the JN2's, thought they were structurally safe and stable if not overloaded and that the substitution of the new JN3 surfaces in place of the JN2 type materially increased the weight-carrying capacity. The changeover from the Curtiss OX to an OXX engine was also believed to have improved the planes; however, they were tested thoroughly after the squadron arrived at San Antonio. Lieutenant Dodd reported on 14 January 1916, that all the JN2-type planes had been eliminated from the service, having been modified to JN3's and that no dangerous defects had been discovered in the two JN3's sent from Fort Sill to Brownsville and flown there some 25 or 30 hours by Lieutenants Willis and Christie and Captain Dodd.[102]

SAN ANTONIO AIR CENTER

In 1915 preparations were again being made to establish the aviation center at San Antonio. On 6 March Foulois was sent from San Diego to Fort Sam Houston to prepare plans and estimates for buildings and roads on the old target range, about 4 miles north of Fort Sam Houston. On 11 March an inspection of the site was made by the Chief Signal Officer, accompanied by Foulois.[103] The sum of $48,200 included in the appropriation for fiscal year 1915 permitted the construction of

quarters for the commanding officer, two six-set bachelor officers' quarters, one barracks building, one garage, a stable, and a machine shop, all of which were already underway. This construction provided quarters for only twelve of the twenty officers to be stationed there, and there was not enough money to build more nor to take care of walks, roads, sewers, and clearing. It was recommended that additional funds to cover these items be included in the 1917 estimates. Two hangars, each capable of housing five planes, were to be built from Signal Corps funds. There were two old hangars on the mounted drill ground which Foulois wanted for temporary use until the squadron could move into its new post. Both were turned over to him, and by 10 January 1916 the two new hangars had been built and he had been authorized to tear down the old ones and move the material to the old target range for the use of the squadron.[104]

From 19 to 26 November 1915 the first squadron cross-country flight since the creation of the Army's air arm was flown by the 1st Aero Squadron from Fort Sill to permanent station at Fort Sam Houston, a distance of 439 miles, in six JN3's. MSE Stephen J. Idzorek and Pfc Westermark were the advance ground echelon. They left on the 17th in the squadron automobile to select the first landing field at Wichita Falls. Enlisted personnel and trucks moved by road and rail. The squadron train of 7 Jeffrey Quad trucks, 1 White truck, and 2 trailmobiles in charge of MSE Marcus and accompanied by four motorcyclists headed by MSE McRae, left on the 19th. The remainder of the ground echelon, under the supervision of Sergeant First Class Vernon L. Burge, left by rail on the 18th, and the surplus equipment was shipped by freight.[105]

On the 19th Lieutenants Carberry, Bowen, Chapman, Rader, Milling, and Captain Foulois* took off at 1-minute intervals, circled over Fort Sill until they reached an altitude of 1,500 feet, and headed for Wichita Falls. The planes and the squadron train arrived at Wichita Falls on the same day. The crowd gathering there made it necessary for each officer to guard his plane, so thereafter Sergeant Idzorek arranged for police protection at all stops. The fliers decided to elimi-

---

*Lieutenants Sutton, FitzGerald, and MacDill had been transferred in October to the Signal Corps Aviation School at San Diego.

nate an intermediate stop which had been planned and to fly through to Fort Worth in one hop the next day. The trip was uneventful and the layover there on Sunday the 21st allowed the squadron train to catch up. The only loss on the trip occurred that evening when one of the Jeffrey trucks was destroyed by fire. On the 22d the planes flew to Waco, Texas, the train arriving the same evening. On the 23d, en route to Austin, Leader Carberry was driven off course by the wind. He was followed by Foulois, Rader, and Chapman, all of whom landed at various places after discovering the error, received directions, and then flew into Austin without any difficulty. Carberry continued flying and finally reached Austin. Milling and Bowen both flew low, followed the railroad, and arrived at their destination without any trouble. Two days were spent at Austin waiting for better weather, and finally at 0945 on the 26th of November, the last plane landed at Fort Sam Houston.[106]

The mobile equipment proved its value on the trip. The trucks, with loads of 1 to 1½ tons, were subjected to a hard test over rough roads and long stretches of deep sand. Some even broke through flimsy bridges, but this possibility had been anticipated and wrecking equipment was carried by each truck. The two trailmobiles loaned by the Sechler Company of Cincinnati, each loaded to its capacity of 1,500 pounds and pulled by Jeffrey trucks, stood up well, and Foulois recommended their purchase. Skilled mechanics, each equipped with a kit of tools, preceded the heavier equipment on motorcycles. These men rode as fast as possible each day to the next landing field and there checked the airplanes and engines, making any minor repairs necessary without waiting for the arrival of the trucks. Both the cyclists and the truck crews worked long hours. They rode all day, worked late at night, and frequently had only one meal a day. The success of the flight was due largely to their efforts.[107]

On 31 December 1915 there were 15 officers of the Aviation Section assigned to Fort Sam Houston: Captain Foulois and Lieutenants Carberry, Bowen, Rader, and Chapman had flown down from Fort Sill;* Captain Dodd and Lieutenants Dargue, Willis, Kilner, Christie, Gorrell, and Gantz, had been ordered to San Antonio in December; the

injured Lieutenant Morrow was on leave of absence; Lieutenants Jones and Harms were on detached service at MIT. In addition to the officers there were 84 enlisted men assigned.[108]

At least three additional planes were sent to San Antonio in December 1915. They were the Burgess-Renaults, Nos. 26 and 27, which had been remodeled at San Diego, and No. 40, the Burgess with a Curtiss 6-cylinder engine built according to the design of the Signal Corps Aviation School at San Diego.[109]

Pursuant to authorization by the War Department, a guidon or flag was designed for the aero squadron during the fall of 1915, but the sketch was not approved by the Secretary of War until the summer of 1916.[110] In November 1915, a board of officers met to select a proper working uniform for the Aviation Section. The outfit worn by army aviators at that time consisted of a helmet, gauntlets, leather jacket, goggles, and a service uniform. No provision had been made heretofore for cold weather flying, and the flying equipment in use at that time was uncomfortable in hot weather. There was no standard clothing for mechanics, and the fatigue uniform was unsuitable. The meetings of the board continued into 1916, and it was finally decided that officers would buy their own clothing while the QMC would furnish that needed by the enlisted men.[111] With the advent of new airplanes equipped with instruments it had become unnecessary for the pilot to carry on his person such things as a watch, compass, and an aneroid barometer.[112]

THE PHILIPPINE SQUADRON AND OTHERS — 1915 AND 1916

On 9 April 1915 it was announced that after an aero squadron had been stationed at San Antonio, the second aero company to be organized would be sent to the Philippine Department for station at Corregidor, the third to the Hawaiian Department for station at Fort Kamehameha, and the fourth to the Canal Zone. The Philippine and Hawaiian companies were to have seaplane equipment but were to have no unit motor vehicle transportation. On 21 April the Chief Signal Officer advised the QMC that provision was being made to equip one aero company for the Philippines with seaplanes by the close of 1915 and asked that plans be made to construct quarters for 9 officers and 40 enlisted men and to build a ma-

---

*Milling, who also had flown down from Fort Sill, had been ordered to San Diego upon his arrival at San Antonio.

chine shop, similar to the one proposed for the San Antonio center. The Signal Corps would provide the necessary hangars.[113]

On 12 May The Adjutant General notified the Chief Signal Officer that the Secretary of War had directed that steps be taken as soon as possible to transfer an aero company to the Philippine Department. The same day the Chief Signal Officer activated the 1st Company, 2d Aero Squadron; however, the company did not begin to function until December 1915.[114] In June the Chief Signal Officer asked the Quartermaster General to include in his 1917 estimates (in addition to NCO quarters for San Antonio, which had not been included in the previous estimates), barracks, quarters, a machine shop, and storehouse for each of the overseas garrisons. The Quartermaster General estimated that housing costs for these squadrons would be:

Philippines	$145,600
Hawaii	141,500
Panama	175,000
San Antonio	10,000
Total	$472,100

These figures were satisfactory to the Chief Signal Officer, but he recommended adding at each station one balloon house and one gas generator building. The Adjutant General directed that only the NCO quarters at San Antonio be included, but on 5 August the Chief Signal Officer asked for reconsideration, since before the close of fiscal year 1917 housing at all three overseas garrisons would be needed—by the end of the current year 1915 a fully equipped seaplane company would be en route to the Philippines, a company would be ready for station in Hawaii in April 1916, and another for Panama three or four months later. Finally, on 18 August, The Adjutant General directed that estimates for barracks and quarters for the entire approved war strength of the garrison of the Philippines, Hawaii, and Panama be added to the estimates for 1917. On 9 October 1915 the Chief of Staff, in order that estimates for barracks and quarters might be included in the appropriation for the next fiscal year, 1917, advised the Quartermaster General that one aero squadron each was approved for the Panama Canal Zone, Hawaiian Islands, and Philippine Islands.[115]

Brig. Gen. C. R. Edwards, Commanding General,

U.S. Troops, Ancon, Canal Zone, on 12 August appealed for a Panama Aero Company at the earliest practicable moment. He stated that the Panama Canal Zone might be considered an isolated fortress and since airplanes were an essential part of fortress defense, it was necessary that the Canal Zone have them. Local conditions seemed to indicate that hydroairplanes would be the most suitable as their greater stability would be a distinct advantage in the reputedly bad flying conditions over the Zone. He suggested the Canal itself and Gatun and Miraflores lakes as ideal locations. Maj. Gen. Leonard Wood, Commanding General of the Eastern Department, favorably indorsed the project and increased the unit to a squadron. General Edwards then wrote that he had been in error—he should have asked for two companies, one for the Atlantic side and the other for the Pacific. He recommended Gatun Lake for the Atlantic company and Miraflores Lake for the Pacific; since neither lake was affected by the tide, hangars could be constructed over the water. Because he considered an aero squadron in Panama of such great importance, General Edwards recommended that if the squadron could be furnished in no other way, the aviation school should be suspended and its personnel and materiel should be used to build up a squadron to be sent at once to Panama. He was informed, however, that no change would be made in the instructions of 9 April, which provided that the first company to be equipped after the one for San Antonio would be sent to the Philippines, the next to Hawaii, and the third to the Canal Zone.[116]

Capt. William L. Patterson, who was to command the company being sent to the Philippines, suggested in October that the machine and repair shop building for the Philippines be planned to permit enlargement in view of the future addition of a second company; that the temporary wooden hangars be rainproofed; that a 5,000-gallon rainwater tank be procured, as the alkaline water at Corregidor could not be used in aircraft engines; and that two reserve fuel storage tanks be provided, one of 5,000-gallon capacity and the other of 2,000 gallon. The Chief Signal Officer informed Patterson that the construction of buildings and the remodeling of the hangars at Corregidor would be left entirely to the commanding officer of the company stationed there and that an allotment of funds would be made for this purpose. As for the tanks, they would have to wait until next year's appropriation became available. The commanding officer would receive full instructions on the program before he departed, and his grasp of the situation plus his ability to meet problems as they arose would determine the success or failure of his administration of a difficult but most important station.[117]

On 1 December 1915 the organization of the 1st Company, 2d Aero Squadron was announced at San Diego. It consisted of 6 officers and 37 enlisted men. The officers were: Capt. William L. Patterson, Commanding, and 1st Lieutenants Douglas B. Netherwood, Redondo B. Sutton, S. W. FitzGerald, Leslie MacDill, and Earl L. Canady. On 16 December the Chief Signal Officer advised The Adjutant General that the unit was under orders to sail for Manila, and on 5 January 1916, 5 officers and 33 men left San Francisco on the U.S. transport *Sheridan*. The remainder of the company arrived in the Philippines on 3 February 1916, except for Lieutenant FitzGerald, who was temporarily on detached service and did not arrive until 6 March. After quarantine at Fort McKinley the company reached its station at Fort Mills on 14 February. No planes had accompanied the unit, but on 13 March two Martin S seaplanes arrived and two more came on 15 April. Flying began on 8 May with S.C. No. 57 and on 29 May with No. 56. Planes 58 and 59 were not set up until a second hangar was ready. A radio transmitter was installed on S.C. No. 59 and by 1917 messages were received from a distance of 29 miles. On 28 June and again on 11 October 1916, the Fort Mills batteries held target practice; and although there was no need for adjustment, the 4 officers on duty at that time flew for practice in spotting and signaling the firing from the air, either as pilots or as observers. The "overs" and "shorts" were noted and records were furnished the artillery commander for comparison with the official figures. Experiments were conducted in an effort to reduce the visibility of Coast Artillery batteries from the air. Observations were made and photographs taken.

The monthly reports of the Department Signal Officer covered a variety of matters. Plane No. 56 was damaged beyond repair on 3 February 1917 in a forced landing. There was continual delay in obtaining materiel. In answer to a letter from Captain Patterson, the Chief Signal Officer stated that the 2d Aero Squadron would be brought to full strength as soon as possible, for it was intended to keep a squadron permanently in the Philippines and plans should be made for a strength of 150 enlisted men. However, the officer strength in November was the same as that of April—the squadron lost two and gained two in that period. Lieutenant Sutton was relieved from the air service and dropped from the company rolls on 25 April 1916. Lieutenant FitzGerald departed on leave on 15 June 1916 and was ordered on detached service to Gloucester, Massachusetts, in September and did not return to the Philippines. Two new officers (1st Lts. M. F. Scanlon and R. B. Barnitz) were sent to the squadron in November 1916.[118]

Thus by the end of 1916 the United States had at least one detachment of its developing air arm, equipped and manned, in operation overseas.

———★———

CHAPTER VIII

The Aviation Section in 1916

AIR LEGISLATION

AS A RESULT of the Goodier court martial and the dissatisfaction of the younger officers with conditions in the Aviation Section, Senator Joseph T. Robinson of Arkansas on 5 January 1916 introduced S. J. Resolution 65 calling for an investigation of the Aviation Section. In his written and oral statements he charged that the true condition of the section had been deliberately withheld from the high authorities in the War Department and that misrepresentations as to the progress made by the aviators were deliberately and repeatedly being made to the Department. In support of these charges he referred to correspondence between Captain Cowan, OIC of the Aviation School, San Diego and Lieutenant Colonel Reber, the chief of the Aviation Section, and to photostatic copies of letters used as evidence in the Goodier court martial purporting to show favoritism toward certain officers. He also filed another statement in which he claimed that despite the Signal Corps report of 46 qualified fliers, an actual investigation would show only 24. The statement charged that the majority of deaths from flying were due to inadequate equipment and that the training of the men was defective in many respects.[1]

S. J. Resolution 65 passed the Senate without opposition on 16 March 1916. After the House of Representatives' Committee on Military Affairs had accepted the Senate committee's report and recommended agreement to the resolution, the subject of investigation of the Aviation Section was debated in the House.[2] Congressman Charles P. Caldwell of New York explained that the purpose of the resolution was to get the information necessary for framing a new law which would put America out in front in aviation. He pointed out that at the time of introduction of the resolution a deplorable condition had existed in the aviation service, but that the situation had been rectified to some extent, since the discussion had served to center attention on the needs of the Aviation Section. The resolution was passed over by the House and nothing further was heard of the investigation in Congress.[3]

As a result of S. J. Resolution 65, the Signal Corps decided to conduct its own investigation of the Aviation Section and called upon its Inspector General, Colonel Shanks, to do the job. On 9 February 1916, General Scriven, the CSO, commented on Shanks' report in a letter to The Adjutant General. The motive behind the "unmilitary insubordination and disloyal acts" of the young and inexperienced aviation officers, declared General Scriven, was an ambition to form a new and independent organization for aviation. Although he strongly denied Senator Robinson's accusations, the Chief Signal Officer recommended that some changes be made in the Aviation Section and that the War Department take action to change the act of 18 July 1914, in order to remove the age and marital status restrictions then imposed on aviation personnel. He thought if this were done it would bring into the aviation service older officers with more military experience and would eliminate many of the difficulties that had beset the progress of aviation in the Army. He also recommended shifts of personnel within the Aviation Section which would change the assignments of Reber and Cowan, against whom most of the charges had been made. In April 1916, Secretary of War Baker censured both Scriven and Reber for failing to enforce and maintain discipline and to observe legal restraints and military regulations. On 5 May, Reber was relieved from duty as chief of the Aviation Section, Signal Corps, but remained on duty in the Office of the Chief Signal Officer. In July Reber took leave of absence for four months on a medical certificate and on expiration of the sick leave in October was assigned as Signal Officer for the Central Department and was not again connected with aviation. On 3 April Captain Cowan was relieved from command of the Signal Corps Aviation School at San Diego and was replaced by Col. William Glassford on the same day. On 6 July Cowan was relieved from duty in the Aviation Section, and in October was detailed to the Southern Department, Canal Zone for assignment.[4]

On 8 April 1916, during hearings on the military appropriation act for fiscal year 1917, Secretary Baker commented on the situation in the Aviation Section before the Committee on Military Affairs. He described the primary difficulty as the impatience of young and eager men in the Aviation Section with the regulations and restrictions imposed by their superiors, who knew little or nothing of flying. He thought that the situation had been largely "tall talk" and had never led to actual insubordination. However, he announced that he had decided to have the General Staff make a study of the Aviation Section and to reorganize it on the basis of their findings. He also announced that Lt. Col. George O. Squier, who had been interested and active in aviation since its inception in the Signal Corps, would be put in charge of the Aviation Section when he returned from his duty as Military Attache in London, and on 20 May 1916 the appointment was made.[5]

While S. J. Resolution 65 was being considered by Congress, Representative Charles Lieb of Indiana introduced a bill to establish a Department of Aviation, headed by a Secretary of Aviation, which would have complete charge of the air arms of both the Army and the Navy. This bill was buried in the Committee on Military Affairs to which it was referred on 28 March 1916.[6]

During this period, military aviation in the United States received its first combat test, when one aero squadron was sent to Mexico with the punitive expedition in the spring of 1916.* The

inefficiency of the planes of this squadron brought to the attention of the country the needs of the aviation service. On 31 March 1916, an urgent deficiency act gave the Aviation Section of the Signal Corps $500,000, but on 29 August, Congress, influenced by the possibility that the United States might be dragged into the European War, allowed $13,281,666 for military aeronautics and in addition appropriated $600,000 for the purchase of land for aviation sites. For the first time the Signal Corps had the money with which to develop aviation, but it was difficult to get planes and engines, and criticism continued. Much of the criticism came from the disgruntled members of the Aero Club of America who were having trouble securing the cooperation of the Signal Corps in their efforts to expand the aviation units of the National Guard.[7] The Club had played an important part in securing the $13,281,666 appropriation, and it understood that $9,640,800 of the sum would be spent on the National Guard. The army officers, to the contrary, maintained that the whole appropriation came to them practically without restrictions, and they felt it was their duty to spend the money in whatever way seemed best to build a real American air service. Mr. Henry Woodhouse and Alan R. Hawley, both members of the Aero Club, attacked the Aviation Section through editorials in the press. They aimed their charges particularly at Maj. William Mitchell, Assistant to Colonel Squier, Chief of the Aviation Section. The charges were to the general effect that the development of military aeronautics was being greatly impeded by the alleged inefficiency and general misconduct of Major Mitchell. The implication was even made that the funds appropriated by Congress for the aviation training of the Guard were being utilized for other purposes. Secretary Baker personally investigated and reported that these allegations were entirely unsubstantiated and that it was unfortunate that the Aero Club could not get along with the Aviation Section.[8]

The National Defense Act was passed on 3 June 1916, and Section 13 of this act particularly benefited the air service. It increased the personnel authorized for the Aviation Section from 60 to 148 officers, consisting of 1 colonel, 1 lieutenant colonel, 8 majors, 24 captains, and 114 first lieutenants, and it gave the President the power to fix the enlisted strength of the Signal Corps. The

---

*See below, Chapter IX.

restrictions relative to the detail of married officers and of officers over 30 years of age were removed. The percentages of flying pay were the same as those in the act of 18 July 1914, but the rank at which Junior Military Aviators and Military Aviators could receive the rank, pay, and allowances of one grade higher than that held in their own branch of the service was raised from first lieutenant to captain. The 35 per cent flying pay of the act of 2 March 1913 was repealed. Provision was made for the appointment of civilians in the grade of "Aviator." Their base pay was to be $150 a month in addition to the allowances of a master signal electrician; they could be discharged if found unsatisfactory.[9] No civilian was appointed in that capacity, however, up to October 1918.[10]

Sections 37 and 55 of the National Defense Act provided for a Signal Officers Reserve Corps and a Signal Enlisted Reserve Corps, comprising 297 officers and 2,000 enlisted men who were to be trained under the direction of the Aviation Section. The Officers Reserve Corps was established for the purpose of providing a reserve of officers available for military service when needed. Its members must be citizens of the United States or the Philippines and must be at least 21 years of age. The appointment was for five years, but in time of war was to continue until six months after the war ended. The Enlisted Reserve Corps was to consist of persons voluntarily enlisted therein for three years. Enlistment was limited to persons eligible for enlistment in the Regular Army who had such military or technical training as was prescribed by the Secretary of War. Under this section more than one hundred civilians were enlisted by the end of 1916 as sergeants in the Aviation Section, Signal Enlisted Reserve Corps (SERC) and ordered to active duty for flying training at the Curtiss schools at Miami and Newport News, and later to the Signal Corps schools at Mineola, Chicago, and Memphis. These flying students of the SERC were enlisted with the understanding that if they successfully completed the required training they would be commissioned and thus would become members of the Signal Officers Reserve Corps. Those who failed to pass the prescribed examination and desired to be relieved from further training would be discharged. Students who, after being transferred to the Aviation Section, Signal Corps from the Regular Army or National Guard, failed to pass the examinations and were relieved from further training for commissions were to be reported to the department commander for transfer to an organization of the same arm of service, corps, or department to which they had belonged originally.[11]

Because this law was an outcome of national development and of the country's increased responsibilities at a time when most of the world was at war, it was impossible to ignore any longer the fact that the strength of the military forces was inadequate. The law had increased the number of Signal Corps officers, and the process of enlargement included plans for successive annual increments to cover a period of five years. The first increment under the act of 3 June 1916 added 1 major and 16 other aviation officers to the Aviation Section giving it a personnel strength on 1 July 1916 of 1 major, 11 captains, and 65 first lieutenants, making a total of 77 officers. On this date, 23 officers of the Regular Army had completed their training in aviation and were serving on duty with the Aviation Section, Signal Corps, and 26 others were under instruction. But less than a year after the first increment was effected, the United States entered the war, and the whole authorized increase was accomplished immediately. The air program adopted by the War Department caused such an extraordinary growth of this heretofore minor branch that a still further reorganization of the Signal Corps was necessary, and a future air service to be separate and distinct from the Signal Corps was projected.[12]

Shortly after the passage of the National Defense Act, several new civilian collaborative agencies, similar to the National Advisory Committee for Aeronautics, which had been established on 2 April 1915, were formed. The National Research Council was organized on 21 September 1916 by the National Academy of Science to further the work of research in the various sciences in their application to both war and peace. This group conducted some investigations in aeronautics; and when the tasks of wartime research became too great and too numerous to be efficiently performed, it was upon their recommendation that the Science and Research Division of the Signal Corps was established in February 1917.[13]

On 29 August 1916, the Council of National Defense was created. It consisted of the Secretaries of War, Navy, Agriculture, Interior, Commerce, and Labor. The law also authorized the establishment of an Advisory Commission made up of seven civilians who possessed special knowledge of the industrial and commercial resources of the country. At the request of President Wilson, the Council of National Defense was reorganized on 3 March 1917 to include the Advisory Commission, composed of Daniel Willard, (president of the B&O Railroad) chairman, Bernard Baruch (banker), Samuel Gompers (president of the American Federation of Labor), Julius Rosenwald (president of Sears, Roebuck & Co.), Dr. Franklin H. Martin (secretary general of the American College of Surgeons, Chicago), Howard E. Coffin (vice president of the Hudson Motor Car Co.), and Dr. Hollis Godfrey (president of Drexel Institute), each of whom was made responsible for a group of activities on which he was well informed. This had hardly been accomplished when the United States entered the war. While there was no army adequate for war, the country had a good basic industrial organization for peace, which served as a foundation for the demands of war, and the newly appointed council applied itself to the task of industrial and economic mobilization.[14]

It was through the efforts of both the National Advisory Committee for Aeronautics and the Council of National Defense, but particularly the former, that the Aircraft Manufacturers Association was formed on 13 February 1917.[15] This association was organized for the purpose of arriving at cross-license agreements that would be satisfactory to all patent holder of patents involving aircraft materiel. Such an agreement was made on 2 March 1917, but it was not effective until July 1917. The government admitted that the Wright-Martin and Curtiss companies held the basic patents on airplanes and that each of them was to receive $2,000,000 for these patents. Each member of the Aircraft Manufacturers Association was to pay the association $200 for each plane built until the two companies had been paid. Later, a supplemental agreement was made which modified the provisions for payments by subscribers and provided that the aggregate payments to the two companies should be $2,000,000 instead of $4,000,000. After both companies had been paid, fees of not more than $25 apiece were to be paid on all airplanes. Other subscriber owners of designs or devices used by another manufacturer

would be paid one per cent of the contract price until the owner received a total of not more than $50,000.[16]

By the cross-license agreement, the subscribers granted to each other licenses under all airplane patents except foreign and certain specified patents; the association was designated as the agent of the subscribers to execute licenses accordingly; and each subscriber agreed "not to enter into any arrangements which would exclude or restrict the operation of the agreement."[17]

THE AVIATION SECTION

The Aviation Section comprised the Aeronautical Division, temporarily headed by a General Staff officer, Capt. William Mitchell;* the Signal Corps Aviation School at San Diego; the 1st Aero Squadron on duty with the expeditionary force in Mexico; and the 1st Company, 2d Aero Squadron on duty in the Philippines. On 12 January 1916, there were in the Aviation Section 46 officers, 243 enlisted men, and 23 planes. Since 1909, a period of just over 6 years, the Signal Corps had purchased 59 airplanes: one of these was in the Smithsonian, 32 had been destroyed or condemned, 3 were out of repair, and 23 were still in service. On 8 April, of these 23, there were 4 seaplanes at Manila, 2 flying boats and 9 trainers at San Diego, and 8 service planes on the Mexican border. In addition, there were 8 planes being tested at Newport News by the Technical Aero Advisory and Inspection Board composed of three officers, Capt. V. E. Clark, Lt. T. D. Milling, and Lt. B. Q. Jones, with two consulting engineers, Jerome C. Hunsaker and Henry Souther. The Board had been appointed to test the new planes bought for use in Mexico as soon as they were delivered, and to inspect aircraft factories.[18]

On 4 May 1916 the Aviation Section's flying personnel consisted of 23 JMA's, 27 aviation students, and 8 enlisted men who were trained aviators. Five JMA's and 5 MA's had been relieved since the organization of the section in 1914. There were 5 officer and 2 civilian instructors at this time and the number of planes had not increased since January.[19]

By 26 June the personnel strength of the Aviation Section was 60 officers and 248 enlisted men.

*He had been appointed to this post on 3 April relieving Capt. George S. Gibbs, who had assumed charge on 17 March during the temporary absence of Lt. Col. Reber. Mitchell was soon promoted to the rank of major.

There were 3 officers in Washington; 10 officers, 24 aviation students, and 92 enlisted men at San Diego; 17 officers and 122 enlisted men on duty with the 1st Aero Squadron on the Mexican border; 5 officers and 34 enlisted men on duty with the 1st Company, 2d Aero Squadron in the Philippines; and 1 officer attending MIT in Boston.[20]

The tactical unit was the squadron, first organized on the basis of 20 officer-aviators and 8 planes, headed by a major; later the number of machines was increased to 12, the personnel remaining the same. Each squadron was divided into three companies of four machines each. The company, commanded by a captain, was composed of four sections, each headed by a first lieutenant, who was charged with keeping the section equipment in condition, supervising repairs, and instructing and training the enlisted men of the section.[21]

A General Staff investigation committee was designated by the Secretary of War on 25 April 1916, to study the organization and methods of administration of the Aviation Section. The committee was composed of Col. C. W. Kennedy, Maj. P. D. Lochridge, Major Palmer, and Captain Moore; they were to make specific recommendations as to reorganization and changes which might be desirable. Their report was completed on 30 June and was approved by the Secretary of War on 5 July. The committee, first considered the development of aeronautics in the European war, where it found that each army was accompanied by organized air units performing the following principal functions: reconnaissance, observation and direction of artillery fire, bombing, and aerial combat; each of these functions required a special type of aircraft. The main objects of the American aviation service, the committee found, were to provide sufficient flying personnel and the necessary types and numbers of aircraft. It was recommended that the Aviation Section be put under a central control in the War Department and completely separated from the Signal Corps; that it be organized as a training-operation agency; and that there should be a military organization for the channeling of machines and personnel into proper tactical units for active military duty.[22] Lt. Col. George Squier, who had become chief of the Aviation Section in May, reported in July that the machinery was complete for the proper

expansion of the air service, provided Congress authorized sufficient personnel and funds. Plans to utilize civilian schools for the training of fliers and to have at least three central government flying schools had been formulated. One of the three schools was already established at San Diego, another was to be near Chicago, and a third would be at Mineola, New York (an aero squadron of the New York National Guard was being trained at Mineola).[23] The San Diego school was to be used primarily for training Regular Army officers and enlisted men; Chicago and Mineola were to be used for advanced training of candidates for the Reserve Corps and National Guard. The civilian schools were to be used for primary and, possibly, advanced training.

Because the air organization was expanding, the emphasis was necessarily on training, and the need for new and better service planes had been evidenced by the 1st Aero Squadron's experiences at Fort Sill and Brownsville. On 24 April 1916 the Chief Signal Officer had issued new specifications for the design, construction, equipment, and requirements of a military airplane adapted to land reconnaissance; and on 1 August Aeronautical Specifications Nos. 1000 and 1001, which covered primary and advanced trainers, were issued by the Aviation Section. The trainers were to be single-engine, 2-place, tandem, tractor biplanes equipped with either Curtiss or Deperdussin duplicate controls, whichever was indicated in the order. Limiting the controls to two specific kinds indicated a tendency toward standardization, and this tendency was more pronounced when Specification No. 1003 of 1 May 1917 appeared, requiring stick controls for all single-seater pursuit planes.[24]

SAN DIEGO DEVELOPMENTS

Beginning in April 1916, after Colonel Glassford became commanding officer there were several transfers of personnel to and from the San Diego School. Lieutenant Lahm was redetailed to the Aviation Section, rated as JMA with rank of captain, and ordered to report to the School on 1 April 1916; Lieutenant Dargue was relieved from the 1st Aero Squadron; and Lieutenant Arnold, who had been assigned to the Infantry since 1913, was redetailed to Aviation as a JMA with rank of captain on 20 May. Going out of the school were Lieutenants B. M. Atkinson, John B. Brooks, Harold S. Martin, and Carl Spaatz, who were ordered to Columbus, New Mexico, for duty with the 1st Aero Squadron.

The Signal Corps Aviation School was reorganized in the spring of 1916 with the following staff:

Col. W. A. Glassford — Commanding Officer
Capt. F. P. Lahm — Secretary
Lt. H. A. Dargue — Officer in Charge of Training
Lt. B. Q. Jones — OIC, Engineering and Repair
Capt. H. H. Arnold — Supply Officer
Capt. H. M. Royden — QM and Disbursing Officer
Capt. C. C. Culver — Meteorological & Radio Officer
Maj. W. R. Ream — Medical Officer

Because of the reorganization and the requirement to furnish personnel for overseas squadrons, little was done at the school in the early part of 1916 other than regular routine training. After the student flying officers had completed their courses in flying and received their ratings, they were either sent to the 1st Aero Squadron for duty or retained in the Aviation School on the permanent staff.[25]

As the school increased its tempo, night flying was inaugurated at San Diego in June. A few experimental night flights had been made earlier, but this was the first training course of its kind given at the school and it was excellent training for young officers who would soon be doing combat flying. At first the fliers went up only on moonlight nights, landing with the aid of searchlights; but later they flew on the darkest of nights and landed with only the aid of the harbor lights.[26]

Between 27 July and 26 October major developments in aircraft radio took place at the San Diego school. On 27 July Captain Culver and Sergeant Ocker in plane No. 50, with a 180-watt transmitter of French design, transmitted messages 119 miles from Santa Monica to San Diego. The receiving was handled by Dr. R. O. Shelton, an enthusiastic amateur at San Diego, who was assisted by Lt. W. A. Robertson from the school. On 18 August, with the same personnel, both sending and receiving were accomplished from the plane over a distance of 11 miles. On the 24th, messages were exchanged over a distance of 20 miles. Plane to plane communication was accomplished for the first time on 2 September, between Cpl. A. D. Smith, piloting No. 50, which was equipped with a small sending set operated by Robertson, and Lieutenant Dargue in No. 51, which had a receiving set operated by Culver. On 26 October, with a 45 pound set constructed at the

school, Culver sent radio signals and messages from a plane to Dr. Shelton at the San Diego station over a distance of 140 miles.[27]

On 15 August Lt. Col. Squier advised Colonel Glassford, commanding officer of the San Diego School, of plans for a field officers' course to give selected officers of the Army at large a limited experience in aeronautics without attempting pilot instruction. The course would occupy much the same position in the Army air service as did the field officers' course at Fort Leavenworth in the education system of the Army ground forces. A limited number of selected officers of field grade and above were needed to fill the higher executive positions required in the development of aeronautics on a scale commensurate with the 1917 appropriation. Colonel Glassford concurred and in November, four officers reported for the course at San Diego—Col. W. L. Kenly, F.A., Lt. Col. H. G. Bishop, F.A., Maj. W. A. Burnside, Inf., and Maj. J. B. Bennet, Inf.*[28] This was the earliest air school of its type.†

By the time the United States entered the war in April 1917, the size and activities of the Signal Corps Aviation School had greatly increased as had the number of airplanes and students to be trained. Between January 1916 and 6 April 1917, 47 planes were delivered at San Diego.†† On 3 October, 45 Army officers were taking flying training there. This was the largest number to date. Two Marine Corps officers and a number of enlisted men were also being trained. The duties of the personnel employed there became correspondingly more important and more exacting. This applied particularly to the Quartermaster Department which, in addition to its other duties, had charge of the construction work to enlarge the school, entailing the erection of additional hangars, shops, storehouses, barracks, and other necessary buildings. Moreover, as soon as a permanent site for the school was selected a permanent school plant was to be built. Heretofore, retired officers had been on duty at the school as quarter-

_____

*After the United States entered World War I Major Burnside returned to his own arm of the service and was lost to aviation as was Lt. Col. Bishop who was in the hospital; but Lt. Col. Bennet became OIC of the Aeronautical Division in 1917 and in 1918 Maj. Gen. Kenly became Director of Military Aeronautics. Thus, 50 per cent of the first class served as air officers.

†A similar school, the Air Command and Staff School, was established as a department of the Air University in March 1946.

††24 Curtiss JN4's, 8 Martins, 9 Curtiss R4's, 2 Standard H8's, and 2 Sturtevant and 2 Curtiss pursuits.

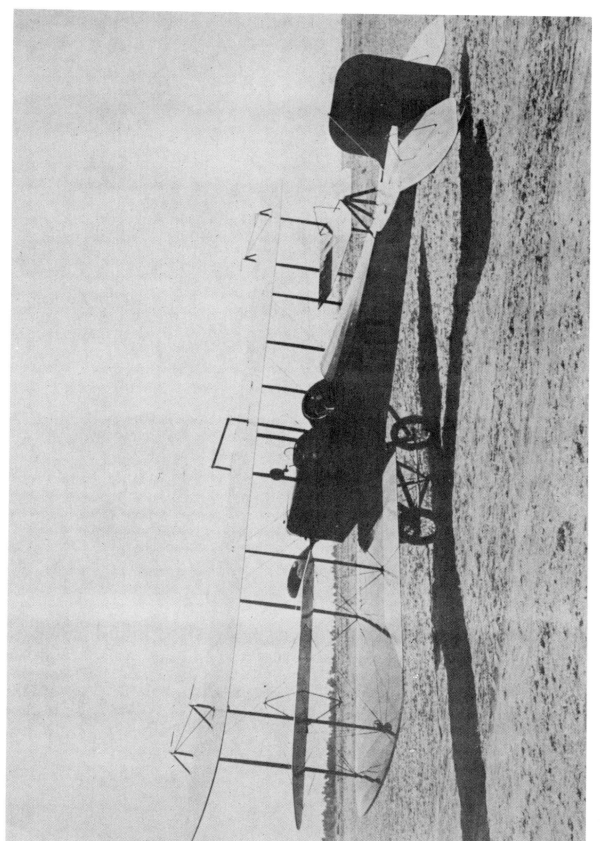

Martin Signal Corps No. 50 equipped with radio, 1916

master, disbursing, and ordnance officers, but Colonel Glassford recommended the detail of a quartermaster officer who was particularly qualified in construction work. The Chief Signal Officer indorsed the request, but still another retired officer was ordered to the school on 11 January 1917, and no regular quartermaster officer appeared on the San Diego rosters through April 1917.[29]

THE AVIATION CENTER AT FORT SAM HOUSTON

On 5 January 1916, just as the 1st Aero Squadron was getting ready to move into new barracks and establish itself in its new post at San Antonio, the commanding officer of Fort Sam Houston requested information as to what jurisdiction he had over the San Antonio Air Center. General Funston indorsed the query to The Adjutant General, recommending that the air center constitute a part of the post of Fort Sam Houston. But Captain Foulois, commanding officer of the 1st Aero Squadron, wired the Chief Signal Officer urgently requesting that the aviation center be placed under the jurisdiction of the department commander and considered as a separate post. The Chief Signal Officer concurred in this opinion and The Adjutant General approved. The technical training and equipment of the 1st Aero Squadron were not to be interfered with by the post commander.[30]

No sooner was that problem taken care of than another arose. On 17 January, air-artillery cooperation was again scheduled at the Fort Sill School of Fire for Field Artillery; the tests were to begin on 20 February. The Adjutant General wrote the commanding general of the Southern Department that the War Department wanted to develop cooperation as soon as possible between the air service and the field artillery, and he requested information as to whether two airplanes and the necessary personnel could be ordered to Fort Sill. Foulois objected to detaching any planes or men for duty at Fort Sill because the squadron's eight airplanes, which had been housed in canvas hangars and had been operating under field service conditions for the past six months, were not in serviceable condition. Two of the planes which had been in Brownsville were being completely overhauled and having new engines installed; the experimental engines with which they had been equipped had been found to be unreliable for military work. The other six planes,

which had been flown to San Antonio after three and a half months at Fort Sill, were badly in need of new covering and it would take until March to put them in good shape. Furthermore the fliers did not have suitable clothing for winter flying at Fort Sill, and the squadron experiments with cold-weather clothing would not be completed for at least two or three months. Foulois believed that air-artillery cooperation could be more quickly, economically and efficiently developed at Fort Sam Houston, and he and the commanding officer of the field artillery troops there were making plans to begin cooperative work in signaling, observation of fire, location of targets, and gun concealment as soon as repairs had been made on the planes.

Actually, in Foulois' opinion, the most important reason for not detaching airplanes from the Squadron for Fort Sill was that the unit was an untried organization without its full quota of men, transport, and technical equipment. Its new officers were practically untrained in the military use of airplanes, and systematic training could not be given them unless the squadron was held together as a unit. It had served as an organized unit only three weeks, when it had been called upon to furnish detachments for border service. Now that all the personnel were back with the squadron, every officer and man was needed to solve the numerous problems of building up a new post; to aid in the development of more suitable types of military planes, instruments for bombing, photographic devices, armor, and firearms for use in airplanes; and to solve problems of supply and transport. General Funston concurred in Foulois' objections and the Chief Signal Officer finally agreed on 15 February 1916 that no planes or personnel would be detached for duty at Fort Sill.[31]

During January all technical work was suspended because the enlisted men were employed in hauling supplies from Fort Sam Houston to the aviation post, four miles away; building roads, walks, and drains; and preparing a landing field. This work would have to be continued for a period of six months to put the post in operating condition, and daily detachments of at least six men would be required. In addition, the detachment of at least 10 more men would be necessary for daily routine in guard and other duties. In view of this personnel requirement, Foulois requested that the enlisted strength be increased from 83 to 100 (his authorized strength was 129), and The Adjutant General ordered 17 men from the SCAS at San Diego to report to San Antonio.[32]

Experiments were conducted at the Aviation Center early in 1916. Tests were made of night flying equipment, furnished by Israel Ludlow and consisting of wing tip lights, a six-inch searchlight operated by a generator and a storage battery, with an automatic cut-out switch to prevent the battery from discharging through the generator when the speed was insufficient to generate over 18 volts. Ludlow mentioned in one of his letters that highly satisfactory tests were made of an electric glove warmer, the current being supplied by a Sperry fan-driven dynamo like that furnished with the searchlight. He also mentioned that a telephoto camera, in which the shutter was tripped and the film advanced one frame by a single pull of a cord, was ready for demonstration. However, Signal Corps files do not mention any action on either the glove warmer or the camera.[33]

RESERVE CORPS EXPANSION

By October 1916 Aviation Section development plans included 24 squadrons—7 for the Regular Army, 12 for National Guard divisions, and 5 for coastal defense, with balloon units for the field and coast artillery. Aero squadrons of 12 airplanes each were approved; the tables of organization provided for each squadron 3 companies with 45 men and 4 machines each, and a squadron headquarters consisting of 14 members.

Also contemplated in the plans was the organization of the new Signal Reserve Corps provided for in the National Defense Act of 3 June 1916. The authorized strength of the Signal Officers Reserve Corps was 296 and the Enlisted Reserve Corps, 2,000. The personnel was to be made up from the regular Reserve Corps and the National Guard. The flying schools recently established at Chicago and Mineola were to be utilized for training the Reserve groups after preliminary training had been given in civilian schools.

National Guard officers and enlisted men could also be detailed to the Signal Corps Aviation schools, and those who desired air training could apply to their state adjutant general, who would forward their applications to the Chief of the Militia Bureau in Washington. On approval by the Bureau, orders were requested from The Adjutant

General of the Army assigning the applicants to duty at the aviation schools; there they were required to pass the prescribed physical and mental examinations.

A similar procedure was followed by those who wished to enter the Signal Officers Reserve Corps. Citizens between 21 and 30 years of age applied to The Adjutant General, stating the grade desired, previous military experience, and educational qualification; they included in the application, letters of recommendation as well as names of persons knowing the applicant. The candidate then appeared before an examining board and was given the same physical examination required for air officers of the Regular Army. The applicant was not given a mental examination but the equivalent of a college education was required. Flying ability was the first consideration and no applicant for commission was to be considered proficient until he was able to pass the flying test for Reserve Military Aviator (RMA) unless especially excepted by the chief of the Aviation Section. The recommendation of the board passed through the chief of the Aviation Section to The Adjutant General. If the candidate was approved he would be commissioned for five years with a possibility of being recommissioned for successive periods of five years each. In time of actual or threatened hostilities officers of the SORC were subject to such duty as the President might prescribe. The officer in charge of the Aviation Section, when authorized by the Secretary of War, might order Reserve officers to duty for a period of not more than 15 days a year, during which period the Reserve Officer would receive the same pay and allowances as an officer of the same rank in the Regular Army. With the consent of the Reserve Officer he might be retained on active duty for such period as the Secretary of War might prescribe.[34]

In order to become a Reserve flying officer, a citizen between 21 and 27 years of age could apply to the officer in charge of the Aviation Section. He then had to meet the conditions which applied to the SORC and state in writing that if he successfully passed his aviation tests he would become an officer in the Aviation Section, SORC. If he passed the board, he was then designated an aviation student and could either attend a flying course as a civilian at his own expense or he could enlist in the Aviation Section, SERC, be made a non-commissioned officer, and be placed on active duty up to the time his course was finished; then he would be discharged to accept a commission in the SORC.[35]

Applicants for commissions as reserve officers who held Aero Club of America (FAI) certificates, after passing the physical examination, were given a flying examination embodying at least the requirements of the preliminary flying test. If the applicant passed this test and was otherwise qualified, he was eligible for further instruction necessary to qualify him as a RMA. If the candidate passed the RMA examination and met the other requirements, he was commissioned in the AS, SORC.[36]

The preliminary flying test consisted of making three figure 8's around pylons 1,600 feet apart, with turns limited to a radius of 800 feet; accomplishing a dead-engine landing from 300 feet and stopping within 150 feet of a previously designated point; making an altitude flight to at least 1,000 feet; and gliding with engine throttled, changing direction of 90° to right and left. Students were encouraged to take the Aero Club of America test for an FAI certificate. The requirements for the Reserve Military Aviator test were: climbing to 500 feet from a 2,000-foot square field, keeping within the area above the field; gliding at normal angles with engine throttled, executing spirals to right and left, and changing direction in gliding; killing the engine at 1,000 feet and landing within 200 feet of a previously designated point; landing over an assumed obstacle 10 feet high and stopping within 1,500 feet; making a cross-country triangular flight of 30 miles, passing over 2 previously designated points, at a minimum of 2,500 feet altitude; making a straightaway cross-country flight of 30 miles at an altitude of 2,500 feet and landing at a designated destination; and flying 45 minutes at 4,000 feet.[37]

Citizens, or those who had declared their intention to become citizens, between the ages of 18 and 45, who could pass the physical examination, speak, read, and write English, and prove good character could enlist in the Aviation Section SERC for four years. Men qualified as aviators, balloonists, or mechanics experienced in the construction and repair of airplanes and engines, were particularly desirable. Candidates had to have a working knowledge of gasoline engines and their accessories and of telegraphy, a fair knowl-

edge of the principles of electricity and photography, and be interested in all these fields. After enlisting, the candidate received a certificate issued by The Adjutant General; the holder could be ordered to active service for instruction not to exceed 15 days a year, or with his consent he could be placed on active duty for such extended period as might be necessary.[38]

BALLOONS AND ZEPPELINS

Although military planners emphasized the heavier-than-air machine, lighter-than-air activities were not neglected. Ballooning had been eliminated as a service activity during the years after 1913, but by 1916 attention was again focused on this method of flying. An aerostatic division was established in the Aviation Section, and a balloon school was to be opened at Fort Omaha where the large airship shed, hydrogen gas plant, and other equipment used from 1908 to 1913 still remained. Captive balloon units were to be equipped as soon as practicable and instruction with airships was to be inaugurated.[39]

Capt. Frederick B. Hennessy of the Field Artillery and a former pilot observed a test of a new Goodyear kite balloon on 19 May 1916 at Cleveland, Ohio. Spanish and Portuguese officers who had been designated by their governments to purchase war supplies were also present. Captain Hennessy reported that the kite balloon was a great improvement over the Drachen model formerly purchased by the Signal Corps, and suggested that each Field Artillery battalion should have at least one kite balloon to be manned by experienced field artillery officers acting as pilots and observers. Since the School of Fire for Field Artillery had been suspended on account of the Mexican situation, Hennessy recommended the immediate purchase of two Goodyear kite balloons at $4,000 each, to be used for experimental purposes at Fort Sam Houston. On 29 May, a board, composed of Capt. V. E. Clark, Lt. T. D. Milling, and Lt. B. Q. Jones, approved Hennessy's recommendation. The two balloons with spare parts were to be under the control of Capt. F. P. Lahm, who was to work with the 3d Regiment, Field Atrillery, at Fort Sam Houston; Hennessy was to be attached for temporary duty as his assistant.[40] No record has been found of the actual purchase of these balloons or of their delivery to Fort Sam Houston, but there were two kite balloons at the Fort Omaha balloon school in 1917 and these may have been the ones bought for Fort Sam Houston.

On 11 November 1916, Capt. Charles deF. Chandler, an ex-balloonist, was relieved as Director of the Signal Corps School at Fort Leavenworth and was ordered to Fort Omaha via Washington to establish a balloon school. He arrived at the Fort on 16 November; on 20 December the organization was designated the "U.S. Army Balloon School." A four-month course of training in operating captive and free balloons was to be given. Physical requirements were the same as those for aviation students, but there were no limitations as to age or rank. Officers who completed the course and qualified as balloon pilots were to be detailed to the Aviation Section until a sufficient number had been secured to permit balloon companies to be formed, while other graduates were to be returned to their regiments for future assignment to the balloon service when required. Graduates considered best qualified would be assigned to developing airships for the military service.[41]

At the end of January 1917, there were at the balloon school 93 enlisted men and 6 officers, the latter assigned as follows:

Capt. C. deF. Chandler, S.C., Commanding
Capt. David H. Bower, S.C., Commanding Officer of the detachment, post adjutant, and summary court officer
Capt. Howard White, P.S., Ret., QM, Ordnance, and Police Officer, Fire Marshal
1st Lt. Lewis C. Davidson, Inf., Student
1st Lt. Paul H. Ellis, MRC, post surgeon, recruiting officer
1st Lt. Aaron F. Eidemiller, dental surgeon

Chandler was relieved for duty in Washington and left Fort Omaha on 5 April 1917. He was succeeded by Capt. H. J. B. McElgin who served until 24 May when Captain Lahm (the only airplane, dirigible, and balloon pilot in the Army) arrived and took command. Captain Bower was not shown as a student on the post returns for this period, but he was on flying status from February, was awarded FAI balloon certificate No. 62, and was rated Junior Military Aeronaut on 24 July 1917. Lieutenant Davidson was relieved on 11 January 1917, after obtaining FAI balloon certificate No. 56. Lieutenant Eidemiller was on detached service at Fort Leavenworth from 19 March. In March and April the following officers joined the balloon school: Capts. H. J. B. McElgin, CAC, James Prentice, CAC, Harold Geiger, CAC, Harry R. Vaughan, CAC, H. LeR. Muller, CAC, and 1st Lts. John H. Jouett, CAC, Byron B. Daggett, SORC, and Arthur Boettcher, Inf. Captain McElgin was awarded FAI balloon pilot certificate No. 57. Captain Prentice received balloon pilot certificate No. 58 and was rated JM Aeronaut on 24 July 1917. Captain Geiger, who was already an airplane pilot and one of the 24 original Military Aviators, did not get any rating on lighter-than-aircraft. Capt. Vaughan received balloon pilot certificate No. 59. Capt. Muller, also an airplane pilot, received FAI balloon pilot certificate No. 60. Lieutenants Jouett, Daggett, and Boettcher received, respectively, balloon pilot certificates Nos. 61, 63, and 65. Jouett and Boettcher also became Junior Military Aeronauts on 24 July 1917.[42]

By March 1917 two kite and two spherical balloons had been delivered at Fort Omaha. Leo Stevens, the well-known civilian balloonist, had been hired as an instructor, and recommendations had been made for the detail of 20 or more junior officers. In the meantime, Stevens was proceeding with the schooling of enlisted men in the operation of free and captive balloons. Besides the fixed equipment of the school (including a hydrogen gas generating plant), field equipment, among which were transport vehicles and mobile gas-charging outfits, was gradually being assembled. Some difficulty was experienced over flying pay, but the Judge Advocate General ruled that student officers at the balloon school would receive the same pay as aviation students; however, the law required that the student be on duty and participate regularly and frequently in aerial flights.[43]

The rigid lighter-than-air ship was another development that interested aviation planners during 1916. The use of the Zeppelin in the European war was closely observed by American Army and Navy officers, especially after these airships were used to bomb England. In October 1916 Lieutenant Colonel Squier raised the problem of whether the Army or Navy or both should have control over the operation of dirigibles in the United States, although the United States had owned only one dirigible, bought in 1908 and long since demolished. After opinions were expressed and discussions had taken place it was finally decided that the development of the Zeppelin should probably be undertaken by the Navy, while the aviation service of the Army would specialize in heavier-than-air machines and captive balloons. However, a joint board of Army and Navy officers was appointed to make the final decision and work out the details. This board, composed of three Navy officers and three Army officers (one of whom was Squier), was later known as the Joint Army and Navy Board on Aeronautic Cognizance, and in 1919 it became the Aeronautical Board. The original board recommended that the Navy start construction of a Zeppelin under the direction of the Chief Constructor of the Navy. The problems involved in this project would be worked out by a joint technical board of officers from both the Army and the Navy. Expenses were to be borne jointly by the two services.* The joint technical board, later known as the Joint Army and Navy Airship Board, consisted of three Navy members in addition to Chief Constructor D. W. Taylor: Lt. J. H. Towers, Lt. W. G. Child, and Asst. Naval Constructor J. C. Hunsaker. The three Army members of the board were Brig. Gen. G. O. Squier, Capt. C. deF. Chandler, and Capt. V. E. Clark. On 19 March 1917, Major Foulois succeeded Captain Chandler and on 12 December Col. H. H. Arnold and Maj. J. C. McCoy were put on the board, apparently relieving Foulois and Clark.[44]

DIVISION OF AUTHORITY

On 27 October 1916 the Office of Naval Operations suggested to the Secretary of the Navy a division of Army-Navy air responsibility. Under this plan the Navy would have jurisdiction over all aircraft operating in conjunction with fleets, all aircraft operating from shore bases for over-sea scouting, and all aircraft for antiaircraft defense of public works of the naval establishment, except those in the immediate vicinity of fortifications and other places requiring protection, irrespective of the naval public works in the immediate vicinity. The Army would be given the responsibility for all aircraft operating in conjunction with the mobile army, all aircraft required for spotting coast defense guns, and all aircraft required for antiaircraft defense of fortifications. All airships for over-sea work were to be provided by the Navy; if they were needed for overland

work, the Joint Airship Board would decide the allocation. Although its study on interservice policy did not appear until 12 March 1917, the Joint Army and Navy Board on Aeronautic Cognizance concurred in these divisions of authority.[45]

SUMMARY

In November 1916 Secretary of War Baker's review of the progress in Army aeronautics revealed an interesting summary of developments. The number of authorized personnel had been increased from 60 officers and 260 men in June 1916 to 77 officers and 1,800 men for 1917. A technical board of officers and civilian engineers had made a study of the airplane industry to learn the productive capacity of the manufacturers, to insure the best equipment possible, and to improve and develop the general design of airplanes. The Signal Corps had established specifications for different types of planes, endeavoring to incorporate in them the military requirements and the lessons in design learned from actual field experience in the European war. Improved power plants, bombs, sights, cameras, machine gun mounts, automatic control devices, navigation instruments and accessories had been produced. A radio set that transmitted messages 140 miles had been developed. Many of these developments had been made possible by the War Department's policy of obtaining assistance from the best civilian specialists in the country. Material assistance had been received from the National Advisory Committee for Aeronautics, the Bureau of Standards, and the American Society of Automotive Engineers. Orders had been placed for reconnaissance, combat, and pursuit planes as well as trainers, seaplanes, and balloons. Schools had been set up and a base for advanced instruction and equipment of land squadrons had been established at San Antonio. As a result of training at these schools, 23 officers had been qualified as Junior Military Aviators after 20 May 1916; 22 of these were Regular Army officers who had qualified at San Diego, the other was a National Guard officer who had qualified at Mineola, New York. Seven Reserve Military Aviators had qualified—3 National Guard officers at Mineola and 4 civilians. In November 62 students were receiving instruction—38 Regular Army Officers at San Diego, 16 National Guard officers at Mineola, 1 National Guard officer and 7 civilians at Chicago.[46]

---

*The Navy did buy a dirigible but there is no record that the Army bore any of the expense. The Army did not buy its second dirigible until after World War I.

By December 1916, a month after Secretary Baker's review, seven Regular Army air squadrons either had been established or were to be organized. The 1st Aero Squadron, which by that time had its full complement of men and planes, was at Columbus, New Mexico. The 1st Company of the 2d Aero Squadron was in Manila and personnel was being collected for the 2d Company also to be stationed in the Philippines. Materiel and equipment for the 3d Aero Squadron were being organized for San Antonio; its enlisted personnel was practically complete, materiel had been ordered, and officers and pilots had been assigned. Immediately upon completion of the 3d Squadron, the 4th and 5th Aero Squadrons were to be organized for San Antonio; the enlisted personnel already were being gathered, officers trained, and materiel ordered. The 6th Aero Squadron was to be organized for Fort Kamehameha, Honolulu, Hawaii, and the 7th for Panama; for each squadron a commander and supply officer had been designated, materiel had been ordered, and enlisted personnel were being selected.

By 6 April 1917, new planes had been ordered for assignment to the San Antonio school and to overseas bases. Three Curtiss JN4's and nine Wright-Martin land reconnaissance planes were to go to San Antonio; two Martin seaplanes were to supplement the four already at Manila; and four Curtiss N9 seaplanes had been ordered— two each to be assigned to Honolulu and Panama.[47]

In the fall of 1916 the War Department had purchased about 700 acres of land on lower Chesapeake Bay near Fort Monroe for an aviation field. The sum of $290,000 was paid for the land from money appropriated by Congress for this purpose. Officials estimated that $1,500,000 would be requested of Congress for buildings and equipment. The tract, located between Back River and Hampton, Virginia, was flat and possessed all the characteristics necessary for a first class airfield. The wisdom of this purchase and the subsequent expenditures were fully justified when this station, later named Langley Field, became one of the major proving grounds for the air arm. By 6 April 1917, four seaplanes had been delivered there and four more were on order.[48]

The reorganization that had taken place in the Aviation Section had improved the Section considerably. The War Department had put the best men available in charge of the section and its components. Brigadier General Squier, who had drawn up the specification for the Army's first airplane, had been recalled from his position as Military Attache in London, where he had had the opportunity to see and study the development of English and French aircraft in wartime, the difficulties they experienced, and the successes they attained. As head of the Aviation Section, Squier was in a position to use the knowledge of organization he had gained in establishing the first Signal Corps school at Fort Leavenworth. Major William Mitchell, who had assisted Squier in organizing the first Signal Corps school at Leavenworth, was his assistant in the Aviation Section. Mitchell had been an instructor in the Infantry and Cavalry School, the Signal School, and the Staff College at Leavenworth. He was a graduate of the Army School of the Line and the United States Army Staff College. He had served in Cuba as Chief Signal Officer in the Spanish American War and on the staff of General MacArthur during the Philippine Insurrection, had visited and studied the armies of Europe, Japan, and China, and had been in charge of running the government telegraph lines through Alaska. As a member of the General Staff in Washington, he had, for the past three years, handled all aviation information from Europe. Another important aviation officer was Capt. V. E. Clark, who served as a member of the Aviation Section's Technical Aero Advisory and Inspection Board. Clark was a graduate of the Naval Academy and the Army's first graduate in aerodynamics from the Massachusetts Institute of Technology. He had been an instructor in the Signal Corps Aviation School, and was one of the leading designers of aircraft in the country. Associated with him on the board was Capt. T. D. Milling, one of the pioneer fliers in the United States, who held many aviation records and was an authority on various types of machines, and controls, and on the employment of planes for military purposes. Lt. Henry W. Harms, also a graduate of MIT, an excellent flier, particularly qualified in aero construction and materials, later was assigned to serve on the board with Clark and Milling.

A number of civilian industrialists and experts had also been called on to work with the Aviation Section, some on a full time basis and others in a strictly advisory capacity. Among these were S. G. Averill, outstanding consulting motor engineer; H. I. Pope of the Pope Manufacturing Company; Henry Souther, pioneer motor engineer; Howard Coffin, prominent motor car expert and manager of Firestone Tire and Rubber Company of Michigan; and Dr. Jerome Hunsaker, employee of the Navy and one of the country's greatest authorities on aerodynamics.[49]

As a result of the formation of the Aviation Section's Technical Aero Advisory and Inspection Board and its attention to all aspects of flying techniques, airplanes, and personnel, Army flying was becoming increasingly safer. From 1 January to 26 December 1916, 6,087 flights had been made, with a total of 3,356 hours in the air and 251,775 miles flown—and there were no fatalities. This safety record was perhaps due

in part to the vastly improved equipment purchased by the government. A total of 149 airplanes had been received between 1909 and the end of 1916; 90 of these were late models which were delivered during 1916.* Colonel Squier attributed the excellent record largely to the Technical Aero Advisory and Inspection Board's inspection department, which was under the supervision of Henry Souther and Capt. L. E. Goodier, Jr., Ret., and consisted of men distributed among all the airplane factories. These men saw to it that government contracts were filled with only the best material, and that the finished product met government specifications.[50]

---

*These figures do not agree with those of Mixter and Emmons, *Aircraft Production Facts,* p. 5. They state that a total of 142 airplanes were received after 1909, 83 of which were delivered in 1916. The author's figures are explained in the last chapter.

———★———

CHAPTER IX

The 1st Squadron With Pershing's Punitive Expedition, 1916

ON 9 MARCH 1916, Francisco (Pancho) Villa, the Mexican revolutionary outlaw, with a force of from 500 to 1,000 men, crossed the international border and raided Columbus, New Mexico, killing 17 Americans. The outlaws were temporarily chased back into Mexico by the United States Cavalry. On 10 March, Brig. Gen. John J. Pershing was directed to organize a force to protect the border, and the 1st Aero Squadron was ordered to Columbus, New Mexico, for duty with Pershing's punitive expedition.[1]

Available records do not spell out the mission of the 1st Aero Squadron as a part of General Pershing's command. It can be deduced, however, from the activities of the squadron south of the border, that the intention was to use the airplanes primarily for observation, both of enemy forces and of advance parties of the expedition, for the carrying of mail and dispatches, and for aerial photography. The request for a bombsight and the ordering of bombs indicate that bombing was contemplated, and the fact that the planes were equipped with machine guns suggests that aerial combat or strafing of enemy ground troops—or both—may have been included in the mission. And, despite the indifferent success the Squadron had had at Fort Sill, it may have been intended to use the planes also for directing artillery fire.

Leaving Lieutenant Harry Gantz in charge of the new air center at Fort Sam Houston,* the squadron left San Antonio on 13 March 1916 and arrived in Columbus, New Mexico two days later. The officers of the 1st Aero Squadron who

moved to Columbus at this time were:[2] Capts. B. D. Foulois, C. O., and T. F. Dodd; 1st Lts. C. G. Chapman, J. E. Carberry, H. A. Dargue, T. S. Bowen, R. H. Willis, Jr., W. G. Kilner, E. S. Gorrell, A. R. Christie, and I. A. Rader. Moving with the unit were 82 enlisted men, one civilian mechanic, Jacob Bailey, and two enlisted medical men. A medical officer, 1st Lt. S. S. Warren, and an additional hospital corpsman joined the squadron on 14 March at El Paso on its route of march. Equipment consisted of 8 Curtiss JN3's (SC Nos. 41 through 45, 48, 52, and 53), 10 trucks and 1 automobile. With the addition of two trucks, which were received from the depot quartermaster at El Paso en route to Columbus, the squadron had about 50 per cent of its necessary motorized transportation. The airplane equipment was assembled immediately after arrival, and the squadron transportation was turned over to the Quartermaster of the Punitive Expedition for hauling supplies to troops in Mexico.[3]

During the period of the 1st Aero Squadron's duty in Mexico and on the border men were transferred in and out of the organization. Several additional officers and enlisted men were added to the rolls of the squadron between March and May 1916: Capt. John F. Curry and Lieutenants B. Q. Jones, H. W. Harms, Ralph Royce, and Roy S. Brown; with the additional enlisted men, the unit had a total of 16 officers and 122 men on the rolls in May. In June four more officers were added: Lieutenants B. M. Atkinson, H. S. Martin, John B. Brooks, and Carl Spaatz. From July to the end of December 1916, the following officers were transferred to the 1st Aero Squadron: 1st Lts. John C. Walker, P. L. Ferron, J. D. von

---

*Lieutenant Gantz was transferred to the SCAS at San Diego in April. The air center seems to have been abandoned later in the year and funds allotted for its completion were diverted in Mineola.

Holtzendorff, George E. Lovell; 2d Lts. G. E. A. Reinburg, John W. Butts, S. H. Wheeler, L. G. Heffernan, Davenport Johnson, M. F. Harmon, C. W. Russell, and Maxwell Kirby.

The December 1916 return of the 1st Aero Squadron at Columbus, New Mexico, showed 23 officers with Captain Dodd commanding. A number of the men carried on the rolls were actually on detached service. Lieutenants Jones and Harms were at MIT and neither saw duty in Mexico with the 1st Aero Squadron. Captain Foulois was on sick leave from 2 September 1916; at the expiration of his leave he was appointed Aviation Officer, Southern Department. Lieutenant Willis was in Washington from 30 September. Lieutenant Gorrell left on 21 September for Washington and MIT; on the same day Lieutenant Rader left for Washington and Mineola. Lieutenant Chapman was ordered to Washington on 13 October. Lieutenant Carberry was on detached service at Mineola from July on. Lieutenants Atkinson and Spaatz were on leave of absence in November 1916 and were transferred to the 3d Aero Squadron on 1 December 1916. Lieutenants Kilner and Martin were relieved and assigned to duty at Mineola in August 1916. Lieutenant Christie was relieved and assigned to Chicago for aviation duty in August 1916.[4]

The 1st Aero Squadron was the first United States tactical air unit to be put in the field. It was in for a rough time. Its planes had been in service for many months and were not in the best condition to engage in combat operations. Furthermore they had not been built for the conditions they were to encounter in Mexico, such as high altitudes (up to 12,000 feet), the comparatively great distances to be flown, and the lack of cultivated areas and resources in general, which made the theater a difficult one in which to operate.[5]

The first reconnaissance flight into Mexico from Columbus was made on 16 March 1916 by Captain Dodd, with Captain Foulois as his observer, in S. C. No. 44. Apparently no further flying other than test flights was done at Columbus. However, the engineer section of the squadron found plenty to do. Twenty-seven Jeffrey truck chassis and an equal number of knocked-down escort wagon bodies had arrived at Columbus for the QMC. Since the QMC had neither the men nor materials to assemble this equipment, the squadron's engineer section with its portable machine shop took over and made the 54 assemblies in 4 days and nights.[6] Half of the enlisted personnel remained at Columbus to do this job while the rest moved, on 19 and 20 March, to Casas Grandes, Mexico; meanwhile, a base was established at Colonia Dublan for immediate operations. The eight planes started the flight to Casas Grandes, but one had to return for engine adjustment, four landed at Las Ascencion, Mexico, because of darkness; and the other three became separated in the night and landed at Ojo Caliente, Janos, and Pearson, Mexico. On the 20th, the four planes which had landed at Las Ascencion, the one which had returned to Columbus, and the one which had landed at Janos, all arrived at Casas Grandes. Lieutenant Willis had damaged his plane No. 41 so badly in landing at Pearson that he abandoned it and walked to Casas Grandes. Lieutenant Gorrell lost his way and when he landed found that he had a leak in his gasoline tank. Several days later near Ojo Caliente Gorrell encountered an Infantry motor truck convoy, obtained fuel from them, and flew on to Casas Grandes. On the 22d a detachment sent to salvage serviceable parts of Willis' wrecked plane turned back after being fired upon by Mexicans near Pearson, but a few days later a second detachment was able to recover the usable parts.

On 20 March Dodd with Foulois as observer in No. 44 reconnoitered south from Casas Grandes toward Cumbre Pass in the heart of the Sierra Madre mountains in an effort to locate troops moving south toward Lake Babicora. Twenty-five miles out they ran into whirlwinds and terrific down drafts which prevented their gaining sufficient altitude to cross the 10,000 foot mountains; hence, they returned to base. On the same day a whirlwind caught Lieutenant Bowen while he was landing No. 48 and demolished the plane; Bowen suffered a broken nose and other minor injuries. This accident and that of Willis in No. 41 left only six airplanes in commission.[8]

On the 21st Dodd and Foulois located Colonel Irwin's troops, and six truckloads of supplies were sent to the column. On the 22d, Lieutenants Kilner and Rader in one plane and Lieutenant Carberry in a second carried out orders to communicate with Colonel G. A. Dodd's command in the Galeana Valley. On the same day Captain Dodd and Lieutenant Christie, flying together, and Lieutenant

Chapman flying alone tried to locate United States troops moving south on the Mexican Northwestern railroad. They flew as far as the northern end of the Cumbre Pass tunnel, but terrific vertical air currents and whirlwinds which drove their planes down to within twenty feet of the treetops forced them to return to Dublan. On 23 March Christie, Carberry, and Chapman located Colonel Dodd's troops at El Valle, as ordered; but they were not able to return to Dublan until 25 March because of high winds, dust, and snow storms. From 27 March through 31 March about twenty flights were made with mail and dispatches, during which the fliers encountered severe rain, hail, and snow storms, which caused several forced landings away from the base at Colonia Dublan.[9]

Because of the difficulties encountered in mountain flying with the JN's, Foulois on 22 March had sent a memo to General Pershing requesting the purchase of 10 new airplanes with spare motors and parts from 5 companies. He asked that the order be placed by telegraph and that immediate delivery by express be specified, with all planes to be completely equipped and ready for immediate use. On 30 March Foulois again appealed for 10 of the highest powered, highest climbing, and best weight-carrying airplanes that could be purchased in the United States.[10]

By the end of March it was obvious that the squadron's six planes were incapable of performing effectively the tasks which they were expected to perform. Their low-powered motors and limited climbing ability with the necessary military load made it impossible to operate them safely in the vicinity of the mountains. These same limitations prohibited operating the machines for more than a few hours each day.[11] The dry atmosphere of the mountains was hard on the wooden propellers; the layers came apart and the wood warped.* In an effort to save the propellers, the 1st Aero Squadron adopted a new policy. As soon as a machine returned to its base the propeller was removed and placed in a humidor to preserve the viscosity of the glue holding together the laminations; another propeller was taken out and attached to each machine when it

was ready to fly again. Despite the efforts of all the commissioned and enlisted personnel the planes could not be made to meet the military needs.[12]

On 30 March Foulois suggested to the Chief of Staff of the Punitive Expedition four plans of operation for the most effective use of the squadron's six airplanes. One of the plans presented was approved and put into effect on 1 April. It provided for the establishment of effective radio-telegraph communications between Namiquipa and Casas Grandes, thus doing away with the need for using planes on this dangerous route; in the meantime the use of airplanes between these two points would be discontinued except in emergencies. Air communication would continue between Namiquipa and El Valle, if radio-telegraph, motorcycles, or other means failed. All available airplanes would be concentrated at Namiquipa for daily communication between this point and advanced troops to the south. Pursuant to this plan, from 1 through 4 April 19, 43 flights were made with mail and dispatches although rain, hail, and snow forced numerous landings at intermediate points.[13]

On 3 April the New York *World* published an article written by Mr. Utrecht, a correspondent at the headquarters of the Punitive Expedition. The article severely criticized the equipment of the 1st Aero Squadron; at the same time it appealed for planes capable of carrying a greater useful load, with more power and with better stability at high altitudes. In presenting his criticisms Utrecht quoted the squadron's flying officers by name. To Foulois he attributed a statement that the pilots risked their lives ten times a day but were not given the equipment they needed to do their work with a minimum of risk. Dargue was quoted as saying: "It is nothing short of criminal to send the aviators up under such conditions as we are meeting here." The story cited the failure to negotiate Cumbre Pass and described the hazardous flights; it reported that two of the flying machines were already condemned; and it stated that the officers blamed Washington for their difficulties. After the article appeared there was an investigation, at which Foulois denied having made the statements attributed to him. About the only concrete result of the affair was that Utrecht's pass was taken away when it was found that he had not submitted the article to censorship.[14]

---

*Every effort was made to correct the trouble: engineering talent was enlisted from all over the country; a propeller factory operated by three Curtiss company civilian employees was set up in Columbus in June 1916; authority was given to prosecute the development of metal propellers and steps were taken to acquire samples of the best foreign models.

On 5 April the squadron headquarters was moved to San Geronimo and further mail and dispatch flights were carried out. During the course of these missions No. 44 was badly damaged in a landing at San Geronimo; the serviceable parts were salvaged but the rest of the plane was condemned and destroyed, leaving five planes in service.[15]

On 7 April 1916 Dargue with Foulois as observer and Carberry with Dodd as observer flew from San Geronimo to Chihuahua City, Mexico, with duplicate dispatches for the United States consul, Marion H. Letcher. By prior arrangement, Dargue and Foulois landed south of the city, while Carberry and Dodd came down to the north. Dargue was then directed to join the other plane, but as he started to take off four mounted rurales opened fire on his machine. Foulois, who had started into town, heard the firing, returned, and stopped the rurales. He was then arrested and taken to the city jail, followed by a mob of several hundred men and boys. Word of his predicament was taken to Letcher by an American bystander. After considerable delay at the jail, Foulois was able to contact Colonel Miranda, chief of staff under General Gutierrez, military governor of Chihuahua. Miranda took Foulois to see the general, who immediately ordered his release. In the meantime, Dodd had gone to the consul with the dispatches. During his absence, natives and Carranzistas surrounded the Dargue and Carberry machines, made insulting remarks, burned holes in the wings of Dargue's plane with cigarettes, slashed the fabric with knives and removed bolts and nuts from both planes. Carberry managed to take off before too much damage was done and flew to an American smelter about six miles away. Dargue got away in the midst of a shower of stones, but had flown only a short distance when the top section of the plane's fuselage blew off, damaging the stabilizer, and forcing an immediate landing. Dargue was able to stand off the crowd until the arrival of a Mexican guard ordered by General Gutierrez. Repairs were made, and on the following day the two flyers, taking off from Chihuahua at 0530 to avoid the threatening crowds, returned to Geronimo.[16]

The squadron headquarters was moved to San Antonio, Mexico, on 8 April. From the 9th through the 13th routine flights were made. On 10 April the squadron was ordered to move to Satevo, Mexico. En route the squadron's truck train was fired on by a band of Villa's men at Cienagas. On the 11th Dargue with Gorrell as his observer flew from San Antonio, Mexico to Columbus, New Mexico, a distance of 315 miles, with only one stop, at Dublan. During a reconnaissance flight from the new base at Satevo, Lieutenant Chapman landed at Santa Rosalia, where he was seized by Carranza troops and carried to the commanding officer of the Carranza garrison. He was finally released, but while he was away from the plane, Mexican soldiers stole his field glasses, goggles, and a considerable amount of ammunition.

On a flight to Chihuahua on the 13th of April, Foulois received the first news of the engagement of United States troops at Parral. He got from the consul the famous ultimatum of the Mexican military governor of Chihuahua that the American troops must be withdrawn. He also delivered General Pershing's reply, which stated in effect that Pershing took his orders from the President of the United States and would withdraw only when ordered to do so by the President or the Secretary of War. During this flight the wings of No. 45 were damaged but were replaced by those of No. 42; the latter then was condemned and destroyed, leaving only four planes in service.[17]

On 14 April 1916, Dargue and Gorrell made a reconnaissance flight to locate a reported large Carranza force. Although the force was not found, the flight set an unofficial American distance record for two persons of 315 miles. It started at Columbus, covered Boca Grande, Pulpit Pass, Oxaca Pass, Carretas, Janos, and Ascencion, and ended at Columbus. On the same day Lieutenant Rader damaged No. 52 while landing on rough ground in hostile country, near Ojito, 100 miles from the nearest base, and had to abandon the plane; thus only three planes were left in operation. Rader then joined Maj. Robert L. Howze's column, which he had been sent out to locate. On 15 April Dargue with Gorrell as observer flew from Columbus to Boca Grande, Pulpit Pass, Dublan, Namiquipa and Satevo, a distance of 415 miles with two stops. On 16 April the monthly return of the 1st Aero Squadron stated that members of the squadron had engaged in a skirmish with Mexican bandits at Cienagas, but there is no mention of any such conflict in Foulois' report. On 17 April suadron headquarters was moved to

Lt. H. A. Dargue guarding his plane, Signal Corps No. 43, at Chihuahua City, Mexico, April 1916

Namiquipa and routine flights were continued.[18]

On 19 April while on a reconnoitering and photographic mission from San Antonio, Mexico, to Chihuahua City, Dargue and Willis in No. 43 made a forced landing in the hills and wrecked the plane. Willis, who was pinned under the wreckage, suffered a severe scalp wound and badly bruised legs and ankles. The flyers burned what was left of their plane (starting a forest fire in the process), administered first aid to Willis' wounds, and set out to walk 65 miles to San Antonio, Mexico. They crossed two mountain ranges, keeping to the thickets and woods rather than using paths where they might be discovered. After two days and nights they arrived at San Antonio on the 21st. On the 23d they proceeded by automobile to Namiquipa and reported to General Pershing. A month later doctors discovered that Willis had walked the 65 miles with a broken ankle.[19]

In the meantime the situation in Europe and the border troubles had caused Congress to pass the urgent deficiency act of 31 March 1916, which gave $500,000 to the Aviation Section. From this appropriation much needed new equipment was purchased for the 1st Aero Squadron. On 5 April, the Technical Aero Advisory and Inspection Board recommended the purchase of 12 planes, all of the same type and same make with all contractors having an equal chance to obtain the contract, but they recommended using the Hall-Scott engine.[20]

Orders were received on 20 April for the squadron to return to Columbus to pick up the new airplanes which were awaiting them there. Of the eight planes taken into Mexico on 19 March, only two were still in commission—Nos. 45 and 53—and these were unsafe for further field service. They were flown to Columbus on the 20th and ultimately condemned and destroyed. The squadron personnel arrived at Columbus on 22 April; there they received four new Curtiss N8* airplanes (S.C. Nos. 60-63) delivered on the 19th. Foulois had not requested N8 planes and flight tests conducted from 23 to 29 April quickly demonstrated that these planes were unsuitable for Mexican field service. During the tests the *New York Times* published a story on the short-

comings of the Curtiss N8's. The article stated that the aviators were observing the rule against talking for publication but that they did not want to fly the four new machines, which were practically the same as those they had been using.[21] The *Times* story was sent to The Adjutant General by the Chief Signal Officer on 28 April with the observation that it spoke in a derogatory way of the equipment and that a casual reading of it might lead one to think that there was something vitally wrong with the manner in which the equipment had been purchased.

Whether the new Curtiss N8's were good, bad, or indifferent, the fact remained that they were the only planes immediately available. Lieutenant Jones, a member of the Technical Aero Advisory and Inspection Board, stated that they had a more efficient engine than the older planes in use in Mexico, that they met Signal Corps' specifications, and that the purchase of any machine had to be considered as an experiment until the plane had been tested in the country in which it was to be flown. Jones later recommended Sturtevant planes although he might have preferred Curtiss R2's but had not recommended buying the latter for three reasons: they could not be quickly delivered, they had not proved their value, and Glenn Curtiss would not recommend them. Later, through tests carried out by the Technical Aero Advisory and Inspection Board of the Signal Corps, the R2 with its 160-horsepower engine had been found most satisfactory by the board and was being purchased for the 1st Aero Squadron in place of the Sturtevants which Jones had recommended.[22]

On 27 April, the El Paso *Herald* published a story by Kent Allerton Hunter which criticized the airplanes and equipment of the 1st Aero Squadron. Hunter denied having received any of his information from the officers and said that the article was inspired by his own observations and impressions gained from having been at Columbus since the early days of the Expedition. Foulois denied that either he or any of his officers had given out the information on which either the *New York Times* or the El Paso *Herald* article was based. He stated that the only action he had taken was official and was contained in the proceedings of a board of officers which had condemned the machines. There was no representative of the *New York Times* at Columbus but there were

---

*The N8's were ordered as JN4's, duplicates of Curtiss' foreign planes, although they were not so called at this time. S.C. No. 63 appeared later at a JN4B.

many other sources of information, especially at El Paso, the distributing point on the border for all news agencies,. where there was no censorship. General Pershing's indorsement of 21 May on Foulois' report from Namiquipa read, "No criticism has ever been permitted by press correspondents with this expedition. They were given to understand from the beginning that nothing that savored of criticism of any department or branch of the army would be permitted to pass the censor."[23] He also stated that it was impossible to maintain strict censorship at Columbus when it was not enforced elsewhere. Pershing said that the officers of the 1st Aero Squadron might have carelessly expressed their disapproval of the machines but that they had "already too often risked their lives in old and often useless machines which they have patched up and worked over in an effort to do their share of the duty this expedition has been called upon to perform." He then testified to the devotion and fearlessness of all the officers of the squadron and said that the recommendations of these men in regard to planes purchased should carry weight because they were in a position to judge the planes' performance.[24]

On 1 May 1916 two Curtiss R2's arrived at Columbus, and by the 25th 12 of this type had been received. They were given Signal Corps numbers 64 through 75.* The Advisory and Inspection Board may have found the R2's satisfactory, but the pilots at Columbus certainly did not. During May, June, and July, there was constant trouble with defective propellers, engine parts, and faulty construction. Every plane required alterations and the replacement of various parts. Nevertheless, Brigadier General Squier reported that the squadron was fully equipped with suitable reconnaissance machines, the best that the country could produce; that the planes were equipped with all auxiliary parts including automatic Lewis machine guns, rifles, automatic cameras, incendiary bombs, destruction bombs, and wireless; and that, within reason, the base at Columbus was capable of repairing any faulty or damaged machine. He reported that the best engineers in the country had worked on the propeller problem and that no further trouble had been experienced.[25]

*No record of the delivery of Signal Corps plane No. 75 has been found, but 12 R2 planes were reported as received by 25 May 1916.

On 9 May 1916, a board of officers at Columbus recommended the condemnation of the old Curtiss N8's S.C. Nos. 60 through 63. The board, composed of Captain Dodd and Lieutenants Dargue, Carberry, and Chapman, declared that the N8's were lacking in proper control and were very slow in climbing with a military load, the landing gear was too weak and the wheels and shock absorbers were too light, the power was inadequate, and the speed too low. There were shortages of equipment and some of the material was found to be defective. These findings were based upon the statement of seven pilots who tested the machines and who stated that unless a great military emergency existed, they would not fly them. Foulois agreed with the board. Although the board had recommended condemnation of the planes they were sent to San Diego to be altered and then to be used there for training and experimental purposes.[26]

On 28 August Major Foulois reported on the operations of the 1st Aero Squadron for the period of 15 March to 15 August 1916. Five hundred and forty flights had been made in Mexico and the United States; they totaled 346 hours and covered 19,533 miles. In his report Foulois made the following suggestions, based on actual experience: that squadrons working in the field should have a convenient base fully equipped for reception, assembly, test, repairs, and alterations, from which all personnel, materiel, and supplies could be drawn, independent of field squadrons; that, since planes had to be ready for service when received, they should be tested under service conditions, in sand and rain, at locations of varying altitude, temperature, and humidity; and that a test station be set up at some point on the Mexican border.

In his report, Foulois also recounted the hardships which the squadron personnel had endured, and praised their performance. All officer pilots on duty with the command during its active service in Mexico, he said, were constantly exposed to personal risk and physical suffering. Because all airplanes of the time had little weight-carrying capability, it was impossible to carry sufficient food, water, or clothing on many of the reconnaissance flights. Pilots in flight were frequently caught in snow, rain, and hail storms which, because of inadequate clothing, invariably caused excessive suffering. Foulois commended the willing spirit shown by every officer in the command in performing this new and hazardous duty. He also commended the enlisted personnel who worked day and night to keep the airplanes in serviceable condition and who often used their time and technical skill to repair automobiles and trucks of the Quartermaster Corps, especially in the earlier days of the Expedition and later as they advanced into Mexico. The enlisted truck drivers, Foulois reported, had performed exceptionally hard service. Because of lack of sufficient motor transportation in the squadron, they were constantly called upon to perform double duty, not only in connection with aviation work, but also frequently in connection with the needs of the entire Expedition for transportation of supplies to advance troops.[27]

At the end of August, the 1st Aero Squadron, with the exception of two airplane sections with necessary personnel and equipment, which were located at division headquarters in Mexico, was still being held at Columbus, New Mexico to test 18 new airplanes. Twelve of these planes were Standard H2's: three planes (S.C. Nos. 76-78) were delivered at Columbus in November 1916, and the remaining nine (S.C. Nos. 85-93) were delivered at San Antonio, the first on 16 September and the remainder by 11 December 1916. In addition there were six Curtiss twin-engine planes (S.C. Nos. 102-107) delivered at Columbus by 20 September 1916. Other planes ordered and delivered at Columbus for the 1st Aero Squadron before 6 April 1917 were: two Martin land reconnaissance machines, S.C. Nos. 108 and 109; two Sturtevant S reconnaissance planes, S.C. Nos. 110 and 111; two LWF reconnaissance planes, S.C. Nos. 112 and 113; two Thomas D5 reconnaissance planes, S.C. Nos. 114 and 115; two Curtiss JN4's of a group of six ordered (S.C. Nos. 130-135), and nine of 16 Curtiss R2 and R4 planes ordered (S.C. Nos. 177-192)—those for Columbus being R2's. Counting the 4 Curtiss N8's, S.C. Nos. 60-63 and the 12 Curtiss R2's, S.C. Nos. 64-75, 51 planes were delivered at Columbus, New Mexico, between January and 6 April 1917.[28]

The first new twin engine Curtiss, was tested at Columbus in September 1916. The average speed of this new plane was 78.8 miles per hour with 2½ hours' fuel and a load of 290 pounds. The rate of climb was 3,400 feet in 14 minutes. The Curtiss-type control was exhausting to the operator and the plane was not adapted for field service in Mexico because of its lack of maneuverability on small fields. The engine mounting was considered dangerous and the plane was reported impracticable for rough air work over deserts and between mountains. However, its twin engines were regarded with favor, as this type of machine was thought to be more reliable and offered advantages that could not be obtained in a single engine machine. By 8 March 1917, Major Foulois reported that there were six of the planes stored at Fort Sam Houston, including the one tested at Columbus.[29]

During its stay at Columbus the squadron carried on extensive experiments with the Brock automatic camera, which was considered one of the most valuable adjuncts for use in aero-reconnaissance. The camera took a continuous string of pictures of the limited section of terrain over which the airplane traveled. These pictures when developed and fitted together provided a strip mosaic of the section traversed.[30]

On 26 May 1916 the squadron asked The Adjutant General for bombs and one Scott-Dodd bombsight.* The Commanding General of the Southern Department stated in his indorsement of the request that no better opportunity could exist for the trial and testing of this materiel than in connection with the activities of the 1st Aero Squadron on the border. The Chief of Ordnance advised that the Scott-Dodd device was unknown to his department and that the Signal Corps was unable to furnish drawings or a description. The arsenal was ordered to make 350 3-inch drop bombs; 100 of these were sent to the 1st Aero Squadron in July, and 240 more in November; the other 10 were never delivered. In September Captain Dodd requested 25 dummy bombs for target practive. Stating that it was impracticable to do accurate bomb dropping by hand, he asked that the drop bombs be changed so that they could be used in the carrier-and-release device then under consideration for use with airplanes. General Crozier of Ordnance replied that these bombs were not intended as standard for airplanes equipped with bomb-dropping devices, but had only been made up to meet a possible emergency. The 1st Aero Squadron also seemed to be proceeding on its own account in the matter of bombs, for a weekly report of the commanding

---

*This was the Riley Scott bombsight. See Chap. III, pp. 45 and 54.

general, Southern Department, dated 17 June 1916, mentioned that for the past four days the railroad shops at Piedras Negras had been engaged in manufacturing about 100 bombs a day. The squadron also had twelve Lewis automatic machine guns, which weighed only 27 pounds each and could be used from the shoulder. Ordnance instructed the personnel in how to use the Lewis guns and the bombs.[31]

Foulois had recommended to the Chief Signal Officer in June 1916, that the Aviation School at San Diego be supplied with one or more airplanes of the same type supplied to field organizations so that officers could be fully trained before they were transferred to the field organizations for duty. He felt that the 1st Aero Squadron was not equipped to handle training and during the emergency should not be required to perform what should be a function of the aviation school. At that time seven new officers who had been assigned to the squadron could not be allowed to fly the R2 planes until they had taken preliminary instruction. One squadron plane had to be set aside for this purpose. Apparently nothing was done about this recommendation, for new officers continued to arrive at Columbus without the proper training.[32]

On 24 July 1916, Foulois suggested to the Chief Signal Officer the following organization for a mobile aero squadron based on the experience of the officers of the 1st Aero Squadron in the preceding two years in garrison and in field service:

Headquarters Section
   1 Major, commanding
   1 Adjutant, flying
  17 Enlisted men
    Transportation
Supply Section
   1 Supply officer
   2 Assistant officers, flying (Supply, Transport)
  29 Enlisted
    Transportation
Engineer Section
   1 Engineer officer, flying
  20 Enlisted
Aeroplane Section
  12 Officers (includes all except Supply Officer)
  94 Enlisted
Total personnel
  18 Commissioned (12 Flying Officers)
 160 Enlisted
 178* Total personnel

*The personnel adds up as above but the original document gives 13 officers and 149 enlisted men under the total.

Transportation was to consist of 25 trucks, 24 trailers, 6 motorcycles, and 1 automobile; among the trucks were to be 1 kitchen, 1 fuel tank, and 4 machine shops.[33]

An aero squadron composed of 12 airplanes, organized as contemplated in the tables of organization, required maintenance of four separate offices, with all the necessary first sergeants, mess and supply sergeants, clerks, etc. Each company had to have its own muster and pay roll, as well as the necessary records to administer a complete unit. The suggested section organization eliminated all first sergeants, all supply sergeants but one, and put the entire squadron directly under the squadron commander's immediate jurisdiction, instead of having three company commanders.

The section organization had been in existence in the 1st Aero Squadron for nearly two years. Its first real test had come at Fort Sill in August 1915, when the squadron had been ordered to send two planes with personnel, equipment, and transportation to Brownsville without delay. Within four hours, two complete sections were loaded and ready to go, although the only order issued by the squadron commander was verbal, directing the chiefs of the sections selected to load immediately their respective sections. The section organization allowed for expansion and reduction without difficulty. The building up of an 8-plane squadron into a 12-plane squadron was effected without any trouble by adding four additional airplanes. Under the company organization this increase would have required the organization of a third company with all of its additional personnel and records. It was necessary to have a nonflying supply officer in the squadron with sufficient men to handle all supplies without having to call on the flying sections for help. On many occasions in Mexico, the supply officer, who was an aviator, was on reconnaissance for days at a time when his services as supply officer were urgently needed.[34]

During the time that Foulois was ill in September 1916, Captain Dodd had assumed command of the squadron. On 25 September Foulois was ordered to Washington for duty in the Office of the Chief Signal Officer, where he was put in charge of the Aviation Section. He was then ordered from Washington back to Fort Sam Houston as Aviation Officer of the Southern Department on 3

November 1916. In the meantime Dodd remained in command of the 1st Aero Squadron until he was relieved by Maj. Ralph Royce.[35]

Two more airplane sections of the 1st Aero Squadron were sent from Columbus on 29 September to join the two already in Mexico; they remained through January 1917*. The strength of the squadron in January 1917 was 17 officers and 128 enlisted men. By March 1917 experienced air officers were in demand for the schools at Chicago and Memphis. It was also considered desirable to have 10 experienced aviators, including Dodd, at San Antonio and 4 more were needed at Columbus. It was proposed to send 7 graduates from the San Diego school to Columbus. On 17 March 1917 Foulois recommended sending Brown to Chicago, Royce to Memphis, and McDonnell, Heffernan, Ferron, Wheeler, and Davidson to San Antonio, while Reinburg, Dunsworth, Lovell, and Kirby were to remain at Columbus.[36]

The accomplishments of the 1st Aero Squadron in Mexico—especially in the light of the

---

*Available evidence indicates that about this time flying over Mexico came to an end. However, the evidence is not final.

conditions under which those accomplishments were achieved—are by no means inconsiderable. Perhaps the best evidence that the Squadron's stay in Mexico was not the fiasco it is sometimes conceived to have been may be found in the message sent to Captain Dodd on 24 December 1916 as a Christmas greeting from General Pershing:

> Please accept for yourself and officers and men of the First Aero Squadron my very cordial greetings and sincere good wishes for the coming year. Please kindly extend my warmest thanks to your command for the faithful and efficient service it has performed as a part of this expedition.

During April and May of 1917, after the U.S. had entered World War I, new officers took an advanced course in flying and the squadron prepared for foreign service. In June and July it was reported as ready for foreign duty; no flying was done, but a course in infantry drill and rifle practice was pursued. On 5 August 1917, the 1st Aero Squadron left Columbus for Europe under command of Maj. Ralph Royce.[37]

———★———

CHAPTER X

Army Flying Training Schools, The National Guard and The Air Reserve

UP TO 1916 the Signal Corps school at San Diego had been adequate for the Aviation Section's flying training needs, but with larger appropriations available and with war threatening the need for other flying schools had become more and more evident. The first of these new schools to be organized was the aviation station at Mineola, Long Island. Later, as United States' involvement in the war seemed imminent, other flying schools were formed, so that by 6 April 1917 there were in existence five United States Army flying schools, located at San Diego; Mineola; Chicago; Memphis; and Essington, Pennsyvanila.

ARMY FLYING TRAINING SCHOOLS

Mineola, N. Y.

On 22 July 1916* the Signal Corps Aviation Station, †Mineola,** later Hazelhurst Field, was inaugurated as the Army's second flying school; 1st Lt. Joseph E. Carberry, who had been transferred from the 1st Aero Squadron, was made commanding officer.

Carberry's primary duty at Mineola was to evaluate flyers for duty with aero squadrons in the field. Orders had been requested for some 15 officers and enlisted men to report to him for duty. The personnel reporting would consist of officers and enlisted men of the organized militia—infantry, cavalry, and field artillery branches. He was

to assign them as he saw fit. He was authorized to hire civilian flyers at a salary of $150 per month in the same manner as the Quartermaster hired civilian scouts. These flyers, known as aero scouts, first had to complete a flying test, which was approximately that required for junior military aviators, and then Carberry had to state that each man who successfully completed the test was qualified. There is no record of any civilian being hired in this capacity. Carberry's duties were entirely independent of the organized militia of any state.[1]

When Carberry assumed control he had no staff. Facilities for airplane upkeep consisted of a group of outmoded hangars, relics of an earlier day of aviation. Aside from the 1st Aero Company, National Guard of New York, there were no military installations, personnel, or equipment under federal control at Mineola. The 1st Aero Company, which had been mustered into federal service on 13 July 1916, received immediate attention from Carberry, who appears to have been on duty prior to 22 July 1916,* for on 18 July he wired the Chief Signal Officer that the private funds of the company would be exhausted at the end of the week. Finally, in August, money was allotted for fuel and oil for the privately owned planes of the company. On 2 November 1916, after less than four months of service, the 1st Aero Company was mustered out of federal service. The 2d Aero Company of New York arrived from Buffalo on 24 July and went into camp, but it was never mustered into federal service and was not under Carberry's jurisdiction.

---

*Colonel Fletcher's Monograph No. 16, AWC, gives the date as 16 June 1916. Colonel Carberry stated in memo to E. L. Jones, 18 March 1951, that 22 July is the correct date.

†Colonel Carberry stated in a letter to E. L. Jones, dated 11 December 1944, that this was the official title of the station throughout his tenure of command. In subsequent War Dept. orders it was referred to as a Signal Corps Aviation School.

**See above, pp. 133, 157, and 164.

---

*Colonel Carberry states he was not at Mineola prior to 22 July 1916 (in a memo to E. L. Jones, 18 March 1951).

In July Carberry hired three civilians—one instructor, Overton Bounds, at $400 a month, and two mechanics, Charles Dauphin and Edwin C. Gorlitz at $125 a month. On 17 August Carberry reported that three flying instructors, seven aviation mechanics, and one inspector of planes and engines were essential to the work of the station, and he was authorized to employ them.[2] The first airplane on government order arrived at Mineola about 1 August 1916. From that time until 6 April 1917 a total of 40 planes was delivered to Mineola. Thirty-three of these were Curtiss JN4's; the other seven consisted of 2 Standard HS's, 2 Sturtevant pursuits, 2 Curtiss pursuits, and 1 Curtiss twin engine JN.[3]

It had been planned to train aviators at Mineola for duty on the Mexican border; but as the likelihood for active border service diminished, the plans were altered and instructions were given by the Aviation Section to train a class of 50 student aviators. A number of militia officers from other states were ordered to Mineola. They came into an understaffed and neglected station. Transportation difficulties were so pressing that Carberry finally slashed the red tape and purchased a Packard truck. He said that for a while it appeared likely that he would become the unwilling donor of this vehicle. Winter was at hand and the men were living in tents. When the weather became extremely cold, some of the personnel were housed in a hangar; the remainder slept in a building which had been used as an office. Bids for buildings were opened on 1 December but they were in excess of the estimate, and building prices were rising rapidly. The QMG, who had allotted $6,150 in November for temporary buildings for the school by diverting funds set aside for completion of the air center at Fort Sam Houston, now recommended that the additional amount necessary to cover the Mineola bids be allotted and if the work could not be done with this sum, suggested that the bids be rejected and that the government buy the material and hire labor for the building. An award was made in January 1917 for a mess hall and barracks and by the end of the month three additional buildings—a Quartermaster storehouse, NCO quarters, and a hospital—were under construction.[4]

On 11 August 1916 two Signal Corps officers were ordered to Mineola to assist Carberry—Lieutenant Walter G. Kilner, who became the officer in charge of training, and Lieutenant Harold S. Martin.* A month later Martin was ordered to MIT to take an engineering course. Capt. Wallace M. Craigie, retired, was made supply officer on 31 August 1916, but was relieved on 28 September. Lt. Ira A. Rader was ordered to Mineola on 19 September 1916. On 27 September 1916, in addition to his other duties, Carberry was designated Acting Aviation Officer, Eastern Department; however, he did not formally report as such until 22 November 1916.[5]

The officers stationed at the Mineola station on 25 September 1916 were divided into two categories. There were three Regular Army officers, Lieutenants Carberry, Kilner, and Rader, and 14 Militia officers:[6]

2d Lt. E. W. Bagnell, N.Y.; 1st Lt. E. G. Benson, N.Y.; 1st Lt. D. B. Byrd, N.C.; 1st Lt. Norbert Carolin, N.Y.; 1st Lt. A. J. Coyle, N.H.; 1st Lt. Barnard Cummings, Colo.; Maj. Thos. W. Hislop, N.Y.; 1st Lt. Henry Ilse, Wash.; 1st Lt. Bee R. Osborne, Ky.; Capt. R. L. Taylor, Conn.; 2d Lt. Forrest Ward, Ark.; 1st Lt. H. F. Wehrle, W.Va.; 2d Lt. Ivan P. Wheaton, N.Y.; 2d Lt. D. R. Wheeler, N.Y.

The post return for the Mineola Aviation Station on 30 November 1916 showed 5 officers and 58 enlisted men, while on 31 December the strength was 8 officers and 110 enlisted men.[7]

As the winter of 1916 approached, the Chief Signal Officer contemplated shifting the training activities from Mineola to the South, but Carberry opposed this idea. He asserted that while preliminary training would have to be suspended at Mineola, valuable experience in winter flying could be gained and it would be possible to organize standard training procedures, programs, and equipment; further, pending the building of the air proving grounds at Hampton Roads, necessary tests and experiments could be conducted at Mineola. This argument probably induced the Chief Signal Officer to change his mind, and thereafter Mineola served largely as a testing ground for methods, equipment, and accessories. It was not until after America entered the war that this station really began to function as a flight school.[8]

Between July and 31 December 1916, numerous tests were made by the flyers at Mineola, some of the most interesting of which were bomb tests.

---

*Colonel Carberry states in memo to E. L. Jones dated 18 March 1951 that Lieutenant Martin's orders must have been revoked as he had no record of his ever having been at Mineola.

On 15 August 1916 Lester P. Barlow, who was at Mineola experimenting with his own bombs, dropped five of the Ordnance-made 3-inch bombs from heights of 1,250 to 2,800 feet. Four failed to function properly but the fifth exploded after penetrating several inches into the ground. After the Ordnance Department had changed the stabilizers, five more bombs with tin stabilizing collars were dropped in September. Four of these detonated upon impact and were surprisingly effective.[9]

On 6 September Barlow tested his own "return-action"* fragmentation bombs at Mineola, primarily to demonstrate the practicability of the mechanical principles involved. The design had been submitted in February 1916 by Barlow, and the Ordnance Department assisted him and allotted $2,000 for the manufacture of a number of the bombs. Although one bomb failed in a test because of a structural defect, the Ordnance Department was convinced that the principles were sound. A subsequent informal test made at Frankford Arsenal demonstrated that the structural defects which had made the previous test a failure had been overcome. Five more bombs were furnished by the Hale and Kilburne Company of Philadelphia, with whom Barlow was associated, for use in service tests. The bombs were loaded with TNT and fused by the Frankford Arsenal at government expense, and were tested at Mineola in November. These were dropped from 2,500 to 3,000 feet but only two of the five were found. They had penetrated firm ground up to about 3 inches of the forward end of the vane. Ordnance felt that these bombs would be satisfactory when equipped with a properly proportioned explosive charge. Frankford Arsenal was instructed to aid Barlow in every way possible in making the necessary shop tests for proper adjustment of the expelling charge. Tests continued into the spring of 1917. Barlow arrived at an agreement with the government whereby the Ordnance Department could manufacture his bombs after an initial payment of $4,000, or if the bombs were furnished by private manufacturers, he was to get a royalty of 10 per cent of the purchase price up to $15,000. The government also was free to use any of his other ideas, such as those on aerial torpedoes, without fear of

infringement because no patents had been issued. At the end of the war a reasonable payment would be made to Barlow. In order to preserve secrecy, the Barlow patents were withheld from publication, for his design was the only one which was known at that time to be sound in principle, had been successfully tried, and had proved that it would detonate well above the ground.[10]

Two tubular-shaped bomb-dropping devices built by Ordnance, were tested at Mineola between 6 and 18 November 1916. With the exception of the releasing clutch they were reported satisfactory. In March 1917 modifications were proposed by Ordnance, but by 1 June the Department stated it was highly improbable that the tubular bomb dropper would be adopted and further work on it was dropped.[11]

In the meantime some winter flying was being done at the Signal Corps station. The first National Guard cross-country formation flight was made from 18 to 20 November 1916 by Mineola flyers in seven JN4 airplanes; the group, led by Capt. R. C. Bolling, flew nonstop from Mineola to Princeton, New Jersey, on the 18th. The participants were: Capts. R. C. Bolling, N.G., N. Y. and Ralph L. Taylor, N.G., Conn.; 1st Lt. A. B. Thaw, N.G., N. Y.; and Sgts. W. P. Willetts, N.G., N. Y., J. H. Stevenson, N.G., N. Y., D. R. Noyes, N.G., N. Y., and H. H. Salmon, N.G., N. Y. The National Guard flyers were joined at a prearranged rendezvous 3,000 feet over the Narrows of New York harbor by three civilians training at the Governors Island Aviation School: Cord Meyer and H. A. H. Baker, observer, in one JN4 and Philip A. Carroll in another. W. H. Bleakley, civilian instructor at Mineola, in an LWF, accompanied the flight to Princeton. All returned on 20 November, again flying nonstop.[12]

On 30 and 31 December 1916 a National Guard-Army group flight was made from Mineola to Philadelphia Navy Yard, a distance of 110 miles. Although this was the second National Guard flight, it was the Guard's first flight in conjunction with the Army. The temperature was zero on the ground and 18 below at 6,000 feet, the altitude at which most of the planes flew. In addition to their own clothing the flyers wore all the experimental clothing which the Army wanted tested; even so, they nearly froze to death. Only eight of the twelve starters arrived in Philadelphia. First Lt. A. J. Coyle and Cpl. H. H.

*The design was secret and no explanation of the meaning of the expression "return-action" has been found.

Salmon, the first to arrive, covered the distance in 97 minutes in the teeth of a bitter wind. Landing after Coyle and Salmon, Instructor W. H. Bleakley and Pvt. C. H. Reynolds hit a flagpole and damaged their plane. They were followed in by Instructor P. C. Millman with Pvt. S. A. Blair, Capt. J. E. Carberry, 1st Lt. James E. Miller, 2d Lt. B. R. Osborne, Instructors L. W. Bonney and A. L. Allan, and 2d Lt. E. W. Bagnell with Sgt. E. A. Kruss.

Four of the planes returned to Mineola from Philadelphia on 31 December 1916 without incident, while three made forced landings but later completed the journey. The last of the eight planes arrived home in a low-lying fog on 2 January 1917.

The four planes which had failed to reach Philadelphia were later accounted for as follows: 1st Lt. Norbert Carolin with 2d Lt. Ivan P. Wheaton, both of the New York National Guard, in a forced landing at Deans, New Jerey, wrecked their plane against a fence. Sgt. D. R. Noyes, N.G., N.Y. with Cadet Russell L. Meredith, USMA, landed without trouble near Monmouth Junction, New Jersey, and flew back to Mineola on 7 January. Capt. Raynal C. Bolling, CO of the 1st Aero Company, N.G., N.Y. was grounded at Monmouth, New Jersey; he flew back to Mineola on 8 January. Lieutenant W. G. Kilner, S.C. and John B. Stetson, Jr., a civilian training at the Army's school at his own expense, abandoned the flight soon after take off and returned to Mineola.

Out of five emergency landings in unfamiliar and difficult territory, only one airplane, that of Carolin and Wheaton, was lost; all others were quickly put back in commission. Some of the difficulties were caused by inexperienced ground crews, one of whom inserted a piece of cardboard on the upper rather than the lower half of the radiators, causing them to overheat.[13]

By January 1917 there were on duty at Mineola the following pilots of the regular establishment: 1st Lts. Carberry, Kilner, Rader, and S. W. Fitz-Gerald, the latter having joined the station in December 1916; 9 militia officers; 110 enlisted men and 35 civilian employees. About this time there were 60 aviators trained or under training:[14]

1st Aero Company, N.G., N.Y.	27
2d Aero Company, N.G., N.Y.	15
Militia, other states	12
Reserve applicants	3
U.S. Army*	2
U.S. Military Academy†	1
Total	60

On 15 January 1917 flying instruction was suspended at Mineola to permit concentration on the systematic overhauling of airplanes and to allow the Supply Department to expand into space vacated by the Technical Department, which had transferred to a new steel building. Certain flying activities were conducted, however, on the 16th, 18th, 26th, and 27th. On the 18th a test was made of a metal propeller and on the 26th and 27th pictures were taken with the Brock airplane camera. It had been expected that the pictures would be completed in time to permit the exhibition of an airplane photographic map at the Pan-American Aeronautic Exposition, 8 to 15 February, but bad weather interfered to such an extent that the project had to be abandoned. On 5 February all tests were discontinued and flying instruction was resumed for the 18 students (8 of whom had soloed) then in training.

As a result of the crisis in foreign relations, stringent security measures were put into effect during this period. Permission was secured from the Wright-Martin Aircraft Corporation, owners of that portion of the field which was not leased, to erect barriers and warning signs. The guard was tripled and the field closed to all except those known by the guard or those who had passes. Plans were made to erect, at central points, four lighting towers equipped with floodlights to light the vicinity of the hangars and all groups of buildings at the station as protection against sabotage.[15]

On 2 February 1917 Lieutenant Carberry reported on the progress of the Mineola station. He stated that 34 men had been tested for the position of instructor. At that time there were 15 instructors on duty at the station, of whom 7 were student instructors in the process of training, the remainder being classed as junior, senior, or chief instructors, depending upon their ability and length of service. In addition, 8 civilians had passed the Reserve Military Aviator (RMA) test, 6 of these having been trained under the supervision of Mr. P. A. Carroll at a private train-

---

*Lt. Follett Bradley and Pvt. K. L. Whitsett, both of the Signal Corps.
†Cadet R. L. Meredith.

ing school at Governors Island, New York.* Little time could be devoted to preliminary training because of the unfavorable weather, although this did not hinder the training of advanced students who were flying alone. For this reason it was not intended that preliminary training would be conducted on a large scale until late spring or early summer. A great deal of work remained to be done toward organizing personnel and methods to be used in training reserve military aviators. In addition to its other work, the station was preparing to issue a loose-leaf administrative manual for the guidance of commanding officers charged with the establishment of other schools. Tables of flight school equipment and organization, which would include a directory of job specifications, were proposed. A program of standardizing equipment and methods in use at an aviation training school was under consideration and standard reports and forms for use in the various departments were being drawn up. Night flying was to be given immediate attention. The station was equipped with a 36-inch searchlight, 12 floodlight projectors, and 6 portable trench searchlights, and the intention was to conduct tests of emergency flares and other means of temporary lighting adapted to field service. Problems would include methods of signaling between aircraft at night, picking up aircraft by searchlight, illuminating the cockpit and the instrument panel of the plane, recognizing the field by code signals, and other phases of night flying.[16]

On 28 February Carberry recommended to the Chief Signal Officer that Mineola be permitted to proceed with an early plan to utilize the station as a proving ground for flight instruction by establishing a camp fully equipped to accommodate 150 students at a time and organizing a system of training to be put into actual practice. Carberry requested that no students be ordered to the station until after 15 May, at which time an active and efficient program could be inaugurated. He guaranteed an output of 40 trained aviators a month, beginning 1 September 1917. The plan of training would allow the school to take in about 50 aviation students and give them as thorough a course in both military and aviation

training as was possible with the personnel and facilities available. In addition to flying instruction the students were to be given such practical military work as infantry drill, camp and march sanitation, first aid, map reading, use of rifle and pistol, and military calisthenics. An order for the erection of an additional building, where lectures and indoor instruction could be given, had already been placed. Hangar accommodations were insufficient and the majority of planes were in storage, but plans for hangars to house 32 planes had been drawn and immediate erection was contemplated.[17]

On 3 April 1917, the Signal Corps Aviation School at Mineola reverted to its original role— that of a school. All experiments, except aviation clothing tests and night flying which were to be continued as a part of the course, were discontinued. The photographic map of Long Island, the selection and marking of landing fields, and air problems already drawn up were turned over to the Department Aeronautical Officer. Correspondence on aviation sites was discontinued. On 30 July 1917,* Captain Carberry was relieved at Mineola and sailed from New York for France with the AEF. Captain Kilner succeeded him as commanding officer.[18]

Ashburn Field, Chicago, and Memphis, Tenn.

The third Army flying school was established in the summer of 1916 at Ashburn Field near Chicago, Illinois. The land was obtained through an arrangement with the Aero Club of Illinois, which had been operating the field. Lt. Joseph C. Morrow, then on leave of absence, was ordered to Washington in July 1916 for consultation and thence to Chicago to establish the school. He was followed in August by Lt. Arthur R. Christie. Capt. E. N. Macon, retired, was ordered to active duty as supply officer; he was relieved in October by 1st Lt. W. R. Van Sant, retired. The first flying student was a member of the Dakota† National Guard, 1st Lt. W. W. Spain, who was ordered to report on 15 August 1916; he passed his RMA test on 3 November. A detachment of four enlisted men headed by Sgt. Charles Chester was ordered to Ashburn Field from San Diego; three others were sent from Fort Leavenworth in October; and four transfers from CAC

---

*It was about this time that an unauthenticated roster of students, instructors, and civilians passing RMA tests at Mineola was compiled. See Appendix No. 18 for this list and see Appendix No. 14 for a complete list of National Guard and Reserve Aviators to 6 April 1917.

*Carberry says he sailed for France on 26 March 1917, although he was not relieved from duty until 30 July 1917.
†The records do not indicate whether this was North Dakota or South Dakota.

arrived in December. In January and February 1917, 23 civilians, enlisted as sergeants in the Aviation Section, SERC, were sent to Chicago for training. By 6 April 1917, 46 planes, 28 of which were JN4's and 18 Standard HS's, had been delivered at Chicago.[19]

On 4 December 1916, Lieutenant Morrow was ordered on temporary duty from Chicago to Memphis, Tennessee, to organize the fourth flying school, which was to be located at the Driving Park, inside a race track. Lieutenants Ralph Royce and Roy S. Brown were relieved in March 1917 at Columbus, New Mexico, for duty at Memphis. They were followed in April by Lt. Warren C. Woodward, AS, SORC. The first regular enlisted man to report was Cpl. Arthur R. Curphey. Nine civilians who had enlisted as sergeants in the AS, SERC reported in February and April, but one of these was relieved in March and ordered home.

Flying had started at Chicago in November but had been stopped on account of cold weather and snow in the latter part of December. Early in 1917, 20 students, their civilian instructors, and a number of enlisted men, were transferred to the Memphis school. Flying at Memphis started about 10 February 1917. At the end of March, 13 planes were in commission with 10 others not yet uncrated because of lack of space. One plane was awaiting condemnation and 4 were temporarily out of commission. A construction and repair department had been organized; and a course in aerodynamics was being given, in addition to classes in infantry drill regulations. Only a few students had soloed because of the danger of using such a small field.

Flying at Memphis stopped in April 1917 and the group was moved back to Chicago; in August it moved from Ashburn to Chanute Field, Rantoul, Illinois, 90 miles away. About 12 planes were flown on this trip.[20]

Essington, Pennsylvania

On 26 January 1917, Lieutenant Colonel Squier, OIC, Aviation Section, recommended that he be authorized to proceed with the organization of an aviation station at Essington, Pennsylvania, where a civilian school had been in operation under Robert Glendinning since early 1916. On 8 February this request was approved and the Army's fifth flying school was established. Capt. William C. Ocker, pilot, recently commissioned in the

Reserve after serving as an enlisted man at San Diego since 1912, was ordered to active duty on 10 February 1917. On 12 March he was relieved from duty in the Office, Chief Signal Officer, and ordered to Essington to organize a temporary aviation station for training and developing the 2d Reserve Aero Squadron for use with the coast defenses of the Philadelphia area.[21] First Lt. William F. Volandt, AS, SORC, and 1st Lt. Joseph N. Barney, Medical Reserve Corps, were ordered to assist Captain Ocker. Ten enlisted men were sent in March and on 1 April flying instruction began. By 6 April 1917, 10 Curtiss N9 seaplanes had been delivered. At a special meeting on 19 April, the board of directors of the Glendinning school agreed to sell the property at Essington to the government for $31,056.55 and to transfer its lease from the city of Philadelphia for $3,000 for the first year. By the 24th of April, Capt L. E. Goodier was at Essington and on 7 July he was commanding officer of the 2d Reserve Aero Squadron. This station was discontinued on 3 November 1917.[22]

THE FLYING SCHOOL PROGRAM, APRIL 1917

The Chief Signal Officer on 3 April 1917 set flying school policy as primarily that of training— all projects of experimentation or other non-flying activity were to be discontinued immediately. The permanent administrative official personnel at all schools was to be reduced to the minimum in time of war and should at no time exceed 1 commanding officer, 1 secretary, 1 disbursing officer, 1 officer in charge of flying, 1 assistant to OIC flying, 1 engineering officer, 1 supply officer. It would not be possible to furnish all of the above staff from Regular Army officers; in most cases reserve officers would have to be used to fill in. As soon as a student aviation officer passed the JMA test, he was to be sent to a squadron for duty; he could not be retained at the school. Training was to be conducted largely by civilians with one flying instructor for every eight students. This constituted the program at flying schools when war was declared.[23]

THE NATIONAL GUARD AND RESERVE UNITS

The National Defense Act of 3 June 1916 had authorized the establishment of a Signal Reserve Corps. It remained only to set up the machinery for recruiting and training the members of an

Aviation Section, Signal Officers and Enlisted Reserve Corps. Recruiting presented no problem as there were any number of men in the country who were anxious to learn to fly; but a training program required time, thought, and money. Of the $13,281,666 appropriated in August 1916, $900,000 was made available for this project. Plans for aviation stations had already been projected, but it was necessary to fit the reserves into these plans. With the advent of war, the air units of the National Guard as such would go out of existence; but prior to the war Guard members could be relieved from their affiliation with this organization and volunteer their services in the Signal Reserve Corps, if they had the necessary qualifications.

In the meantime, the Aero Club of America furnished money from its National Airplane Fund for the training of National Guard members. On 22 March 1916, Alan R. Hawley, the Club's president, reported to the Secretary of War that the Aero Club had mobilized 15 licensed aviators and was sending them to aviation schools for special training so that they could volunteer for the Mexican campaign.[24] On 20 June, 26 officers and 12 enlisted men were receiving this training. These men would be eligible for aviation duty when they were mustered into the service; however, the Aviation Section recommended that the trainees at the Curtiss school at Newport News and the Thomas school at Ithaca be taken into service at the schools and continue their training until they had received their aviator's certificates. This recommendation was approved by the Signal Corps and from time to time groups of officers from the two schools were ordered to report to Mineola for examination as to proficiency in aeronautics.

The Aero Club also had helped finance the 1st Aero Company of the New York National Guard. When this company was mustered out of federal service on 2 November 1916, many of its members remained in camp the rest of the winter in order to complete their flying training. The 1st Aero Company was disbanded on 23 May 1917, but nearly all of its members saw active service in the war; many of them were commissioned in the air service.[25]

The Governors Island aviation school was an outgrowth of the Military Training Camp for Business Men at Plattsburg, as was the 1st Aero Com-

pany, National Guard, N. Y. On 5 April 1916, the Governors Island Training Corps was organized by Philip A. Carroll, who undertook the training of a group of civilians at the military post on Governors Island, New York. A few wealthy business men in New York City purchased several airplanes and seaplanes to be used to train volunteers. In June 1916, Maj. Gen. Leonard Wood, Commanding General Eastern Department, issued regulations to govern enrollments and operations at Governors Island.* Enrollments were controlled by instructions issued to Carroll. The hours of flight were 0530 to 0800 and 1630 to dark in the afternoons except on Sunday when no flying was permitted before 1630. No one other than an enrolled member of the corps or an officer of the Army was allowed to fly without special permission from the Department Commander, and no sensational or fancy flying was allowed. Col. J. B. Bellinger, QMC, Maj. C. F. Hartman, S.C., and Capt. C. E. Kilbourne, G.S. were appointed as a committee to represent the Department Commander in all matters pertaining to the Governors Island Training Corps.

The first instruction flights were made on 2 May 1916. There were seven men in training, one of whom soloed in June. At that time the planes used at this school were two Curtiss JN4's with OX2 Curtiss 90-horsepower engines. A Sturtevant with 140-horsepower engine was being tested; it was not accepted and a Curtiss JN4 with a 100-horsepower engine was substituted. Filip A. Bjorklund was the only civilian instructor from April to December 1916. Of the 17 who trained there, 10 completed the course, 6 passed the RMA test and 1 passed the JMA test.† By March 1917, three other candidates either had passed the RMA test or were capable of passing it with some further practice. By this time only two planes remained in service.[26]

From the Governors Island school and members of the 1st Aero Company, which had been mustered out of federal service, was formed the 1st Reserve Aero Squadron in May 1917. The officers of this squadron were: Major Raynall C. Bolling, Capts. Philip A. Carroll and James E. Miller; and 1st Lts. D. R. Noyes, Frederick T.

---

*The commanding officer of Fort Jay was responsible for attending to the grass, landing markers, signs, and obstructions.
†For a list of Reserve and National Guard pilots in the U.S. Army to 6 April 1917, see Appendix No. 14.

Blakeman, Charles Reed, H. A. H. Baker, and Edwin M. Post, Jr.

Under Bolling's direction a part of the squadron proceeded to Mineola with Captain Carroll, while the rest remained in New York to recruit personnel. Early in June, Bolling was sent to Europe. He left the squadron under the command of Carroll, who conducted its training until 23 August 1917, when it sailed for Europe on the *S. S. Baltic*. On this ship also were the 30th and 37th Aero Squadrons commanded by Maj. Carl Spaatz; they had been shipped from Kelly Field, Texas. After the 1st Reserve Aero Squadron arrived in France it was redesignated the 26th Aero Squadron and its equipment and personnel formed the basis for the organization of the famous aviation school at Issoudun.[27]

The same order that provided for the organization of the 1st Reserve Aero Squadron on 3 May 1917 also provided for the establishment of the 2d Reserve Aero Squadron at Essington, Pennsylvania; and the commanding general of the Eastern Department was ordered to complete these organizations by the assignment of officers and enlisted men of the Aviation Section, Signal Reserve Corps.[28]

The 2d Aero Company, New York National Guard, which was never federalized, trained at Mineola with the 1st Aero Company. Capt. J. M. Satterfield, commanding officer of the 2d, attempted to form a third reserve aero squadron, but an order from the Adjutant General of New York disbanded the 2d Aero Company and ordered the discharge of the men. Satterfield and five lieutenants were placed on the National Guard reserve list, and Satterfield then was informed that it was no longer the policy of the War Department to proceed with the organization of reserve squadrons as originally intended. The problem of what to do with the officers and the men immediately arose. The Chief Signal Officer stated that if the former officers of the 2d Aero Company were free to volunteer, they might do so; the enlisted men could do the same, provided additional enlisted personnel were needed and that recruiting was resumed.[29]

A number of other organizations formed flying groups in 1916 to train aviators. The Harvard Flying Club was established through funds solicited by alumni headed by Robert Bacon. The undergraduates were trained at the Curtiss Buffalo school

under Phil Rader, the Thomas school at Ithaca, and the Wright Company's school at Mineola. Both Bacon and the Aero Club of America offered a bonus of $50 for each student who obtained his FAI certificate. Of the 17 men sent to these schools, 12 qualified for their FAI pilot's licenses, 4 had not yet completed their 400-minute course before the opening of college that fall, and one was unable to qualify because of bad weather.[30]

Yale also had an Aero Club, headed by F. Trubee Davison, who induced most of its members to become students in the Aerial Coast Patrol School at Port Washington, L. I. in the spring of 1917.

The 1st and 2d Battalions of the New York Naval Militia did some flying training at Bay Shore, Long Island. Seven men of the Massachusetts Militia trained at Marblehead. The Rhode Island and Michigan militias also had some flying training. Earl W. Dodge offered to train 16 college men at Jacksonville, Florida,* and Robert Glendinning trained Navy pilots at Essington, Pennsylvania.[31]

On 20 June 1917, the Chief Signal Officer stated the policy of his office in regard to reserves, to which no exception would be made. The two squadrons already organized (1st and 2d Aero Reserve Squadrons) would become a part of the Regular or National Army, and no other reserve squadrons would be organized. All other squadrons would be organized by the Regular or National Army and the first ones would be training squadrons whose officers and men would be of the Regular or National Army. Reserve flying officers would be commissioned after completing a full theoretical and practical course of instruction and passing the RMA test. The theoretical course was to consist of four to eight weeks at a designated university, the length of the course depending on previous military training of the students. Successful graduates of schools of military aeronautics would be assigned to government aviation schools for training and as soon as they were qualified would be commissioned and assigned to squadrons. The grade of Master Signal Electrician and Sergeant First Class would be filled by competitive examinations in the squadron, while vacancies in an organized squadron below the grade of Sergeant first class would be filled by promotion without examination. The squadron commander would

---

*Whether any men were trained at Jacksonville is unknown.

make promotions and the Department Aeronautical Officer, on request of the squadron commander, might assign qualified men to fill vacancies below the grade of Sergeant first class. Enlisted men would not be enlisted in any grade above that of private and would not be promoted or assigned to any other grade, prior to reporting to the squadron commander. The designated strength of non-commissioned personnel in squadron organizations was not to be exceeded. Reserve officers and enlisted men would be assigned to organizations in which their services were desired by military authorities. No guarantee or assurance was to be given any prospective flying officer or enlisted man as to rank, station, or duties prior to his acceptance in the military service. No aviation organization was to be accepted or incorporated as an organization into the Regular service or National Army; all entries of Reserve officers and enlisted men would be the result of individual applications and subsequent acceptance in accordance with the above policy. Non-flying officers duly qualified for administrative duties were exempted from training at schools of military aeronautics.[32]

THE SIGNAL RESERVE CORPS

In July 1916, the President had authorized the following number and grades for officers of the Aviation Section, Signal Officers Reserve Corps and enlisted men of the Signal Enlisted Reserve Corps:

Majors	16	Master Signal Electricians	40
Captains	48	Sergeants, first class	140
1st Lts.	232	Sergeants	200
	—	Corporals	400
Total	296	Privates, first class	305
		Privates	915

Total 2000

He approved utilizing the services of civilian schools for preliminary training of flyers who then would finish their training in United States Army flying schools. After the reserve officers and enlisted men had been brought into the service, the OIC, AS, SC would make recommendations to the Secretary of War for calling into active service as many men as were needed for aviation instruction.[33]

Several opinions were handed down in regard to pay and the use of funds for instruction at civilian schools. In August 1916, the Judge Advocate General decided that members of the National Guard, while attending maneuvers or encampments or when in the service of the United States, were entitled to the same pay and allowances, including flying pay, as officers and enlisted men of corresponding grades in the Regular Army.[34] On 31 March 1917, the Comptroller of the Treasury ruled that no part of the $900,000 appropriation made earlier for the Aviation Section was available for flying instruction of Regular Army officers. In May 1917, the Comptroller rendered the opinion that this fund was available for preliminary training at civilian aviation schools of personnel of the Officers Reserve Corps and the Enlisted Reserve Corps of the Aviation Section of the Signal Corps.[35]

On 14 November 1916, the first civilian pilot students of the Signal Enlisted Reserve Corps were sent to the Curtiss school at Newport News, Virginia. This school had been established in the fall of 1915 when the Curtiss Canadian school was transferred there from Canada. It was known as the Atlantic Coast Aeronautical Station and Curtiss School of Aviation and was under the management of T. S. Baldwin, who had built the Signal Corps' Dirigible No. 1. Civilians with the necessary qualifications (a college education was desirable) were enlisted as sergeants in the Aviation Section, Signal Enlisted Reserve Corps and assigned to active duty for the purpose of undergoing a course of instruction to obtain a commission. Transportation expenses to the school were paid by the government. The base pay of a sergeant was $36.00 a month and each candidate received medical attention free of charge. The Quartermaster Corps paid commutation of quarters at the rate of $15.00 a month and rations at $1.00 a day.

The students at Newport News learned to fly and land under adverse conditions, the field being short and narrow with obstructions on the sides; cross-wind landings were necessary about 90 per cent of the time. By March 1917, the first graduate, H. M. Gallup, was commissioned as a first lieutenant, RMA, and ordered to the 3d Aero Squadron at Fort Sam Houston.[36]

Major William Mitchell, a Regular Signal Corps officer who had been ordered to air duty in the Office of the Chief Signal Officer, learned to fly at Newport News in the fall of 1916 by attending the school on official orders on week ends. Mitchell received instruction from several of the Curtiss Company instructors: Victor Carlstrom, Stewart W. Cogswell, James M. Johnson, Walter E. Lees, and Victor Vernon. Capt. Milling also gave him a flight or two during an official visit to Newport News in December 1916. Mitchell made his first flight with S. W. Cogswell, but he gave Walter Lees credit for soloing him. Lees said of this flight, "Mitchell was very erratic. One day he would be O.K. and the next lousy and I just happened to catch him on one of his good days. He made two perfect flights this day."[37] Mitchell was later rated a JMA from 19 July 1917. The bill for his instruction, which amounted to $1,470, was not paid by the government because of the ruling that none of the appropriation could be used for instruction of Regular Army officers at civilian schools. It was sent to Mitchell at the American Embassy in Paris on 13 April 1917.[38]

The Curtiss school at Miami did not get into operation until December 1916, and the first civilian student ordered to active duty as a sergeant in the AS, SERC reported on 25 January 1917. By April 1917, there were 126 SERC students at Newport News and Miami; of these, 25 were later commissioned as 1st lieutenants in the Aviation Section and the others were sent to ground and flying schools, which were organized at universities; the contract training system was discontinued on 22 May 1917.[39]

As nearly as can be determined, under the contract system flight training consisted of 600 minutes dual and 200 minutes solo instruction. The 600 minutes for dual training compared very favorably with the 400 minutes usually given for civilian training. After completion of this training the student then took the RMA test under the observation of a Signal Corps officer. Those who failed to qualify as candidates for final training were discharged and returned to the jurisdiction of their local draft boards. Under General Order 55 of 16 October 1916, $500 was to be paid the civilian schools for each student qualifying in the preliminary or FAI tests conducted by an officer or agent of the Aviation Section, Signal Corps. An additional $300 was to be paid for any aviation student who qualified as a Reserve Military Aviator upon graduation. Other suggestions were made as to the price the government should pay for this

training. It is difficult to determine just what it did pay, but some idea of the government's laxity in this matter can be obtained from a statement of J. W. Scott of the Curtiss Company, who said that up to 12 March 1917, no contract had been made between the government and Curtiss, although several thousand dollars were already due the company for training Reserve aviators. Government vouchers show that finally on 19 July 1917, the Curtiss Company was paid $100,523 for training 131 enlisted reservists.[40]

At first considerable confusion arose at the aviation stations when candidates for the Enlisted Reserve Corps arrived for enlistment. In order to put these men on active duty after they had enlisted, it was necessary for the commanding officer of the aviation station to request authority from The Adjutant General of the Army through the Chief Signal Officer. It took a week or ten days for the authority to come through and during the intervening period the newly enlisted men either had to return to their homes or stay at the aviation station at their own expense. Since the Office of Chief Signal Officer was qualified to authorize the enlistment of these men, it was requested on 22 January 1917 that the office also be authorized to order them on active duty. This would take care of the confusion resulting from the unnecessary waiting period. The Adjutant General replied that he had the matter under consideration, but the records do not indicate what if any action was taken.[41]

THE NATIONAL GUARD

On 24 February 1917, certain National Guard officers and enlisted men were reported as still being on duty at Mineola and Memphis. The Chief of the Militia Bureau recommended that the commanding general, Eastern Department be directed to muster these men out of federal service and that the Chief of the Aviation Section of the Signal Corps be directed to submit immediately the names of officers and enlisted men, whose instruction he desired to continue after the mustering out process. This was done and a number of the officers and men were later taken into the Army.[42]

By 6 April 1917, when the United States entered World War I, volunteering for aviation service in the Signal Reserve Corps had become an individual matter and continued so until it was prohibited by the draft act of 18 May 1917. Only one National Guard squadron had been mustered into federal service and it had been mustered out months before the United States entered the war. An earlier plan to take in reserve aviation units was dropped, although the 1st and 2d Aero Reserve Squadrons were already in federal serv- ice. Civilian flying schools were functioning and the Army had five flying training schools of its own. The number of Reserve Military Aviators turned out by 6 April 1917 was negligible, but at least some semblance of a training plan had been put into effect.

———————★———————

CHAPTER XI

The Aviation Section to 6 April 1917

B Y THE FIRST of January 1917, the aviation school at San Diego—the only school in the United States Army where officers of the regular service were sent for aviation instruction—had grown considerably in size and importance. Thirty-five officers had been graduated and assigned to duty with operating units in the field. Eight graduates were still on duty at San Diego awaiting assignments, and 51 student officers were receiving instruction. The enlisted personnel had been increased to 240. There were 32 airplanes on hand. By the end of January the school staff had increased to nine officers.[1]

In addition to regular officers some National Guard and Reserve officers were sent to San Diego. The first of a number of National Guard aviation students, 1st Lt. James P. Kelly of Connecticut, reported on 2 January; apparently he had had no flying instruction and was dropped from the roster in February. There were nine other National Guard officers at San Diego through March 1917.[2]

Early in January, Colonel Squier, looking ahead for the next two years, told the House Committee on Military Affairs that by the end of 1917 there would be 78 Regular Army officers in the Aviation Section; and with an increase of 18 lieutenants each year, there would be 96 by the end of 1918. It was expected that the Aviation Section would have in 1917: 4 squadrons for the Regular Army in the United States (2 at San Antonio), 3 squadrons for overseas possessions, and 6 reserve squadrons for coast defense. These 13 squadrons would require about 286 officers; the vacancies would be filled from the Reserve Corps. The President had authorized 1,800 enlisted men for 1917 and 3,200 men for 1918;

there were presently on duty about 800, who had either been transferred from the Army or were enlisted civilians. It had been estimated that the 13 squadrons could be maintained at a cost of $600,000 each for the next fiscal year and 4 more were to be added at an original cost of $800,000 each. It had been found that under war conditions an airplane would wear out after an average of three months' service; consequently, a squadron which consisted of 12 planes would use up 48 planes per year. The life of an engine was about 300 hours and several engines costing about $50 per horsepower would be needed for each plane. It took five trained men to take care of each plane. All these things had to be considered in figuring the cost of maintenance of a squadron for a year.[3]

In January, an incident occurred at the San Diego school which ended in an organizational shake-up. On the morning of the 10th, Lt. W. A. Robertson, with Lt. Col. H. G. Bishop of the Field Officers School as passenger, took off from North Island in training plane No. 62 for a cross-country flight to Yuma, Arizona. Shortly after noon they ran out of gas and made a forced landing; the plane turned over but neither man was injured. They came down on what they believed to be the shore of the Salton Sea in southern California, but they soon realized—after observing that the tide was coming in—that their plane had been blown far to the south of their course and that they actually were in Mexico, on the Gulf of California along the southern edge of the Sonora Desert, miles from any habitation. With two sandwiches and two oranges apiece, a gallon oil can filled with water from the radiator, and the plane's compass, they set out to follow the shore line west to the Colorado River, but the going was so rough that they soon decided to head straight north across the desert, hoping to reach the Southern Pacific Railroad near Yuma.[4]

On the fifth day their meager supply of food and water ran out; thereafter, they had no food and their only water was the dew which collected on cactus plants early in the morning. Fortunately, the January days were not hot; fortunately, too, the men had their flying jackets so that they were able to survive the cold nights. By the morning of the eighth day Bishop could go no farther, but Robertson, who was younger and huskier, stumbled on in a final effort to reach the railroad. On the morning of the ninth day he found automobile tracks which led him to two Mexicans. They proved to be members of a Wellton, Arizona, searching party which had been sent out by John Greenway of Ajo, Arizona, at the request of his friend Colonel Wilder, a Cavalry officer who was in charge of the border patrol at Calexico. The Mexicans found Bishop weak but still alive about 30 miles to the south in the Rosario Mountains. They took the two flyers to Wellton and put them on a train.*

Bishop had injured his foot on the long tramp through the desert and gangrene had set in; he was taken to a hospital where several toes were amputated. Later he returned to duty, completed his Army career, and retired as a Major General. Robertson seemed none the worse for his harrowing experience—he was playing polo four days after the rescue—but evidently the trip had taken its toll for not long afterward he became ill and eventually was retired for physical disability.[5]

On the surface it would appear that the men should have been found by one of the more than 30 planes which were at the San Diego school. That they were not was due, at least in part, to a series of circumstances beyond the control of the school. The usual crop of rumors and reports that the missing plane had been seen here, there, or yonder came in; these had to be checked, so that several days passed before San Diego was reasonably certain that the men were down either in Arizona, Lower California, or Sonora. A relief party then was organized under Major Lahm and Lt. Jack W. Heard with instructions to proceed

to Calexico on the 14th and there to establish a camp which would serve as a base for search planes. At Calexico Lahm received news which indicated that the search could be limited to the Sonora Desert; accordingly, it was decided to establish the camp and clear a landing field at Black Butte, about 18 miles below the border.[6]

This latest plan of action promptly ran into trouble. The Mexicans, in part, no doubt, because at that time relations between the United States and Mexico were strained, were anything but cooperative. Governor Cantu of Lower California could not be located and his staff interposed numerous obstacles before they finally agreed that the planes could be pushed by hand across the border, inspected by Mexican customs officials, and then could start their search. Then the Mexican official who had to grant permission for the truck train to cross the border could not be found, but this problem was solved when the American Consul persuaded the authorities at a second border town to let the train through at daylight on the 16th. By noon of that day a field had been cleared, barely in time for Lieutenant Dargue to land his search plane. Dargue reported that he and Cpl. A. D. Smith searched the desert by alternating at the controls and on the wings, but saw nothing of the missing men. Bishop and Robertson later said that they had seen the plane and had tried to signal to it, but without success.[7]

The scanty records of this episode do not show conclusively that any plane except Dargue's participated in the search, although the January roster of the aviation school lists a number of officers on detached service in Mexico.* When, on the 19th, word was received that the flyers had been found, Lahm's relief party and the truck train returned to San Diego, arriving there on the 21st.[8]

Even with the extenuating circumstances described above it seems rather evident that the aerial search should have been started sooner than it was and should have been much more thorough. Certainly some of the officers and men of the aviation school thought so. The permanent staff was divided in opinion. Some thought that Colonel Glassford, the commanding officer, might have backed a far more aggressive search for the lost airmen; the others, members of the headquarters staff, were inclined to let nature take its

---

*The wrecked plane was brought from Mexico much later; Arnold states in his History of Rockwell Field that it was returned to service at Kelly Field in March 1918.

---

*In a picture taken during the search, two planes are shown.

Rescue expedition from SCAS at Black Butte, Mexico, 17 Jan 1917. Major Lahm, Captain Culver, Lieutenant Dargue, Corporal Smith, Mr. Wildman, Mr. Hayes, and Sergeant Coe

course and assume no responsibility. The younger airmen composed the first group, and there was so much comment on the lack of activity by Colonel Glassford that he was retired on 11 April and replaced by Col. A. L. Dade. Other, but less important, changes in personnel also resulted from the affair.[9]

On 25 January 1917, before he was retired, Glassford wrote the Chief Signal Officer that Col. W. L. Kenly and Lt. Col. H. G. Bishop, who were attending the Field Officers course at the aviation school, were drawing 25 per cent flying pay and if this was proper he would like for Capt. C. C. Culver to draw similar pay for the hazardous risks he took as a passenger in his airplane radio work. The QMG rendered the opinion that the drawing of flying pay by Kenley and Bishop was "unlawful and the amounts should be refunded to the U.S."[10] The Judge Advocate General was not convinced that the two men had been detailed as officers of the Aviation Section, and unless they had been so detailed they were not entitled to the increase in pay. Nor was he able to determine whether the officers were on duty that required them to "participate regularly and frequently in aerial flights."[11] The Chief Signal Officer finally agreed that the officers had not been detailed to aviation and The Adjutant General directed a refund. But Colonel Kenly, who became executive officer of the aviation school in February, asked that the refund be held in abeyance as he believed that the flight pay was in the nature of government insurance, as no commercial companies would insure aviators, and he felt it should apply to all who had occasion to make official flights, whether as pilots or observers, and he mentioned that he himself had 27 hours in the air. Colonel Dade, the new commanding officer of the school, recommended approval of Colonel Kenly's request and here the matter seems to have rested.[12]

In order to tighten up the requirements for flying pay, Change No. 51 to Army Regulation 1269, issued on 5 February 1917, stated that there would be announced in special orders of the War Department the names of Military Aviators, Junior Military Aviators, and aviation officers who were on duty requiring them to participate regularly and frequently in aerial flights. An officer announced in such orders was entitled to pay and allowances authorized under the terms of the act of Congress approved 18 July 1914 and the Na-

tional Defense Act approved 3 June 1916. The order was to specify the date on which such duty was begun and a subsequent order would specify the date on which the duty was terminated. The change further stated that when the commander of an aviation station or aeronautical organization in the field was entitled to pay and allowances of his grade under either of the acts named, it was the duty of the officer in charge of the Aviation Section, Signal Corps, to make the recommendations and certificates prescribed for such commanders, and these commanders in turn would do the same for officers under their command. No officer would be continued on such duty except as authorized by one of the two acts. There was also a statement regarding enlisted men incorporated in AR 1342½, 24 November 1915, which read, "It is the duty of the commander of an aviation station or aeronautical organization in the field to recommend the issue of orders announcing the commencement and termination of rating or additional pay of enlisted men of his command."[13]

On 14 February 1917, Lt. Col. George O. Squier, who was Chief of the Aviation Section, received the rank of Brigadier General and became Chief Signal Officer, relieving Brig. Gen. George. P. Scriven who retired at his own request after more than 42 years of service. On 19 February Lt. Col. John B. Bennet, who had attended the Field Officers course at San Diego, became Chief of the Aeronautical Division, and head of the Aviation Section.[14]

On 26 February 1917, Bennet submitted plans for Aviation Section personnel as of 1 July 1917:

Total authorized by 1916 increment	77
Total authorized by 2d increment, 1 July 1917	17
Total	**94**
Total detailed with Aviation Section	50
Students under instruction, San Diego	50
Balloon School	1
Total	**101**

Thus there was a surplus of 7 officers who could not be absorbed by 1 July 1917.

The 50 officers detailed with the Aviation Section were assigned as follows:

Detailed from squadrons for duty at San Diego, Mineola, and Chicago Aviation schools	11
War Department	6

*London		1
Boston, MIT		2
	Total	20

On duty with squadrons:

1st Aero Squadron, Columbus, N.M.	14
2d Aero Squadron, Manila, P.I.	7
3d, organizing, San Antonio	5
6th, organizing, Honolulu	2
7th, organizing, Panama	2
Total	30

Officers for the 4th and 5th squadrons were yet to be assigned. Counting squadrons expected to be organized by 1 July 1917, there was a total shortage of 116 officers. Under the law at that time, only 44 of the vacancies could be filled after including the second increment intended to supply the deficiencies by the assignment of AS, SORC members who were to be called to active service as fast as they became available. The full allotment for the 4th squadron was made from the first increment. After a readjustment, the allowance of enlisted personnel permitted the allotment of 76 men to the 5th squadron; immediately after 1 July 1917, the remaining 74 men required could be allotted from the second increment. Existing appropriations permitted complete equipment of both the 4th and 5th squadrons.[15]

General Order No. 21 of 9 February 1917, had authorized the organization of the 3d Aero Squadron near San Antonio. However, active organization had already begun, for a return of the 3d Aero Squadron for October 1916 signed by 1st Lt. John C. Hineman, reported 22 enlisted men on duty. On 23 October, 1st Lt. Thomas S. Bowen was relieved from duty with the 1st Aero Squadron and ordered to San Antonio in connection with the organization of the 3d Aero Squadron. He was assigned to the squadron on 4 November and became Supply and Engineer Officer on the 10th. Major Foulois became commanding officer on 1 November 1916, by verbal order of the Chief Signal Officer. By the end of November, the strength was 2 officers and 79 enlisted men, one group of which came from the 1st Aero Squadron at Columbus. On 6 December Captain Bowen became commanding officer while Foulois was absent on leave. Capt. Carl Spaatz and

Capt. B. M. Atkinson, both from the 1st Aero Squadron, arrived for duty in December. On 31 December, the squadron strength was 4 officers and 162 enlisted men. Other officers added up to 6 April 1917 were:[16] 1st Lts. Bee R. Osborne, Edgar W. Bagnell, B. B. Lewis, Harold M. Gallup, and Wm. G Schauffler, Jr., all AS, SORC.

On 8 January, Foulois, who was also the Department Aviation Officer, Southern Department, reported on San Antonio sites for the 3d Aero Squadron, selecting one out of six, a tract of about 677 acres located five miles southwest of the center of San Antonio, between the Frio City Road and the Southern Pacific Railway. General Funston approved and the land was leased in order to expedite aviation work.[17]

On 9 January 1917, Capt. John F. Curry, JMA, was relieved from duty with the 1st Aero Squadron in New Mexico and ordered to Fort Kamehameha, Hawaii to organize and command the 6th Aero Squadron. Curry was given no opportunity to visit Washington for conferences and instructions but ordered to proceed at once. He arrived in Honolulu on 13 February, with orders to establish a seaplane base for Curtiss N9's. He was followed by Capt. John B. Brooks and 49 men, who sailed on the March transport. They were stationed temporarily at Fort Kamehameha while Curry, who was appointed Department Aeronautical Officer on 21 March, surveyed possible sites. He finally decided on Ford Island in Pearl Harbor. The survey was approved by the Department Commander and the War Department; Curry arranged with the owner for the purchase of the land for $235,162, half of which was to be paid by the Navy. He advised the Joint Army-Navy Board of the results of his survey and the purchase was approved by the Secretary of War in September 1917. Major Curry left Hawaii on 10 July 1917, for duty in the Office of the Chief Signal Officer, and was succeeded as commanding officer of the squadron by Captain Brooks.[18]

Also on 9 January 1917, Capt. H. H. Arnold was relieved from duty at San Diego and ordered to Panama to organize and command the 7th Aero Squadron. He was followed by 1st Lt. C. W. Russell in March. Arnold did not stay long, for in April he was en route to the United States, and in May was on duty in the Office, Chief Signal Officer.[19]

---

*Captain C. G. Chapman was an observer with the British in London in March 1917.

In February the NACA passed a resolution urging that the Secretaries of War and Navy designate the aeronautic divisions of the Army and Navy, "Army Air Service" and "Naval Air Service," respectively, and that the aeronautic stations be termed "air stations;" apparently these titles were put into use.[20]

In March, the Joint Army and Navy Board on Aeronautic Cognizance reported to the Secretaries of War and Navy that the development of aeronautical resources of the United States and their application in war to the maximum national advantage could be best accomplished through the formulation of plans and regulations for the joint development, organization, and operation of the aeronautical services of the Army and the Navy instead of by the separate development of each service within delimited exact areas of responsibility.[21] While air operations of the Navy and Army were principally over water and land respectively, war would find the two services constantly operating together, with the Navy air service taking precedence prior to invasion and the Army air service being more important should a hostile landing be accomplished; but in either case each service would support the other. Consequently, the board felt that pilots and observers for both services should be trained together on or near the coast and that their equipment should be standardized as much as possible. In general, the Army would defend harbors, cities, factories, and utilities on shore, while the operations of the Navy air service would be principally over the sea, with bases on shore. Army and Navy commanders in coastal districts would have to familiarize themselves with each other's plans for effective cooperation on land and sea. The two services should coordinate their plans with those of local commanders, with the Army plans taking precedence. The Army aircraft mission over the sea was for the purpose of security and to obtain information for the territorial commander, as well as to furnish fire control for local Coast Artillery commanders and to afford aid and assistance to both the Army and Navy in scouting and offensive measures when the enemy was operating in the immediate vicinity of the coast. The Navy aircraft mission from shore stations was to scout and report movements of enemy forces at sea and to assist the Army when the enemy was operating in the immediate vicinity of the coast. Local Army

and Navy commanders in need of assistance were to communicate directly with one another. The report of the Joint Army-Navy Board—composed of Brig. Gen. G. O. Squier, CSO; Capt. G. R. Marvel, USN; Capt. Hugh Rodman, USN; Maj. S. D. Embick, CAC; Capt. J. S. McKean, USN; and Maj. D. T. Moore, G.S.—was approved by Secretaries Daniels and Baker.[22]

In the meantime a reorganization of the Aeronautical Division, suggested by Lieutenant Colonel Bennet and approved on 16 March 1917 by General Squier, provided for the following organization:[23]

Advisory Board

Personnel
　General Correspondence and Records
　Instruction, Organization, Training
　Intelligence

Materiel
　Inspection and Equipment
　Supply and Disbursement, H/A, L/A*
　Engineering, H/A
　Engineering, L/A

Because of the increase in the aviation activity in the Signal Corps, Bennet on 12 March 1917 had recommended additional personnel for the Aeronautical Division. His recommendations, exactly in line with those of the Assistant Chief of Staff, which had been approved by the Secretary of War on 5 July 1916, listed personnel required as follows:

Headquarters, Aeronautical Division
　1 Colonel, in charge
　1 Major, Supply Officer
　1 Major, Personnel and Record Officer
　1 Captain　　　) Intelligence Officers
　1 1st Lieutenant (
　1 Captain　　　)
　1 1st Lieutenant (Inspectors
Department of Inspection and Experiments
　(1) Headquarters
　　　1 Major, Commanding
　　　1 Captain, Adjutant and Intelligence Officer
　　　1 Captain, Chief Inspector
　　　1 Captain, Assistant Inspector
　　　4 Officers attached from squadrons
　(2) Airplane Design, Construction and Testing:
　　　1 Captain, in charge, Aeronautical Engineer
　(3) Radio and Electrical Apparatus:
　　　1 Captain, in charge, Electrical Engineer
　(4) Ordnance and Instruments:
　　　1 Captain, in charge

---

*H/A: Heavier-than-air (airplanes); L/A: Lighter-than-air (balloons).

(5) Motor Development and Testing:
    1 Captain, in charge
(6) Supply Section:
    1 1st Lieutenant, Supply Officer

This made a total of 1 colonel, 3 majors, 9 captains, and 7 first lieutenants, or 20 officers, for Headquarters, Aeronautical Division. The Department of Inspection and Experiments had not been organized and some personnel had not been assigned to the Headquarters, Aeronautical Division. It was intended to complete these organizations by the detail of aviation officers from time to time. The experimental work was to be carried on later at Hampton, Virginia, but in the meantime it was necessary to develop this branch in Washington.[24]

On 23 March a fourth indorsement to a report from the OCSO to The Adjutant General stated that the following officers were required in the Office, Chief Signal Officer in order to conduct the business of the organization:

Administration Division —
    Lt. Col. C. McK. Saltzman ....Present
Personnel Division —
    Major George S. Gibbs ....On Detached Service
    (Signal Corps, commissioned and enlisted SORC,
        SERC) Capt. Aubrey Lippincott ....Present
    (Aviation Section, commisisoned and enlisted,
        AS, SORC, AS, SERC)
Aeronautical Division — The General Staff plan
    approved by the Secretary of War on 5 July 1916
    provided 15 officers for duty in the headquarters
    offices. Five of these officers were en route at
    that time, but the work could not be efficiently
    carried on by this number. It was believed that
    the following officers could perform the work:
        Chief of Division — Lt. Col. John B. Bennet..Present
        Executive Assistant — Maj. B. D. Foulois ....En route
        Executive Assistant ....Vacancy
        Chief, Sub-division Materiel ....Vacancy
        Chief, Sub-division, Instruction, Organization,
            Training — Capt. T. D. Milling ....Present
        Chief, Sub-division, Intelligence ....Vacancy
        Chief, Sub-division, Inspection, Equipment —
            Capt. H. W. Harms ....Present
        Assistant to above ....Vacancy

It was impossible to prescribe grades of officers required for the vacant positions or to recommend their assignments until the names of officers competent to fill the positions could be decided. In addition to the above the following officers were required for temporary duty in the Department of Experiments, pending organization of the Experimental Station at Hampton, Virginia:

1 Aero engineer (H/A) — Capt. V. E. Clark ....Present
1 Aero engineer (L/A) — to be held vacant until
    Capt. C. deF. Chandler became available ....Vacancy
1 Radio engineer — to be held vacant for
    Capt. C. C. Culver ....Vacancy
Disbursing Division — OIC, Maj. C. S. Wallace ....Present
    Assistant and Supply Officer —
        Capt. A. C. Voris ....Present
    Disbursing Officer — Lt. A. G. Gutensohn ......Present
    Aviation Officer, Aviation Supplies,
        Equipment — Lt. G. H. Brett ....Present

Orders were requested for the return of Major Gibbs from detached service to the Office, Chief Signal Officer, the assignment of Lieutenant Brett to permanent duty, and the transfer of Capt. Edgar S. Gorrell from MIT to OCSO.[25]

By 6 April 1917, when America entered the war, the organization of the Aeronautical Division was as follows:[26]

Aeronautical Division — Lt. Col. John B. Bennet
    Correspondence — Maj. B. D. Foulois
        Instruction, Organization, and Training —
            Capt. T. D. Milling
        Intelligence — Capt. E. S. Gorrell
    Advisory Board — Maj. B. D. Foulois
    Materiel — vacancy
        Inspection and Equipment — Capt. H. W. Harms
        Experiments, Engineering, H/A — Capt. V. E. Clark
        Experiments, Engineering, L/A —
            Maj. C. deF. Chandler
        Experiments, Engineering, Radio —
            Capt. C. C. Culver

In order to relieve inequities in the rank and pay of certain flying officers, 1st Lt. Davenport Johnson on 16 March 1917 urged that legislation be enacted for the relief of officers on the Detached Officer List (DOL) attached to the Aviation Section. The following six officers were concerned:

1st Lt. William A. Robertson, Cav.   13 October 1916
1st Lt. Clinton W. Russell, Inf.   14 October 1916
1st Lt. Millard F. Harmon, Jr., Inf. 15 October 1916
1st Lt. Maxwell Kirby, Cav.   15 October 1916
1st Lt. Davenport Johnson, Inf.   16 October 1916
1st Lt. Howard C. Davidson, Inf.   16 October 1916

These officers had been detailed in the Aviation Section as of the dates shown above and rated JMA's by SO 240-49, 13 October 1916; but this order had been revoked on 15 November 1916, because officers whose names were on the Detached Officer List were not eligible for detail in the several staff corps and departments. The officers had passed the JMA test on 10 September

1916 and since that date had performed the duties of a JMA but were not allowed the rank, pay, and allowances of other JMA's who were not on the Detached Officer List.[27] Colonel Bennet reported that there was a bill before Congress that would remedy this situation, but in the meantime the Secretary of War ordered that "Acts of Congress forbidding the detachment from duty with their proper commands of officers of the line . . . who have not been actually present for duty for 2 years out of the last 6 years with organizations of the respective arms of the service in which they hold permanent commissions, being in force only in time of peace, the suspension of the operation thereof because of the imminence of hostilities is announced."[28] The draft act of 18 May 1917, then provided that "all existing restrictions upon the detail, detachment, and employment of officers and enlisted men of the Regular Army are hereby suspended for the period of the present emergency."[29]

On 31 March, SO 74-46 again detailed Lieutenant Robertson and rated him JMA with no date of rating, but on 29 August, SO 201-165 amended SO 74-46, giving Robertson his original rating date of 13 October 1916. On 15 June, SO 138-9 detailed and rated the other five officers from 16 June 1917. On 29 August SO 201-166 amended SO 138-9 of 15 June 1917; the new order reinstated the other five officers as JMA's as of the original date of 13 October given in SO 240.

On 17 March 1917, General Squier, Chief Signal Officer, stated that the necessary number of regular aviation officers on duty with tactical units in the completed organization of 7 squadrons would be 154. The 20 attached officers at the balloon school, which was being organized, would be students and instructors. The duties performed by officers regularly detailed or attached to the Aviation Section were:

	Detailed in Section	Attached to Section
Stationed at Washington	5	1
For duty: France	2	2
London	1	0
San Diego	4	53
Mineola	4	0
Memphis	2	0
MIT	2	0
Fort Omaha	----	3
Hq., Southern Dept.	1	0
	21	59

Proposed new tables of organization for aero squadrons provided 1 major, 9 captains, and 12 first lieutenants for duty with each squadron. The Chief of Staff on 3 March had authorized:

5 squadrons forming part of tactical organizations in the U.S.; 12 squadrons for cooperation with coast defenses in the U.S.; 3 squadrons at overseas stations, the 20 squadrons requiring:

20 Majors
180 Captains
240 First Lieutenants

440 Total

It was believed that three officers were necessary at each department headquarters. One officer could take care of supply and disbursement at the Experimental Station. One officer was necessary in Washington for personnel and one for intelligence. On 28 May, The Adjutant General approved the attachment to the section of the officers requested with the understanding that application for orders for them would be made only when the instruction facilities were adequate and when the growth of the aeronautical service required the full number of administrative officers estimated.[30]

The organization of the air service under a 7-squadron policy—4 squadrons equipped with land planes and 3 with sea planes—was in process. In order to equalize the number of experienced officers for duty with regular squadrons and to provide assistance at the two schools it was proposed to transfer four officers from Columbus to Fort Sam Houston for the three squadrons being organized there, and two officers to Chicago and Memphis, where other schools had been organized.[31]

On 22 March 1917, the formation of the Reserve Corps was authorized under the National Defense Act, and on 29 March, the first War Program was drawn up at a meeting of the National Advisory Committee for Aeronautics. This was a project for the production of 19,070 training and service airplanes for the Army and the Navy. It was approved by the Chief Signal Officer but was not sanctioned by the War and Navy departments. A personnel program of the same date called for an appropriation of $54,000,250 for a force of 1,850 aviators and 300 balloonists comprising 16 aero squadrons and 16 balloon companies. The fund also would provide 9 aviation schools, each of which would turn out 150 pilots a year; civilian schools were counted on to train the remaining 500 pilots and 300 balloonists in a year. The money requested was reduced to $43,450,000 and this amount was appropriated for aviation on 15 June 1917.[32]

General Squier proposed that aircraft production be taken over by a group of experts and on 5 April 1917, he appointed Mr. Sidney D. Waldon, Inspector of Airplanes and Airplane Motors, Signal Service at Large, to head a committee to put the aircraft building program on an up-to-date practical business basis and to speed up production of the necessary types as quickly as possible, keeping in mind the needs of the entire service of the United States rather than those of the War Department alone. The committee was to cooperate with the Council of National Defense, the National Advisory Committee for Aeronautics, and all other activities authorized and prescribed by law, with the single purpose of placing the industry on a sound basis at the earliest possible time. Mr. Waldon was to select a small staff of experts on the various phases of production and present their names to the Chief Signal Officer so that their hiring might be expedited. Out of this committee came the Aircraft Production Board, which was created on 16 May 1917.[33]

In April 1917, the Curtiss Company's annual production capacity of land planes was reported to be 2,500 JN's and 700 R's a year. Its existing British orders would be completed by September. Working one shift only, the Curtiss Company's deliveries to the United States government were expected to be 130 a month in April, May, and June; 200 in July; 250 in August, September, and October; 275 in November; 300 in December; and 350 a month in January and February 1918. A second shift could increase the output by more than 50 per cent and a third shift by 100 per cent. At this time the total output of all aircraft factories in England was about 300 machines a week.[34]

Although the Aero Club of America by 6 April 1917 had certified 689 airplane pilots—and many other pilots were flying without the Aero Club's card—the NACA reported that there were only about 25 good flying instructors in the United

States. The small number might be explained by the fact that a number of American aviators already were in the European War, having enlisted in the aviation corps of various European countries as well as that of Canada; a number of these men later became members of the United States Air Service in the AEF. Even so, the NACA figures are puzzling; for other sources show 51 civilian instructors at Army flying schools on 6 April 1917 and this number increased as time went on. The average period of preliminary instruction at the schools was estimated at about two months to fit recruits to be sent overseas; there a second period of three months' instruction was necessary to qualify them for active service. Advanced training for military fliers could not be given in the United States, but could only be given at schools in England and France.[35]

On 6 April 1917, America declared war on Germany. Because aeronautics had been sorely neglected, the outbreak of war found the United States with but a handful of fliers and very few training machines. The Navy had 48 officers, 230 enlisted men,* 54 planes, 2 kite balloons, and 1 unsatisfactory dirigible. The Army air officer strength on this date was 131.† This figure included all officers on air duty, airplane and balloon pilots, flying and non-flying officers, and Reserve and retired officers ordered to active duty, with the exception of Quartermaster and Medical officers. In addition to the above there were a number of Reserve students taking flight instruction at Newport News, Miami, Chicago or Memphis, and Mineola. These men had enlisted as sergeants in the SERC and many of them were rated shortly after 6 April. A number of officer pilots who held JMA or MA ratings were not on air duty at this time, and also a group of enlisted pilots with FAI ratings. In addition to the officers, there were 1,087 enlisted men in the air service.** The Army airplane strength was given as "less than 300 training planes, all of inferior types"; and the experience on the Mexican border had demon-

---

*NACA figures in Aircraft Hearings before the President's Aircraft Board (Morrow), 5 Dec. 1925, Vol. IV, p. 1716 give 38 naval aviators and 163 enlisted men.

†The figure 65 is usually given for the number of air officers on duty at this time. This figure represents only the Regular Army officers detailed to or working with the Aviation Section, Signal Corps. Of the 131 officers, 56 were airplane pilots and 51 were student pilots.

**Two sources give this figure: Fletcher, Monograph #16, AWC 1922 and Hearings on H.R. 11273, 1928.

strated the unsuitability of the planes for combat operations.[36]

According to the "Consolidated List of Aircraft Contracts and Deliveries," from the purchase of the first plane in 1909 to 1 November 1919, the Signal Corps bought and received 14,274 airplanes.[37] Of these, 13,894 were delivered on orders made between 6 April 1917 and 1 November 1919,[38] leaving 380 planes received between 1909 and 6 April 1917. But there is no assurance that the figure of 380 is correct. The sources all agree that 59 airplanes were delivered between 1909 and 31 December 1915, but at that point any similarity between figures ends, so that it is impossible to make a complete and accurate list of either orders or deliveries for the period 1 January 1916 to 6 April 1917. Mixter and Emmons of the Bureau of Aircraft Production state that during the year 1916, 83 airplanes were received.[39] This figure can be broken down as follows:[40]

    68 Curtiss JN4's
     6 Curtiss Twin Engine Reconnaissance planes
     3 Standard H2's
     2 Lowe-Willard Fowler (LWF) VI's
     2 Martins
     2 Sturtevants
    ──
    83 Total

This total plus the original 59 planes adds up to 142 airplanes received by 31 December 1916. However, the above list does not agree with the figures given by the General Accounting Office (GAO) records nor those of James C. Fahey in *U.S. Army Aircraft 1908-1946*. It does not include 12 Curtiss R2 planes received at Columbus, New Mexico and 13 Standard H2's—9 delivered at San Antonio and 2 each at Mineola and San Diego. It shows 16 Curtiss JN4's and 2 Martins that GAO records do not list as delivered until 1917.

After consulting every available source, the most accurate of which seem to be the GAO records and Fahey, the figure which the author has arrived at for planes delivered in 1916 is 90. This, plus

the 59 planes delivered through 1915, makes a total of 149 planes received through 1916, leaving 231 of the 380 planes to be accounted for in the period 1 January to 6 April 1917. Counting only those planes which there is good reason to believe were delivered, the author can account for only about 165 received during this time, leaving an excess of 66 planes. This discrepancy can only be explained by gaps in the orders, cancellations, and the possibility that some planes which were ordered were not delivered. Also the figure of 13,894 planes delivered between 6 April 1917 and 1 November 1919 covered only the planes delivered on orders made after 6 April 1917 and doubtless there were a number of planes ordered before that date which were not delivered until later. In fact, General Scriven reported on 5 January 1917 that there were 302 planes on order but not delivered.[41]

At least one thing is certain: at the outbreak of war little or nothing was on hand, either of planes, fields, instructors, curricula, or—most important of all—experience that would indicate what was needed. The United States had never trained an aviator for actual combat overseas; and there was no one who knew what kind of instruction was necessary for radio operators, photographers, or regular run-of-the-mill enlisted personnel. Consequently, the first men charged with the training program had to learn by the trial and error method before teaching others.[42]

The tactical units were distributed among seven aero squadrons, most of which were still in the process of organizing and being equipped. There was no regular balloon company in existence. In January 1917, an estimate calling for the organization of six National Guard squadrons was in the Military Affairs Committee but no National Guard units and only two Reserve Aero Squadrons were in existence when the United States entered the war,[43] and no more of either were ever authorized. Probably no one in aviation realized what difficulties lay ahead.

──────────★──────────

Notes

Chapter I

1. F. Stansbury Haydon, *Aeronautics in the Union and Confederate Armies* (Baltimore, 1941), pp. 39–47 (hereinafter cited as Haydon).

2. *Ibid.*, pp. 48–56.

3. *Ibid.*, pp. 47–71; Charles deF. Chandler and Frank P. Lahm, *How Our Army Grew Wings* (New York, 1943), p. 15 (hereinafter cited as Chandler and Lahm).

4. Chandler and Lahm, pp. 16–17; Haydon, pp. 71–74.

5. Haydon, pp. 75–81.

6. *Ibid.*, pp. 82–94.

7. *Ibid.*, pp. 95–97.

8. *Ibid.*, pp. 116–27.

9. *Ibid.*, pp. 127–53.

10. *Ibid.*, pp. 162–67; Chandler and Lahm, pp. 22–23.

11. Haydon, pp. 168–86.

12. *Ibid.*, pp. 190–93; War of the Rebellion: Compilation of the Official Records of the Union and Confederate armies (U.S. War Dept., Washington, D.C., 1880–1901) 3, III, 256–58 (hereinafter cited as O. R.)

13. Historical Office of the AAF, *The Official Pictorial History of the AAF* (New York, 1947), p. 13 (hereinafter cited as *AAF Pictorial History*); Haydon, pp. 194–95.

14. Haydon, pp. 194–95.

15. *Ibid.*, pp. 195–98; Lowe's Report to Sec. of War Stanton, 26 May 1863, in O. R., 3, III, 258–59.

16. Haydon, pp. 199–204.

17. *Ibid.*, pp. 205–18; Chandler and Lahm, pp. 30–31.

18. Chandler and Lahm, pp. 31–32; Haydon, pp. 218–27.

19. Ltr., Brig. Gen. Montgomery C. Meigs to Lowe, 25 Sep 1861, in O. R., 3, III, 269.

20. Haydon, pp. 247–54.

21. *Ibid.*, pp. 233–46.

22. *Ibid.*, pp. 256–58.

23. *Ibid.*, pp. 258–68.

24. *Ibid.*, pp. 269–79.

25. *Ibid.*, pp. 293–307.

26. Ernest L. Jones, Chronology of Military Aeronautics (1793–1948) (hereinafter cited as Jones Chronology), 168.6501, in USAFHD Archives. This is an unpublished chronology compiled by the late Ernest L. Jones, formerly of the USAF Historical Division.

27. T. S. C. Lowe, *The Latest Development in Aerial Navigation* (Los Angeles, 1910), p. 25, USAFHD Archives; General James Longstreet, "Story of the Civil War," *Century Magazine,* cited in Lowe, *The Latest Development in Aerial Navigation,* p. 23; Lt. Col. W. A. Glassford, "Our Army and Aerial Warfare," *Aeronautics,* January 1908.

28. Special Order No. 157, Army of the Potomac, 25 May 1862.

29. Haydon, pp. 280–292; Chandler and Lahm, pp. 33–34.

30. Haydon, pp. 187–88.

31. *Ibid.*, pp. 217–18.

32. *Ibid.*, p. 360.

33. Chandler and Lahm, p. 32 .

34. General James Longstreet, "Story of the Civil War," *Century Magazine,* quoted in Lowe, *The Latest Development in Aerial Navigation,* pp. 32–33.

35. Chandler and Lahm, pp. 32–33.

36. Article by Edward Wellman Serrell in *Science,* XIX (1904), 952.

37. *Ibid.*

38. Files of the Smithsonian Institution; *Encyclopedia Americana,* "Submarines: Their History, Development and Equipment."

39. Jones Chronology; *AAF Pictorial History,* pp 14–15; Chief Signal Officer's Annual Report, 1894 (hereinafter cited CSO Annual Report). These reports for the years 1894 through 1908 are located in the Office, Chief Signal Officer; those from 1908 on are found in the USAF Library in the Office of the Air Adjutant General.

40. *AAF Pictorial History,* p. 17; Jones Chronology; CSO Annual Report, 1898; Gen. A. W. Greely, "Balloons in Warfare," *Harpers,* XLIV (1900), 46.

41. CSO Annual Report, 1898; Gen. A. W. Greely, "Balloons in Warfare," *Harpers,* XLIV (1900), 47.

42. Jones Chronology; *AAF Pictorial History,* p. 17.

43. *AAF Pictorial History,* p. 17; CSO Annual Report, 1898; Gen. A. W. Greely, "Balloons in Warfare," *Harpers,* XLIV (1900), 47.

44. Jones Chronology, June 1898.

45. *Ibid.*; Chandler and Lahm, pp. 50–51.

46. *Aeronautical World,* 1 Sep 1902 and 1 May 1903, in

Ernest L. Jones' personal file; ltr, Baldwin to E. L. Jones, 20 Apr 1950, in Jones' personal file.

47. CSO Annual Report, 1903.

48. CSO Annual Report, 1906.

49. CSO Annual Report, 1907.

50. Chandler and Lahm, pp. 52–66; *AAF Pictorial History,* p. 18.

51. Chandler and Lahm, pp. 76–77.

52. *American Magazine of Aeronautics,* November 1907, p. 34; *AAF Pictorial History,* p. 18; Yearbook, *Aero Club of America,* 1908, p. 29, in National Aeronautics Association files and in USAFHD Archives.

53. War Dept. Special Order No. 154, 2 Jul 1907.

54. Office Memo No. 6, OCSO, 1 Aug 1907, in Central Files, AAG, 321.914, Signal Corps Organization.

55. Chandler and Lahm, pp. 79–84; *AAF Pictorial History,* p. 19.

56. WDSO No. 86, Washington, D.C., 11 Apr 1908, in Army Library.

57. Chandler and Lahm, p. 101; *American Magazine of Aeronautics,* November 1907, p. 39.

58. CSO Annual Report, 1908.

59. Rept., C. H. Claudy to CSO, in Signal Corps file No. 452.2, Airplanes 1907–1915, in National Archives; *Aeronautics,* June 1908, pp. 5, 31 and 50; Chandler and Lahm, pp. 83–84; Gen. A. W. Greely, "Balloons in Warfare," *Harpers,* XLIV (1900), 48. (All Signal Corps files cited hereinafter are in the National Archives.)

60. Chandler and Lahm, pp. 107–10.

61. *Ibid.,* pp. 110–11.

62. *Ibid.,* pp. 111–13, App. 4, p. 291; Jones Chronology, August 1908.

63. Chandler and Lahm, App. 4, pp. 291–93; Jones Chronology, August 1908.

64. *Aeronautics,* February 1908, p. 33, March 1908, pp. 26, 40–41, July 1908, pp. 13, 41, September 1908, p. 8; CSO Annual Report 1908; Chandler and Lahm, pp. 111–12; Diary of Events, Aeronautical Div., Office of the CSO, written by 1st Lt. Frank P. Lahm to CSO, November 1908 in E. L. Jones files.

65. Maj. George O. Squier, "Present Status of Military Aeronautics 1908," paper presented 2 Dec 1908 before the American Society of Mechanical Engineers, in *Journal of the American Society of Mechanical Engineers,* pp. 1589–90, in USAFHD Archives.

66. *Aeronautics,* July 1909, p. 10, August 1909, p. 52; WDSO No. 114, Washington, D.C., 8 May 1909 and WDSO No. 252, 29 Oct 1909; Aero Club of America records, in National Aeronautics Association files; Chandler and Lahm, p. 120; Yearbook, *Aero Club of America,* 1910.

67. CSO Annual Report, 1912.

68. Special Order No. 46, Army Signal School, Fort Leavenworth, Kansas, 17 May 1911; Chandler and Lahm, p. 86.

69. Repts, Major Russel and Captain Chandler, in Signal Corps file No. 27170; Annual Report, Commandant, Army Service Schools, 1911, in Signal Corps file No. 28735.

70. WDSO No. 132, Washington, D.C., 7 June 1911.

71. *Aeronautics,* August 1911, p. 67, October 1911, p. 138, November 1911, p. 159; Chandler and Lahm, pp. 103–5; Yearbook, *Aero Club of America,* 1912.

72. Messages in Signal Corps file No. 39759.

73. CSO Annual Report, 15 Oct 1912; Aero Club of America records in National Aeronautics Association files; Chandler and Lahm, pp. 122–23; *Aeronautics,* January 1910, p. 27.

74. Ernest Lehmann and Howard Mingos, *The Zeppelins,* The Development of the Airship with the Story of the Zeppelin Air Raids in World War (New York, 1927), p. 16.

CHAPTER II

1. Chandler and Lahm, p. 124; AFROTC Textbook, *Introduction to Aviation,* Air Science, Vol. II, Chap. VI.

2. Chandler and Lahm, pp. 93–95; *Dictionary of American Biography; Smithsonian Contributions to Knowledge,* XXVII, No. 3; *Langley Memoirs on Mechanical Flight,* 1911; Signal Corps file No. 452, Langley Airplane.

3. Description of the Langley aerodrome in the files of the Smithsonian Institution. The plane was carefully examined by the author.

4. S. Paul Johnston, "Aide in Aerodynamics: Charles Matthews Manly, assistant to Samuel Langley," *The Technology Review,* XLIV (1942), 218–36, in files of the Smithsonian Institution.

5. Chandler and Lahm, pp. 95–98; Langley aerodrome papers in files of the Smithsonian Institution.

6. Chandler and Lahm, pp. 125–30; Fred C. Kelly, *The Wright Brothers* (New York, 1943), pp. 70–78.

7. Chandler and Lahm, p. 133; Description of the 1903 Wright Flyer in the files of the Smithsonian Institution. This plane was also carefully examined by the author.

8. Chandler and Lahm, p. 132; Description of the 1903 Wright Flyer in the files of the Smithsonian Institution; Kelly, *The Wright Brothers,* pp. 84–86.

9. Chandler and Lahm, pp. 133–35; Orville Wright, "How We Made the First Flight," *Flying Maga-*

zine, II (1913), 10–12; *New York Times,* 11 Dec 1938.

10. *The Washington Post,* 21 Oct and 23 Nov 1948; *The Miracle of Kitty Hawk,* ed. Fred C. Kelly (New York, 1951), pp. 442–44. The author saw the *Kitty Hawk* returned to the Smithsonian on 22 November 1948.

11. Chandler and Lahm, pp. 135–40; Kelly, *The Wright Brothers,* pp. 121–37.

12. Board of Ordnance and Fortification files in National Archives; Chandler and Lahm, pp. 141–42; Early Bird Assn., *Chirp,* ed. E. L. Jones, August 1948, No. 38, pp. 1 and 7, in E. L. Jones' personal files; Kelly, *The Wright Brothers,* pp. 147–65.

13. Board of Ordnance and Fortification files in National Archives; *Chirp,* August 1948, No. 38, p. 7; Kelly, *The Wright Brothers,* pp. 157, 162–65.

14. Jones Chronology. At the close of 1907 only 12 men in the world had flown an airplane (certain doubtful flights are omitted). None of the other flyers had approached the Wright brothers in duration and distances of flights.
    1. Orville Wright (U.S.)
    2. Wilbur Wright (U.S.)
    3. T. Vuia (France)
    4. J. C. H. Ellehammer (Denmark)
    5. Santos-Dumont (France)
    6. Charles Voisin (France)
    7. Louis Bleriot (France)
    8. Henri Farman (France)
    9. Robert Esnault-Pelterie (France)
    10. Leon Delagrange (France)
    11. Henri de la Vaulx (France)
    12. M. de Pischoff (France)

15. Kelly, *The Wright Brothers,* pp. 194–213.

16. Board of Ordnance and Fortification files in National Archives.

17. Chandler and Lahm, pp. 295–98.

18. *American Magazine of Aeronautics,* II (1908), 5–7; Chandler and Lahm pp. 146–47; Kelly, *The Wright Brothers,* pp. 191–93 and 209–11; New York *Herald,* 22, 25, 28, and 29 November 1906.

19. Chandler and Lahm, pp. 148–50; Board of Ordnance and Fortification files in National Archives.

20. Chandler and Lahm, pp. 150 and 167–68; Board of Ordnance and Fortification files in National Archives.

21. Chandler and Lahm, pp. 150–51; Kelly, *The Wright Brothers,* pp. 216–25; ltr., Orville Wright to E. L. Jones, 15 Nov. 1928, in E. L. Jones' personal files; Board of Ordnance and Fortification files in National Archives.

22. Chandler and Lahm, pp. 150–51; *Aeronautics,* II (1908), 129; D. B. Salley messages, in E. L. Jones' personal file; Kelly, *The Wright Brothers,* pp. 216–25; Norfolk *Landmark,* 9–17 May 1908; New York

Herald, 9–20 May 1908; Arthur Ruhl, "History of Kill Devil Hill," *Colliers,* LVII (30 May 1908), 18–19, 26.

23. Chandler and Lahm, pp. 152–54; Kelly, *The Wright Brothers,* pp. 226–32; Signal Corps file No. 19621.

24. Chandler and Lahm, pp. 154–55; Signal Corps file Nos. 20279, 21340, and 20852; *Proceedings of the Board of Regents, Smithsonian Institution,* 1910, Publications Numbers 1916, 2000, and 2001 in Smithsonian Institution; Kelly, *The Wright Brothers,* pp. 258–59, 302; *Aeronautics,* V (1909), 25–27.

25. Chandler and Lahm, p. 155 and App. 7, pp. 299–302.

26. Signal Corps file No. 22246; Chandler and Lahm, App. 7, pp. 299–302.

27. Chandler and Lahm, pp. 156–61; *The Evening Star,* Washington, D.C., 31 Jul 1909; Kelly, *The Wright Brothers,* pp. 260–61. The information that Lahm flew as an observer and Foulois as an observer and navigator came from General B. D. Foulois, who reviewed this manuscript.

28. Chandler and Lahm, p. 167; Board of Ordnance and Fortification Proceedings, p. 35, in National Archives.

29. Chandler and Lahm, pp. 162–63; Kelly, *The Wright Brothers,* pp. 265–66; Jones Chronology. By October 1909 at least 13 men had flown in the United States:

Orville Wright	Carl S. Bates
Wilbur Wright	Hugh A. Robinson
F. W. Baldwin	Charles F. Willard
Lt. T. E. Selfridge	B. Russell Shaw
Glenn Curtiss	G. Francis Myers
J. A. D. McCurdy	Charles Crout
M. B. Sellers	

30. Office, Chief Signal Officer, Memo No. 18, in Signal Corps file No. 21347.21; yearbooks, *Aero Club of America,* 1910, p. 58 and 1913, p. 71.

31. Chandler and Lahm, pp. 163–65 and App. 8, pp. 303–4; Kelly, *The Wright Brothers,* pp. 265–66.

32. Chandler and Lahm, pp. 169–76.

33. House Comm., 68th Cong., 1st Sess., [Report] on Inquiry into . . . The United States air service, pp. 180, 350, 3176, 3184, and 3185; affidavits of William W. Christmas, Robert N. Ions, and David B. Fawcett, 29 Aug 1929, in regard to Christmas' claim before the Chief of Air Service in Air Force files, Patent Branch, in National Archives.

34. J. A. D. McCurdy, *Canadian Aviation,* XIII (October 1940), 30.

CHAPTER III

1. Chandler and Lahm, pp. 166–67.

2. *Ibid.,* p. 166.

3. *Ibid.,* pp. 158 and 180–84; *Aeronautics,* VI (1910),

164 and 200; VII (1910), 48 and 132; San Antonio *Express,* 11, 20, and 23 Aug 1910; Signal Corps files No. 23631, 23905, and 24905.

4. Chandler and Lahm, p. 182.

5. *Ibid.,* p. 183, note 6.

6. *Ibid.,* pp. 182–83.

7. Signal Corps file Nos. 26547, 26476, 23631, and 26574; Chandler and Lahm, p. 184.

8. Chandler and Lahm, pp. 185–86; Signal Corps file Nos. 26672, 26559, and 23631; San Antonio *Express,* 4 and 6 Mar 1911.

9. Chandler and Lahm, p. 187.

10. Chandler and Lahm, p. 194; Ernest L. Jones' compilations of first airplanes bought by United States government, in USAFHD Archives.

11. Signal Corps file No. 26464.

12. *Aeronautics,* VIII (1911), 100–3 and 121–22; Ernest L. Jones' compilations of first airplanes bought by United States government, in USAFHD Archives; Signal Corps file Nos. 27286 and 27278.

13. Chandler and Lahm, pp. 188; ltr., Frank T. Coffyn to E. L. Jones, 10 Oct 1945, in Jones' personal file; Signal Corps file No. 27098.

14. San Antonio *Express,* 23 Apr 1911.

15. Signal Corps file Nos. 27434 and 27368; *Aeronautics,* VIII (1911), 202.

16. Chandler and Lahm, pp. 189–90.

17. Chandler and Lahm, pp. 190–91; Board Report G. E. M. Kelly 201 file in AAG 201 files; *Aeronautics,* VIII (1911), 213; San Antonio *Express,* 11 and 12 May 1911; General Foulois' report of his aviation experiences for The Air Force Historical Foundation, 1955, and interview, author with General Foulois, August 1954.

18. Ltr., Frank T. Coffyn to E. L. Jones, 10 Oct 1945, in Jones' personal file; Chandler and Lahm, p. 191; Signal Corps file No. 27098.

19. Chandler and Lahm, pp. 191–92, 198; Frank M. Kennedy 201 File in AAG 201 files; WDSO No. 139–6, 15 Jun 1911.

20. WDSO No. 160, Washington, D.C., 11 Jul 1911.

21. Ernest L. Jones, Chronology, January 1910, in USAFHD Archives; Chandler and Lahm, pp. 87–89; Signal Corps file No. 22634; WDSO No. 298, Washington, D.C., 23 Dec 1909.

22. *Aeronautics,* VI (1910), 106; Chandler and Lahm, pp. 89–90; Signal Corps file No. 26064; ltr., Myron Crissy to E. L. Jones, 28 Dec 1943, in E. L. Jones' personal file; Capt. Paul Beck in *Hearings on H.R. 5304,* House Committee on Military Affairs, 12 Aug 1913, p. 38.

23. New York *Herald,* 16 Jan 1911.

24. San Francisco *Call,* 17 Jan 1911; Signal Corps file No. 26064.

25. Albert F. Zahm, *Aerial Navigation* (New York, 1911), pp. 284–286, 298–300.

26. Signal Corps file No. 24555; *Aeronautics,* VII (1910), 49; Jones Chronology, 30 Jun 1910.

27. Chandler and Lahm, pp. 90–91; *Aeronautics,* VII (1910), 128; Glenn H. Curtiss' personal chronology, cited in Jones Chronology, 20 Aug 1910.

28. Chandler and Lahm, p. 195; Signal Corps file Nos. 27146 and 27198; WDSO No. 72, 28 March 1911.

29. Chandler and Lahm, p. 196; WDSO No. 132, 7 Jun 1911.

30. WDSO No. 139, 15 Jun 1911.

31. WDSO No. 143, 20 Jun 1911; Chandler and Lahm, pp. 196, 198.

32. WDSO No. 161, 12 Jul 1911.

33. Signal Corps file No. 27699; Chandler and Lahm, pp. 196–97.

34. Chandler and Lahm, p. 196.

35. *Ibid.,* pp. 197–98.

36. *Ibid.,* pp. 198–99; College Park file 452.1–43 in WD Records Branch, Alexandria, Va.; Signal Corps file Nos. 31638 and 31209.

37. Chandler and Lahm, pp. 199–203; *Aeronautics,* X (1912), 29; Signal Corps file Nos. 28153 and 28158; Compilation of Plane Acceptance dates in File D52.1/308 in USAF Library.

38. Chandler and Lahm, p. 199.

39. Chandler and Lahm, pp. 200–1; Aero Club of America records; Signal Corps file Nos. 28259 and 29214.

40. Frank M. Kennedy 201 File in AAG 201 Files.

41. Central Files 353.9, Rockwell Field Training, in AGO Files.

42. Frank M. Kennedy 201 File in AAG 201 Files.

43. Signal Corps Office Memo No. 13, 3 Jul 1911, in Signal Corps file No. 27836.

44. Chandler and Lahm, p. 198.

45. Chandler and Lahm, pp. 204–5.

46. CSO Annual Report, 1913.

47. Signal Corps file Nos. 32515 and 28215.

48. Signal Corps file Nos. 29378 and 30340.

49. Signal Corps file No. 29378; Chandler and Lahm, pp. 206–7; "Military Aviation," *House Document 718,* 62d Congress, 2d Session.

50. Chandler and Lahm, pp. 204, 209; *Aeronautics,* IX (1911), 89–91, 134–36; Glenn H. Curtiss' Chronology, cited in Jones Chronology, 23–30 Sep 1911.

51. Chandler and Lahm, p. 195; Signal Corps file No.

28852; *Aeronautics,* VIII (1911), 159. The Chief Signal Officer had invited civilians to use the Army's flying field during the previous winter, and the land at College Park had been used by Rexford Smith for experiments with airplanes of his own design. In March 1912 Adolph Richter, pilot of the Rex Smith Airplane Company, received permission to erect a tent hangar and instruct students at Augusta while the Signal Corps Aviation School was there.

52. Chandler and Lahm, pp. 210–11; Signal Corps file Nos. 31323 and 28849.

53. Chandler and Lahm, pp. 212 and 215; Signal Corps file No. 29214.

54. Signal Corps file No. 32567.

55. Chandler and Lahm, p. 215; Signal Corps file No. 29214.

56. Chandler and Lahm, pp. 213–14; Signal Corps file No. 29214.

57. Signal Corps file Nos. 29105, 29214, and 29222.

58. Chandler and Lahm, p. 214; Signal Corps file No. 29214.

59. Signal Corps file Nos. 29449, 29214, and 29516; Chandler and Lahm, pp. 214–15.

60. Signal Corps file No. 29214; Chandler and Lahm, p. 216.

61. Chandler and Lahm, pp. 217, 221; Signal Corps file Nos. 29449 and 29214.

62. Signal Corps file No. 29427; "Military Aviation," *House Document No. 718,* 62d Congress, 2d Session; CSO Annual Report 1912; Chandler and Lahm, pp. 209–10; *Aeronautics,* X (1912), 67.

63. Chandler and Lahm, p. 216; Signal Corps file Nos. 10772 and 29427.

64. "Military Aviation," *House Documetn No. 718,* 62d Cong., 2d Sess., 1912; War Dept. Bulletin No. 2, 23 Feb. 1912; Signal Corps file Nos. 28851 and 30753; Chandler and Lahm, p. 306.

65. Circular No. 11, OCSO, 26 Oct 1912, as cited in Chandler and Lahm, p. 307.

66. Signal Corps file No. 31180.

67. WDGO No. 40, 9 Jun 1913 (amended by GO No. 54, 2 Sep 1913).

68. Memo, CSO to Chief of Staff, 28 Mar 1913, in Central Files 421A-Insignia, in AAG; memo, CSO to Chief of Staff in Central Files No. 211-Aviators, etc. in AAG.

69. WDGO No. 39, 27 May 1913; WDGO No. 48, 22 Jul 1913.

70. Central Files No. 421A-Insignia and 211-Aviators, etc., in AAG; R. D. Ewin, *Insignia and Decorations of the U.S. Armed Forces,* National Geographic Society, 1944.

71. WDGO No. 54, 12 Sep 1913, which amended GO No. 40, 9 Jun 1913; GO No. 61, 15 Oct 1913; GO No. 72, 24 Nov 1913; GO No. 2, 15 Jan 1914; GO No. 5, 5 Feb 1914.

72. Signal Corps file Nos. 352-San Diego Aviation School 1913–18, 32350 and 32428; yearbook, *Aero Club of America,* 1912, p. 49 and 1913, pp. 63–64; CSO Brig. Gen. George P. Scriven, 12 Aug. 1913, in *Hearings on H.R. 5304;* SO No. 57, SCAS, San Diego, Calif., 26 Dec 1913.

CHAPTER IV

1. WDSO No. 73, Par. 8, 27 Mar 1912.

2. Chandler and Lahm, p. 219; Signal Corps file No. 29993.

3. Signal Corps file No. 29993; WDSO No. 115–2, 15 May 1912; Chandler and Lahm, pp. 219, 232.

4. WDSO No. 161–19, 10 Jul 1912.

5. WDSO No. 228–23, 27 Sep 1912.

6. WDSO No. 228–3, 27 Sep 1912.

7. WDSO No. 110, 9 May 1912, No. 213–11, 10 Sep 1912, and No. 202–5, 27 Aug 1912.

8. WDSO No. 248–22, 21 Oct 1912.

9. Chandler and Lahm, pp. 240–41.

10. WDSO No. 252–26, 25 Oct 1912; WDSO 268–3, 14 Nov 1912.

11. Chandler and Lahm, pp. 241–42; ltr., Frank Coffyn to Chandler, 18 Apr 1938, Lahm Mss., Vol. V, in USAFHD Archives; Signal Corps file Nos. 31732, 34257, 31285, 32126, and 32158.

12. Chandler and Lahm, pp. 219–20.

13. Chandler and Lahm, pp. 233–34; Signal Corps file No. 30856; WDSO 208–30, 3 Sep 1912.

14. *Ciba Symposia,* December 1943, of Ciba Pharmaceutical Products, Summit, N.J.; WDGO No. 66, 1910; Signal Corps file Nos. 28551 and 31264; "Military Aviation," *House Document No. 718,* 1912.

15. Chandler and Lahm, pp. 225–27; *New York Times,* 2 Jun 1912.

16. CSO Annual Reports, 1912 and 1913; Chandler and Lahm, pp. 222–25; Signal Corps file No. 35404.

17. Chandler and Lahm, pp. 220–21; Central File 704.5A—Mortality Reports, in AAG; College Park file 452.1–43, in War Dept. Rec. Br., Alexandria, Va.; *Army Navy Journal,* 15 Jun 1912, p. 1302.

18. Chandler and Lahm, pp. 230–31.

19. Signal Corps file Nos. 30814, 30721, 31464, and 29269; CSO Annual Report, 1913.

20. CSO Annual Report, 1913; ltr., Beckwith Havens to E. L. Jones, 19 Oct 1948, in E. L. Jones' personal file.

21. Chandler and Lahm, pp. 229–30; CSO Annual Report, 1913.

22. Chandler and Lahm, p. 229; CSO Annual Report, 1913.

23. Chandler and Lahm, pp. 229–31 and 233; Signal Corps file No. 30251; ltr. F. M. Kennedy to E. L. Jones, 1946, in E. L. Jones' personal file.

24. Ltr., H. A. Dargue to Fiorella La Guardia, 15 Aug 1928, in E. L. Jones' personal file; College Park file 451–1–43, in War Dept. Rec. Br., AGO, Alexandria, Va.; Chandler and Lahm, pp. 232–33.

25. Signal Corps file No. 31243.

26. CSO Annual Report, 1913; *NAA Review,* April 1926, p. 57; Chandler and Lahm, pp. 236–37.

27. Chandler and Lahm, pp. 237–38; Signal Corps file Nos. 30340 and 31367.

28. Ltr., Follett Bradley to General Menoher, 14 Dec 1919 in Bradley 201 file, in AGO 201 files; Signal Corps file No. 30340.

29. Jones Chronology, 5 Nov 1912.

30. App. 4 to *Report on Progress in Army Aeronautics,* CSO, Annual Report, 1913; *Hearings on H.R. 5304,* 1913; Chandler and Lahm, pp. 237–38.

31. Signal Corps file No. 30340.

32. H. H. Arnold, *Global Mission* (New York, 1949), pp. 41–45.

33. Signal Corps file Nos. 30340 and 31563.

34. Chandler and Lahm, p. 242; Signal Corps file Nos. 32237 and 31412.

35. Signal Corps file No. 31399.

36. OCSO Circular No. 11, 26 Oct 1912; OCSO Circular No. 9, 18 Oct 1913.

37. E. L. Jones' compilation of planes purchased by the Signal Corps, in USAFHD Archives.

38. Chandler and Lahm, pp. 242–43; CSO Annual Report, 1913.

39. Signal Corps file Nos. 32087 and 32168; CSO Annual Report, 1913; *Hearings on H.R. 5304,* 12 Aug 1913, pp. 35–36.

40. Signal Corps file Nos. 28309 and 31323; CSO Annual Report, 1913; Chandler and Lahm, p. 251.

41. Signal Corps file Nos. 31892, 28309, 32237, 32306, 35568, and 143.6; GAO, R&C Division files 47912 and 48059; Central Files 425.1A—Rockwell Field; File No. D52.1/308 in AF Library; CSO Report of 7 Jul 1913 in *Hearings on H.R. 5304.*

42. Chandler and Lahm, p. 253–54.

43. Signal Corps file No. 34257.

44. Signal Corps file Nos. 28309 and 32463; Chandler and Lahm, p. 254.

45. Central Files 322, 172A, in AGO.

46. Field Order No. 1, Hq. First Aero Squadron, 5 Mar 1913, in file C22.32/44 in AF Library, "History of Organization of Aero Squadrons" (a collection of brief histories in manuscript form).

47. WDSO No. 53, 6 Mar 1913.

48. WDSO No. 61, 15 Mar 1913.

49. WDSO No. 63, 18 Mar 1913; U.S. Congress, House Committee on Military Affairs, 63d Cong., 1st Sess., *Hearings on H.R. 5304,* p. 32.

50. WDSO No. 70, 26 Mar 1913; WDSO No. 107, 8 May 1913; WDSO No. 108, 9 May 1913.

51. WDSO Nos. 71–40, 27 Mar 1913 and 113–6, 15 May 1913; Chandler and Lahm, p. 256.

52. Signal Corps file No. 28309.

53. Signal Corps file Nos. 32637, 32487, and 28309.

54. Signal Corps file No. 28309; General Scriven, "Report on Progress Made in Aeronautics in the Army Since About 1 March 1913," 7 Jul 1913, in *Hearings on H.R. 5304,* p. 107.

55. Signal Corps file No. 32637.

56. Signal Corps file No. 32487.

57. Jones Chronology, 10 May 1913.

58. Signal Corps file Nos. 35032, 33263, and 33326; ltr., A. B. Lambert to E. L. Jones, 25 Sep 1913, in E. L. Jones' personal file; CSO Annual Report, 1913, p. 69.

59. *Aero,* 15 Oct 1910; *Aeronautics,* X (1912), 106.

60. Signal Corps file Nos. 28716, 35060, 32139, 36474, and 33263; CSO Annual Report, 1913, p. 69.

61. Signal Corps file No. 32487; Chandler and Lahm, p. 256; Central Files "Aviation Fields," 686 Southern Dept., in AGO Files.

62. Signal Corps file No. 32752.

63. Ltr., H. A. Dargue to Fiorella La Guardia, 15 Aug 1928, in Dargue's personal file, cited in Jones Chronology; *Army Navy Journal,* 13 Jul 1913, p. 1304; Chandler and Lahm, pp. 256–57.

64. Signal Corps file No. 32733; SO No. 190, Hq. 2d Div., Texas City, 28 Nov 1913.

65. Signal Corps file Nos. 28378 and 28666; Chandler and Lahm, p. 244.

66. Chandler and Lahm, pp. 244–45; *Aeronautics,* X (1912), 153.

67. Signal Corps file Nos. 21371 and 23830; Chandler and Lahm, pp. 245–46.

68. Signal Corps file No. 31402.

69. Signal Corps file No. 32796; CSO Annual Report, 1914; Chandler and Lahm, p. 246.

70. Signal Corps file No. 31166.

71. Ltr., F. P. Lahm to E. L. Jones, 1 Sep 1945, in E. L. Jones' personal file.

72. Signal Corps file Nos. 21371 and 32796; CSO Annual Report, 1914; Chandler and Lahm, p. 246.

73. Signal Corps file No. 21471.

74. Signal Corps file No. 32796.

75. Central Files 143.6 in AAG; Signal Corps file No. 21471; Chandler and Lahm, p. 247; CSO Annual Report, 1913.

76. Signal Corps file No. 21471; Lt. C. Perry Rich 201 file, in AGO 201 files; Chandler and Lahm, pp. 247–48.

77. Signal Corps file No. 34160; Chandler and Lahm, p. 284; ltrs., Dargue to La Guardia, 15 Aug 1918, and Dargue to J. K. Spencer, 21 Jul 1918, in Dargue's personal file, cited in Jones Chronology, November 1914.

78. Signal Corps file Nos. 33406, 33502, 33503, 35718, and 34160; Chandler and Lahm, p. 249; CSO Annual Report, 1914; Dargue's personal file, cited in Jones Chronology, November 1914.

79. Signal Corps file Nos. 34160 and 35718.

80. Signal Corps file Nos. 34160, 37999, 38154, 37828, 35375, and 36723.

81. Address by Maj. Gen. J. O. Mauborgne, USA Ret., delivered to American Signal Corps Assn. and Veteran Wireless Operators Assn., 25 Oct 1941, in file B13.41/213 in USAF Library; ltr., Dargue to C. deF. Chandler, 26 Feb 1938, in Lahm MSS, Vol. V.

82. Ltr., General Mauborgne to George H. Clark, Sec., Veteran Wireless Operators Assn., 29 Jan. 1941, in file B13.41/213 in USAF Library; Address by General Mauborgne to American Signal Corps Assn. and Veteran Wireless Operators Assn., 25 Oct 1941, in file B13.41/213 in USAF Library.

83. CSO Annual Report, 1914; Signal Corps file Nos. 37233, 37234, and 38413.

84. CSO Annual Report, 1913; Signal Corps file No. 32696; Chandler and Lahm, p. 265.

85. Signal Corps file No. 32696.

86. Signal Corps file Nos. 32696, 35075, 35826, 35820, 35613, and 143.6.

Chapter V

1. Signal Corps file Nos. 26607, 29233, and 31342.

2. Maj. H. H. Arnold, History of Rockwell Field, p. 22, in USAFHD Archives; WDSO No. 268–19, 14 Nov 1912; WDSO No. 268–20, 14 Nov 1912.

3. Signal Corps file No. 32796.

4. Ltr., Col. L. E. Goodier, Jr., to E. L. Jones, 24 Mar 1945, in Goodier 201 file, AGO; Maj. H. H. Arnold, History of Rockwell Field, p. 22.

5. Signal Corps file No. 31256; Chandler and Lahm, pp. 261–62.

6. Signal Corps file Nos. 32144, 28309, and 32487; ltr., Goodier to Chandler, 1 Apr 1938, Lahm MSS, Vol. V, in USAFHD Archives; Goodier letter in Goodier 201 file in AGO; Chandler and Lahm, pp. 272–74.

7. WDSO No. 61–13, 15 Mar 1913; WDSO No. 63–21, 18 Mar 1913.

8. Rex Chandler 201 file in AGO; Signal Corps file Nos. 32237 and 32487; Chandler and Lahm, pp. 262–63; Central Files 704.5A, Mortality Reports, in AGO.

9. Signal Corps file No. 28309; WDSO No. 146–31, 24 Jun 1913.

10. Signal Corps file Nos. 28309 and 31383; *Aeronautics,* XIV (1914), 37; XV (1914), 12.

11. Signal Corps file No. 28309.

12. Signal Corps file Nos. 28309 and 32408.

13. *Aeronautics,* XII (1913), 96.

14. Chandler and Lahm, p. 264; Statement of Brig. Gen. T. D. Milling to E. L. Jones, 23 Jun 1944, in Jones' personal file.

15. Signal Corps file No. 32487; Progress Report in *Hearings on H.R. 5304;* CSO Annual Report, 1913; WDSO No. 89–25, 17 Apr 1913.

16. Signal Corps file No. 28309; CSO Annual Report, 1913.

17. Ltr., L. E. Goodier to E. L. Jones, 24 Mar 1945, in Goodier 201 file, AGO; Chandler and Lahm, p. 264; *Aeronautics,* XII (1913), 194; Central Files 704.5A, Mortality Reports, in AGO; Joseph D. Park 201 file in AGO.

18. Central Files 353.9—Rockwell Field Training, in AGO.

19. *Ibid.*

20. WDSO No. 131–14, 6 Jun 1913; WDSO No. 135–17, 6 Jun 1913.

21. WDSO No. 122–19, 26 May 1913.

22. Central Files 353.9—Fockwell Field, Training, in AGO.

23. *Ibid.*

24. WDSO No. 146–30, 24 Jun 1913.

25. Signal Corps file No. 28309.

26. Chandler and Lahm, pp. 265–66; Signal Corps file Nos. 44130, 41803, and 35718.

27. Signal Corps file Nos. 33068 and 32941.

28. *The Official Pictorial History of the AAF,* p. 32; Signal Corps file No. 32984.

29. Signal Corps file No. 32944.

30. WDSO No. 164–18, 16 Jul 1913; WDSO No. 174–12, 28 Jul 1913; Signal Corps file Nos. 37939 and 36314; ltr., L. E. Goodier to E. L. Jones, 24 Mar 1945, in Goodier 201 file in AGO; ltr., Joseph E.

Carberry to E. L. Jones, 27 Oct 1947, in Jones' personal file.

31. "Aeronautics in the Army," Part II, "Progress in Aeronautics," in *Hearings on H.R. 5304,* 12 Aug 1913, p. 263.

32. *Aeronautics,* XII (1913), 72.

33. Chandler and Lahm, p. 267; ltr., H. A. Dargue to Fiorella La Guardia, 15 Aug 1928, in Dargue's personal file, cited in Jones Chronology; Signal Corps file No. 33602; Moss L. Love 201 file, in AGO.

34. Signal Corps file No. 33187; *Aeronautics,* XIII (1913), 112.

35. WDSO No. 211–18, 10 Sep 1913; *Aeronautics,* XIII (1913), 110 and 148.

36. Ltr., CSO Scriven to Chief of Staff, 11 Apr 1913, in Central Files 686, 360.04—Old Records, in AGO.

37. CSO Annual Report, 1913; Memo, Chief of Staff to CSO, 9 May 1913, in Central Files, Aviation Fields 686—Southern Dept.

38. WDSO No. 158–5, 7 Sep 1913; WDSO No. 213–8, 12 Sep 1913.

39. WDSO No. 210–23, 9 Sep 1913.

40. WDSO No. 202–27, 29 Aug 1913; WDSO No. 298, 22 Dec 1913.

41. WDSO 217–41, 17 Sep 1913; WDSO No. 224–25, 25 Sep 1913.

42. WDSO No. 274–3, 22 Nov 1913; WDSO No. 52–6, 14 Mar 1914.

43. *Aeronautics,* XIII (1913), 182.

44. WDSO No. 284–15, 5 Dec 1913; WDSO No. 288–16, 10 Dec 1913.

45. WDSO No. 272–2, 20 Nov 1913; WDSO 284–9, 5 Dec 1913.

46. *Hearings on H.R. 5304,* pp. 122 and 125; *Aeronautics,* XII (1913), 74 and 106; Signal Corps file No. 32125.

47. Yearbook, *Aero Club of America,* 1913, pp. 61–62.

48. OCSO Circular No. 10, 27 Oct 1913, in Signal Corps file No. 33177; *Aeronautics,* XIII (1913), 211.

49. Signal Corps file Nos. 33910, 35733, 35718, 35742, and 33591.

50. WDGO No. 79, 13 Dec 1913.

51. Signal Corps Aviation School (SCAS) GO No. 4, 1 Apr 1914; interview, by author with Col. Claude Burch, editor of *The Armoured Cavalry Journal,* 15 Dec 1948.

52. Signal Corps file Nos. 32420, 33828, 13175, and 33922; Central Files 452.1—Burgess Tractor, in AGO; Central Files 452.1A—Rockwell Field, in AGO.

53. Signal Corps file No. 34219; *Aeronautics,* XIII (1913), 130.

54. Central Files 704.5A—Mortality Reports, in AGO; H. M. Kelly 201 file, in AGO; ltr., Dargue to La Guardia. 15 Aug 1928, in Dargue's personal file, cited in Jones Chronology; Arnold, History of Rockwell Field, p. 24; Chandler and Lahm, p. 268.

55. Signal Corps file No. 33927; *Aeronautics,* XIII (1913), 216; *Aero and Hydro,* 3 Jan 1914, p. 171.

56. Ltr., J. E. Carberry to E. L. Jones, 27 Oct 1947, in E. L. Jones' personal file; Arnold, History of Rockwell Field, p. 25.

57. Ltr., J. E. Carberry to E. L. Jones, 27 Oct 1947, in E. L. Jones' personal file; Arnold, History of Rockwell Field, p. 27; National Aeronautics Association, *N.A.A. Review,* April 1926, p. 57; *Aeronautics,* XIV (1914), 12.

58. WDGO No. 75, 4 Dec 1914.

59. Central Files 322, 172—Rockwell Field Squadrons, in AGO.

60. Signal Corps file No. 33959.

61. Signal Corps file No. 34168.

62. Signal Corps file No. 30446.

63. *Ibid.;* WDSO No. 115, 17 May 1913; WDSO No. 134, 10 Jun 1915.

64. WDSO No. 286, 6 Dec 1912; Signal Corps file No. 30446.

65. Signal Corps file No. 34874.

66. WDSO No. 22, 27 Jan 1917; WDSO No. 34, 10 Feb 1917; Signal Corps file No. 30446.

67. WDSO No. 113, 16 May 1917; WDSO No. 270, 30 Nov 1920; Signal Corps file No. 30446.

68. Signal Corps file No. 34307.

69. Signal Corps file No. 34358; ltr., Capt. Stephen J. Idzorek to General Lahm, 7 Sep 1931, in Lahm MSS, Vol. VI, in USAFHD Archives.

70. Signal Corps file Nos. 34105 and 34646.

71. Signal Corps file Nos. 34874 and 34358; ltr., Arthur S. Cowan to E. L. Jones, 6 Feb 1946, in Jones' personal file.

72. SCAS GO No. 1, 7 Jan 1914, in Signal Corps file No. 352—San Diego Aviation School.

73. SCAS GO No. 2, 15 Jan 1914, in Signal Corps file No. 352—San Diego Aviation School.

74. Signal Corps file No. 34907; CSO Annual Report, 1914.

75. Signal Corps file No. 34169; *Aeronautics,* XIV (1914), 30.

76. Signal Corps file No. 34169; Los Angeles *Examiner and Times,* 13 and 14 Jan 1914; ltr., J. E. Carberry to E. L. Jones, 20 Nov 1947, in Jones' personal file.

77. Signal Corps file No. 34410; Central Files 452.1A—Rockwell Field, in AGO; CSO Annual Report, 1914; *Aeronautics,* XIV (1914), 44.

78. Signal Corps file Nos. 34541 and 34746; *Aeronautics,* XIV (1914), 74.

79. Ltr., J. E. Carberry to E. L. Jones, 27 Oct 1914, in Jones' personal file.

80. Signal Corps file Nos. 34935 and 35718; CSO Annual Report, 1914; Arnold, History of Rockwell Field, p. 50.

81. Central Files 704.5A—Mortality Reports, in AGO; Henry B. Post 201 file, in AGO; *Aeronautics,* XIV (1914), 44 and 74.

82. CSO Annual Report, 1913; Signal Corps file No. 32898; ltr., Dargue to La Guardia, 15 Aug 1928, in Dargue's personal file, cited in Jones Chronology.

83. Arnold, History of Rockwell Field, pp. 26, 29.

84. Signal Corps file No. 35013.

85. CSO Annual Report, 1914.

86. *Ibid.;* Signal Corps file Nos. 34548 and 33831; Central Files 452.1A—Rockwell Field, in AGO; Wright Brothers' papers in the Library of Congress.

87. CSO Annual Report, 1914.

88. Signal Corps file No. 35013.

89. *Ibid.*

90. Chandler and Lahm, pp. 275–76.

91. *Aeronautics,* XIV (1914), 21 and 57.

92. Signal Corps file No. 34300.

93. *Ibid.; Aeronautics,* XIV (1914), 58.

94. *Aeronautics,* XIV (1914), 137; File D52–1/308, in USAF Library.

95. *Aeronautics,* XIV (1914), 108 and 137.

96. Signal Corps file No. 35718.

97. Signal Corps file No. 34791.

98. Signal Corps file Nos. 40416 and 471.6—Bombs; CSO Annual Report, 1914; Arnold, History of Rockwell Field, p. 31; *Aeronautics,* XV (1914), 74, 87.

99. Chandler and Lahm, p. 276; Signal Corps file Nos. 35935, 35145, 35197, 35517, 35284, and 352—San Diego Avn. School, 1913–1918.

100. Signal Corps file Nos. 35517, 35169, and 352—San Diego Avn. School, 1913–1918.

101. Signal Corps file Nos. 35721 and 39792; Central Files 353.9—Rockwell Field Training, in AGO.

CHAPTER VI

1. *Cong. Rec.,* 60th Cong., 2d Sess. 1453 (26 Jan 1909); 61st Cong., 1st Sess., 132 (22 Mar 1909); 61st Cong., 2d Sess., 353 (5 Jan 1910).

2. Organization of Military Aeronautics 1907–1935 (USAFHS–25), pp. 7–8; Signal Corps file No. 29751.

3. CSO Annual Report, 1912; "Military Aviation," *House Doc. 718,* 62d Cong., 2d Sess., 1912; USAFHS–25, p. 8; *Hearings on 1912 Army Appropriations Bill.*

4. *Cong. Rec.,* 62d Cong., 2d Sess., 736 (8 Jan 1912).

5. USAFHS–25, pp. 8–9.

6. *Ibid.,* p. 10; *Cong. Rec.,* 62d Cong., 2d Sess., 10245 (5 Aug 1912).

7. *Hearings on 1914 Army Appropriation Bill,* 5 Dec 1912; Signal Corps file No. 111, Estimates 1910–1914.

8. *Aeronautics,* XII (1913), 108, XIII (1913), 62 and 128, and XVI (1915), 36; Signal Corps file No. 33831.

9. *Cong. Rec.,* 62d Cong., 3rd Sess., 3025 (11 Feb 1913); USAFHS–25, p. 10.

10. Ltr., Lt. B. D. Foulois to CSO, 17 Feb 1913, in Signal Corps file No. 29278.

11. Memo, Chief, War College Div., to Sec. of War, 15 Feb 1913, in Signal Corps file No. 29278.

12. Undated manuscript (apparently a summary of officer's opinions) in Signal Corps file No. 29278.

13. USAFHS–25, pp. 12–13; War Dept. Bulletin No. 7, 15 Mar 1913; *Cong. Rec.,* 62d Cong., 3d Sess., 4468 (1 Mar 1913), 4379 (1 Mar 1913), 4855 (4 Mar 1913).

14. OCSO Office Memo No. 7, 24 Feb 1913, in Signal Corps file No. 360, AC Folder No. 1; Proposed bill in Signal Corps file No. 360—Air Service.

15. *Cong. Rec.,* 63d Cong., 1st Sess., 1623 (16 May 1913); *Hearings on H.R. 5304,* 22–93; ltr., Actg. Sec. of War Breckinridge to Representative Hay, 18 Aug 1913, in Signal Corps file No. 29278; USAFHS–25, pp. 14–17.

16. House Report No. 5304, 63d Cong., 2d Sess.

17. *Cong. Rec.,* 63d Cong., 2d Sess., 11893 (9 Jul 1914), 12433 (21 Jul 1914); USAFHS–25, p. 18.

18. Signal Corps file No. 29278; Senate Report No. 576, 63d Cong., 2d Sess.; Public Law No. 143, 63d Cong.; CSO Annual Report, 1914, p. 9.

19. Jones Chronology, 27 Apr 1914.

20. Signal Corps file No. 29278; Senate Report No. 576, 63d Cong., 2d Sess.; Public Law No. 143, 63d Cong.

21. *Hearings before H. R. Committee on Military Affairs,* 70th Cong., 1st Sess., H. R. 11273, 3 Apr 1928, p. 31.

22. WDGO No. 68, 17 Sep 1914; Army Regulation No. 51, 5 Feb 1917 (Changes to Compilation of Orders [CCO] 12 Mar 1917); Signal Corps file No. 322.082, Air Service.

23. Signal Corps file No. 322.082, Air Service.

24. Signal Corps file Nos. 35911 and 300.6; Report, "Pioneer Aviators," *Hearings before the H. R. Committee on Military Affairs,* 70th Cong., 1st Sess., 3 Apr 1928; WDSO 238, 9 Oct 1914.

25. WDSO 229–77, 6 Aug 1917; Roy C. Kirtland's testimony in Goodier Court-martial Proceedings, in Judge Advocate General Files, in National Archives.

26. WDSO 238, 9 Oct 1914.

27. WDSO 196–46, 20 Aug 1913, and WDSO 238, 9 Oct 1914.

28. WDSO 241, 13 Oct 1914.

29. WDSO 219–37, 17 Sep 1914, and WDSO 265, 10 Nov 1914.

30. OCSO Office Memo No. 12, 29 Jul 1914, in Signal Corps file Nos. 35911 and 300.6.

31. WDGO No. 68, 17 Sep 1914; Changes, Army Regulations, No. 51, 5 Feb. 1917 (CCO, 12 Mar 1917); Signal Corps file No. 36786.

32. OCSO Circular No. 5, 22 Jul 1914.

33. Files of Special Orders in the War Department.

34. WDSO 284–34, 2 Dec 1914; Maj. A. D. Smith in *Air Corps News Letter (ACNL),* 15 Jan 1938, in USAF Library.

35. Signal Corps file Nos. 37415 and 36645.

36. Signal Corps file Nos. 36665 and 35979.

37. Signal Corps file No. 36789.

38. General Accounting Office (GAO), R&C Div., file No. 57490; USAF Library file No. D52.1/308; Central Files 580.851—1st Aero Sq.; Signal Corps file Nos. 143.6 and 142.3—1st Aero Sq.

39. Signal Corps file No. 39825; USAF Library D52.1/308; Central Files 452.1A—Rockwell Field.

40. Signal Corps file Nos. 35749, 36223, 39792, and 35692; *Aeronautics,* XV (1914), 10.

41. Signal Corps file Nos. 36223, 36262, 39792, 39231, 39232, 143.6, and 352—San Diego Aviation School; GAO, R&C Div file No. 58454; SCAS GO, No. 22, 1914, San Diego, Calif; USAF Library D52.1/308.

42. Signal Corps file Nos. 36262, 39231, 39792, 143.6, and 352; Central Files 452.1A—Rockwell Field; USAF Library D52.1/308.

43. Signal Corps file Nos. 39792 and 37109.

44. Signal Corps file Nos. 39792, 35749, 39744, 36394, and 352; GAO, R&C Div. file Nos. 57489 and 58403; Central Files 452.1–43; Thomas S. Bowen 201 file in AGO 201 Files; ltr., Col. B. Q. Jones to E. L. Jones, May 1949, in E. L. Jones' personal file.

45. Signal Corps file Nos. 39792, 36317, 40005, and 143.6; SCAS GO No. 22, 1914, San Diego; USAF Library D52.1/308; Central Files 452.2—Curtiss.

46. Signal Corps file Nos. 36820, 36767, 36921, 36540, and 36212; SCAS GO No. 26, 1914, San Diego; USAF Library D52.1/308.

47. Signal Corps file Nos. 39792, 32337, 32420, 33342, and 3443; GAO, R&C Div. file Nos. 52975 and 62718; *Aeronautics,* XV (1914), 88, XIV (1914), 120 and 108; Advertisement of Burgess Co. in *Aeronautics,* XVI (1915), 10 and 32.

48. Advertisement of Burgess Co. in *Aeronautics,* XVI (1915), 32.

49. USAF Library D52.1/308; *Aeronautics,* XIV (1914), 58 and 83; Grover C. Loening, *Military Airplanes,* pp. 23–27, 168–69; Arnold, History of Rockwell Field, p. 34.

50. Signal Corps file Nos. 32337, 32421, and 32422; GAO, R&C Div., file No. 52621; *Aeronautics,* XIII (1913), 74 and 184.

51. Ltr., Grover C. Loening to E. L. Jones, 17 Jan 1949, in E. L. Jones' personal file; Signal Corps file Nos. 31160, 35692, 33260, 39792, and 143.6; Central Files 452.1A—Rockwell Field; *Aeronautics,* XIV (1914), 58 and 69.

52. Signal Corps file No. 35549.

53. CSO Annual Report, 1914, pp. 20–21.

54. *Ibid.,* p. 23; *Aeronautics,* XV (1914), 9; Signal Corps file No. 35742.

55. Signal Corps file No. 35742; CSO Annual Report, 1914, pp. 20–23; *Aeronautics,* XV (1914), 74 and 90; *Flight,* VI (1914), 1133.

56. Signal Corps file No. 35721; CSO Annual Report, 1914, p. 19.

57. CSO Annual Report, 1914, pp. 24–25; Jones Chronology, 5 Aug and Arnold, History of Rockwell Field, p. 42; Signal Corps file No. 39792.

58. Signal Corps file No. 352, San Diego Avn. School; AAF Photographic Library file AC No. 24761.

59. Signal Corps file No. 39792.

60. Signal Corps file No. 41803; Arnold, History of Rockwell Field, p. 32.

61. CSO Annual Report, 1914; Signal Corps File No. 39461.

62. Grover C. Loening, *Our Wings Grow Faster;* Jones Chronology, 15 Jul 1914; ltr., Schofield, Chief Clerk, War Dept. to Grover C. Loening, 14 Jul 1914, cited in Jones Chronology, 15 Jul 1914; Signal Corps file Nos. 39896 and 39792; Annual Report CO, SCAS, 1915.

63. Signal Corps file Nos. 36395 and 36843.

64. Maj. A. D. Smith in *Air Corps News Letter,* 15 Jan 1938, in USAF Library; Arnold, History of Rockwell Field, pp. 35–37.

65. Signal Corps file No. 36280; Arnold, History of Rockwell Field, p. 32; Goodier Court-martial Pro-

ceedings in Judge Advocate General Files in National Archives.

66. Signal Corps File No. 36332; ltr., A. S. Cowan to Samuel Reber, 8 Dec 1914, in Goodier Court-martial Proceedings in Judge Advocate General Files in National Archives.

67. CSO Annual Report, 1915, p. 2; Arnold, History of Rockwell Field, p. 33; General Scriven in *Hearings before House Military Affairs Committee,* 18 Jan. 1916, p. 348; *Aeronautics,* XV (1914), 91; Signal Corps file Nos. 39792 and 36394.

68. Ltr., L. E. Goodier to Col. C. deF. Chandler, 1 Apr 1938, Lahm MSS, Vol. V, in USAFHD Archives; Arnold, History of Rockwell Field, p. 33; ltr., Goodier to E. L. Jones, 24 Mar 1945, in Goodier 201 file in AGO 201 files; Maj. A. D. Smith in *Air Corps News Letter,* 15 Jan. 1938.

69. WDSO 150–48, 29 Jun 1915, WDSO 153, 1 Jul 1916 and WDSO 160, 11 Jul 1916.

70. Signal Corps file Nos. 37841, 40031, 40894, and 37120; WDSO 215–20, 13 Sep 1915.

71. Signal Corps file No. 38057.

72. Signal Corps file No. 111, Estimates for 1915.

73. Signal Corps file Nos. 39792 and 37109; Arnold, History of Rockwell Field, p. 34; ltr., Dargue to La Guardia, 15 Aug 1928, in Dargue's personal file, cited in Jones Chronology.

74. Signal Corps file No. 143.6.

75. *Ibid.;* Annual Report CO, SCAS 1914–1915; Signal Corps file No. 352, San Diego Aviation School, 39702, and 38014.

76. Annual Report SCAS 1914–1915; Signal Corps file Nos. 39707 and 38014.

77. John R. Cuneo, *The Air Weapon 1914–1916* (Harrisburg, Pa., 1947), p. 16.

78. *New York Times,* 5 Aug. 1914, p. 7.

79. John R. Cuneo, *The Air Weapon 1914–1916,* pp. 354–361, 366–67, and 31; *Hearings on Bill to Increase the Efficiency of the Military Establishment,* p. 333, House Military Affairs Committee, 18 Jan 1916; ltr., Military Attache Georges Thenault to E. L. Jones; Walter Raleigh, *The War in the Air* (Oxford, England, 1922), I, 307; Ernest Lehmann and Howard Mingos, *The Zeppelins,* pp. 14–15.

80. Signal Corps file No. 40416 and Ordnance file No. 471.6—Bombs; General Scriven in *Hearings on Army Appropriation Bill for 1916,* 8 Dec 1914, p. 651; *Aeronautics,* XV (1914), 87 and 74.

81. *Hearings on Army Appropriation Bill for 1916,* 8 Dec 1914, p. 651; Signal Corps files No. 35781 and Ordnance file No. 471.6—Bombs; *Aeronautics,* XV (1914), 74 and 87; *New York Times,* 27 Sep 1914.

82. Signal Corps file Nos. 35046, 40029, and 36713.

83. Signal Corps file Nos. 37266, 33787, and 40576.

84. Arnold, History of Rockwell Field, p. 33.

85. *Ibid.,* pp. 35–37; Signal Corps file No. 352-–San Diego School.

CHAPTER VII

1. House of Representatives: *Hearings on 1916 Army Appropriation Bill,* 8 Dec 1914, pp. 642–3 and 653–4; 111—Estimates 1916, in National Archives; War Dept. Bulletin No. 12, 31 March 1915; Public Law No. 292, 63d Cong.; Jones Chronology, 8 Dec 1914.

2. War Dept. Bulletin No. 12, 31 March 1915; Arnold, History of Rockwell Field, p. 47.

3. Signal Corps file Nos. 37348 and 111—Estimates 1916; General Scriven in House *Hearings on Army Appropriation Bill 1916,* 8 Dec. 1914, p. 643.

4. CSO Annual Report, 1915, 10 Sep 1915, p. 8; Signal Corps File Nos. 452.1 and 000.71, box 1, and 360–AC Folder No. 1.

5. Signal Corps Nos. 37427 and 38079.

6. Air Ministry, *A Short History of the RAF* (Oxford Univ. Press, 1922), Air Publication 125, pp. 73 and 81; Walter Raleigh, *The War in the Air,* I, 266.

7. Signal Corps file No. 38884; OCSO Circular No. 8, 1915, p. 21; CSO Annual Report, 1915, pp. 6–8; *Aerial Age Weekly,* I (1915), 160; *Army Navy Journal,* LII (1915), 1563.

8. Comdr. Thomas Drayton Parker, "From An Air Fleet: Our Pressing Naval Want," in *U.S. Naval Institute Proceedings,* XLI, 739; *Flight,* VII (1915), 544.

9. CSO Annual Report, 1915, 10 Sep 1915.

10. *Aeronautics,* XVI (1915), 36; Signal Corps file No. 334.8; NACA Folder No. 1.

11. Signal Corps file No. 334.8; NACA Folder No. 1; Jones Chronology, 3 Mar 1915; ltr., G. W. Lewis, ex-officer of NACA, to E. L. Jones, 4 Oct 1920, in E. L. Jones' personal file.

12. Signal Corps file No. 334.8, NACA folder No. 1; Jones Chronology; ltr., G. W. Lewis, ex-officer of NACA, to E. L. Jones, 4 Oct 1920, in E. L. Jones' personal file.

13. *New York Times,* 22 May and 3 July 1915; *The Aeroplane,* IV (1915), 44.

14. Signal Corps file Nos. 38487, 39346, 39266, and 360, AC Folder No. 1; *Flight,* VII (1915), 274 and 504; *Aeronautics* (London), IX (1915), 347.

15. Signal Corps file Nos. 37262 and 41271; *Army Navy Journal,* 6 June 1914.

16. Signal Corps file No. 36955.

17. Signal Corps file Nos. 40104 and 40247; T. F. Ward 201 File in AAG; E. L. Jones' personal file.

18. Signal Corps file Nos. 41006 and 41003.

19. *Aerial Age Weekly,* II (1915), 223; *Flying,* IV (1915), 767; Signal Corps file Nos. 40759 and 360, AC Folder No. 1.

20. Ltr., J. E. Miller to Capt. J. E. Carberry, 7 March 1917, in Central Files 314.7, in AAG; ltr., F. A. Bjorklund to E. L. Jones, 19 April 1948, in E. L. Jones' personal file; Henry G. Pearson, *A Business Man in Uniform, Raynal Cawthorne Bolling* (New York, 1923), pp. 57–65.

21. Pearson, *A Business Man in Uniform, Raynal Cawthorne Bolling,* pp. 68–72; *Chirp,* December, 1914; ltr., F. A. Bjorklund to E. L. Jones, 10 Apr 1948, in E. L. Jones' personal file; ltr., J. E. Miller to Captain Carberry, 7 Mar 1917, in Central Files 314.7, in AAG.

22. Signal Corps file Nos. 39304 and 39458; *Aeronautics,* XVII (1915), 24.

23. Signal Corps file Nos. 40233, 40075, and 352—San Diego Aviation School.

24. Signal Corps file Nos. 41349, 40836, and 40019.

25. Signal Corps file No. 38939.

26. Signal Corps file No. 38919.

27. Verbal statement of Col. B. Q. Jones to E. L. Jones in 1949; Jones Chronology, 20 Mar 1916; Arnold, History of Rockwell Field, p. 40; Aero Club of America (ACA) Records; Signal Corps file Nos. 39792, 37472, 37286, and 38549.

28. Signal Corps file Nos. 38014 and 39792; CSO Annual Report, 1915; Central Files 452.1A—Rockwell Field, in AAG; USAF Library file D52.1/308.

29. Signal Corps file Nos. 39792, 37206, 37407, 38376, 38242, 38461, and 37417.

30. Signal Corps file No. 143.6; Central Files 452.1A—Rockwell Field and 580.851—1st Aero Squadron, in AAG.

31. Signal Corps file No. 38802; Central Files 452.1A—Curtiss, in AAG; *Aeronautics,* XVII (1915), 4; Army Airplane Receipts 1908–1915, compiled by E. L. Jones.

32. *Aeronautics,* XVII (1915), 4.

33. Memo, CSO to TAG, 6 Oct 1915, in Central Files 452.1A—Curtiss, in AAG; GAO, R&C Div., No. 65238.

34. *Aeronautics,* XVI (1915), 104; XVII (1915), 4; Signal Corps file Nos. 38802, 143.6 and 40480; telegram from Capt. B. D. Foulois, 24 April 1916, in Central Files 580.851 and 452.1A—Curtiss, in AAG; USAF Library file D52.1/308.

35. Signal Corps file Nos. 39792, 39420, and 352—San Diego Aviation School; SCAS GO No. 24, 23 Jul 1915; *Aeronautics,* XVII (1915), 4.

36. Signal Corps file No. 40894; telegram from Foulois, 24 Apr 1916, in Central Files 580.851; USAF Library file D52.1/308; Report of Operations, 1st Aero Sq., pp. 7 and 8, in USAF Library file 22.32/44.

37. Signal Corps file No. 39805; GAO, R&C Div., No. 68487; Central Files 452.1A—Rockwell Field, in AAG; Army Airplane Receipts 1908–1915, compiled by E. L. Jones.

38. USAF Library file D52.1/308.

39. Signal Corps file No. 41301.

40. Arnold, History of Rockwell Field, p. 37.

41. Signal Corps file No. 37369.

42. Arnold, History of Rockwell Field, p. 37.

43. Signal Corps file Nos. 37653, 37912, 18346, 38705, 38347, 38706, 387919, and 38348.

44. CSO Annual Report, 1915, p. 12; Arnold, History of Rockwell Field, p. 45.

45. Signal Corps file Nos. 37287, 36956, 35980, and 38092.

46. Grover Loening, *Our Wings Grow Faster;* Signal Corps file No. 14316.

47. Central Files 452.1A—Rockwell Field, in AAG; Annual Report of CO, SCAS, San Diego, 30 Jun 1915, in Signal Corps file 39792.

48. Signal Corps file Nos. 38014, 37206, and 39792; Arnold, History of Rockwell Field, p. 40; CSO Anual Report 1915, p. 12.

49. Signal Corps file Nos. 39792, 37864, and 352—San Diego Aviation School; *Aeronautics,* XVI (1915), 104; CSO Annual Report, 1915; *Aviation,* I (1917), 389.

50. Arnold, History of Rockwell Field, p. 41.

51. Signal Corps Aviation School Memo, 31 Dec 1916.

52. Arnold, History of Rockwell Field, p. 41.

53. Signal Corps file Nos. 38303 and 39669.

54. Signal Corps file Nos. 39387, 38936, 38444, 38542, 39787, and 40059.

55. Signal Corps file No. 37817.

56. Signal Corps file Nos. 38134, 37932, and 37947.

57. Signal Corps file Nos. 38118 and 38155.

58. ACA records; Arnold, History of Rockwell Field, p. 54; CSO Annual Report, 1915; *NAA Review,* April 1926, p. 27.

59. Signal Corps file Nos. 38681 and 39320.

60. Signal Corps file No. 37940.

61. Central Files 352.12—Rockwell Field, in AAG; *Aeronautics,* XVI (1915), 104.

62. Signal Corps file No. 39346.

63. Central Files 321.91A—Organization, in AAG.

64. *Aeronautics,* XVI (1915), 127.

65. Signal Corps file No. 39087.

66. Signal Corps file No. 41803.

67. Signal Corps file No. 38886.

68. Signal Corps file No. 39054.

69. Signal Corps file No. 352—San Diego Avn. School; *Aeronautics,* XVI (1915), 104 and 127; CSO Annual Report, 1915, p. 12; Annual Report CO, SCAS, San Diego, 1915, in Signal Corps file Nos. 39792 and 35718.

70. Annual Report, CO, SCAS, San Diego, 1915, in Signal Corps file Nos. 39792 and 35718; CSO Annual Report, 1915, p. 12.

71. Annual Report CO, SCAS, San Diego, 1915, in Signal Corps file Nos. 39792 and 35718; CSO Annual Report, 1915, p. 12; Arnold, History of Rockwell Field, pp. 45 and 46.

72. Annual Report CO, SCAS, San Diego, 1915, in Signal Corps file Nos. 39792 and 35718.

73. Signal Corps file No. 39792; Arnold, History of Rockwell Field, pp. 45–46.

74. Signal Corps file No. 37404.

75. Annual Report CO, SCAS, 9 Aug 1915, in Signal Corps file No. 39792.

76. Signal Corps file No. 39703.

77. Signal Corps file Nos. 39047, 39749, and 40294; Arnold, History of Rockwell Field, p. 49; Correspondence of C. C. Culver with E. L. Jones in Jones' personal file; Aero Club Certificate No. 689, 4 Apr 1917; WDSO 172, 26 Jul 1917.

78. Signal Corps file No. 39926 and Post Returns of SCAS, in National Archives.

79. Arnold, History of Rockwell Field, p. 51.

80. Signal Corps file Nos. 40618, 352—San Diego Aviation School, and 143.6; ltr., Dargue to J. K. Spencer, 21 Jul 1928, and to La Guardia, 15 Aug 1928, in Dargue's personal file, cited in Jones Chronology.

81. Goodier Court-martial Proceedings in JAG Files, in National Archives; *Army and Navy News,* San Francisco, December 1915; San Francisco *Chronicle,* 19 Oct 1915; San Francisco *Examiner,* 19 Oct 1915.

82. JAG's review of the case on Goodier Court-martial Proceedings in JAG File, in National Archives; Memo for Sec. of War, 30 Dec 1915 and Reprimand from President Wilson, 17 Apr 1916.

83. Goodier Court-martial Proceedings in JAG file, in National Archives; San Francisco *Chronicle,* 27 Oct 1915; San Francisco *Examiner,* 26–28 Oct and 4 Nov 1915; Signal Corps file No. 032.09—Aviation.

84. Goodier Court-martial Proceedings in JAG file, in National Archives; Memo for Sec. of War from JAG, "The pay of Capt. Wm. L. Patterson as junior military aviator," 7 Sep 1915, in JAG files in National Archives.

85. House Committee on Military Affairs, 64th Cong., 1st Sess., *Hearings on Bill to Increase the Efficiency of the Military Establishment of U.S.,* 18 Jan 1916.

86. Arnold, History of Rockwell Field, p. 51; Signal Corps file Nos. 40839 and 005.2; Yearbook, *Aero Club of America,* 1917, pp. 88–89.

87. Arnold, History of Rockwell Field, pp. 52–54; Signal Corps file Nos. 41130 and 41803.

88. Signal Corps file Nos. 38340, 38769, and 38566.

89. Signal Corps file Nos. 38479, 38546, 38549, and 39792.

90. Signal Corps file Nos. 38769 and 39792.

91. Signal Corps file Nos. 38340, 38566, and 38340.

92. *Chirp,* December 1930; Signal Corps file No. 38562.

93. Signal Corps file Nos. 38438 and 39792; Central Files 319.9—Rockwell Field, 322–172, and 452.1, in AAG; *Aeronautics,* XVI (1915), 104.

94. Signal Corps file Nos. 39489, 40894, 37472, and 352—San Diego Aviation School; Arnold, History of Rockwell Field, p. 47; *Aeronautics,* XVII (1915), 4.

95. Signal Corps file Nos. 40894, 49894, and 40110; Central Files 451.1A—Curtiss Planes, in AAG.

96. Signal Corps file Nos. 38823, 41851, and 40894; Monthly Squadron Returns, 1st Aero Sq., in National Archives; CSO Annual Report, 1915, pp. 6–8 and 13; Foulois Report of Operations, 1st Aero Sq. 1916, in Signal Corps file 40894.

97. Signal Corps file No. 40894.

98. Central Files 451.1A—Curtiss Planes, in AAG.

99. *Ibid.*

100. Signal Corps file Nos. 40007; Central Files 458.1A—Curtiss, in AAG.

101. Central Files 452.1A—Curtiss Planes, in AAG.

102. Signal Corps file Nos. 40007 and 40930; Central Files 452.1A—Curtiss Planes, in AAG.

103. Signal Corps file Nos. 39304, 38134, 37932, and 37947.

104. Signal Corps file Nos. 39073, 40746, and 41389; *Aeronautics,* XVII (1915), 25.

105. Report of Capt. B. D. Foulois in Signal Corps file No. 40755; Central Files 452.1A, in AAG.

106. *Ibid.*

107. *Ibid.*

108. Monthly squadron returns, 1st Aero Sq., in National Archives; WDSO files.

109. Signal Corps file Nos. 40279 and 39792.

110. Signal Corps file Nos. 38391 and 38520.

111. Signal Corps file No. 40877; QMG Annual Report, 1916.

112. *Aeronautics*, XVII (1915), 104.

113. CSO Annual Report 1915, p. 15; Central Files "Old Records" 322.122—Panama, Hawaii, and P.I. and 360.01—Development of Aviation, in AAG; Signal Corps file No. 38455.

114. Signal Corps file No. 38818.

115. Signal Corps file Nos. 111.05—Army Appropriations 1917, and 39195.

116. Signal Corps file Nos. 39891, 41055, and 41043.

117. Signal Corps file No. 40446.

118. Company Returns, 1st Co., 2d Aero Sq., in National Archives; Arnold, History of Rockwell Field, p. 52; Signal Corps file Nos. 121.25, 319.1—Philippines No. 1 in Philippines Annual Reports, and .061—Corregidor.

CHAPTER VIII

1. *Cong. Rec.*, 64th Cong., 1st Sess., 494 (5 Jan 1916); S. Rept. No. 153, 64th Cong., 1st Sess.; Signal Corps file No. 41804.

2. H.R. Report No. 368, 64th Cong., 1st Sess.; *Cong. Rec.*, 64th Cong., 1st Sess., 7420 (4 May 1916).

3. *Cong. Rec.*, 64th Cong., 1st Sess., 7420, (4 May 1916).

4. *Cong. Rec.*, 64th Cong., 1st Sess. 494 (5 Jan 1916); S. Rept. No. 153, 64th Cong., 1st Sess.; Signal Corps file No. 41804; Special Order File; Central Files 360.01—Old Records, in AAG; *New York Times*, 18 Apr 1916, p. 7; WDSO 64–19, 3 Apr 1916.

5. House of Representatives Committee on Military Arfairs, 1917, 64th Cong., 1st Sess., 837–838, 8 Apr 1916.

6. *Cong. Rec.*, 64th Cong., 1st Sess. (28 Mar 1916).

7. Ltr., Alan R. Hawley, president of Aero Club of America, to Col. George O. Squier, 28 Jul 1916, in Signal Corps file No. 360.03.

8. *Aviation*, I (1916), 192; *New York Times*, 1 Oct 1916, p. 20:1 and 4 Oct 1916, p. 10:7.

9. The National Defense Act, Public Law 85, 64th Cong.; 39 *Stat*. 174.

10. Memo of Control Board to Executive Officer, DMA, 16 Oct 1918; Central Files 211.32—RMA's in AAG.

11. WDSO files; Central Files 321.91A—Organization, in AAG; 39 *Stat*. 195; *Flying*, III (1914), 220–21.

12. Col. R. H. Fletcher, Monograph No. 16, Hist. Sec., Army War College, 1922, "The Signal Corps and Air Service," pp. 1–2 (hereinafter cited as Fletcher); CSO Annual Rept. 17 Oct 1916, p. 6.

13. Fletcher, pp. 35–36; *Aviation*, I (1916), 157.

14. Fletcher, pp. 36–37; W. D. Bulletin No. 33, 9 Sep 1916; Annual Report of Secretary of War, 1916; *Aerial Age Weekly*, IV (1916), 141.

15. Fletcher, p. 36; Signal Corps file No. 334.8, NACA Folder No. 1; Annual Report, Exec. Com., NACA, 1917.

16. Annual Report of NACA, Senate Doc. 123, 65th Cong., 2d Sess., 1918; Charles Evans Hughes, "Report on Aircraft Production Inquiry," in *The Official U.S. Bulletin*, Wednesday, 6 Nov 1918, p. 48.

17. Hughes, "Report on Aircraft Production Inquiry," in *The Official U.S. Bulletin*, Wednesday, 6 Nov 1918, p. 48.

18. House Committee on Military Affairs, 64th Cong., 2d Sess., Hearings on Army Appropriation Bill, 1918, 8 Apr 1916, pp. 829–838.

19. Ltr., Capt. Wm. Mitchell to F. La Guardia, 4 May 1916, in Signal Corps file No. 000.71, box 1; Office Memo No. 5 (OCSO) in Signal Corps file No. 300.6 OM's.

20. Signal Corps file No. 210.6—Aviation.

21. Central Files No. 321.9A—Organization, in AAG.

22. Signal Corps file No. 580.3, box 880.

23. Memo, Lt. Col. G. O. Squier to TAG, 20 Jul 1916; Central Files No. 321.91—Organization, and 322.172A in AAG; Signal Corps file No. 360—AC Folder No. 1.

24. Memo, Lt. Col. G. O. Squier to TAG, 20 Jul 1916; Central Files No. 321.91—Organization and 322.172A in AAG; Signal Corps file No. 360—AC Folder No. 1; Rept. of Brig. Gen. C. McK. Saltzman, Acting CSO, 17 Oct 1917, p. 6, filed with contract No. 914, order No. 4545 to Sloane Mfg. Co., in WD Rec. Br., Alexandria, Va.

25. WDSO 77, 1 Apr 1916; WDSO 127, 31 May 1916; WDSO 119, 20 May 1916; *New York Times*, 3 Jun 1916, p. 7; Arnold, History of Rockwell Field, p. 55.

26. Ltr., Dargue to J. K. Spencer, 21 Jul 1928, in Dargue Special File.

27. Arnold, History of Rockwell Field, p. 57; ltr., C. C. Cole to E. L. Jones, 12 Aug 1946, in E. L. Jones' personal file; *Aviation*, I (1916–17), 127, 395.

28. Signal Corps file No. 352—San Diego Aviation School.

29. Signal Corps file No. 352—San Diego Aviation School; WDSO 47–37, 11 Jan 1917; SCAS, San Diego rosters; CSO Annual Report, 3 Oct 1916, p. 27; GAO, R&C Div. Files.

30. Signal Corps file No. 41548.

31. Signal Corps file Nos. 41628, 41807, and 42940.

32. Signal Corps file Nos. 41722 and 41180.

33. Signal Corps file No. 41780.

34. WDGO No. 55, 16 Oct 1916.

35. WDGO No. 55, 16 Oct 1916.

36. *Ibid.*

37. *Ibid.*

38. *Ibid.*

39. CSO Annual Report, 3 Oct 1916; WDGO No. 55, 16 Oct 1916.

40. Signal Corps file No. 452.3—Kite Balloons No. 1, 1916.

41. Fletcher, p. 34; CSO Annual Report, 10 Oct 1913, p. 16; W.D. Bulletin No. 55, 20 Dec 1916.

42. Fort Omaha roster, WDSO files; National Aeronautic Association (NAA) Records.

43. Signal Corps file No. 373—General Folder No. 1; WD Bulletin No. 26, 7 May 1917.

44. Central Files 334.7—Army and Navy Joint Bds.; Signal Corps file No. 334.7—Army and Navy Jt. Bd. in Aero Folder No. 1; *Aircraft,* February 1917, p. 64; A. D. Turnbull and C. L. Lord, *History of United States Naval Aviation* (New Haven, 1949), p. 75.

45. Central Files 334.7—Joint Boards, in AAG; Turnbull and Lord, *History of United States Naval Aviation,* pp. 76–77.

46. Annual Report of Secretary of War, 20 Nov 1916; *The Aeroplane* (London), XI (1916), 1058.

47. Signal Corps file No. 580.82—Policy, Location Aviation Sites; GAO, R&C Div. files.

48. *Aerial Age Weekly,* IV (1916), 384; GAO, R&C Div. files.

49. Ltr., Frank C. Page in the *New York Times,* 30 Aug 1916, p. 8.

50. House Comm. on Military Affairs, 64th Cong., 2d Sess., Hearings on 1918 Army Appropriation Bill, 5 Jan 1917, pp. 1008–9; Mixter and Emmons, *U.S. Army Aircraft Production Facts,* p. 5.

CHAPTER IX

1. Report of Maj. B. D. Foulois, 28 Aug 1916, "Operations of First Aero Squadron, S.C. with Punitive Expedition, USA, 15 March to 15 Aug 1916," p. 1 (Foulois Rept.), in C22.32/44 in USAF Library.

2. Signal Corps file No. 37657.

3. Signal Corps file No. 37657; Foulois Rept., p. 1.

4. Foulois Rept.; WD Special Order files; Monthly Squadron Returns, in National Archives.

5. CSO Annual Report, 1916, p. 26.

6. Foulois Report.

7. *Ibid.,* p. 2; Clayton L. Bissell, "Brief History of the Air Corps and Its Late Development" (Air Corps Tactical School, Langley Field, Va.), (1927), pp. 16–17; A. W. Sweetser, *The American Air Service,* p. 33; *San Antonio Express,* 28 March 1916.

8. Foulois Rept., p. 4.

9. *Ibid.,* p. 5.

10. *Ibid.,* p. 2.

11. *Ibid.,* pp. 4–6.

12. *Ibid.,* p. 8; CSO Annual Report, 1916, p. 26; Signal Corps file Nos. 047.22—Forest Service, and 360—AC Folder No. 1; *Aviation,* I (1916), 77; Memo Lt. Col. George O. Squier to TAG, 20 Jul 1916; Central Files Nos. 321.91—Organization, and 322.172 in AAG.

13. Foulois Rept., pp. 4–6.

14. New York *World,* 3 Apr 1916; Signal Corps file No. 000.75—N.Y. *World.*

15. Foulois Rept., pp. 4–6.

16. *Ibid.,* p. 6.

17. *Ibid.,* p. 7.

18. *Ibid.;* Monthly Return, 1st Aero Squadron, 1–22 Apr 1916, in National Archives.

19. Ltr., H. A. Dargue to J. K. Spencer, 21 Jul 1928, in Dargue's personal file; Foulois Rept., p. 8.

20. Signal Corps file No. 580.3—Avn. Sec.

21. *New York Times,* 26 Apr 1916; Signal Corps file No. 000.75—*N.Y. Times;* S. C. Order No. 4208, contract No. 870, GAO, R&C Div. file No. 69532; W.D. Rec. Br., Alexandria, Va.

22. Signal Corps file No. 000.75—*New York Times.*

23. Signal Corps file 000.75—*New York Times* and *El Paso Herald.*

24. *Ibid.*

25. Foulois Rept., p. 8; WD Records Br., Alexandria, Va.; USAF Library Files No. D52.1/308; Signal Corps file No. 158—Curtiss; House Committee on Military Affairs, 64th Cong., 2d Sess., *Hearings on 1918 Army Appropriation Bill,* 5 Jan 1917, pp. 1018–1020.

26. Signal Corps file No. 000.75—*New York Times* and *New York World.*

27. Foulois Report.

28. *Ibid.; Aviation,* I (1916), 77; SC Order No. 4545, contract No. 914, GAO, R&C Div. file No. 77383; S. C. Order No. 5138, contract No. 989, in GAO, R&C Div. file No. 74214; GAO, R&C Div. file Nos. 74192, 76712, 73648, 83599, and 76048; WD Records Branch, Alexandria, Va.

29. Squadron Returns, in National Archives.

30. Foulois Rept., p. 8.

31. Signal Corps file No. 400.112—Inventions, and Ordnance file Nos. 471.6—Bombs and 471.6, 1–99.

32. Central Files, 360.04—Old Records, in AAG.

33. Signal Corps file No. 360—AC Folder No. 1.

34. *Ibid.*

35. WDSO Files.

36. WDSO Files.

37. Squadron Returns, 1st Aero Sq., in National Archives; Signal Corps file No. 400.112—Inventions.

CHAPTER X

1. Ltr., G. O. Squier to J. E. Carberry, 27 Jun 1916, in Central Files 314.7, in AAG; WDSO 150–37, 28 Jun 1916.

2. Signal Corps file No. 121.25—Aviation Employees and 121.2—Eastern Dept.; Central Files No. 230.14 —Hazelhurst Field, in AAG.

3. Ltrs., J. E. Carberry to E. L. Jones in Central Files 314.7 and Central Files No. 230.14—Hazlehurst Field, in AAG; GAO, R&C Div. Files; Signal Corps file No. 121.2—Eastern Dept.

4. Ltr., Col. J. E. Carberry to E. L. Jones, 11 Dec 1944, in Central Files 314.7, in AAG; Signal Corps file No. 121.25—Mineola.

5. WDSO Files.

6. Ltr., Col. J. E. Carberry to E. L. Jones, 11 Dec 1944, in Central Files 314.7, in AAG.

7. Monthly post returns Aviation Station, Mineola, N.Y., November and December 1916, in National Archives.

8. Mineola Station Memo, 31 Dec 1916, in Central Files 314.7, in AAG; ltr., Col. Carberry to E. L. Jones, 11 Dec 1944 in Central Files 314.7, in AAG.

9. Ordnance file No. 471.6, 1–99, in National Archives.

10. *Ibid.;* Ordnance file No. 471.6, 200–299, in National Archives.

11. Ordnance file Nos. 471.6, 1–99 and 471.6, 100–199, in National Archives.

12. *Aviation,* I (1916) 294; ltrs., Col. J. E. Carberry and Col. P. A. Carroll to E. L. Jones, 1945, in Central Files 314.7, in AAG.

13. Ltr., Ivan P. Wheaton to E. L. Jones, 1945, in Central Files 314.7, in AAG; SCAS Mineola, Bulletin No. 1, 1917, in Central Files 314.7, in AAG.

14. Bulletin No. 1, Mineola Aviation Station, 1917, in Central Files 314.7, in AAG; ltr., J. E. Carberry to E. L. Jones, 11 Dec 1944, in Central Files 314.7, in AAG.

15. Bulletins No. 2 and 3, SCAS Mineola, 1917, in Central Files 314.7, in AAG.

16. Memo, Lt. J. E. Carberry to CSO, 2 Feb 1917, in Carberry's personal file; SCAS Mineola Memo, 15 Feb 1917, in Central Files 314.7, in AAG.

17. Central Files No. 352.9—Miscellaneous Schools and 353.9—Hazelhurst Field, in AAG.

18. Central Files 352.9—Miscellaneous Schools, in AAG; WDSO 175–10, 30 Jul 1917.

19. WDSO Files; *Aviation,* I (1916), 195; *Aerial Age Weekly,* IV (1917), 504; Signal Corps file No. 240—Chicago; GAO, R&C Div. Files.

20. WDSO Files: File No. 220.3A—Central Dept. W. D. Records Br., Alexandria, Va.; ltr., Captain Christie to OCSO, 4 Apr 1917, Central Files 353.9—Park Field Training, in AAG; ltr., Victor Vernon, Civ. Instructor at Ashburn Field, to E. L. Jones, March 1948, in E. L. Jones' file; ltr., F. A. Hoover, Civ. Instructor, Ashburn Field, to E. L. Jones, 13 May 1948, in E. L. Jones' file.

21. Signal Corps file No. 580–82—Policy, Loc. Avn. Sites; memo of Chief WCD to CofS, 1 Mar 1917, 7112–35 in War College Division Files; WDSO 57–35, 12 Mar 1917.

22. WDSO Files; Fletcher; Central Files 352.9A—Schools Miscellaneous, in AAG; Signal Corps file No. 360—AC Folder No. 1; GAO, R&C Div. Files.

23. Central Files 352.9A—Schools Miscellaneous, in AAG.

24. Central Files 322.172A, in AAG.

25. Signal Corps file Nos. 2415717 and 28487; *Chirp,* 1 Dec 1941.

26. Central Files 314.7—Carroll and 211—Aviators, etc., in AAG; ltr., F. A. Bjorklund to E. L. Jones, 19 Apr 1948 and ltr., P. A. Carroll to E. L. Jones, 28 Apr 1948, in E. L. Jones' file.

27. Central Files 314.7, in AAG; Pearson, *A Business Man in Uniform, Raynal Cawthorne Bolling,* p. 228.

28. WDGO 54–2, 3 May 1917; Signal Corps file No. 352 —AS Schools Gen.; Central Files 322.172A, in AAG.

29. Central Files 314.7—Second Aero Co., N.G., in AAG; J. M. Satterfield 201 File, in AAG.

30. *Aviation,* I (1916), 92, 127, and 296; Signal Corps file No. 37432½.

31. *Aviation,* I (1917), 392; Pearson, *A Business Man in Uniform, Raynal Cawthorne Bolling,* p. 228.

32. Central Files 314.7—Second Aero Co., N.G., in AAG; J. M. Satterfield 201 File, in AAG.

33. Central Files 326.64—Reserve Officers, in AAG; Signal Corps file No. 280.82—Policy SC; War College Div. 9521–21 in War College Div. Files; File No. 2411280–B in AGO.

34. W.D. Bulletin No. 34, 1916; JAG 58–211, 25 Aug 1916; WDSO 15–22, 18 Jan 1917.

35. Signal Corps file No. 132.2.

36. Central Files No. 353.9, in AAG; WDSO 73–17, 30 Mar 1917.

37. Ltr., Walter E. Lees to E. L. Jones, 15 Apr 1948, in Jones' personal files.

38. WDSO files; ltrs., Victor Vernon to E. L. Jones, 7 Apr 1948 and 13 May 1948, in E. L. Jones' file;

Signal Corps file Nos. 016.3—Instruction and 300.6 —Office Memos in 1917.

39. Signal Corps file No. 029.21—Avn. Sec.; Central Files 353.9, in AAG; WDSO files.

40. Signal Corps file No. 029.21—Avn. Sec.; Vouchers 18907, 18908, 18909, Check No. 9335, files of GAO; ltr., GAO to Hq USAF, 11 Apr 1950.

41. Signal Corps file No. 320.

42. Signal Corps file No. 352—Air Service Schools, General.

CHAPTER XI

1. Arnold, History of Rockwell Field, p. 58; SCAS, San Diego rosters, January to March 1917, in National Archives.

2. *Ibid.*

3. House Comm. on Mil. Att., 64th Cong., 2d Sess., Hearings on Army Appropriation Bill, 1918, 5–8 Jan 1917.

4. General Lahm's report, in E. L. Jones' personal files.

5. *Ibid.*

6. *Ibid.;* Arnold, History of Rockwell Field, pp. 59–60.

7. General Lahm's report; ltr., H. A. Dargue to J. K. Spencer, 21 Jul 1928, in Dargue's Special File.

8. January 1917 roster of SCAS, San Diego, in National Archives; General Lahm's report.

9. Ltr., C. C. Cole (then a sergeant at San Diego) to E. L. Jones, 11 Feb 1950, in E. L. Jones' personal files; Arnold, History of Rockwell Field, pp. 59–60; Arnold, *Global Mission,* pp. 45–46.

10. Signal Corps file No. 352—San Diego Avn. School.

11. *Ibid.*

12. *Ibid.;* WDSO No. 79, 6 Apr 1917; SCAS GO No. 1, 12 Feb 1917.

13. Change No. 51, 5 Feb 1917, to AR 1342½, 24 Nov 1915.

14. CSO Annual Report, 1917; WDSO No. 43, 5 Jan 1917; *The Order of Battle of the U.S. Land Forces in the World War* (1917–1919), Zone of Interior, GPO, prepared by OCMH, Dept. of the Army, III (Pt. 1), 92–93.

15. Signal Corps file No. 360—AC Folder No. 1.

16. WDGO 1, 9 Feb 1917; October and December 1916 3d Aero Sq. returns, in National Archives; WDSO files.

17. Signal Corps file No. 580.82—Policy, Locations Avn. Sites; WDSO No. 258–39, 3 Nov 1916.

18. WDSO 7–39, 9 Jan 1917; Central Files No. 334.7— Jt. Army and Navy Bds.; Statement, Maj. Gen. John F. Curry to E. L. Jones, 1947.

19. WDSO 7–38, 9 Jan 1917; WDSO files.

20. Signal Corps file No. 334.8—NACA Folder No. 1.

21. Sec. of Navy Ltr. 26983–663; 3 Ops 17, ML of 21 Feb 1917.

22. Memo, Col. Wm. L. Patterson, ASA, in charge of Aerial Coast Defenses, 1919, in Central Files 323.5C.

23. Signal Corps file No. 320—Org. of Army; Jones Chronology, 16 Mar 1917.

24. Signal Corps file No. 210.3—1913–1916.

25. *Ibid.*

26. Collation of Air Technical Intelligence Information of the Army Air Arm, 1916–1947, Vol. I, Doc. 145, in USAFHD Archives.

27. Signal Corps file No. 029.21—Avn. Sec.

28. War Dept. Bulletin 20–II, 18 Apr 1917.

29. War Dept. Bulletin 32, 24 May 1917.

30. Signal Corps file No. 210—General and 210–6— Aviation.

31. Signal Corps file No. 210.6—Aviation.

32. Ltr., AGO to CSO, 22 Mar 1917, in Fletcher, p. 5; Arnold, Outline of History of Avn. Section and Div. of Mil. Aeronautics, April 1917–October, 1918, in E. L. Jones' personal file.

33. Signal Corps file No. 300.6—Office Memos and 334.7—Aircraft Production Board; CSO Annual Report, 1917, p. 4.

34. Signal Corps file No. 334.8—NACA Folder No. 1.

35. *Ibid.;* Yearbook, *Aero Club of America,* 1917; Arnold, Outline of History Avn. Sec., S.C. and Div. of Mil. Aeronautics, April 1917—October 1918, p. 5.

36. CSO Annual Report 1918, in USAF Library; Fletcher, pp. 33–34; Arnold, Outline of History of Avn. Section, S.C. & Div. of Mil. Aeronautics, April 1917-October 1918; Sec. of War Annual Rept., I, 62; Turnbull and Lord, *History of United States Naval Aviation,* pp. 91, 97.

37. Consolidated List of Aircraft Contracts and Deliveries, File No. A–00.2/22, in USAF Library.

38. *Report of Aircraft Surveys* (as corrected by Information Division of Air Service Intelligence), H. R. Document 621, 66th Cong., 2d Sess., 19 Jan 1920.

39. Mixter and Emmons, *U.S. Army Aircraft Production Facts,* p. 5.

40. Consolidated List of Aircraft Contracts and Deliveries, File No. A–00.2/22, in USAF Library.

31. House Comm. on Mil. Aff., 64th Cong., 2d Sess., Hearings on Army Appropriation Bill for FY 1918, 5 Jan 1917.

42. Director of Military Aeronautics Report 1918, in USAF Library.

43. Fletcher, pp. 33–34; Arnold, Outline of History Avn. Section, S.C. and Div. of Mil. Aeronautics, April 1917–October 1918.

APPENDICES

Appendix 1

WAR DEPARTMENT*

Office of the Chief Signal Officer,

Washington

August 1, 1907

OFFICE MEMORANDUM NO. 6

An Aeronautical Division of this office is hereby established, to take effect this date.

This division will have charge of all matters pertaining to military ballooning, air machines, and all kindred subjects. All data on hand will be carefully classified and plans perfected for future tests and experiments. The operations of this division are strictly confidential, and no information will be given out by any party except through the Chief Signal Officer of the Army or his authorized representative.

Captain Charles DeF. Chandler, Signal Corps, is detailed in charge of this division, and Corporal Edward Ward and First-class Private Joseph E. Barrett will report to Captain Chandler for duty in this division under his immediate direction.

J. Allen,

Brigadier General,

Chief Signal Officer of the Army.

*Central Files 321.91A "S. C. Organ." (USAF Library).

Appendix 2

REQUIREMENTS FOR SPHERICAL BALLOON PILOT, F.A.I. - 1909*

Applicant must be 21 years of age

10 ascensions

- 1 at night

- 1 alone

- 2 conducted by applicant under supervision of licensed pilots (with no interference) who report on handling to board

*[Briefed from ACA Yearbook 1909.] Changes were made subsequently as can be seen from 1911 requirements: †

Applicant must pass the following tests:

(A) Five ascensions without any conditions.

(B) An ascension of one hour's minimum duration undertaken by the candidate alone.

(C) A night ascension of two hours' minimum duration, completed between the setting and the rising of the sun.
The issue of a certificate is always discretionary.

*Chandler and Lahm, *How Our Army Grew Wings*, p. 286 (taken from ACA Yearbook 1911).

Appendix 3

Brief of General Specification #483 for an Army Airship

Proposals to be opened 15 Feb. 1908*

The length must not be over 120 feet, for use with hydrogen; the envelope fabric was to test not less than 62½ pounds per inch width and require no varnish; one or two ballonets with total capacity of at least 1/6 total volume of bag, with a centrifugal blower; adjustable automatic valve in ballonet and bag or a ballonet air tube near the gas bag; a second such valve on under side of gas bag to release hydrogen; a ripping panel in the upper portion of the bag.

The suspension system and frame were to have a factor of safety of at least three, considering wind strains as well as weight suspended.

A frame capable of quick mounting and demounting will be considered advantageous.

The airship must carry two persons of combined weight of 350 pounds and at least 100 pounds of ballast.

The designated speed shall be 20 m. p. h. in still air; but bidders must submit quotations depending on speed attained during trial flight on the following schedule: 20 m.p.h. 100%, 19 m.p.h. 85%, 18 m.p.h. 70%, 17 m.p.h. 55%, 16 m.p.h. 40%; less than 16 m.p.h., rejected.

For 21 m.p.h. 115%, 22 m.p.h. 130%, 23 m.p.h. 145% and 24 m.p.h. 160%.

The speed to be determined by an average over a measured course of between 2 and 5 miles, against and with the wind, subject to such additional details as the C.S.O. may prescribe at the time.

Fuel capacity for at least 2 hours, determined by a 2-hour flight at a speed at least 70% of that developed in the speed test.

Three trials are allowed each for speed and endurance, both within 30 days of delivery.

Ascent, descent, and equilibrium to be regulated by shifting weight, movable planes, using 2 ballonets or other method. For direction, a rudder.

A manometer must be provided to show pressure within the bag, and all other fittings and appurtenances "for successful and continuous flights."

Certified check for 15% of the 20-mile price must be enclosed with bid; successful bidder to furnish bond equal to the 20-mile bid.

Bidders must also submit drawings to scale; description of engine; size, pitch and r.p.m. of propellers; drawings of suspension system; description of blower; volume of bag and ballonets; description of bag fabric, valves, etc.

They must also furnish evidence that the Government has lawful right to use all patented devices and that the manufacturers are authorized to convey the same to the Government.

The price was to include instruction of 2 men in the handling and operating of the airship.

*Condensed from Appendix 3, Chandler and Lahm, pp. 287-90.

Appendix 4

REQUIREMENTS FOR DIRIGIBLE BALLOON PILOT, F.A.I., 1910*

Applicant must be over 21 years of age.

At least 10 ascents must be proved

On 5 a licensed dirigible pilot must have accompanied him and make a report describing his handling of dirigible.

On 2 of these trips he must have operated the dirigible on his own responsibility completely and on both voyages he must have flown a distance of at least 5 kilometers, including a return trip to the point from which he started.

REQUIREMENTS FOR DIRIGIBLE BALLOON PILOT, F.A.I., 1913†

The applicant must:

(a) Hold a spherical balloon pilot certificate.

(b) Furnish proof of having made six voyages in a dirigible balloon on different dates, of which one, at least, must have been of an hour's duration; on at least three of these occasions the dirigible must have been handled by the candidate himself.

The application for a certificate must be endorsed by two Dirigible Balloon Pilots who have assisted at least three of the starts and landings of the candidate.

The issue of a certificate is always discretionary.

---

*Brief from ACA Yearbook, 1910, p. 68.
†Appendix 5, Chandler and Lahm, *How Our Army Grew Wings*, p. 294, taken from ACA Yearbook, 1913.

Appendix 5*

Wilbur Wright
  Orville Wright

Van Cleve

Established in 1892

Mfrs of WRIGHT CYCLE COMPANY
Bicycles

1127 West Third Street,
Dayton, Ohio,
January 18, 1905.

Hon. R. M. Nevin,
  Washington, D. C.

Dear Sir:

The series of aeronautical experiments upon which we have been engaged for the past five years has ended in the production of a flying machine of a type fitted for practical use. It not only flies through the air at high speed, but it also lands without being wrecked. During the year 1904 one hundred and five flights were made at our experimenting station on the Huffman prairie, east of this city, and though our experience in handling the machine has been too short to give any high degree of skill, we nevertheless succeeded, toward the end of the season, in making two flights of five minutes each, in which we sailed round and round the field until a distance of about three miles had been covered, at a speed of thirty-five miles an hour. The first of these record flights was made on November 9th, in celebration of the phenomenal political victory of the preceding day, and the second on December 1st, in honor of the one hundredth flight of the season.

The numerous flights in straight lines, in circles, and over "S" shaped courses, in calm and in winds, have made it quite certain that flying has been brought to a point where it can be made of great practical use in various ways, one of which is that of scouting and carrying messages in time of war. If the latter features are of interest to our Government, we shall be pleased to take up the matter either on a basis of providing machines of agreed specification, at a contract price, or, of furnishing all the scientific and practical information we have accumulated in these years of experience, together with a license to use our patents; thus putting the Government in a position to operate on its own account.

If you can find it convenient to ascertain this is a subject of interest to our own Government, it would oblige us greatly, as early information on this point will aid us in making our plans for the future.

Respectfully yours,

(Sgd. in ink)   WILBUR and ORVILLE WRIGHT
(Initialed in ink) O.W.

COMMITTEE ON THE JUDICIARY
House of Representatives U.S.
Washington, D.C. Jan. 21, 1905.

My dear Mr. Secretary:

I have been skeptical as to the practicability and value of any so called "flying machine" or "air ship" that I did not give much heed to the request made sometime since by the gentlemen whose letter I attach hereto, until I was convinced by others who had seen their experiments, the result of their labor, and there was really something in their ideas.

I do not know whether you, or the proper officer of the Government to whom this matter will be referred, will care to take it up or not, but as I am advised, they only want to present, without expense of any consequence to the Government, the result of their labors, and as I am satisfied they have at least succeeded in inventing a machine worthy of investigation, I would respectfully ask that this matter be referred to the proper officer and that he may grant them, at any rate, the privilege of demonstrating to him what they have and what they can do. I assume that the Government is interested in the matter at least to that extent, providing its officers be convinced that here is something of value and something that would be of practicable use.

Will you kindly advise me, that I may let them know at the earliest opportunity.

Very truly yours,

(Sgd. in ink)   R. M. Nevin

Hon. William H. Taft,
    Secretary of War,
        Washington, D.C.

WAR DEPARTMENT
BOARD OF ORDNANCE & FORTIFICATION

Washington, D.C.,
January 24, 1905.

Hon. R. M. Nevin, etc.

My dear Sir:

Referring to your letter of the 21st instant to the Honorable Secretary of War inviting attention to the experiments in mechanical flight conducted by Messrs. Wilbur and Orville Wright, which has been referred to the Board of Ordnance and Fortification for action, I have the honor to inform you that, as many requests have been made for financial assistance in the development of designs for flying machines, the Board has found it necessary to decline to make allotments for the experimental development of devices for mechanical flight, and has determined that, before suggestions with that object in view will be considered, the device must have been brought to the stage of practical operation without expense to the United States.

It appears from the letter of Messrs. Wilbur and Orville Wright that their machine has not been brought to the stage of practical operation, but as soon as it shall have been perfected, the Board would be pleased to receive further representations from them in regard to it.

Very respectfully,

G. L. Gillespie,
Major General, General Staff,
President of the Board.

Wilbur Wright
  Orville Wright

Established in 1892.

WRIGHT CYCLE COMPANY

1127 West Third Street

Dayton, Ohio

October 9, 1905.

The Honorable Secretary of War,
    Washington, D.C.

Dear Sir:

Some months ago we made an informal offer to furnish to the War Department practical flying machines suitable for scouting purposes. The matter was referred to the Board of Ordnance and Fortification, which seems to have given it scant consideration. We do not wish to take this invention abroad, unless we find it necessary to do so, and therefore write again, renewing the offer.

We are prepared to furnish a machine on contract, to be accepted only after trial trips in which the conditions of the contract have been fulfilled; the machine to carry an operator and supplies of fuel, etc., sufficient for a flight of one hundred miles; the price of the machine to be regulated according to a sliding scale based on the performance of the machine in the trial trips; the minimum performance to be a flight of at least twenty-five miles at a speed of not less than thirty miles an hour.

We are also willing to take contracts to build machines carrying more than one man.

Respectfully yours,

(Sgd. in ink)   Wilbur and Orville Wright

(Initialed in ink)   O.W.

Washington, D.C.,

October 16, 1905.

Messrs. Wilbur and Orville Wright,
    1127 West Third Street,
    Dayton, Ohio.

Gentlemen:

Your letter of the 9th instant to the Honorable Secretary of War has been referred to this Board for action. I have the honor to inform you that, as many requests have been made for financial assistance in the development of designs for flying machines the Board has found it necessary to decline to make allotments for the experimental development of devices for mechanical flight, and has determined that, before suggestions with that object in view will be considered, the device must have been brought to the stage of practical operation without expense to the United States.

Before the question of making a contract with you for the furnishing of a flying machine is considered it will be necessary for you to furnish this Board with the approximate cost of the completed machine, the date upon which it would be delivered, and with such drawings and descriptions thereof as are necessary to enable its construction to be understood and a definite conclusion as to its practicability to be arrived at. Upon the receipt of this information, the matter will receive the careful consideration of the Board.

Very respectfully,

(Sgd.)   J. G. Bates

Major General, General Staff,

President of Board.

Wilbur Wright
   Orville Wright

Established in 1892.

WRIGHT CYCLE COMPANY

1127 West Third Street

Dayton, Ohio

October 19, 1905.

President of Board, Ordnance and Fortification,

   War Department,

     Washington, D.C.

Dear Sir:

Your communication of October 16th has been received. We have no thought of asking financial assistance from the Government. We propose to sell the results of experiments finished at our own expense.

In order that we may submit a proposition conforming as nearly as possible to the ideas of your Board, it is desirable that we be informed what conditions you would wish to lay down as to the performance of the machine in the official trials, prior to acceptance of the machine. We can not well fix a price, nor a time for delivery, till we have your idea of the qualifications necessary to such a machine. We ought also to know whether you would wish to reserve a monopoly on the use of the invention, or whether you would permit us to accept orders for similar machines from other governments, and give public exhibitions, etc.

Proof of our ability to execute an undertaking of the nature proposed will be furnished whenever desired.

Respectfully yours,

(Sgd. in ink)   Wilbur and Orville Wright

(Initialed in ink)   O.W.

At its meeting of 24 Oct. 1905 the Board considered the Wright's letter of 19 October and recommended:

"That Messrs. Wright be informed that the Board does not care to formulate any requirements for the performance of a flying machine or to take any further action on the subject until a machine is produced which by actual operation is shown to be able to produce horizontal flight and to carry an operator."

---

*Board of Ordnance and Fortification files, National Archives.

Appendix 6

Brief of
Specification No. 486 of Heavier-than-air Flying Machine

Bids to be in by 1 Feb. 1908*

Bidders were asked to submit dimensional drawings to scale, describe power plant, state speed, surface area, weight and material of frame, planes and propellers. There is required assembly in about one hour and quick demountability for transport in Army wagons.

The machine must be capable of taking off in any country encountered in field service and landing undamaged in a field without requiring a specially prepared spot.

It will carry two persons of a combined weight of 350 pounds with sufficient fuel for a flight of 125 miles and should have a speed of 40 miles a hour.

Besides a simple and transportable starting device, the machine is to be equipped with some device to permit of a safe descent in case of an accident to the propelling machinery.

It will be sufficiently simple in construction and operation to permit an intelligent man to become proficient in its use within a reasonable length of time. The price to be quoted includes instruction of two men.

Bidders are required to furnish evidence that the Government has the lawful right to use all patented devices or appurtenances which may be a part of the flying machine, and that the manufacturers of the flying machine are authorized to convey the same to the Government, but does not contemplate the exclusive purchase of patent rights for duplicating the flying machine.

A premium of 10% of the contract price is to be paid for each additional mile-per-hour of speed over 40, with a similar deduction for each mile of less speed. The speed is to be determined by taking an average of the time over a measured course of more than 5 miles, against and with the wind. An endurance flight of at least one hour is required, the machine to land in condition to at once start on another flight, demonstrate steering in all directions without difficulty and be at all time under perfect control and equilibrium.

Bidders must state time required for delivery after receipt of order and furnish with their proposal a certified check amounting to 10% of the price stated for the 40-mile speed. Upon award, the check would be returned to the bidders and successful bidder will be required to furnish a bond in the amount equal to the price stated.

---

*Condensed from Appendix 6, Chandler and Lahm, pp. 295-98.

Appendix 7

Requirements for Aviation Pilot, F.A.I., 1910*

Three separate flights, each of 5 kilometers, in a closed circuit without coming to the ground, but not necessarily on same day. On completion of each 5 kilometer circuit the engine must be stopped and a landing effected within 150 yards of a given spot, previously designated. Each trial must be vouched for by officials appointed by the Aero Club of America and a separate official certificate must be obtained for each flight.

Requirements for Aviation Pilot, F.A.I., 1913†

Applicants must pass the three following tests:

(A) Two distance tests, each consisting of covering, without touching the ground or the water, a closed circuit not less than five kilometers in length (length measured as indicated below).

(B) An altitude test consisting of rising to a minimum height of 50 meters above the starting point.

(C) The (B) test may be made at the same time as one of the (A) tests.

Starting from and landing on the water are authorized for only one of the tests (A).

The course over which the aviator shall accomplish the aforesaid two circuits must be marked by two posts or buoys situated not more than 500 meters from each other.

After each turn made around a post or buoy the aviator will change his direction to turn around the other. The circuit will thus consist of an uninterrupted series of figure 8's, each loop of the figure 8 containing alternately one of the two posts or one of the two buoys.

For each of these three tests the landing shall be made:

(1) By stopping the motor not later than the time when the machine touches the ground.

(2) At a distance of less than 50 meters from a point designated by the applicant before the test.

Landings must be made properly and the official observer shall indicate in his report the way in which they were made, the issue of the certificate being always discretionary.

Official observers must be chosen from a list drawn up by the governing organization of each country.

---

*Brief of Requirements in ACA *Yearbook* for 1910. These were changed in 1913 and again in 1915.
†Appendix 9, Chandler and Lahm, p. 305, taken from ACA *Yearbook* for 1913.

Appendix 8

REQUIREMENTS FOR MILITARY AVIATOR RATING, 1912, SIGNAL CORPS*

1. Attain an altitude of at least 2,500 feet as recorded by a barograph.
2. Make a flight of at least five minutes' duration in a wind of at least 15 m.p.h. as indicated by an anemometer near the ground.
3. Carry a passenger to a height of at least 500 feet, and on landing bring the machine to rest within 150 feet of a previously designated point, the engine being completely shut off prior to touching the ground; combined weight of pilot and passenger, at least 250 pounds.
4. Execute a volplane from an altitude of at least 500 feet with engine cut off, and cause the airplane to come to rest within 300 feet of a previously designated point on the ground.
5. Make a military reconnaissance flight of at least 20 miles cross-country at an average altitude of 1,500 feet, for the purpose of observing and reporting information concerning features of the ground or other matter which the candidate was instructed to report upon.

These requirements were changed twice in 1913 and were changed thereafter.

---

*Appendix 10, Chandler and Lahm, p. 306, taken from Report of Chief Signal Officer, U.S. Army to Sec. of War, 1912.

Appendix 9

REQUIREMENTS FOR EXPERT AVIATOR, AERO CLUB OF AMERICA, 1913*

Each applicant must pass a thorough physical examination by a reputable, competent physician, designated by the Contest Committee of the Aero Club of America. The applicant must possess normal heart and lungs as well as normal sight and hearing and shall be free from all nervous affections. In case the physician is in doubt as to the physical stability of the applicant, the examination shall be made immediately following a trial flight to determine this point.

After passing the physical examination the applicant must pass the following tests:

1. A Cross-country flight, from a designated starting point to a point at least 25 miles distant and return to the starting point without alighting.

2. A glide, without power, from a height of 2,500 feet, coming to rest within 50 meters of a previously designated point without the use of brakes.

3. A Figure Eight around two marks, 500 meters apart. In making turns, the aviator must keep all parts of his apparatus within semi-circles of 50 meters radius from each turning mark as a center.

The issuance of the certificate is discretionary with the Aero Club of America.

---

*Appendix 12, Chandler and Lahm, p. 309; ACA Yearbook for 1913, p. 63.

Appendix 10**

TWENTY-FOUR ORIGINAL MILITARY AVIATORS
UNDER GENERAL ORDER NO. 39

May 27, 1913

	Name	Qualification Date
#	1st Lt. H. H. Arnold, Inf.	5 July 1912
	Capt. Charles DeF. Chandler, S.C.	5 July 1912
*	2d Lt. Thomas DeW. Milling, Cav.	5 July 1912
R	Capt. Paul W. Beck, Inf.	12 July 1912
*	1st Lt. B. D. Foulois, Inf.	13 July 1912
K*	1st Lt. Harold Geiger, CAC	8 November 1912
*	1st Lt. Roy C. Kirtland, Inf.	17 January 1913
R*	1st Lt. Lewis E. Goodier, Jr., CAC	14 February 1913
R	1st Lt. Samuel H. McLeary, CAC	11 March 1913
†	2d Lt. Lewis H. Brereton, CAC	27 March 1913
K	1st Lt. Joseph D. Park, Cav.	7 May 1913
K	1st Lt. Eric L. Ellington, Cav.	11 August 1913
*	2d Lt. Carleton G. Chapman, Cav.	26 June 1913
#	1st Lt. Frank P. Lahm, Cav.	19 July 1913
K*	2d Lt. Herbert A. Dargue, CAC	19 July 1913
*#	2d Lt. Joseph E. Carberry, Inf.	25 September 1913
K*	2d Lt. Walter R. Taliaferro, Inf.	25 September 1913
K	2d Lt. Henry B. Post, Inf.	11 November 1913
K	1st Lt. Hugh M. Kelly, Inf.	18 November 1913
*	1st Lt. H. LeR. Miller, CAC	19 December 1913
#	2d Lt. Robert H. Willis, Jr., Inf.	26 December 1913
*	2d Lt. Joseph C. Morrow, Inf.	27 December 1913
K*	1st Lt. Townsend F. Dodd, CAC	30 December 1913
R	2d Lt. Fred Seydel, CAC	31 December 1913

K—Killed in airplane accident.
R—Relieved.
*—Rated JMA, Act of 18 July 1914.
†—Rated MA by distinguished service in World War I.
#—Rated MA after three years as a JMA because of an absence from the air service by return to original branch.
**Appendix 1, Chandler and Lahm, pp. 282-85.

Appendix 11*

REQUIREMENTS FOR MILITARY AVIATOR RATING
1914, WAR DEPARTMENT

Circular}
No. 10. }

WAR DEPARTMENT
Office of the Chief Signal Officer,

Washington, October 27, 1913.

The following requirements for a military aviator, effective January 1, 1914, having been approved by the Secretary of War, are published for the information and guidance of all concerned:

1. Make a cross-country flight over a triangular course not less than 100 miles in perimeter with two intermediate landings; this flight to be completed within 48 hours after the start, the same machine being used during the flight.

2. Make a straight-away cross-country flight, without landing, of at least 60 miles, over a previously designated course; return flight to be made either on the same day or on the first subsequent day that the weather permits.

3. During the flight prescribed in paragraphs 1 and 2, the candidate shall remain at least 1,500 feet above the surface of the ground.

4. Make a flight during which the machine shall remain for at least 30 minutes at an altitude of between 2,500 and 3,000 feet above the surface of the ground. This requirement may be accomplished during one of the cross-country flights if practicable.

5. Execute a volplane, with motor cut out completely, at an altitude of 1,500 feet, the motor to be cut out when aeroplane is over the landing field, and on landing cause the aeroplane to come to rest within 300 feet of a previously designated point.

6. Reports will be submitted giving the main military features observed during the flights made under paragraphs 1 and 2.

7. No tests shall be made with passengers. Time of arrival at and departure from the various points may be attested by military or civil authorities; if none of these are present, by the aviators themselves.

8. The candidate will then be examined theoretically and practically on his ability to read maps; his knowledge of the compass, and how to steer thereby; his knowledge of the aeroplane, i.e., what constitutes safe construction; how to make the ordinary repairs of an aeroplane; the action of the machine under ordinary flying conditions, covering the points on the action of the controls, how the angles of lift on the wings change in making turns, how the pressures change both on the main planes, rear elevator, and vertical rudder; and what constitutes safe flying as far as gliding, banking, etc., is concerned.

He will be examined on his knowledge of gasoline motors; carburetors; the most common troubles that occur to motors and how to correct them. He shall be able to make simple repairs, dismantle and assemble motors, and shall show a thorough knowledge of all motors in use at the school.

He shall be examined in meteorology and topography in so far as they relate to aviation.

---

*Appendix 14, Chandler and Lahm, pp. 312-13.

9. Any aviator who has gained his military aviator's certificate previous to January 1, 1914, and who is on duty with the Aeronautical Branch of the Signal Corps from January 1 to July 1, 1914, and who during this period does not make flights the equal or better than those contained in paragraphs 1 to 5, and who does not show himself conversant with the repair of motors and machines and general knowledge of them will be required to pass the above tests.

GEORGE P. SCRIVEN,
Brigadier General, Chief Signal Officer.

Appendix 12*

ARMY AND SIGNAL CORPS AVIATION FATALITIES
17 September 1908–6 April 1917

1.	17 September 1908	Lt. T. E. Selfridge, passenger with Orville Wright during delivery trials of Wright airplane at Fort Myer, Va.
2.	10 May 1911	Lt. G. E. M. Kelly in a Curtiss pusher, S.C. No. 2, at San Antonio, Texas.
3.	11 June 1912	Lt. L. W. Hazelhurst, passenger with civilian pilot, A. L. Welch, both killed in tests of Wright C, S.C. No. 10, College Park, Md.
4 & 5.	28 September 1912	Lt. Lewis C. Rockwell, pilot and Cpl. Frank S. Scott, passenger in Wright B, S.C. No. 4, at College Park, Md.
6.	8 April 1913	Lt. Rex Chandler, passenger with Lt. Lewis H. Brereton, who escaped, in Curtiss flying boat, S.C. No. 15, at San Diego, Calif.
7.	9 May 1913	Lt. Joseph D. Park in Curtiss, Type IV "Military," S.C. No. 2, Olive, Calif.
8.	8 July 1913	Lt. Loren H. Call, in Wright C, S.C. No. 11, Texas City, Tex.
9.	4 September 1913	Lt. Moss L. Love in a Burgess Wright C, S.C. No. 18, at San Diego, Calif.
10.	14 November 1913	Lt. C. Perry Rich in Wright C, S.C. No. 12, Manila, P.I.
11 & 12.	24 November 1913	Lt. E. L. Ellington, pilot, and Lt. H. M. Kelly, passenger, in Wright C, S.C. No. 14, San Diego, Calif.
13.	9 February 1914	Lt. Henry B. Post in Wright C seaplane, S.C. No. 10, San Diego, Calif.
14.	21 December 1914	Lt. F. J. Gerstner, passenger with Lt. L. H. Muller, who escaped, in Curtiss J tractor, S.C. No. 29, San Diego, Calif.
15.	12 August 1915	Capt. G. H. Knox, QMC, passenger with Lt. R. B. Sutton, who escaped, in Curtiss JN2, S.C. No. 47, Fort Sill, Okla.
16.	11 October 1915	Lt. W. R. Taliaferro in Curtiss J, S.C. No. 30, San Diego, Calif.

*Appendix 1, Chandler and Lahm, pp. 282-85; Jones, Chronology.

Appendix 13*

CREATION OF AVIATION SECTION, SIGNAL CORPS
SIXTY-THIRD CONGRESS
Sess. II

July 18, 1914. (H.R. 5304) An Act To Increase The Efficiency of the Aviation Service of the Army, and for Other Purposes.

Be it enacted by the Senate and House of Representatives of the United States of America in Congress assembled, That there shall hereafter be, and there is hereby created, an aviation section, which shall be a part of the Signal Corps of the Army, and which shall be, and is hereby, charged with the duty of operating or supervising the operation of all military aircraft, including balloons and aeroplanes, all appliances pertaining to said craft, and signaling apparatus of any kind when installed on said craft; also with the duty of training officers and enlisted men in matters pertaining to military aviation.

SEC. 2. That, in addition to such officers and enlisted men as shall be assigned from the Signal Corps at large to executive, administrative, scientific, or other duty in or for the aviation section, there shall be in said section aviation officers not to exceed sixty in number, and two hundred and sixty aviation enlisted men of all grades; and said aviation officers and aviation enlisted men, all of whom shall be engaged on duties pertaining to said aviation section, shall be additional to the officers and enlisted men now allotted by law to the Signal Corps, the commissioned and enlisted strengths of which are hereby increased accordingly.

The aviation officers provided for in this section shall, except as hereinafter prescribed specifically to the contrary, be selected from among officers holding commissions in the line of the Army with rank below that of captain, and shall be detailed to serve as such aviation officers for periods of four years, unless sooner relieved, and the provisions of section twenty-seven of the Act of Congress approved February second, nineteen hundred and one (Thirty-first Statutes, page seven hundred and fifty-five) are hereby extended so as to apply to said aviation officers and to the vacancies created in the line of the Army by the detail of said officers therefrom, but nothing in said Act or in any other law now in force shall be held to prevent the detail or redetail at any time to fill a vacancy among the aviation officers authorized by this Act, of any officer holding a commission in the line of the Army with rank below that of captain, and who, during prior service as an aviation officer in the aviation section, shall have become especially proficient in military aviation.

There shall also be constantly attached to the aviation section a sufficient number of aviation students to make, with the aviation officers actually detailed in said section under the provisions of this Act, a total number of sixty aviation officers and aviation students constantly under assignment to, or detail in, said section. Said aviation students, all of whom shall be selected on the recommendation of the Chief Signal Officer from among unmarried lieutenants of the line of the Army not over thirty years of age, shall remain attached to the aviation section for a sufficient time, but in no case to exceed one year, to determine their fitness or unfitness for detail as aviation officers in said section, and their detachment from their respective arms of service which under assignment to said section shall not be held to create in said arms vacancies that may be filled by promotions or original appointments: Provided, That no person, except in time of war, shall be assigned or detailed against his will to duty as an aviation student or an aviation officer: Provided further, That when-

233

ever, under such regulations as the Secretary of War shall prescribe and publish to the Army, an officer assigned or detailed to duty of any kind in or with the aviation section shall have been found to be inattentive to his duties, inefficient, or incapacitated from any cause whatever for the full and efficient discharge of all duties that might properly be imposed upon him if he should be continued on duty in or with said section, said officer shall be returned forthwith to the branch of the service in which he shall hold a commission.

SEC. 3. That the aviation officers hereinbefore provided for shall be rated in two classes, to wit, as junior military aviators and as military aviators. Within sixty days after this Act shall take effect the Secretary of War may, upon the recommendation of the Chief Signal Officer, rate as junior military aviators any officers with rank below that of captain, who are now on aviation duty and who have, or shall have before the date of rating so authorized, shown by practical tests, including aerial flights, that they are especially well qualified for military aviation service; and after said rating shall have been made the rating of junior military aviator shall not be conferred upon any person except as hereinafter provided.

Each aviation student authorized by this Act shall, while on duty that requires him to participate regularly and frequently in aerial flights, receive an increase of 25 per centum in the pay of his grade and length of service under his line commission. Each duly qualified junior military aviator shall, while so serving, have the rank, pay, and allowances of one grade higher than that held by him under his line commission, provided that his rank under said commission be not higher than that of first lieutenant, and, while on duty requiring him to participate regularly and frequently in aerial flights, he shall receive in addition an increase of 50 per centum in the pay of his grade and length of service under his line commission. The rating of military aviator shall not be hereafter conferred upon or held by any person except as hereinafter provided, and the number of officers with that rating shall at no time exceed fifteen. Each military aviator who shall hereafter have duly qualified as such under the provisions of this Act shall, while so serving, have the rank, pay, and allowances of one grade higher than that held by him under his line commission, provided that his rank under said commission be not higher than that of first lieutenant, and while on duty requiring him to participate regularly and frequently in aerial flights, he shall receive in addition an increase of 75 per centum of the pay of his grade and length of service under his line commission.

The aviation enlisted men hereinbefore provided for shall consist of twelve master signal electricians, twelve first-class sergeants, twenty-four sergeants, seventy-eight corporals, eight cooks, eighty-two first-class privates, and forty-four privates. Not to exceed forty of said enlisted men shall at any one time have the rating of aviation mechanician, which rating is hereby established, and said rating shall not be conferred upon any person except as hereinafter provided; Provided, That twelve enlisted men at a time shall, in the discretion of the officer in command of the aviation section, be instructed in the art of flying, and no enlisted man shall be assigned to duty as an aerial flyer against his will except in time of war. Each aviation enlisted man, while on duty that requires him to participate regularly and frequently in aerial flights, or while holding the rating of aviation mechanician, shall receive an increase of 50 per centum in his pay: Provided further, That, except as hereinafter provided in the cases of officers now on aviation duty, no person shall be detailed as an aviation officer, or rated as a junior military aviator, or as a military aviator, or as an aviation mechanician, until there shall have been issued to him a certificate to the effect, that he is qualified for the detail or rating, or for both the detail and the rating, sought or proposed in his case, and no such certificate shall be issued to any person until an aviation examining board, which shall be composed of three officers of experience in the aviation service and two medical officers, shall have examined him, under general regulations to be prescribed by the Secretary of War and published to the Army by the War Department, and shall have reported him to be qualified for the detail or rating, or for both the detail and the rating, sought or proposed in his case: Provided further, That the Secretary of War shall cause approrpiate certificates of qualification to be issued by the Adjutant General of the Army to all officers and enlisted men who shall have been found and reported by aviation examining boards in accordance with the terms of this Act, to be qualified for the details and ratings for which said officers and enlisted men shall have been examined: Provided further, That except as hereinbefore provided in the cases of officers who are now on aviation duty and who shall be rated as junior military aviators as hereinbefore authorized, no person shall be detailed for service as an aviation officer in the aviation section until he shall have served creditably as an aviation student for a period to be fixed by the Secertary of War; and no person shall receive the rating of military aviator until he shall have served creditably for at least three years as an aviation officer with the rating of junior military aviator: Provided further, That there shall be paid to the widow of any officer or enlisted man who shall die as the result of an aviation accident, not the result of his own misconduct, or to any other person designated by him in writing, an amount equal to one year's pay at the rate to which such officer or enlisted man was entitled at the time of the accident resulting in his death, but any payment made in accordance with the terms of this proviso on account of the death of any officer or enlisted man shall be in lieu of and a bar to any payment under the Acts of Congress approved May eleventh, nineteen hundred and eight, and March third, nineteen hundred and nine (Thirty-fifth Statutes, pages one hundred and eight and seven hundred and fifty-five), on account of death of said officer or enlisted man.

Approved, July 18, 1914.

*Appendix 16, Chandler and Lahm, pp. 316-19.

Appendix 14

ARMY OFFICERS AND ENLISTED PILOTS ON AERONAUTICAL DUTY CHRONOLOGICALLY ARRANGED TO 1917

Name, Rank, and Organization	No. and Date of Balloon and Airship Pilot Certificates*	Date and/or No. Airplane Pilot Cert. and Ratings*	Killed in Airplane Accident	Left the Service
1st Lt. Frank P. Lahm, 6th Cav.	B. No. 4, 1905 D. No. 2, Aug 1908	A. No. 2, Oct 1909 M.A., 19 Jul 1913 E. No. 15, Jul 1913 J.M.A., Apr 1916		
Capt. Charles DeF. Chandler, S.C.	B. No. 8, 1907 D. 1909	A. No. 59, Sep 1911 M.A., Jul 1912 E. No. 5, 1912		
1st Lt. Thomas E. Selfridge, Jr., 1st F.A.	D. Aug 1908		17 Sep 1908	
1st Lt. Benjamin D. Foulois, 7th Inf.	D. Aug 1908	A. No. 140, 26 Jun 1912 M.A., 13 Jul 1912 E. No. 7, 1912 JMA, 23 Jul 1914		
2d Lt. John G. Winter, 6th Cav.	D. 1909			
1st Lt. Raymond S. Bamberger, 7th Cav.	D. 1909	None (Retired 1915)		12 Apr 1915 (Retired)
2nd Lt. Oliver A. Dickinson, 5th Inf.	D. 1909			
2d Lt. Frederic E. Humphreys, C.E.**	None (Resigned 1910)			1 Aug 1910
Capt. Arthur S. Cowan, S.C.	None			
1st Lt. Paul W. Beck, S.C.		A. No. 39, Aug 1911 M.A., Jul 1912 E. No. 6, 1912		
2d Lt. John C. Walker, Jr., 8th Inf.		A. No. 554, Aug 1916		
2d Lt. G. E. M. Kelly, 30th Inf.	None		10 May 1911	
1st Lt. Roy C. Kirtland, 14th Inf.**		A. No. 45, Aug 1911 M.A., Jan 1913 E. No. 11, 1913 J.M.A., Jul 1914		
2d Lt. Henry H. Arnold, 29th Inf.		A. No. 29, Jul 1911 M.A., Jul 1912 E. No. 4, Sep 1912 J.M.A., May 1916		
2d Lt. Thomas DeW. Milling, 15th Cav.		A. No. 30, Jul 1911 M.A., Jul 1912 E. No. 3, Sep 1912 J.M.A., Jul 1914		
2d Lt. Frank M. Kennedy, 10th Inf.**		A. No. 97, Feb 1912		
Maj. Samuel Reber, S.C.	B. No. 43, Oct 1911			
2d Lt. Leighton W. Hazlehurst, Jr., 17th Inf.		None	11 June 1912	
2d Lt. William C. Sherman, C.E.**		A. No. 151, Aug 1912 J.M.A., Apr 1920		
1st Lt. Harry Graham, 22d Inf.**		A. No. 152, Aug 1912 J.M.A., Feb 1919		
Capt. Frederick B. Hennessy, 3d F.A.		A. No. 153, Aug 1912		
Sgt. Vernon L. Burge, S.C.		A. No. 154, Aug 1912		

*A—F.A.I. airplane pilot certificate; B—Balloon, F.A.I. certificate; D—Airship or Dirigible, F.A.I. certificate; M.A.—Military Aviator, War Dept. 1912-1914; E—Expert Aviator, Aero Club of America; JMA—Junior Military Aviator, Act of 18 July 1914.

**Redetailed during World War I.

ARMY OFFICERS AND ENLISTED PILOTS ON AERONAUTICAL DUTY
CHRONOLOGICALLY ARRANGED TO 1917

Name, Rank, and Organization	No. and Date of Balloon and Airship Pilot Certificates*	Date and/or No. Airplane Pilot Cert. and Ratings*	Killed in Airplane Accident	Left the Service
2d Lt. Moss L. Love, S.C.		A. No. 155, Aug 1912	4 Sep 1913	
2d Lt. Lewis C. Rockwell, 10th Inf.		A. No. 165, Sep 1912	28 Sep 1912	
1st Lt. Harold Geiger, CAC**		A. No. 166, Sep 1912 M.A., Nov 1912 E. No. 9, 1912 J.M.A., Jul 1914		
Cpl. William A. Lamkey, S.C.		A. No. 183, Nov. 1912		
1st Lt. Samuel H. McLeary, CAC		A. No. 210, Mar 1913 M.A., Mar 1913 E. No. 12, 1913		
2d Lt. Lewis H. Brereton, CAC		A. No. 211, Mar 1913 M.A., Mar 1913 E. No. 13, 1913 J.M.A., Jun 1917		
2d Lt. Rex Chandler, CAC		None	8 Apr 1913	
1st Lt. Lewis E. Goodier, Jr., CAC**		A. No. 200, Jan 1913 M.A., Feb 1913 E. No. 10, 1913 J.M.A., Jul 1914		1 July 1916 (Retired)
1st Lt. Joseph D. Park, 14th Cav.		A. No. 223, Apr 1913 M.A., May 1913	9 May 1913	
1st Lt. Loren H. Call, CAC		None	8 Jul 1913	
2d Lt. Eric L. Ellington, 3d Cav.		M.A., Aug 1913	24 Nov 1913	
2d Lt. Carleton G. Chapman, 7th Cav.		A. No. 241, Jul 1913 M.A., Jun 1913 E. No. 14, 1913 J.M.A., Jul 1914		
2d Lt. Herbert A. Dargue, CAC		A. No. 242, Jul 1913 M.A., Jul 1913 E. No. 16, 1913 J.M.A., Jul 1914		
2d Lt. C. Perry Rich, Philippine Scouts		A. No. 243, Jul 1913	14 Nov 1913	
2d Lt. Walter R. Taliaferro, 21st Inf.		A. No. 250, Jul 1913 M.A., Sep 1913 E. No. 18, 1913 J.M.A., Jul 1914	11 Oct 1915	
2d Lt. Joseph E. Carberry, 6th Inf.		A. No. 251, Jul 1913 M.A., Sep 1913 E. No. 17, 1913 J.M.A., Jul 1914		
2d Lt. Frederick J. Gerstner		None	21 Dec 1914	
2d Lt. Ralph E. Jones, 17th Inf.		None		
1st Lt. Hugh M. Kelly, 26th Inf.		M.A., Nov 1913	24 Nov 1913	
2d Lt. Henry B. Post, 25th Inf.		A. No. 264, Sep 1913 M.A., Nov 1913 E. No. 19, 1913	9 Feb 1914	

*A—F.A.I. airplane pilot certificate; B—Balloon, F.A.I. certificate; D—Airship or Dirigible, F.A.I. certificate; M.A.—Military Aviator, War Dept. 1912-1914; E—Expert Aviator, Aero Club of America; JMA—Junior Military Aviator, Act of 18 July 1914.

**Redetailed during World War I.

ARMY OFFICERS AND ENLISTED PILOTS ON AERONAUTICAL DUTY
CHRONOLOGICALLY ARRANGED TO 1917

Name, Rank, and Organization	No. and Date of Balloon and Airship Pilot Certificates*	Date and/or No. Airplane Pilot Cert. and Ratings*	Killed in Airplane Accident	Left the Service
1st Lt. Hollis LeR. Muller, CAC**		A. No. 272, Nov 1913 M.A., Dec 1913 E. No. 21, 1914 J.M.A., Nov 1914		
1st Lt. Virginius E. Clark, CAC		A. No. 273, Nov 1913 J.M.A., Oct 1914		
2d Lt. Stanley W. Wood, 7th Inf.†		None		22 Dec 1914 (Resigned)
2d Lt. Leon R. Cole, CAC		None		
2d Lt. Robert H. Willis, Jr., 6th Inf.		A. No. 275, Dec 1913 M.A., Dec 1913 E. No. 22, 1914 J.M.A., Nov 1914		
2d Lt. Frederick S. Snyder, 2d Cav.		None		
2d Lt. John P. Edgerly, 2d Inf.**		None		
1st Lt. William C. F. Nicholson, 9th Cav.		None		
1st Lt. Townsend F. Dodd, CAC		A. No. 280, Jan 1914 M.A., Dec 1913 E. No. 23, 1914 J.M.A., Jul 1914		
2d Lt. Joseph C. Morrow, Jr., 23d Inf.		A. No. 288, Jan 1914 M.A., Dec 1913 E. No. 25, 1914 J.M.A., Jul 1914		
2d Lt. Fred Seydel, CAC**		A. No. 289, Feb 1914 M.A., Dec 1913 E. No. 24, 1914		
Sgt. Wm. C. Ocker††		A. No. 293, Apr 1914 J.M.A., Nov 1917		
2d Lt. Byron Q. Jones, 14th Cav.		A. No. 308, Sep 1914 J.M.A., Aug 1914		
2d Lt. Douglas B. Netherwood, CAC		A. No. 312, Oct 1914 J.M.A., Aug 1914 E. No. 41, 1915		
2d Lt. R. B. Sutton		A. No. 316, Mar 1915 J.M.A., Jun 1915		
2d Lt. Thomas S. Bowen, 6th Inf.		J.M.A., Aug 1914		
Capt. Wm. L. Patterson, 7th Inf.		A. No. 390, Jan 1916 J.M.A., Sep 1914		
2d Lt. W. G. Kilner, Inf.		A. No. 317, Mar 1915 J.M.A., Jun 1915		
2d Lt. R. C. Holliday, Inf.		None		
2d Lt. S. W. Fitzgerald, CAC		A. No. 318, Apr 1915 J.M.A., Jun 1915		

*A—F.A.I. airplane pilot certificate; B—Balloon, F.A.I. certificate; D—Airship or Dirigible, F.A.I. certificate; M.A.—Military Aviator, War Dept. 1912-1914; E—Expert Aviator, Aero Club of America; JMA—Junior Military Aviator, Act of 18 July 1914.

**Redetailed during World War I.

†Killed in action in France 13 June 1916 while serving as an officer of the 1st Canadian Division.

††Discharged to accept commission as Captain, ordered to active duty Avn. Sec. 10 Feb. 1917.

ARMY OFFICERS AND ENLISTED PILOTS ON AERONAUTICAL DUTY
CHRONOLOGICALLY ARRANGED TO 1917

Name, Rank, and Organization	No. and Date of Balloon and Airship Pilot Certificates*	Date and/or No. Airplane Pilot Cert. and Ratings*	Killed in Airplane Accident	Left the Service
2d Lt. Leslie MacDill, Cav.		A. No. 319, Apr 1915 J.M.A., Jun 1915		
2d Lt. Arthur R. Christie, Inf.		A. No. 323, May 1915 J.M.A., Jul 1915		
2d Lt. E. S. Gorrell, Inf.		A. No. 324, Jun 1915 J.M.A., Jul 1915		
2d Lt. Ira A. Rader, Inf.		A. No. 327, Jun 1915 J.M.A., Jul 1915		
2d Lt. Harry Gantz, Inf.		A. No. 328, Jun 1915 J.M.A., Jul 1915		
2d Lt. H. W. Harms, Cav.		A. No. 326, Jun 1915 J.M.A., Jul 1915		
Sgt. Herbert Marcus, S.C.***		None		
2d Lt. W. W. Vautsmeier, CAC**		None		
2d Lt. Dana Palmer, Inf.		None		
Cpl. J. S. Krull, S.C.†		A. No. 360, Oct 1915		16 May 1917 (Discharged)
2d Lt. E. L. Canady, Cav.		A. No. 342, Sep 1915 J.M.A., Oct 1915		
Cpl. A. D. Smith, S.C.††		A. No. 354, Oct 1915 J.M.A., Mar 1918		11 Aug 1916 (Purchased Discharge)
2d Lt. Sumner Waite, Inf.		None		
Cpl. Ira O. Biffle S.C.†††		A. No. 396, Jan 1916		12 Jul 1917 (Discharged)
2d Lt. Roy S. Brown, Cav.		A. No. 394, Jan 1916 J.M.A., May 1916		
2d Lt. H. H. C. Richards, Cav.		A. No. 391, Jan 1916 J.M.A., Aug 1918		
1st Lt. J. F. Curry, Inf.		A. No. 392, Jan 1916 J.M.A., May 1916		
2d Lt. Ralph Royce, Inf.		A. No. 393, Jan 1916 J.M.A., May 1916		
Sgt. A. A. Adamson, S.C.#		A. No. 395, Jan 1916		
2d Lt. Jack W. Heard, Cav.		A. No. 485, May 1916 J.M.A., Jun 1917		
2d Lt. John B. Brooks, Cav.		A. No. 429, Mar 1916 J.M.A., Jun 1916		
Cpl. S. V. Coyle, S.C.†††		A. No. 431, Mar 1916		18 Jul 1917 (Discharged)
2d Lt. H. S. Martin, Inf.		A. No. 427, Mar 1916 J.M.A., Jun 1916		

*A—F.A.I. airplane pilot certificate; B—Balloon, F.A.I. certificate; D—Airship or Dirigible, F.A.I. certificate; M.A.—Military Aviator, War Dept. 1912-1914; E—Expert Aviator, Aero Club of America; JMA—Junior Military Aviator, Act of 18 July 1914.

**Redetailed during World War I.

***Assigned to active duty at 1st Lt., SORC, 21 Nov 1917.

†Discharged to become civilian instructor, later 1st Lt, Air Service.

††Became civilian instructor at San Diego and was ordered to active duty as a captain Avn. Sec., SORC, 13 Aug 1917.

†††Discharged to become civilian instructor.

#Attached to Air Service, AEF, as 1st Lt. in July 1917.

ARMY OFFICERS AND ENLISTED PILOTS ON AERONAUTICAL DUTY

CHRONOLOGICALLY ARRANGED TO 1917

Name, Rank, and Organization	No. and Date of Balloon and Airship Pilot Certificates*	Date and/or No. Airplane Pilot Cert. and Ratings*	Killed in Airplane Accident	Left the Service
2d Lt. B. M. Atkinson, Inf.		A. No. 430, Mar 1916 J.M.A., Jun 1916		
2d Lt. Carl Spaatz, Inf.		A. No. 428, Mar 1916 J.M.A., Jun 1916		
2d Lt. S. H. Wheeler, Inf.		A. No. 455, Apr 1916 J.M.A., Sep 1916		
2d Lt. G. E. A. Reinburg, Cav.		A. No. 454, Apr 1916 J.M.A., Sep 1916		
2d Lt. G. H. Brett, Cav.		A. No. 476, May 1916 J.M.A., Sep 1916		
2d Lt. J. C. McDonnell, Cav.		A. No. 477, May 1916 J.M.A., Sep 1916		
Cpl. Leo G. Flint, S.C.		None		
2d Lt. J. W. Butts, Cav.		A. No. 488, May 1916 J.M.A., Sep 1916		
2d Lt. L. G. Heffernan, Cav.		A. No. 489, May 1916 J.M.A., Sep 1916		
2d Lt. J. C. P. Bartholf, Inf.		A. No. 501, Jun 1916 J.M.A., Sep 1916		
2d Lt. H. C. Davidson, Inf.		A. No. 528, Jul 1916 J.M.A., Oct 1916		
2d Lt. C. W. Russell, Inf.		A. No. 533, Jul 1916 J.M.A., Oct 1916		
2d Lt. Maxwell Kirby, Cav.		A. 529, Jul 1916 J.M.A., Oct 1916		
2d Lt. W. A. Robertson, Cav.		A. No. 527, Jul 1916 J.M.A., Oct. 1916		
2d Lt. Davenport Johnson, Cav.		A. No. 534, Jul 1916 J.M.A., Oct 1916		
2d Lt. M. F. Harmon, Inf.		A. No. 535, Jul 1916 J.M.A., Oct 1916		
2d Lt. R. B. Barnitz, Cav.		A. No. 560, Aug 1916 J.M.A., Oct 1916		
2d Lt. M. F. Scanlon, Inf.		A. No. 591, Sep 1916 J.M.A., Oct 1916		
Sgt. Felix Steinle, S.C.†		A. No. 779, Jul 1917		
2d Lt. J. D. V. Holtzendorff, F.A.		A. No. 592, Sep 1916		
1st Lt. P. L. Ferron, CAC		A. No. 594, Sep 1916 J.M.A., Oct 1916		
2d Lt. G. E. Lovel, Cav.		A. No. 611, Oct 1916 J.M.A., Oct 1916		
1st Lt. J. L. Dunsworth, CAC		A. No. 612, Oct 1916 J.M.A., Nov 1916		

*A—F.A.I. airplane pilot certificate; B—Balloon, F.A.I. certificate; D—Airship or Dirigible, F.A.I. certificate; M.A.—Military Aviator, War Dept. 1912-1914; E—Expert Aviator, Aero Club of America; JMA—Junior Military Aviator, Act of 18 July 1914.

†Applied for discharge to become civilian instructor 3 Oct 1917. Assigned to active duty as 1st Lt., Avn. Sec., SORC, 4 Jan 1918.

ARMY OFFICERS AND ENLISTED PILOTS ON AERONAUTICAL DUTY
CHRONOLOGICALLY ARRANGED TO 1917

Name, Rank, and Organization	No. and Date of Balloon and Airship Pilot Certificates*	Date and/or No. Airplane Pilot Cert. and Ratings*	Killed in Airplane Accident	Left the Service
1st Lt. Follett Bradley, F.A.†		None		
1st Lt. W. W. Wynne, Cav.		A. No. 664, Feb 1917 J.M.A., Apr 1917		
1st Lt. J. F. Byrom, Inf.		A. No. 663, Feb 1917 J.M.A., Apr 1917		
1st Lt. B. G. Weir, Inf.		A. No. 653, Feb 1917 J.M.A., Apr 1917		
1st Lt. E. L. Naiden, Cav.		A. No. 655, Feb 1917 J.M.A., Apr 1917		
1st Lt. B. W. Mills, Inf.		A. No. 654, Feb 1917 J.M.A., Apr 1917		
1st Lt. J. T. McNarney, Inf.		A. No. 657, Feb 1917 J.M.A., Apr 1917		
1st Lt. C. W. Howard, F.A.		A. No. 656, Feb 1917 J.M.A., Apr 1917		
1st Lt. L. C. Davidson, Inf.		None		
1st Lt. George Pulsifer, Jr., Inf.		A. No. 662, Feb 1917 J.M.A., Apr 1917		
1st Lt. H. B. Anderson, Cav.		A. No. 666, Feb 1917 J.M.A., Apr 1917		
1st Lt. T. J. Hanley, Inf.		A. No. 665, Feb 1917 J.M.A., Apr 1917		
1st Lt. R. P. Cousins, Cav.		A. No. 680, Mar 1917 J.M.A., May 1917		
1st Lt. M. McE. Eberts, Inf.		A. No. 688, Apr 1917 J.M.A., May 1917	15 May 1917	
1st Lt. W. O. Ryan, Cav.		A. No. 681, Mar 1917 J.M.A., May 1917		
1st Lt. H. J. Damm, Inf.		A. No. 678, Mar 1917 J.M.A.,May 1917		
Capt. Seth W. Cook, Cav.		A. No. 684, Mar 1917 J.M.A., May 1917		
1st Lt. J. R. Alfonte, Inf.		A. No. 701, Apr 1917 J.M.A., Jun 1917		
1st Lt. L. S. Churchill, Inf.		A. No. 686, Apr 1917 J.M.A.,May 1917		
1st Lt. G. W. Krapf, Inf.		A. No. 687, Apr 1917 J.M.A., May 1917		
1st Lt. C. C. Benedict, Jr., Inf.		A. No. 682, Mar 1917 J.M.A., May 1917		
1st Lt. G. E. Stratemeyer, Inf.		A. No. 683, Mar 1917 J.M.A., May 1917		
1st Lt. H. M. Clark, Cav.		A. No. 679, Mar 1917 J.M.A., May 1917		

*A—F.A.I. airplane pilot certificate; B—Balloon, F.A.I. certificate; D—Airship or Dirigible, F.A.I. certificate; M.A.—Military Aviator, War Dept. 1912-1914; E—Expert Aviator, Aero Club of America; JMA—Junior Military Aviator, Act of 18 July 1914.

†Received flying training at Mineola and elsewhere on his own time. Order for JMA issued 1 Mar 1920 but revoked. He was rated Airplane Pilot 23 Aug 1920.

ARMY OFFICERS AND ENLISTED PILOTS ON AERONAUTICAL DUTY
CHRONOLOGICALLY ARRANGED TO 1917

Name, Rank, and Organization	No. and Date of Balloon and Airship Pilot Certificates*	Date and/or No. Airplane Pilot Cert. and Ratings*	Killed in Airplane Accident	Left the Service
1st Lt. W. J. East, Inf.		A. No. 705, Apr 1917 J.M.A., Jun 1917		
1st Lt. M. F. Davis, Inf.		A. No.700, Apr 1917 J.M.A., Jun 1917		
1st Lt. A. H. Gilkeson, Inf.		A. No. 702, Apr 1917 J.M.A., Jun 1917		
Capt. C. C. Culver, S.C.		A. No. 689, Apr 1917 J.M.A., Jul 1917		
1st Lt. A. N. Krogstad, Inf.		A. No. 704, Apr 1917 J.M.A., Jun 1917		
1st Lt. W. B. Peebles, Cav.		A. No. 738, Jun 1917 J.M.A., Jul 1917		
2d Lt. R. S. Kimball, Inf.		None		
1st Lt. P. Frissell, Inf.		A. No. 703, Apr 1917 J.M.A., Jun 1917		
1st Lt. Thorne Deuel, Jr., Cav.		A. No. 741, Jun 1917 J.M.A., Jul 1917		
Cpl. Kirby L. Whitsett, S.C.		None		
1st Lt. H. M. Brown, Inf.		A. No. 707, Apr 1917 J.M.A., Jun 1917		
Capt. G. L. Gearhart, CAC		A. No. 739, Jun 1917 J.M.A., Jul 1917		
Capt. J. N. Reynolds, CAC		A. No. 706, Apr 1917 J.M.A., Jun 1917		
1st Lt. T. H. Bane, Cav.		A. No. 743, Jun 1917 J.M.A., Jul 1917		
1st Lt. J. E. Rossell, Inf.		A. No. 753, Jun 1917 J.M.A., Jul 1917		
1st Lt. W. P. Jernigan, Cav.		A. No. 740, Jun 1917 J.M.A., Jul 1917		
1st Lt. J. Kennard, Cav.		None		
1st Lt. H. R. Harmon, CAC		A. No. 717, May 1917 J.M.A., Jun 1917		
1st Lt. N. W. Peek, Inf.		A. No. 737, Jun 1917 J.M.A., Jul 1917		
1st Lt. J. C. Prince, Cav.		A. No. 786, Jul 1917		
1st Lt. E. L. Hoffman, Inf.		A. No. 772, Jul 1917 J.M.A., Jul 1917		
1st Lt. H. B. S. Burwell, Cav.		A. No. 744, Jun 1917 J.M.A., Jul 1917		
1st Lt. A. Boettcher, S.C.†		None		
1st Lt. E. M. Owen, Cav.		None		
Capt. C. K. Rhinehardt, S.C.		A. No. 736, Jun 1917 J.M.A., Jul 1917		
Capt. N. J. Boots, S.C.		A. No. 742, Jun 1917 J.M.A., Jul 1917		

*A—F.A.I. airplane pilot certificate; B—Balloon, F.A.I. certificate; D—Airship or Dirigible, F.A.I. certificate; M.A.—Military Aviator, War Dept. 1912-1914; E—Expert Aviator, Aero Club of America; JMA—Junior Military Aviator, Act of 18 July 1914.

†Relieved from SCAS and sent to Balloon School, Ft. Omaha, 9 Apr 1917.

ARMY OFFICERS AND ENLISTED PILOTS ON AERONAUTICAL DUTY
CHRONOLOGICALLY ARRANGED TO 1917

Name, Rank, and Organization	No. and Date of Balloon and Airship Pilot Certificates*	Date and/or No. Airplane Pilot Cert. and Ratings*	Killed in Airplane Accident	Left the Service
Sgt. A. E. Simonin†		A. No. 1015, Nov 1917		
Sgt. B. S. Robertson, S.C.††		None		
Sgt. A. J. Ralph, S.C.††		None		
Cpl. R. K. Smith, S.C.††		A. No. 1772, Jun 1918		
Cpl. G. D. Floyd, S.C.††		None		
Cpl. H. A. Chandler, S.C.††		None		
Pfc. C. B. Coombs, S.C.		A. No. 870, Oct 1917		
1st Lt. E. B. Lyon, S.C.		A. No. 771, Jul 1917 J.M.A., Jul 1917		
1st Lt. D. C. Emmons, Inf.		A. No. 770, Jul 1917 J.M.A., Jul 1917		
1st Lt. L. A. Walton, S.C.		A. No. 769, Jul 1917 J.M.A., Jul 1917		
Maj. William Mitchell, S.C.**		J.M.A., Jul 1917		
Sgt. D. M. Jones, S.C.†††		None		
Cpl. H. D. McLean, S.C.†††		A. No. 909, Nov 1917		
Cpl. Ray A. Willis, S.C.†††		A. No. 914, Nov 1917		

*A—F.A.I. airplane pilot certificate; B—Balloon, F.A.I. certificate; D—Airship or Dirigible, F.A.I. certificate; M.A.—Military Aviator, War Dept. 1912-1914; E—Expert Aviator, Aero Club of America; JMA—Junior Military Aviator, Act of 18 July 1914.

†Ordered to active duty as 1st Lt., SORC, 20 Sep 1917.

††Commissioned 1st or 2d Lt., SORC, and ordered to active duty.

**Major Mitchell began instruction on his own time at the Curtiss School.

†††Commissioned 1st or 2d Lt., SORC and ordered to active duty.

NOTE: In addition there were some U.S. Reserve and U.S. National Guard Aviators ordered to active duty prior to 6 April 1917, as well as some few commissioned in the Reserve from civil life. There was also one cadet from the U.S. Military Academy who took flying instruction at SCAS, Mineola, during a furlough from West Point and upon graduation was made a Captain in the Air Service.

This list was compiled from General and Special Orders, and records from every conceivable source by E. L. Jones. See his list, which is more complete. Some information was obtained from Chandler and Lahm, App. 1, pp. 282-285.

U.S. RESERVE AVIATORS TO APRIL 6, 1917

Name and Rank	Airplane Pilot Certificate and Ratings	Killed in Airplane Accident	Left the Service
San Diego			
Sgt. C. C. Cole			
Newport News — 1916			
W. V. Barnaby			
1st Lt. H. M. Gallup	FAI No. 575, RMA		
1st Lt. W. G. Schauffler	RMA		
1st Lt. H. P. Culver	FAI No. 673, RMA		
1st Lt. W. T. Rolph	RMA		
1st Lt. C. W. Connell	RMA		
E. G. Schultz	FAI No. 545	29 Jul 1943 (Killed in Action)	
1st Lt. R. H. Jones	FAI No. 671, RMA		
1st Lt. E. R. Kenneson	FAI No. 631, RMA		
1st Lt. W. B. Wright	RMA		
1st Lt. St. C. Streett	FAI No. 4871, RMA		
1st Lt. J. G. Colgan	FAI No. 685, RMA		

Name and Rank	Airplane Pilot Certificate and Ratings	Killed in Airplane Accident	Left the Service
1917			
1st Lt. F. K. Lane	FAI No. 718, RMA		
1st Lt. L. Schenk	FAI No. 756, RMA		
1st Lt. H. W. Schulz	RMA	23 Aug 1918	
1st Lt. R. Olds	FAI No. 8803, RMA		
1st Lt. S. H. Noyes	FAI No. 543, RMA, JMA		
1st Lt. F. L. Isbell	FAI No. 3894, RMA		
1st Lt. M. L. Newhall	RMA		
Sgt. C. E. Neidig	FAI No. 500		Relieved 10 May 1917
M. P. Lane	FAI No. 626		
A. R. Collins			
E. W. Hubbard	FAI No. 748		
W. A. Lord	FAI No. 380		
1st Lt. P. V. Burwell	RMA		
D. K. Steele			
1st Lt. S. B. Eckert	SP No. 52,* RMA		
1st Lt. D. H. Young	FAI No. 758, RMA		
1st Lt. W. A. Munn	RMA		
1st Lt. H. E. Mensch			
1st Lt. C. G. Sellers	FAI No. 757, RMA		
1st Lt. J. A. Hamleton	RMA	8 Jun 1929	
1st Lt. T. E. P. Rice	RMA		
H. M. McCuistion			
1st Lt. G. T. Tilbrook	N.F.†		Relieved from flying 16 May 1917
1st Lt. L. L. Harvey	FAI No. 2199, RMA		
1st Lt. L. Richardson	FAI No. 745, RMA		
1st Lt. W. E. Lewis	RMA, N.F.		
2d Lt. A. H. Williams			
2d Lt. H. N. Murphy	RMA		
1st Lt. R. G. Page	FAI No. 6393, RMA		
1st Lt. J. W. Watts	RMA		
1st Lt. E. M. Welch	FAI No. 1480, RMA		
1st Lt. S. P. Mandell	FAI, No. 766, RMA	5 Nov 1918 (Shot by Germans after crash)	
1st Lt. D. Buckley	RMA, N.F.		
G. I. Sullivan			Relieved from flying 3 May 1917
1st Lt. T. M. Ring	FAI No. 765, RMA		
1st Lt. A. W. Lawson	RMA		
H. F. Gates			
A. T. Wiederhold			
H. V. Lucas			
1st Lt. A. R. Metzger, Jr.	RMA	10 May 1919	
2d Lt. E. H. Tonkin	FAI No. 4812, RMA, N.F.		Relieved from flying 3 May 1917
1st Lt. R. B. Quick	FAI No. 4229a, RMA		
1st Lt. C. E. Wright	FAI No. 1003, RMA		
1st Lt. B. A. Law	FAI No. 1230, RMA		
1st Lt. J. F. Brown, Jr.	RMA		
E. B. Koger			
2d Lt. H. C. Smith	RMA		
1st Lt. W. A. Cheney	RMA	20 Jan 1918	

*SP—FAI seaplane or hydroaeroplane certificate.

†N.F.—Nonflying.

Note: Others ordered to active duty for flying training by April 6, 1917, but whose instruction began later were: Howard W. French and A. R. Gaffney. The latter was listed in Colonel Carberry's roster of the SCAS, Mineola, 2 Dec. 1917 as being in training as a Reserve applicant.

Name and Rank	Airplane Pilot Certificate and Ratings	Killed in Airplane Accident	Left the Service
Chicago and Memphis			
1st Lt. A. C. Adams	RMA		
1st Lt. C. W. Browne	FAI No. 885, RMA		
1st Lt. M. F. Gerlowski	RMA		
1st Lt. A. E. Gibson	RMA		
1st Lt. G. J. Kinberg	FAI No. 1195, RMA		
V. J. Pickard	RMA		
1st Lt. G. W. Sawyer	NF		
1st Lt. R. W. Schroeder	FAI No. 2265, RMA		
1st Lt. W. A. Thompson	RMA		
1st Lt. J. Van Walchshauser	RMA		
1st Lt. G. C. Melvin	RMA		
1st Lt. J. H. Zoerman	RMA		
1st Lt. R. H. Harper	RMA		
1st Lt. F. L. McCordic	FAI No. 622, RMA		
1st Lt. Carlyle Rhodes	RMA		
1st Lt. H. M. Sanford	FAI No. 891, RMA		
G. E. Knight			
1st Lt. O. E. Wolf	RMA		
1st Lt. C. B. Stevens	RMA		
2d Lt. H. W. Powers			
S. A. Herrick			
1st Lt. J. M. Foote	RMA		
1st Lt. F. W. Alsip	RMA		
1st Lt. E. B. Jones	RMA	13 Sep 1918 (Killed in combat)	
1st Lt. Alex McLeod	FAI No. 4762, RMA		
1st Lt. G. F. Fisher	RMA		
1st Lt. P. N. Hollowell	RMA		
E. E. Leonard			
1st Lt. Donald Lyle	RMA		
1st Lt. Arthur Mitchell	RMA		
1st Lt. A. C. Ortmayer	RMA	8 Mar 1918	
1st Lt. T. C. Taylor	RMA		
Miami			
Robert Matter			
2d Lt. J. W. Junkin	FAI No. 1933, RMA		
2d Lt. L. H. DeGarmo	FAI No. 764, RMA	16 Feb 1918	
1st Lt. O. S. Ferson	FAI No. 747, RMA		
2d Lt. E. H. Holterman	FAI No. 677, RMA		
1st Lt. E. S. Hoag	FAI No. 1126, RMA		
2d Lt. E. P. Jones	RMA		
1st Lt. T. B. Belsjoe	FAI No. 4731, RMA		
J. F. Neale			13 Apr 1917
2d Lt. G. R. King	NF		Relieved from flying 25 Apr 1917
S. T. Vanderbilt	NF		10 May 1917
1st Lt. J. R. Graham	FAI No. 7460, RMA		
1st Lt. W. J. Foy	RMA		
2d Lt. F. D. Croxford	FAI No. 2094, RMA		
1st Lt. A. F. Horn	RMA		
G. E. Olmstead			12 Apr 1917
W. B. Rodgers	French brevet*		
H. A. Theed			25 Apr 1917
1st Lt. J. G. Trees	FAI No. 461, RMA	13 Jun 1918	

*French pilot's license.

Name and Rank	Airplane Pilot Certificate and Ratings	Killed in Airplane Accident	Left the Service
1st Lt. Hamilton Coolidge	FAI No. 572, RMA	27 Oct 1918 (in air action)	
1st Lt. F. H. Harvey	RMA	19 Apr 1936	
1st Lt. W. A. Hoeveler	RMA		
1st Lt. John L. Mitchell	RMA		
1st Lt. A. L. Richmond	FAI No. 726, RMA		
1st Lt. E. E. Bates	FAI No. 578, RMA		
A. R. Jennings			10 May 1917
1st Lt. R. C. Taylor	RMA	16 Sep 1918 (in combat in air)	
2d Lt. R. B. Barry	RMA		
W. B. Culbertson*	FAI No. 4874, RMA		10 May 1917
1st Lt. Thomas C. Nathan	RMA	20 Mar 1918	
2d Lt. W. N. Dewald	FAI No. 4201, RMA		
1st Lt. Russell MacDonald	FAI No. 4607		
1st Lt. J. I. Moore	FAI No. 763, RMA		
B. T. Myers			
Mineola			
Philip Boyer†			15 Jun 1917
1st Lt. Ray A. Dunn	RMA		

*Sgt. Culbertson was discharged at Miami on 10 May 1917, after 13 hours of flying training. Incomplete records show him as a civilian instructor at Mineola and Wichita Falls in December. In 1918 he was commissioned a 2d Lt. in the Marine Corps.

†Discharged at his own request and later commissioned in CWS. He was a graduate of the Wright Company school at Mineola in 1916.

Note: Others ordered to active duty at Miami by 6 April but whose flight records began later were: Wm. R. Becker, Chas. S. Chase, Jr., Marcus H. Rice, George D. Selden, Jr., and Oscar J. Gude.

Note: Irad M. Hidden was a third enlisted man ordered to active duty as Sgt., SERC by 6 April 1917, but his flying began later and he was discharged on 15 June 1917.

U.S. Reserve Aviators
Commissioned from Civil Life

1st Lt. B. B. Lewis	FAI No. 345, RMA
1st Lt. Cord Meyer	FAI No. 176, RMA
1st Lt. Seth Low	FAI No. 548, RMA
1st Lt. Charles Reed	FAI No. 480, RMA
1st Lt. F. T. Blakeman	FAI No. 614, RMA

Note: Philip A. Carroll, H.A.H. Baker, and Lawrence B. Sperry took their RMA tests at Mineola, but Sperry was not commissioned in the army. Philip Carroll passed his RMA test on 22 Oct. 1916, but was not commissioned until 3 May 1917. H.A.H. Baker was not commissioned until 30 April 1917.

U.S. Military Academy

Cadet R. L. Meredith	FAI No. 6879, RMA, Capt.

Note: Cadet Meredith took flying instruction at the SCAS, Mineola, during a furlough from West Point. He was commissioned a 2d Lt. in the F.A. and ordered to the School of Military Aeronautics at the University of Texas on 1 Feb. 1918. He was detailed to the ASSC upon graduation and appointed Captain in the Air Service on 21 Sept. 1918. Although he passed the test for FAI certificate in 1918 at Kelly Field, the certificate was not issued until 1928.

These lists do not include American members of the Lafayette Escadrille or other Americans flying with the Allies and not members of the U.S. Air Forces on or before 6 April 1917.

U.S. National Guard Aviators
to 6 April 1917

1912
Pfc. Beckwith Haven, N.Y.	FAI No. 127
Lt. Col C. B. Winder, Ohio	FAI No. 130

1914
Pvt. S. A. Blair, N.Y.	RMA, 1st Lt.

Name and Rank	Airplane Pilot Certificate and Ratings	Killed in Airplane Accident	Left the Service
1916			
1st Lt. A. B. Thaw, N.Y.	FAI No. 441	18 Aug 1918	
Ferd. Eggena, N.Y.	FAI No. 333		
Capt. R. L. Taylor, Conn.	FAI No. 517, RMA	2 Aug 1917	
1st Lt. H. F. Wehrle, W.Va.	FAI No. 658, RMA, Capt.		
1st Lt. Barnard Cummings, Colo.	FAI No. 525, RMA		
1st Lt. M. B. More, N.Y.	FAI No. 506, RMA		
Sgt. W. G. Hickman, N.Y.	FAI No. 503, RMA, 2d Lt.		
2d Lt. B. F. Briggs, Wyo.	FAI No. 511, RMA, Capt.		
2d Lt. E. W. Bagnell, Neb.	FAI No. 515, RMA, 1st Lt.		
Cpl. John D. Sullivan, N.Y.	RMA 1st Lt.		
Cpl. Thos. F. Ward, N.Y.	FAI No. 785 RMA, 1st Lt.		
1st Lt. Frank W. Wright, Ore.	FAI No. 524, JMA		
W. C. Miller, N.Y.			
Charles Wald, N.Y.			
2d Lt. Ivan P. Wheaton, N.Y.	FAI No. 632		
Capt. R. C. Bolling, N.Y.	FAI No. 536, RMA, Maj.		
1st Lt. James E. Miller, N.Y.	FAI No. 538, RMA, Capt.	9 Mar 1918 (Killed in Action)	
Sgt. Wm. P. Willetts, N.Y.	FAI No. 539, RMA, 1st Lt.		
1st Lt. D. B. Byrd, N.C.			Relieved 3 Oct 1916
1st Lt. A. J. Coyle, N.H.	RMA		
Cpl. R. M. Olyphant, N.Y.	RMA, 1st Lt.		
Pfc. R. S. Knowlson, N.Y.	FAI No. 780, RMA, JMA, 1st Lt.		
Pfc. G. J. Dwyer, N.Y.	RMA, 1st Lt.		
1st Lt. Norbert Carolin, N.Y.	FAI No. 668, RMA		
Cpl. H. H. Salmon, N.Y.	RMA, 1st Lt.		
Sgt. J. H. Stevenson, N.Y.	RMA, 1st Lt.		
1st Lt. R. W. Bryant, N.Y.	Capt.		
2d Lt. B. R. Osborne, Ky.	FAI No. 623, RMA, 1st Lt.		
Pvt. C. H. Reynolds, N.Y.	RMA, 1st Lt.		
Sgt. D. G. Frost, N.Y.	RMA, 1st Lt.		
Sgt. L. V. Smith, Ga.	FAI No. 1800, RMA, 1st Lt.		
Sgt. W. T. Odell, N.Y.	1st Lt.		
Cpl. Raymond F. Fox, N.Y.	RMA, 2d Lt.	1 Oct 1918 (Killed in Action)	
Pfc. Wm. M. Conant, N.Y.	RMA, 1st Lt.		
Cpl. Arthur L. Lewis, N.Y.	RMA, 1st Lt.		
Capt. J. M. Satterfield, N.Y.	NF		
Sgt. Theodore C. Knight, N.Y.	RMA, 1st Lt.		
Pvt. D. P. Morse, N.Y.	FAI No. 730, RMA, 1st Lt.		
Pvt. H. H. Simons, N.Y.	RMA, 1st Lt.		
Pfc. W. C. Jenkins, N.Y.			
Cpl. Chas. S. Lyon, N.Y.	FAI No. 1100, RMA, 1st Lt.		
1st Lt. Henry Ilse, Wash.	FAI No. 613		
2d Lt. Forrest Ward, Ark.			Relieved 15 Oct 1916
Pvt. E. M. Post, N.Y.	FAI No. 593, RMA, 1st Lt.		
Cpl. B. O. Watkins, Ala.	RMA, 1st Lt.		
2d Lt. Dean Smith, N.M.	FAI No. 599, JMA, Capt.		
Capt. W. W. Spain, S.D.	RMA, 1st Lt.		
Sgt. E. A. Kruss, N.Y.	FAI No. 752, RMA, 1st Lt.		
D. R. Noyes, N.Y.	RMA, 1st Lt.		
Capt. L. P. Billard, Kan.	FAI No. 636, RMA, 1st Lt.	24 Jul 1918	
1917			
1st Lt. James P. Kelly			26 Feb 1917
Pvt. James F. Carr, Va.	RMA, 1st Lt.		

Name and Rank	Airplane Pilot Certificate and Ratings	Killed in Airplane Accident	Left the Service
Geo. L. Argus, N.Y.	2d Lt.		
K. L. Burns, N.Y.			
R. J. Gilmore, N.Y.			
Cpl. E. B. Hagerty, N.Y.	RMA, 1st Lt.		
F. S. Hoppin, N.Y.			
J. F. Hubbard, N.Y.			
Philip D. Smith, N.Y.			
Sgt. Paul R. Stockton, N.Y.	FAI No. 774, RMA, 1st Lt.		
Cpl. E. L. Thomas, N.Y.	1st Lt.		
Sgt. R. H. Tifft, N.Y.	RMA, 2d Lt.		
W. W. Waring, N.Y.	RMA, 1st Lt.		
1st Lt. Ernest Clark, Ind.	FAI No. 799, JMA, 1st Lt.		
2d Lt. E. G. Horigan, Me.	FAI No. 796		Relieved for duty with his regiment 25 Sep 1917

E. Martin, N.Y.

NOTE: A bulletin No. 157 of the Aero Club of America lists in addition to others included above, the following Guardsmen training with the assistance of the Club's fund, on whom no information has been disclosed in Army records:

Lt. Ralph Baker, N.M.
Lt. R. H. Hoyer, Ohio
Cpl. Charles Robbins, Ark.
2d Lt. Fay Ross, S.D.
Cadet Capt. L. H. White, Nev.

Pvt. George Bambaugh, Ind.
Cpl. Greenhow Johnson, Va.
Lt. B. S. Ketcham, N.Y.
Lt. H. P. Sheldon, Vt.
Capt. R. E. McMillen, Neb.

Sgt. Harrison Handley, Okla.
Lt. Curry McDaniels, Tenn.
2d Lt. E. M. Romberger, Miss.
Capt. A. Sunderland, Conn.

Still other National Guard personnel were trained but their flying as Guardsmen appears to have begun after 6 April 1917. So far as records are available these were as follows:

Capt. J. B. Alexander, Wash.
MSE H. E. Bardwell, N.Y.
Reed M. Chambers, Tenn.
1st Lt. Fred. I. Eglin, Ind.
Capt. R. H. Fleet, Wash.
1st Lt. George C. Furrow, Tenn.

Capt. E. E. Newbold, Neb.
Sgt. Harold H. George, N.Y.
Pvt. Raymond B. Messer, Mass.
Capt. R. L. Noggle, Hawaii
Sgt. George M. Palmer, Minn.
1st Lt. K. G. Pulliam, Ky.

1st Lt. Bryan McMullen, Tex.
1st Lt. A. R. Scheleen, Kan.
1st Lt. Ernest E. Shields, Ind.
Capt. Almon Stroupe, Ark.
Capt. John N. Thorp, N.J.
2d Lt. Francis E. Walton, N.Y.
1st Lt. Wm. W. Waring, N.Y.

Appendix 15

SOLDIER PILOTS, REGULAR ARMY UP TO THE OUTBREAK OF WORLD WAR I

Enlisted men of the Regular Army who became pilots arranged in order of flying, so far as it has been possible to determine, regardless of orders on flying status for pay purposes or of rating.

Name	First Order on Flying Status*	F.A.I. Certificate	J.M.A. Rating
1912			
Sgt. V. L. Burge[1]	6 Oct 1914, SO 304	No. 154, 14 Aug 1912	----------------------
Cpl. W. A. Lamkey[2]	6 Oct 1914, SO 241	No. 183, 6 Nov 1912	----------------------
1914			
Sgt. W. C. Ocker[3]	6 Oct 1914, SO 243	No. 293, 29 Apr 1914	2 Nov 1917, SO 266
Cpl. J. S. Krull[4]	12 Apr 1915, SO 93	No. 360, 24 Oct 1915	----------------------
1915			
Sgt. Herbert Marcus[5]		----------------------	----------------------
Cpl. A. D. Smith[6]	7 Jul 1915, SO 163	No. 354, 17 Oct 1915	8 Mar 1918, SO 77
Sgt. A. A. Adamson[7]		No. 395, 19 Jan 1916	----------------------
Cpl. Ira O. Biffle[8]	25 Aug 1915, SO 205	No. 396, 19 Jan 1916	----------------------
Cpl. S. V. Coyle[9]	18 Nov 1915, SO 279	No. 431, 15 Mar 1916	----------------------
Cpl. L. G. Flint[10]		----------------------	----------------------
1916			
Sgt. Felix Steinle[11]	11 Apr 1916, SO 94	No. 779, 11 Jul 1917	----------------------
Sgt. B. S. Robertson[12]	15 Feb 1917, SO 55	----------------------	----------------------
Cpl. G. D. Floyd[13]	15 Feb 1917, SO 55	----------------------	----------------------
Cpl. H. A. Chandler[14]	15 Feb 1917, SO 55	----------------------	----------------------
Sgt. D. M. Jones[15]	5 Jul 1917, SO 181	----------------------	----------------------
Sgt. A. J. Ralph[16]	15 Feb 1917, SO 55	----------------------	----------------------
Pfc. C. B. Coombs[17]	15 Feb 1917, SO 55	No. 870, 17 Oct 1917	----------------------
1917 (to 6 Apr)			
Cpl. K. L. Whitsett[18]	4 Jan 1917, SO 55	----------------------	----------------------
Sgt. A. E. Simonin[19]	15 Feb 1917, SO 55	No. 1015, 28 Nov 1917	----------------------
Cpl. R. K. Smith[20]	15 Feb 1917, SO 55	No. 1772, 26 Jun 1918	----------------------
Cpl. H. D. McLean[21]	5 Jul 1917, SO 181	No. 909, 7 Nov 1917	----------------------
Cpl. R. A. Willis[22]	4 Sep 1917, SO 279	No. 914, 7 Nov 1917	----------------------

*Generally, such orders cannot be taken as evidence of flying instruction or piloting, as enlisted men were ordered on and off flying status according to their duties, and such duty did not necessarily entail any flying instruction.

[1]Instructed by Lt. Lahm in Philippines and passed FAI test 14 June 1912. Rated by ACA 14 August 1912.

[2]Cpl. Lamkey was graduated from the Moisant school with FAI certificate in 1912. He enlisted in the Signal Corps and was ordered to the SCAS, San Diego, on 17 May 1913, SO #115, where he had further flying instruction under civilian instructor Oscar Brindley. He purchased his discharge to become a civilian aviator on 10 June 1915, SO #134. After flying for Villa in Mexico, he became a naval pilot in the AEF.

[3]Pvt. Ocker was ordered to SCAS, San Diego (6 Dec 1912, SO #286), where he became an instructor. He was discharged 27 Jan 1917, SO #22, to accept a commission as Captain, AS, SORC, and was ordered to active duty 10 Feb 1917, SO #34.

[4]Cpl. Krull was flying in the spring of 1914. Rockwell Field Monthly Progress Report of 31 Dec 1915 stated he could pass the JMA test. He was discharged 16 May 1917, SO #113, to become a civilian instructor. He was discharged as 1st Lt., A.S. (Aeronautics) 30 Nov 1920, SO #270.

[5]Sgt. Marcus was on flying status from 6 Oct 1914, SO #241, but it is not certain that he was a pilot at that time. However, he was flying solo by 19 March 1915 as mentioned by Major A. D. Smith in ACNL 15 Jan 1938. He was assigned to active duty at a 1st Lt., AS, SORC on 21 Nov 1917, SO #272.

[6]Cpl. Smith purchased his discharge on 11 Aug 1916, SO #187, to become a civilian instructor at SCAS, San Diego, 29 Aug 1916. He was ordered to active duty as a Captain AS, SORC, 13 Aug 1917, SO #187. He was retired in 1930.

[7]Sgt. Adamson was on flying status from 26 Feb 1915, SO #57, but it is not certain whether or not he was a pilot at that time. Reported ready for pilot test 31 Dec 1915, ready for JMA test 29 Feb 1916 in Rockwell Field Monthly Progress Reports. He was attached to Air Service, AEF, as 1st Lt. in July 1917.

[8]Cpl. Biffle was ordered to SCAS, San Diego on 6 July 1914, SO #156, to accept appointment as flying instructor on 12 July 1917, SO #160.

[9]Sgt. Coyle was discharged 18 July 1917, SO #165, to become a civilian instructor. He was killed in a crash on 4 June 1918.

[10]Cpl. Flint was on flying status from 12 April 1915, SO #93, but it is not known whether or not as a pilot. He was ready for his pilot test on 31 December 1915, Rockwell Field Monthly Progress Report.

[11]Sgt. Steinle was flying from 3 March 1916. He became a flying instructor in July and qualified as JMA, on 7 July 1917, but was not so rated. He applied for discharge to become a civilian instructor on 3 Oct 1917. He was assigned to active duty at 1st Lt., AS. SC, 4 Jan 1918, SO #3, discharged on 30 Nov 1919, SO #269.

[12]Sgt. Robertson began flying at Mineola on 19 Sep 1916 and later became an instructor. He passed the RMA test on 18 June 1917. He was commissioned 1st Lt., AS SORC. 31 Aug 1917, and was ordered to active duty 7 Sep 1917, SO #208. Returned to active duty as a Major in 1942.

[13]Cpl. Floyd began flying at Mineola on 14 Sep 1916, passed his RMA test on 23 July 1917. He was commissioned 1st Lt., AS, SORC on 13 Nov 1917 and was put on active duty 15 Nov 1917, SO #301.

[14]Cpl. Chandler began flying at Mineola 14 Sep 1916, and passed his RMA test 24 Jul 1917. He was commissioned 1st Lt., AS SORC, 2 Nov 1917 and ordered to active duty on 7 Nov 1917, SO #260.

[15]Sgt. Jones began flying at Mineola on 26 Sep 1916 and passed his RMA test on 14 Aug 1917. He was commissioned 1st Lt., AS, SORC, 12 Sep 1917 and ordered to active duty on 18 Oct 1917, SO #243.

[16]Sgt. Ralph began flying at Mineola on 21 Oct 1916 and passed his RMA test on 21 July 1917. He was commissioned 1st Lt., AS, SORC, on 22 Aug 1917 and was ordered to active duty 29 Aug 1917, SO #201.

[17]Pfc. Coombs began flying at Mineola on 25 November 1916. He passed his RMA test 18 July 1917.

[18]Cpl. Whitsett began flying at Mineola on 4 Jan 1917 and passed the RMA test on 15 July 1917, but he was not so rated because of the policy of rating only officers as JMA's. He was transferred to Essington on 24 Aug 1917.

[19]Sgt. Simonin began flying at Mineola on 15 Jan 1917 and passed the RMA test 22 June 1917, but was not so rated. He was commissioned 1st Lt., AS, SORC, on 12 Sep 1917 and was ordered to active duty 20 Sep 1917, SO #219.

[20]Cpl. Smith began flying at Mineola on 17 Feb 1917 and later became an instructor. He passed the RMA test on 23 July 1917 and was commissioned as a 2d Lt, AS (Aeronautics) on 26 Sep 1918.

[21]Cpl. McLean began flying at Mineola on 31 March 1917 and he passed his RMA test on 11 Aug 1917. He was commissioned 1st Lt., AS, SORC 16 Jan 1918.

[22]Cpl. Willis enlisted in the AS, SC on 3 Jan 1917 and was assigned to the SCAS, Mineola, where he began flying in March 1917. He became an instructor, passed the RMA test on 4 Sep 1917 and was commissioned 2d Lt., AS (A) on 5 Nov 1918, and was put on active duty the same day.

NOTE: This list may not be complete, but it consists of the names of all enlisted pilots that the records show as having become pilots by 6 April 1917.

Appendix 16

ENLISTED MEN RATED AVIATION MECHANICIANS UNDER THE ACT
OF 18 JULY 1914 UP TO THE OUTBREAK OF WORLD WAR I

MSE Herbert Marcus	S.O. 36–24, 12 Feb 1915
Sgt. 1st Cl. Thomas Boland	" "
MSE Stephen J. Idzorek	" "
Sgt. Alvah E. Baxter	" "
Sgt. William C. Ocker	" "
MSE John McRae	" "
Sgt. 1st Cl. Asa J. Etheridge	" "
Sgt. Charles Payne	" "
Sgt. Wm. A. Bechtold	" "
Cpl. Leland D. Bradshaw	" "
Sgt. Walter Brewer	" "
MSE Henry J. Darnbrush	" "
MSE Earl S. Schofield	" "
Cpl. Glenn R. Modale	" "
Cpl. Wilfred G. Threader	" "
Sgt. 1st Cl. Walter L. Costenborder	" "
Sgt. Fred Parkins	" "
Sgt. Robert Robinson	" "
Cpl. Clarence P. Young	" "
Cpl. Wm. O. Bosworth	" "
Sgt. 1st Cl. Vernon L. Burge	S.O. 205–21, 2 Sept 1915
Sgt. Charles W. Winters	" "
Cpl. W. R. Morrison	" "
Cpl. Clarence F. Adams	" "
Cpl. Jakob Kuhn	" "
Cpl. Arnold Ruef	" "
Cpl. Ward H. Rice	" "
Cpl. Wilburn C. Dodd	" "
Cpl. Frank H. Covell	" "
Cpl. Frank Krick	" "
Cpl. Robert W. Houser	" "
Pvt. Victor H. Miller	" "
Sgt. W. C. Hunter	S.O. 274–1, 24 Nov 1915
Sgt. John W. Corcoran	" "
Cpl. Calvin T. Stephenson	" "
Cpl. John Dolan	" "
Cpl. John A. Downey	S.O. 242–3, 16 Oct 1916

NOTE: This list may not be complete.

Appendix 17

ALLOCATIONS AND APPROPRIATIONS FOR AERONAUTICS, U.S. ARMY, TO 6 APRIL 1917*

1899	Board of Ordnance & Fortification allotted 9 Nov 1898		$ 25,000[1]
1899	Board of Ordnance & Fortification allotted 9 Dec 1898		25,000[1]
1909	Board of Ordnance & Fortification allotted 1 Oct 1908		25,000[2]
1909	Board of Ordnance & Fortification allotted 4 Nov 1909		5,000[2]
1912	Signal Service of the Army	Act of 3 Mar 1911	125,000
	($25,000 immediately available)		
1913	Signal Service of the Army	Act of 24 Aug 1912	100,000
1914	Signal Service of the Army	Act of 2 Mar 1913	125,000
1915	Signal Service of the Army	Act of 27 Apr 1914	250,000
1916	Signal Service of the Army	Act of 4 Mar 1915	301,000
1916–17	Signal Service of the Army	Emergency Act, 31 Mar 1916	500,000
1917	Signal Service of the Army	Act of 29 Aug 1916	13,881,666[3]
1917	Aviation Seacoast Defenses, U.S.	Fortification Act	3,600,000
1917	Aviation Seacoast Defenses, Hawaii	of	600,000
1917	Aviation Seacoast Defenses, P.I.	14 Feb 1917	600,000

[1]Allotted to Dr. S. P. Langley for his experiments in aerodynamics.
[2]Allotted to pay for Wright airplane which completed tests in 1909.
[3]Includes $600,000 for purchase of aviation sites.
*Air Corps Tabulation of Finance Division, 12 Oct 1935.

Appendix 18

UNAUTHENTICATED LIST OF STUDENTS AND INSTRUCTORS UNDERGOING TRAINING AT MINEOLA, FEBRUARY 1917*

Pupils	1st Aero Co.	2d Aero Co.	Militia	Reserve Applicants	Training Incomplete	Under Training	RMA
Argus, George		x			x		
Bagnell, E. W.			x				x
Bradley, Follett[1]						x	
Bryant, R. W.		x			x		
Burns, K. L.[2]	x				x		
Byrd, D. B.[3]			x		x		
Chapman, Capt. C. G.[4]						x	
Conant, W. M.	x					x	
Carolin, Norbert	x			x			x
Coyle, A. J.			x				x
Cummings, Barnard[3]			x		x		
Dwyer, Geoffrey J.	x				x		
Eggena, Ferdinand		x			x		
Frost, Donald	x			x	x		
Fox, R. F.		x					
Gaffney, A. R.				x		x	
Gilmore, R. J.	x				x		
Hagerty, Edwin	x			x		x	
Hickman, W. G.		x			x		
Hoppin, F. S.	x				x		
Hubbard, J. F.	x				x		
Ilse, Henry[3]			x		x		
Knight, Theodore		x				x	
Knowlson, R. S.	x					x	
Kruss, E. A.	x						x
Lewis, A. L.		x			x		
Lyon, C. S.		x				x	
Martin, E.	x				x		
Meredith, R. L.[5]					x		
Miller, W. C.		x			x		
More, M. B.		x			x		
Morse, D. P., Jr.	x			x		x	
Noyes, D. R.	x						x
Odell, Walter	x				x		
Olyphant, R. M.	x					x	
Osborne, B. R.			x				x
Satterfield, J. M.		x			x		
Salmon, H. H., Jr.	x			x	x		
Simons, H. H.		x				x	
Smith, L. V.			x			x	
Smith, P. D.[6]	x				x		
Stetson, J. B., Jr.				x		x	
Stevenson, J. H.	x			x			x
Stockton, P. R.	x					x	
Sullivan, J. D.	x				x		
Taylor, R. L.			x				x

[1]Ordnance Capt. USA, Lt. Bradley began flying at Mineola while temporarily present in connection with certain ordnance tests, but not officially assigned to aviation duty.
[2]Dropped from flying list.
[3]Relieved.
[4]AS, SC.
[5]Cadet, USMA.
[6]Taken off flying list.

Pupils	1st Aero Co.	2d Aero Co.	Militia	Reserve Appli-cants	Training Incom-plete	Under Train-ing	RMA
Thomas, E. L.		x			x		
Tifft, R. H.		x			x		
Tiffany, C. S.				x	x		
Ward, T. F.	x			x		x	
Wald, Chas.		x			x		
Waring, W. W.		x			x		
Ward, Forrest[7]			x		x		
Watkins, B. O.			x	x		x	
Wehrle, H. F.			x	x		x	
Wheaton, I. P.			x	x		x	
Willetts, W. P.	x						x
Whitsett, K. L., Cpl.[8]						x	
Bolling, R. C.	x						x
Thaw, A. B.	x						x
Miller, J. E.	x						x

[7]Relieved.
[8]Regular Army.
*List compiled by Lt. J. E. Carberry and sent to E. L. Jones by Col. Carberry.

APPLICANT STUDENT INSTRUCTORS

Student Instructors	Failed	Student Instructor	Junior Instructor	Senior Instructor	Chief Instructor
Allan, A. L.					x
Atwater, W. B.					
Acosta, B. B.			x		
Bleakley, Wm. H.		x			
Bonney, W. L.			x		
Briggs, A. W.			x		
Bjorklund, F. A.			x		
Fish, Farnum	x				
Fuller, E. G.	x				
Gray, G. A.	x				
Hewitt, H. M.		x			
Heinrich, J. O.[1]					
Hill, J. D.			x		
Holt, L. E.	x				
Jenkins, W. C.		x			
Johnson, E. A.			x		
LaGrone, J. K.	x				
Leon, Lawrence	x				
Manning, Douglas	x				
Mead, R. H.		x			
Nicholson, A.	x				
Norton, N. J.		x			
Page, G. A.	x				
Patterson, Dwight	x				
Probst, J. D.	x				
Reynolds, C. H.		x			
Rinehart, H. M.					
Sherwood, O. B.	x				
Toncray, Henry	x				
Wall, C. A.		x			
Bergquist, E.	x				
Bounds, Overton[2]					
Millman, P. C.					
Nyegaard[3]				x	

[1]Tried out and reported on favorably.

[2]Resigned.

[3]Nyegaard's connection was severed. He was later in France in the French uniform. His first name is unknown.

Bibliographical Note

This history of early aviation in the United States Army has drawn heavily on the records and research of Lt. Col. Ernest L. Jones, who for many years collected notes for a chronology of the Army's air arm. Colonel Jones published the magazine **Aeronautics** in the early days of aviation, served with the Air Service in World War I and the Air Forces in World War II, and for many years was the editor of **Chirp,** the magazine of the Early Birds. After World War II he served as a civilian historian with the Air Force Historical Division until he retired in August 1952. At the time of his death he was one of the most widely recognized authorities on early Air Force history.

The National Archives, in which early Signal Corps records are housed, is perhaps the most important source for the material in this history. From the creation of the Signal Corps on 1 July 1891 to 1894, the numbers of the Signal Corps reports are consecutive for each year; with each new year numbering began again from 1. In 1894 the Office, Chief Signal Officer, arbitrarily began numbering reports consecutively from 1; by 1917 the numbers had reached 40,091. In 1917, the Dewey decimal system was put into use, and this system has been followed since. It is not necessary, however, to use the Dewey index with the Signal Corps report numbers used in this history. The annual reports of the Chief Signal Officer for the year 1908 and earlier are found in the Office of the Chief Signal Officer. From 1909 on these annual reports are located in the Air Force Library in the Air Adjutant General's office.

For the early history the above records were used as well as the Official Records of the War of the Rebellion, and newspapers and aeronautical magazines of the day. A few books were also used, among them F. Stansbury Haydon's **Aeronautics in the Union and Confederate Armies.** The one book which has been used more than any other is **How Our Army Grew Wings,** by Charles deForest Chandler and Frank P. Lahm, both of whom were early army aviators and wrote of the period through which they lived. Although in the present work there are minor disagreements with this book, they are mainly in the matter of dates. The book has proved itself invaluable for the period it covers. Books, unpublished histories, and articles written by H. H. Arnold and other air officers have furnished an excellent source of information. The author has also had access to General B. D. Foulois' collection of records.

Congressional records, committee hearings, reports, and government pamphlets have been used for that part of the history which concerns legislation, appropriations, and aircraft production. The files of the General Accounting Office have been used as a source for deliveries of airplanes. The Air Force Library also contains some early air force records that are not to be found elsewhere. General and special orders files as well as AGO records have furnished a great deal of information about administration and personnel. Letters from and conversations with early air force personnel obtained by Ernest L. Jones have solved a great many problems. The records of the Smithsonian Institution have been consulted from time to time for construction particulars of early planes. Various books on individuals, such as Fred C. Kelley's **The Wright Brothers** and **Miracle at Kitty Hawk** have been most helpful. The Aero Club records have furnished information on official records established by various individuals, as well as on balloon, dirigible, and airplane pilot certificates and requirements.

Index

257

Air Force (581316) McGregor & Werner, Inc., Atlanta, Ga.   12/5/58   500

☆U.S. GOVERNMENT PRINTING OFFICE: 1 9 8 6   4 8 6   9 8 ᵒ